Also by Raymond Ibrahim

Sword and Scimitar: Fourteen Centuries of War between Islam and the West (2018)

Defenders of the West: The Christian Heroes Who Stood Against Islam (2022)

Crucified Again: Exposing Islam's New War on Christians (2013)

The Al Qaeda Reader (2007)

The Battle of Yarmuk: An Assessment of the Immediate Factors behind the Islamic Conquests (2002)

THE TWO SWORDS OF CHRIST

THE TWO SWORDS OF CHRIST

Five Centuries of War Between Islam and the Warrior Monks of Christendom

RAYMOND IBRAHIM

Published by Bombardier Books
An Imprint of Post Hill Press
ISBN: 979-8-88845-723-8
ISBN (eBook): 979-8-88845-724-5

The Two Swords of Christ:
Five Centuries of War Between Islam and the Warrior Monks of Christendom

Cover Design by Jim Villaflores

Post Hill Press
New York • Nashville
posthillpress.com

Published in the United States of America
3 4 5 6 7 8 9 10

To all the forgotten and unsung heroes who sacrificed much—sometimes all—for righteousness' sake.

TABLE OF CONTENTS

"Then said he unto them, 'But now ... he that hath no sword, let him sell his garment, and buy one'.... And they said, 'Lord, behold, here are two swords.' And he said unto them, 'It is enough.'" (Luke 22:36, 38 KJV).

CHRISTENDOM AND ISLAM
12TH ~ 17TH CENTURIES
ATLANTIC OCEAN
Clermont
PARIS
PAYNS
Troyes
VÉZELAY
Poitiers
FRANCE
HOLY ROMAN EMPIRE (GERMANY 962-1648)
Vienne
Avignon
PROVENCE
Milan
GENOA
REPUBLIC OF VENICE
León
CASTILE
ARAGON
PORTUGAL
Lisbon
THE SPAINS
AL-ANDALUS
Barcelona
Valencia
Granada
Peñon de Vélez de la Gomera
ALMORAVIDS (1055-1130)
ALMOHADS (1147-1228)
Algiers
BARBARY
Goletta
Tunis
Mahdia
Tripoli
Sirte
ITALY
ROME
Naples
AMALFI
Lipari
MESSINA
SICILY
MALTA
OTRANTO
Buda
KINGDOM OF HUNGARY
Belgrade
TRANSYLVANIA
WALLACHIA
SERBIAN LANDS
Adrianople
BOLGARS
CONSTANTINOPLE
BLACK SEA
Dorylaeum
EASTERN ROMAN EMPIRE (330-1453)
OTTOMANS (1299-1923)
SELJUKS (1071-1308)
TARTARS
LESBOS
EUBOEA
Smyrna
Athens
Corinth
Ephesus
Mt. Cadmus
CILICIAN ARMENIA
Candia
CRETE
RHODES
CYPRUS
Limassol
Antioch
Aleppo
Tripoli
Tyre
Acre
Jerusalem
Gaza
MEDITERRANEAN SEA
Damietta
Alexandria
MANSOURA
CAIRO
EGYPT
FATIMIDS (969-1171)
AYYUBIDS (1171-1250)
MAMLUKS (1250-1517)
OTTOMANS (1517-1923)
N
0 Miles
500
0 Kilometers
500
1000

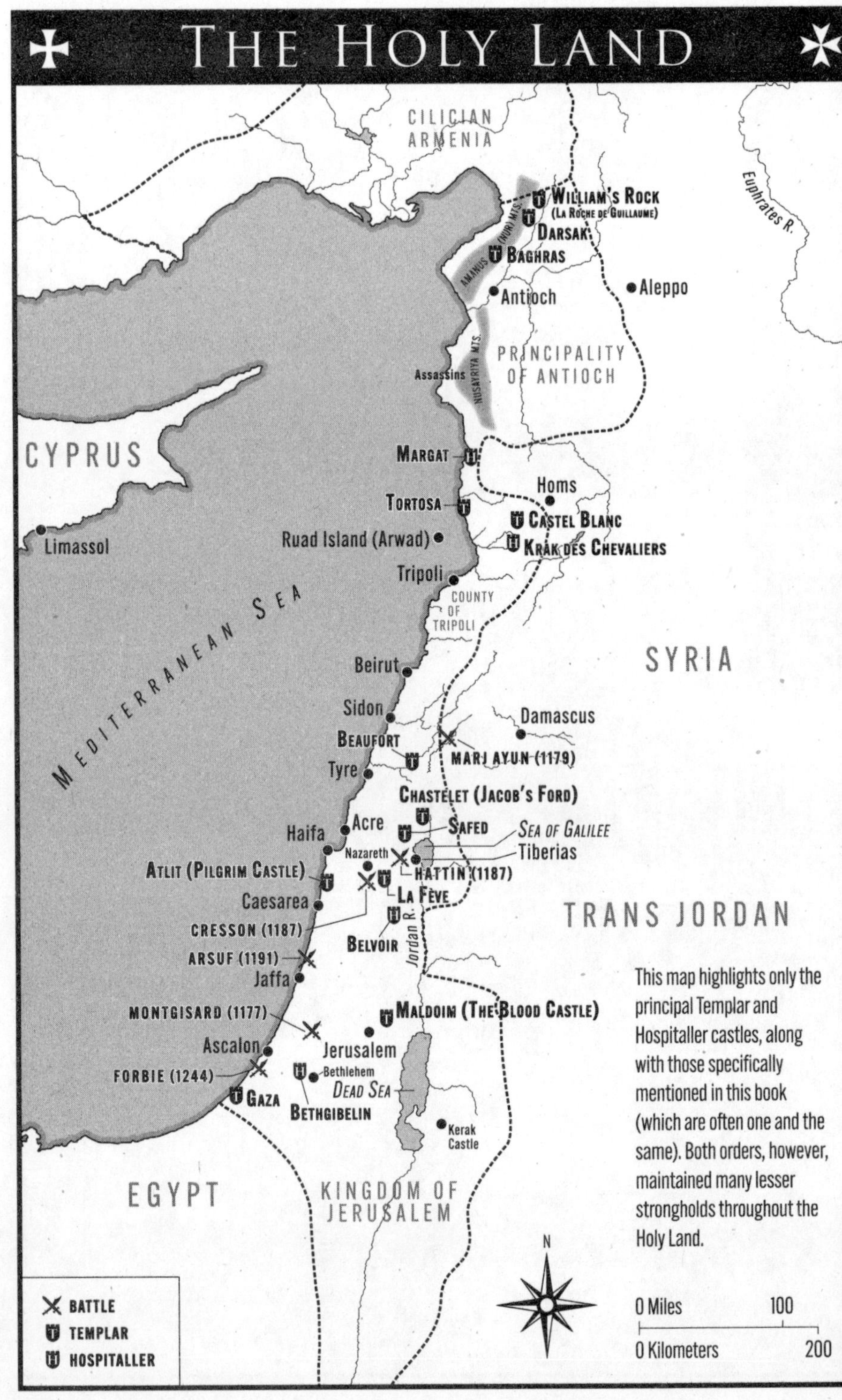
THE HOLY LAND
CILICIAN ARMENIA
William's Rock (La Roche de Guillaume)
Darsak
Baghras
Amanus (Nur) Mts.
Antioch
Aleppo
Euphrates R.
Principality of Antioch
Nusayriya Mts.
Assassins
Cyprus
Margat
Homs
Tortosa
Castel Blanc
Ruad Island (Arwad)
Krak des Chevaliers
Limassol
Tripoli
County of Tripoli
Mediterranean Sea
Syria
Beirut
Sidon
Damascus
Beaufort
Marj Ayun (1179)
Tyre
Chastelet (Jacob's Ford)
Acre
Safed
Haifa
Sea of Galilee
Nazareth
Tiberias
Atlit (Pilgrim Castle)
Hattin (1187)
La Fève
Caesarea
Trans Jordan
Cresson (1187)
Belvoir
Jordan R.
Arsuf (1191)
Jaffa
Montgisard (1177)
Maldoim (The Blood Castle)
Ascalon
Jerusalem
Forbie (1244)
Bethlehem
Dead Sea
Gaza
Bethgibelin
Kerak Castle
Egypt
Kingdom of Jerusalem
This map highlights only the principal Templar and Hospitaller castles, along with those specifically mentioned in this book (which are often one and the same). Both orders, however, maintained many lesser strongholds throughout the Holy Land.
N
Battle
Templar
Hospitaller
0 Miles 100
0 Kilometers 200

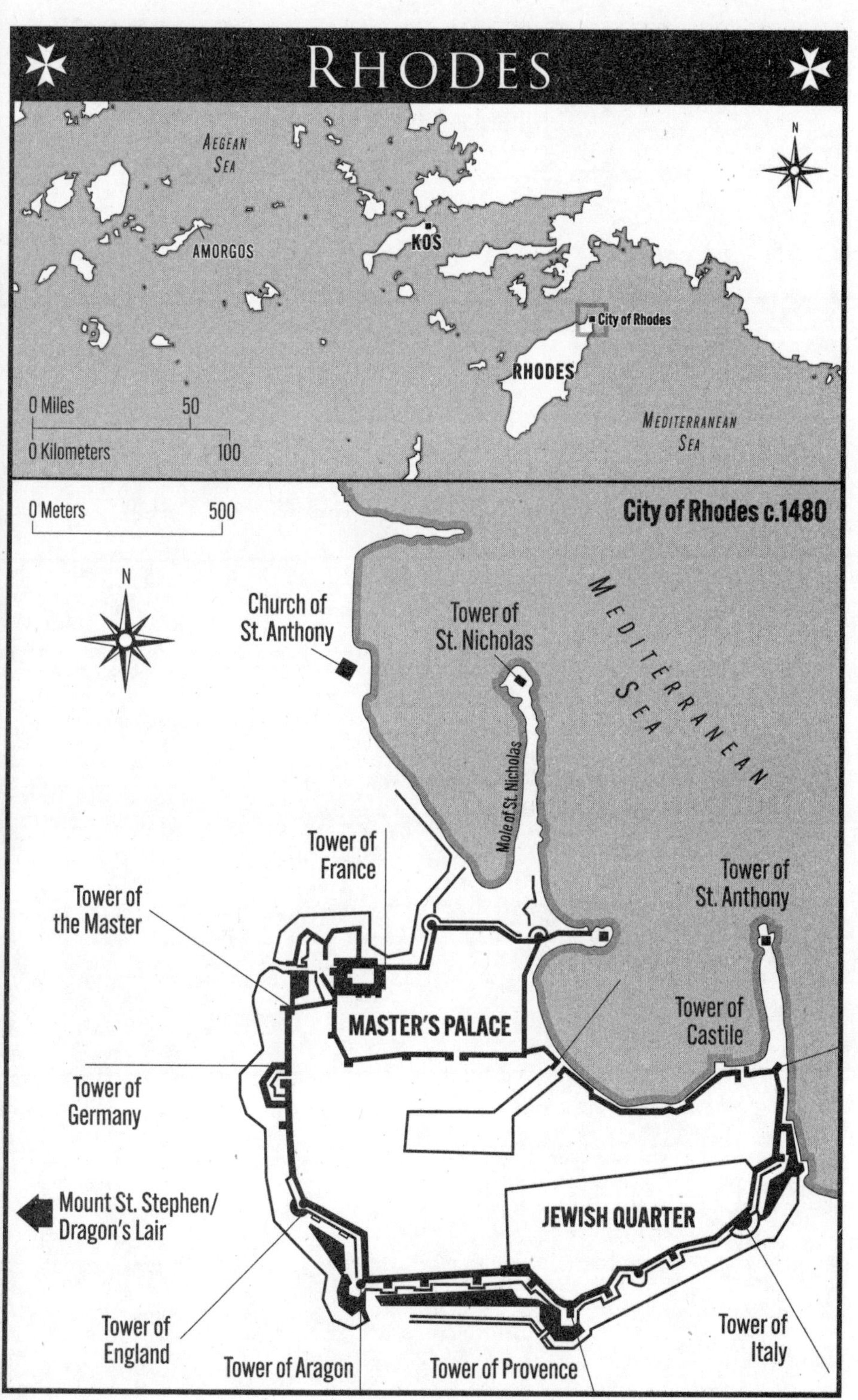
RHODES
AEGEAN SEA
AMORGOS
KOS
City of Rhodes
RHODES
MEDITERRANEAN SEA
0 Miles 50
0 Kilometers 100
N
City of Rhodes c.1480
0 Meters 500
N
Church of St. Anthony
Tower of St. Nicholas
MEDITERRANEAN SEA
Mole of St. Nicholas
Tower of France
Tower of the Master
Tower of St. Anthony
MASTER'S PALACE
Tower of Castile
Tower of Germany
Mount St. Stephen/ Dragon's Lair
JEWISH QUARTER
Tower of England
Tower of Aragon
Tower of Provence
Tower of Italy

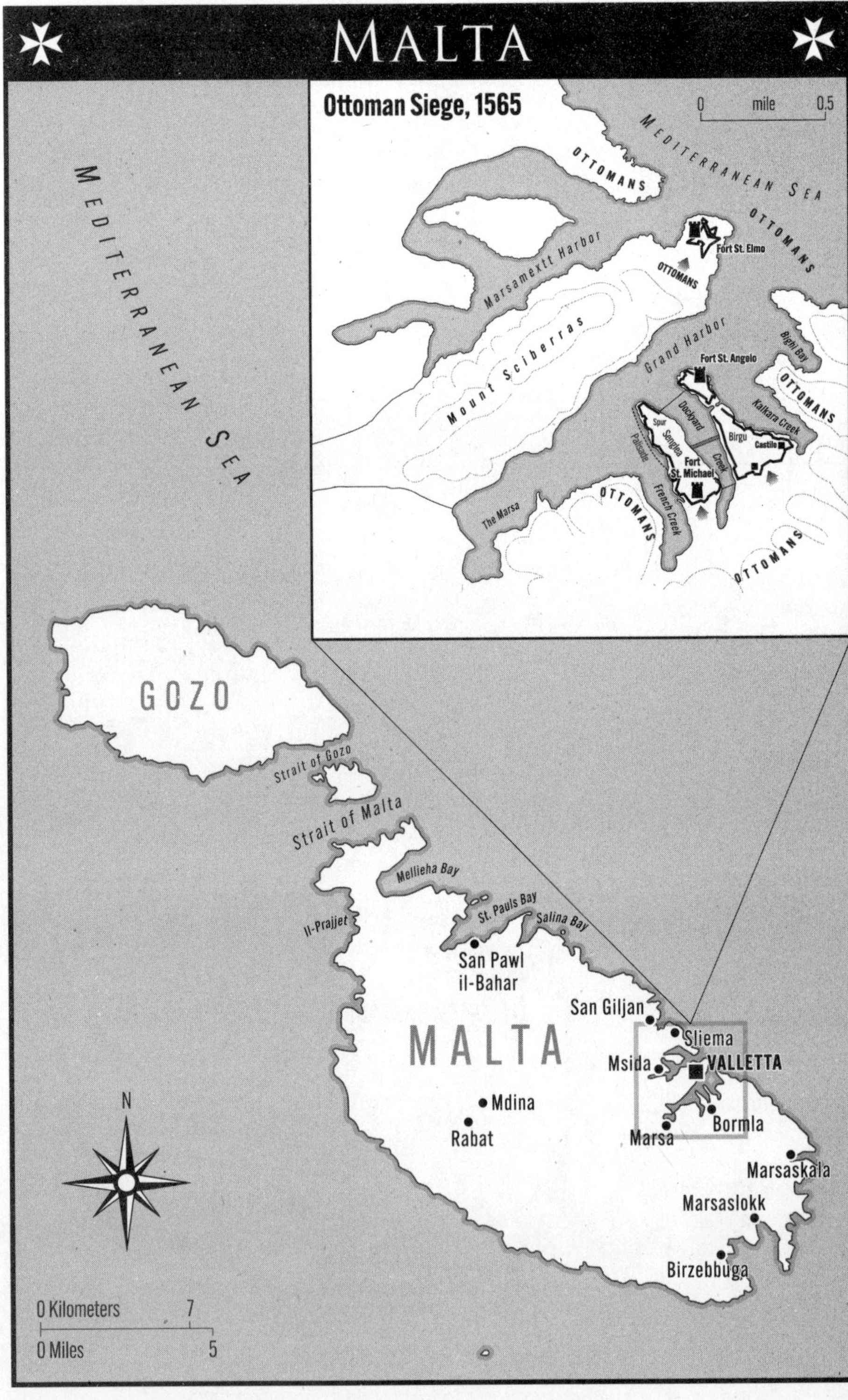

MALTA
Ottoman Siege, 1565
0 mile 0.5
MEDITERRANEAN SEA
OTTOMANS
Fort St. Elmo
Marsamextt Harbor
Mount Sciberras
Grand Harbor
Fort St. Angelo
Bighi Bay
Kalkara Creek
Dockyard
Spur
Senglea
Birgu
Castile
Fort St. Michael
Creek
Palisade
French Creek
The Marsa
MEDITERRANEAN SEA
GOZO
Strait of Gozo
Strait of Malta
Mellieha Bay
St. Pauls Bay
Salina Bay
Il-Prajjet
San Pawl il-Bahar
San Giljan
Sliema
MALTA
Msida
VALLETTA
Mdina
Rabat
Marsa
Bormla
Marsaskala
Marsaslokk
Birzebbuga
N
0 Kilometers 7
0 Miles 5

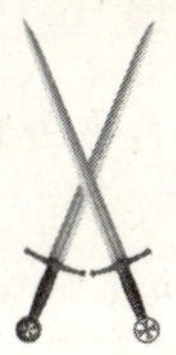

AUTHOR'S NOTE

This book tells the tale of history's great military orders—namely, the Knights of the Temple and the Hospital—who stood at the forefront of Christendom's long struggle against Islam.

These knights were unique and worthy of remembrance in that they were and remain the chief paragons of "Muscular Christianity"—an unapologetically masculine form of the faith that dominated much of the premodern era. Embodying a fierce, sacred resolve, these men were neither mere soldiers nor cloistered monks: They were both—*holy warriors*—men who believed that to defend the faith was to serve God.

Their entire raison d'être was rooted in scripture, beginning with the biblical concept of Just War: They fought not for conquest, but to protect the innocent, uphold the sacred, and defend Christian civilization.

While many modern Christians believe their faith begins and ends with being passive and non-confrontational—"turning the other cheek," never judging, and being tolerant of everything (including unadulterated evil)—these men took into account and tried to act on *all* of Christ's words.

Take Jesus's talk of *swords*. He tells his disciples that "he that hath no sword, let him sell his garment, and buy one." They respond, "Lord, behold, here are two swords," to which Christ concludes, "It is enough" (Luke 22:36, 38 KJV).

Whereas most modern-day Christians allegorize this verse into meaninglessness, for most premodern and especially medieval Christians, its meaning was clear: Christians are to fight two sorts of evils with two sorts of swords—a spiritual sword against spiritual enemies, and a physical sword against physical enemies. Taken together, these two swords were, and are, "enough."

Even the Knights' surreal feats of heroism were rooted in scripture. The biblical verse that told of how, if it was God's will, even one man could "chase a thousand, and two put ten thousand to flight" (Deuteronomy 32:30 KJV) inspired and actuated these men to no end.

It is for all these reasons and more that their story deserves to be told—especially to those Christians who insist, to their own detriment, that faith and force are exact opposites. The example of these Knights—whose blend of Christian piety and martial discipline remains unmatched—proves otherwise, hearkening back to a time of moral clarity, conviction, and courage.

The power of the Templars and Hospitallers rests in the fact that they *believed in*—and thus in many ways *became*—the Two Swords of Christ.

*****

A few words on stylistic and editorial decisions. My guiding principle throughout the writing of this book has been, in a word, *simplification*—taking stylistic and editorial liberties for the sake of clarity, consistency, and readability, while scrupulously preserving the substance of the material.

Proper names have been standardized in spelling (*Mohamet*, *Muhamad*, and *Mohammed*, have been rendered as *Muhammad*). British spellings have been Americanized (*honour*, *valour*, and *defence* have become *honor*, *valor*, and *defense)*. For familiarity's sake, personal names have generally been anglicized (*Jean* becomes *John*, *Carlos* becomes *Charles*, *Guillaume* becomes *William*).

Except when left for feel or atmosphere, archaic spellings and terminology have generally been modernized (*Musselmen* becomes *Muslims*, *Alcoran* becomes *Koran*, and *Grand Seignor* becomes *Sultan*).

When quoting from (typically older) English translations of Arabic, Turkish, or Persian texts, I have rendered certain translations into transliterations. Thus, if an English-language source of an Arabic text translates "Allah" to "God," I returned it to "Allah"; if it translates "jihad" to "Holy War," I returned it to "jihad"; if it translates sharia to "Holy Law," I returned it to sharia; if it translates "Allahu Akbar" to "God is Greatest"—which is also a wrong translation in that the Arabic is a comparative, not superlative—I returned it to "Allahu Akbar."

Dates—birth and death, or years of reign—have occasionally been added in parentheses following the names of select (usually notable) personages, when knowledge of such years adds context to the events and figures under discussion.

Another key editorial decision concerns terminology for leadership titles. In their origins, the supreme leaders of both the Temple and Hospital were referred to as *masters*. As these organizations grew and expanded across Europe, local administrative centers (commanderies or preceptories) developed and were headed by commanders and preceptors, respectively, who also came to be known as (regional) masters. To differentiate between the supreme and lesser masters, the former eventually took on the title of *grand master*. However, because the sources frequently refer to these supreme heads of both organizations by both terms (masters and grandmasters), to prevent confusion, I have opted for uniformity and always refer to the supreme leaders as *masters*, while referring to the lesser, regional leaders as priors, preceptors, and commanders. In short, *master* throughout this text should be understood to mean the highest-ranked leader of the Temple or Hospital, also known as *grand master*.

A final caveat: Towards the end of his magisterial history of the Hospitallers, the historian René-Aubert Vertot remarked, "I may have just reason to fear that the reader will be tired with the repetitions of so many assaults, so little different from one another."[1] His concern is not unwarranted. Because both the military orders, and Islam, were true to their mandate—the former constantly defending, the latter constantly attacking Christians—the histories of the Temple and Hospital have something of a repetitive quality to them. From another perspective, it is also a reminder that, from the moment they entered the Temple or Hospital, the lives of these knights were constantly marked by war, sieges, valor, and death—rinse and repeat, *ad nauseam.*

This is, incidentally, why so many of the knights mentioned in the forthcoming history, especially the masters, seem to blend into one another, appearing as the selfsame man, with only their personal names differentiating them. Even the Islamic sect of Assassins recognized this perpetual, unchanging nature of both orders. Though known for targeting and terrorizing high-profile leaders, the *Hashashin* never bothered trying to assassinate the masters of the Temple or Hospital (and even opted to pay them tribute instead). As the Muslims themselves admitted, assassinating any master was pointless, since another master would simply take his place and continue prosecuting the war—though with a renewed vengeance.

*****

This book constitutes the third of a trilogy, following *Sword and Scimitar* (2018) and *Defenders of the West* (2022). Like the former, it traces the centuries-long conflict between Islam and the West—now through the lens of Christendom's original commando forces. Like the latter, it highlights the unprecedented level of heroism and sacrifice—often unto martyrdom—that defined these Knights of God.

1

A LAND CALLED HOLY

Between the 320s and 330s, Constantine the Great, the first Roman emperor to convert to and legalize Christianity, heavily invested in Jerusalem and the adjoining Holy Land, including by constructing the Holy Sepulchre, a then-massive church structure built over the sites of Christ's crucifixion and entombment (hence its alternative name, the Church of the Resurrection).

Building places of worship atop holy sites cemented the already popular idea of *sacred territory*, which was well articulated by Eusebius, a contemporary of Constantine. This father of church history "directed attention, for the first time in Christian history, to the religious and theological significance of space. He was interested in Jerusalem not as a symbol of something else, that is, the heavenly Jerusalem, but because it is the site of places associated with the life of Jesus."[1]

Such ideas were hardly new. As Robert L. Wilken writes, "In a way that is difficult for moderns to grasp, religion in the ancient world was wedded to place."[2]

> Christians realized that seeing the holy places was a way of "renewing the image" of what had happened, that is, representing the saving events of the past in the present, of allowing believers through "memory" to "become

> spectators of history." If there were no places that could be seen and touched, the claim that God had entered human history would become a chimera. Sanctification of place was inevitable in a religion founded on history and on the belief that God "became flesh" in a human being. The holy places and the tombs of the patriarchs and prophets as well as the sites in Jerusalem and Bethlehem became witnesses to the truth of the biblical history and of the Christian religion.... By "exposing to sight" the tomb of Christ Constantine unveiled the "deeds of God".... [Christians were able to] see for the first time the scenes of biblical history, to touch the actual places where Jesus lived and died, to tread the same streets and roads that he walked.[3]

Because pilgrimages to holy sites are as old as mankind—Christians were already making pilgrimages to Jerusalem within a century of Christ's crucifixion[4]—after Constantine redesigned the Holy Land in a manner that was conducive to pilgrimage, they exploded. In response, John Chrysostom, who was born less than twenty years after the building of the Holy Sepulchre, could write about how "the whole world runs to see the tomb which has no body."[5]

Then Islam came. Around 634, the "great Arab conquests" of history began. Jerusalem was among the first Christian cities to be conquered in 637. After it, the whole of the Middle East and North Africa—which then represented the larger, older, and more sophisticated part of Christendom—was permanently conquered.

Although all forms of persecution were unleashed on the now-conquered Christian populations—massacres, enslavements, church desecrations, and systematic extortion (jizya)—for the purposes of this history, we focus primarily on the treatment of Christian pilgrims.*

---

* The first ninety or so pages of *Sword and Scimitar: Fourteen Centuries of War between Islam and the West* (chapters 1, 2, and 3) closely document the persecution Christians experienced during that first century in the Middle East, North Africa, Spain, and further into Europe.

The new Muslim conquerors of the Holy Land appreciated its importance to Christians and allowed pilgrims to visit—for a price: namely, that they pay for the privilege. But while Muslim rulers stood to gain from Christian pilgrims, the general Muslim populace saw only a nuisance. As such, random outbursts against the visiting Christians were a common occurrence.

Thus, in the early eighth century in Jerusalem, some Arabs—described as "untamed and beastly, illogical in mind and maniacs in their desires"—captured, tortured, and executed seventy Christian pilgrims for refusing to convert to Islam (minus seven who complied under torture). Shortly after that, another sixty pilgrims were crucified in Jerusalem. In 1022, Gerald of Thouars, a French abbot, was "martyred by Muslims before he reached Jerusalem." Four years later, another Frenchman, Richard of St. Vanne, was stoned to death by Muslims for openly saying mass. In 1040, Ulrich of Breisgau, a German pilgrim, was also stoned to death near the Jordan River.[6]

So much for visiting pilgrims. As for treatment of the Holy Land's native Christians, in the late eighth century, Muslims destroyed two churches and a monastery near Bethlehem and slaughtered its monks. In 796, Muslims burned another twenty monks to death. In 809, and again in 813, multiple monasteries, convents, and churches were attacked in and around Jerusalem; Christians of both sexes were gang-raped and massacred. In 929, on Palm Sunday, another wave of atrocities broke out: Churches were destroyed and Christians were slaughtered. In 936, "the Muslims in Jerusalem made a rising…and burnt down the church of the Resurrection [the Holy Sepulchre], which they plundered, and destroyed all they could of it."[7] In short, "Almost generation after generation, Christian writers recorded acts of persecution and harassment, to the point of slaughter and destruction, suffered at the hands of Muslim rulers."[8]

And that was *before* the advent of the Turks. In the years preceding but especially after the Turks' great victory against the Christian Roman Empire ("Byzantium") in 1071 at Manzikert, the persecution reached apocalyptic levels. "Far and wide they [Muslim Turks] ravaged cities and castles together with their settlements," wrote a Frankish eyewitness.

"Churches were razed down to the ground. Of the clergymen and monks whom they captured, some were slaughtered while others were with unspeakable wickedness given up, priests and all, to their dire dominion, and nuns—alas for the sorrow of it!—were subjected to their lusts."[9]

Emperor Alexios I Komnenos elaborated on this in a letter:

> The holy places are desecrated and destroyed in countless ways.... Noble matrons and their daughters, robbed of everything, are violated, one after another, like animals. Some [of their attackers] shamelessly place virgins in front of their own mothers and force them to sing wicked and obscene songs until they have finished having their way with them...men of every age and description, boys, youths, old men, nobles, peasants and what is worse still and yet more distressing, clerics and monks and woe of unprecedented woes, even bishops are defiled with the sin of sodomy and it is now trumpeted abroad that one bishop has succumbed to this abominable sin.[10]

Similar atrocities were meted out against pilgrims: "As the Turks were ruling the lands of Syria and Palestine, they inflicted injuries on Christians who went to pray in Jerusalem, beat them, pillaged them, [and] levied the poll tax [jizya]," writes chronicler Michael the Syrian. Moreover, "every time they saw a caravan of Christians, particularly of those from Rome and the lands of Italy, they made every effort to cause their death in diverse ways."[11] Such was the fate of one large German pilgrimage in 1064. After explaining how those Christians "endured many snares set by the pagans [Muslims] and lost many of their companions and their possessions" during their arduous trek to the Holy Land, a contemporary recorded a particularly savage atrocity:

> Accompanying this journey was a noble abbess of graceful body and of a religious outlook. Setting aside the cares of the sisters committed to her and against the advice of the wise, she undertook this great and

> dangerous pilgrimage. The pagans captured her, and in the sight of all, these shameless men raped her until she breathed her last, to the dishonor of all Christians. Christ's enemies performed such abuses and others like them on the Christians.[12]

Such are the origins of the First Crusade, which Pope Urban II called for in 1095. By then, the Turks, according to contemporary chroniclers such as Matthew of Edessa, had slaughtered and enslaved tens of thousands of Christians (Armenians, Greeks, Syriacs, and European pilgrims), and desecrated and destroyed thousands of churches throughout Anatolia (today, Turkey). In the words of historian Charles G. Addison,

> Under the iron yoke of [the Turks], the Christians were fearfully oppressed; they were driven from their churches; divine worship was ridiculed and interrupted; and the patriarch of the Holy City was dragged by the hair of his head over the sacred pavement of the Church of the Resurrection, and cast into a dungeon, to extort a ransom from the sympathy of his flock. The pilgrims who, through innumerable perils, had reached the gates of the Holy City, were plundered, imprisoned, and frequently massacred; an *aureus*, or piece of gold, was exacted as the price of admission to the Holy Sepulchre, and many, unable to pay the tax, were driven by the swords of the Turcomans* from the very threshold of the object of all their hopes, the borne of their long pilgrimage, and were compelled to retrace their weary steps in sorrow and anguish to their distant homes. The melancholy intelligence of the profanation of the holy places, and

* The term "Turcoman" is often used by historians to distinguish the unsettled, nomadic Turkic peoples of Central Asia—who arrived in various violent waves between the tenth and thirteenth centuries—from the more settled "Turks," an appellation typically reserved for established empire-builders such as the Seljuks and Ottomans.

> of the oppression and cruelty of the Turcomans, aroused the religious chivalry of Christendom; "a nerve was touched of exquisite feeling, and the sensation vibrated to the heart of Europe." Then arose the wild enthusiasm of the crusades; men of all ranks, and even monks and priests, animated by the exhortations of the pope and the preachings of Peter the Hermit, flew to arms, and enthusiastically undertook "the pious and glorious enterprise" of rescuing the Holy Sepulchre of Christ from the foul abominations of the heathen.[13]

By the summer of 1099—after nearly three years of untold sufferings and battles on their long and grueling march to the Holy Land—the First Crusaders had accomplished their mission and liberated Jerusalem and other ancient Christian cities, such as Edessa and Antioch, from Muslim control and abuse.

Incidentally, and despite modern-day characterizations, theirs was a *just war*: "The crusaders regarded their conquests as a part of Christendom that had been temporarily captured by Islam but was now restored to its rightful owners."[14] The indigenous Christians, especially Armenian and Syriacs, hailed them as liberators and saviors.

Once Europe learned that the holy sites, including the Church of the Sepulchre, or Resurrection, were now under the care of fellow Christians, pilgrimaging, which had never stopped, experienced a mass resurgence. However, because the pilgrimage routes still had to cross through Muslim regions—the Crusader Kingdom of Jerusalem was, in fact, a Christian island surrounded by a hostile Muslim sea—attacks on Christian pilgrims not only continued but were marked with a special cruelty by vengeful Muslims still smarting over the Christian victory.

After writing that the victory of the First Crusade caused the "zeal of pilgrimage to blaze forth with increased fierceness," Addison continues:

> Crowds of both sexes, old men and children, virgins and matrons, thinking the road then open and the journey practicable, successively pressed forwards towards the Holy City.... The infidels had indeed been driven out of

> Jerusalem, but not out of Palestine. The lofty mountains bordering the sea-coast were infested by warlike bands of fugitive Muslims, who maintained themselves in various impregnable castles and strongholds, from whence they issued forth upon the high-roads, cut off the communication between Jerusalem and the sea-ports, and revenged themselves...by the indiscriminate pillage of all travelers. The Bedouin horsemen, moreover, making rapid incursions from beyond the Jordan, frequently kept up a desultory and irregular warfare in the plains; and the pilgrims, consequently, whether they approached the Holy City by land or by sea, were alike exposed to almost daily hostility, to plunder, and to death.[15]

Every surviving pilgrim account supports this dismal description. Of his journey from the port of Jaffa to Jerusalem, the route which virtually every pilgrim took, Saewulf, the first English pilgrim to visit the Holy Land in 1103, wrote that the "The Saracens [Muslims] are always seeking to ambush the Christians: they lie concealed in the caverns of the mountains and the caves of the rocks, on the lookout night and day for anyone they can easily attack, either pilgrims traveling in small bands or exhausted stragglers separated from their companions."[16]

Three years later, Daniel, a Russian abbot, described the dangers he encountered to reach the church of Lydda near Jaffa: "There are many springs here; travelers rest by the water but with great fear, for it is a deserted place and nearby is the town of Ascalon from which Saracens sally forth and kill travelers on these roads. There is a great fear too going up from that place to the hills."[17]

Of his visit to Galilee, he wrote, "This place is very dreadful and dangerous...for here live fierce pagan Saracens who attack travelers."[18]

2

THE POOR FELLOW-SOLDIERS OF CHRIST

Although Jerusalem was secure and under Frankish control following the First Crusade, reaching it remained an even more hazardous undertaking for Western pilgrims than in previous centuries—not least due to vengeful Muslims committed to the utter annihilation of Christian pilgrims.

One man, Hugh of Payns (1070–1136), a knight who had fought with distinction in the First Crusade before returning home to Champagne, came back to and settled in the Holy Land in 1104. The ongoing savaging of pilgrims sorely troubled him. Walter Map (b. 1130), a Welsh cleric, offers the following anecdote:

> A knight called Payns from a village of that name in Burgundy went to Jerusalem on pilgrimage. Having heard that at a cistern just outside Jerusalem Christians watering their horses were frequently ambushed and killed in pagan attacks, he took pity on them. Moved by a strong feeling of justice, he defended them to the best of his ability, often lying in ambush himself and then coming to their aid, killing several of the enemy.

> The pagans were shaken by this and they set up camp in such numbers that nobody would be able to counter their attacks. The result was that the cistern had to be abandoned. But Payns, who was a man of energy and not easily defeated, obtained help for himself and for God after a lot of effort.[1]

Hugh took counsel with another knight, Godfrey of St. Omer. Together, they decided to form a brotherhood of guardians consisting of themselves and seven other knights of like mind. They would dedicate their lives to escorting and guarding pilgrims along the roads to and from Jerusalem (especially the port of Jaffa, which had long been harried by the Muslim garrison of Ascalon in Gaza). Described as a formidable band of knights, we know that "two at least of the original nine members, Hugh of Payns and Godfrey of St. Omer, were warriors of repute who had won high praise for their conduct in the First Crusade, and all of them had a knowledge of the country and of the wiles of the Muslim bandits of which newcomers from the West were naturally ignorant."[2]

Their altruistic proposal was enthusiastically welcomed by both secular and religious authorities. But because they were committing themselves to a distinctly Christian cause—loving their neighbor as themselves—they did it the Christian way. And so, sometime in late 1119 or early 1120—some say on Christmas Day[3]—Hugh, Godfrey, and the seven other nameless knights took vows of poverty, chastity, and obedience before Warmund, the patriarch of the Church of the Holy Sepulchre. Then and there, on their birthdate, they referred to themselves, and are referred to in the earliest documents, as the "Poor Fellow-Soldiers of Jesus Christ."

They could not have come any sooner; in the months preceding their vows, "a party of 700 unarmed pilgrims traveling from Jerusalem to the River Jordan in Holy Week of 1119 was ambushed by Saracens: 300 were killed and 60 taken off as slaves. It is quite possible that this incident was the catalyst for Hugh's idea of creating a brotherhood of guardians. Marauding Saracens had reached as far as the walls of

Jerusalem, and it had become dangerous to leave the city without an armed escort."[4] This is to say nothing of the "regular" Muslim raids on newly arrived Europeans in general, for example, the "Field of Blood," also in 1119, where "atabeg Togtekin gave Frankish prisoners to his soldiers for archery practice or hacked off their legs and arms, leaving them in the streets of Aleppo for the townsmen to finish off."[5]

As a reward for their pious intentions and self-sacrificial services to Christians, King Baldwin II bestowed upon them the al-Aqsa Mosque on the Temple Mount as a residence and headquarters. Although the mosque was built over a church dedicated to the Virgin Mary in 543 (the once-famous Nea Church), the Crusaders referred to the entire mount as Solomon's Temple—and so the nine quickly became known as the "Knights of the Temple," or, more simply, "Templars." Walter Map continues:

> He [Hugh of Payns] lived there [in the Temple] poorly dressed and ill-fed, spending everything he had on horses and arms, using all means of persuasion and pleading to enlist whatever pilgrim-soldiers he could either for permanent service there to the Lord or at least for temporary duty. Then, strictly according to rank and duty he fixed for himself and his fellow knights the insignia of the cross on the shield, imposing on his men a regime of chastity and sobriety.[6]

Having given away everything toward the cause, and as an indication of their poverty, Hugh and Godfrey were, for a time, reduced to sharing a single horse between them in their sorties to protect pilgrims from Muslim attacks (as is reflected by the original Templar seal, which depicts two knights riding atop one horse).

Along with offering some nuances concerning the rise of the Templars, the one thing all contemporary and near-contemporary chroniclers agree on is that the Poor Fellow-Soldiers of Jesus Christ were sincerely pious and self-sacrificing. Writing around 1135, one of the earliest entries comes from Simon, a monk of St. Bertin:

> On the advice of the princes of God's army they vowed themselves to God's Temple under this rule: they would renounce the world, give up personal goods, free themselves to pursue chastity, and lead a communal life wearing a poor habit, only using weapons to defend the land against the attacks of the insurgent pagans when necessity demanded.[7]

Writing between 1165 and 1184, William the archbishop of Tyre, whose chronicle of the First Crusade and his own era is invaluable, introduced them as follows:

> Some noblemen of knightly rank, devoted to God, pious and God-fearing, placed themselves in the hands of the lord patriarch for the service of Christ, professing the wish to live perpetually in the manner of regular canons in chastity, and obedience, without personal belongings. The leading and most eminent of these men were the venerable Hugh of Payns and Godfrey of Saint-Omer.... Their main duty, something that was imposed on them by the patriarch and the other bishops for the remission of their sins, was that they should maintain the safety of the roads and highways to the best of their ability, for the benefit of pilgrims in particular, against attacks of bandits and marauders.[8]

In short, and to quote James (or Jacques) of Vitry, bishop of Acre from 1214–1240, the Templars were committed "to defend pilgrims against brigands and rapists," as well as to observe "poverty, chastity and obedience according to the rules of ordinary priests."[9]

Little is known of the original brotherhood of nine other than that they still numbered nine a decade later, at least according to William of Tyre (though they may have had mercenaries and/or auxiliaries working alongside them). All that changed in 1129.

Enter Bernard of Clairvaux (1090–1153), founder of the Cistercian order (a reformed version of the Benedictine order) and Clairvaux

Abbey. Renowned for his robust piety, "Bernard was a monk who sincerely longed for a life of solitude and quiet prayer. It was not to be. His high energy, intense religious fervor, and the demands of those who called upon him for help constantly pulled him out of his monastery and involved him in the major moral, theological, and ecclesiastical issues of his day, including the crusades."[10] And his influence was considerable. In the words of a modern-day Benedictine historian,

> [Bernard was] one of the small class of supremely great men whose gifts and opportunities have been exactly matched. As a leader, as a writer, as a preacher and as a saint his personal magnetism and his spiritual power were far-reaching and irresistible. Men came from the ends of Europe to Clairvaux, and were sent out again all over the continent.... For forty years Citeaux-Clairvaux was the spiritual centre of Europe.[11]

Bernard, who was referred to as a "Doctor of the Church" and "the Last of the Fathers" by Pope Pius XII, was a keen supporter of the Templars and their mission to protect pilgrims. When, in 1124, a fellow Cistercian proposed the founding of yet another monastery in the Holy Land, Bernard rebuked the idea in a letter to the pope, adding, "Who cannot see that the necessities there are fighting knights not singing and wailing monks?"[12] A firm believer that only a true man of God can wage a successful war against the enemies of God,

> St. Bernard had no patience with men who tried to tackle tasks for which they were unsuited, and he did not share the current opinion that any undisciplined soldier, provided that he wore the cross, was fit to fight the Muslims. He criticized the priests who, after spending their lives in sedentary tasks, wanted to go to war against Islam, and he was later to thunder that the Army of the Lord must not be burdened with such but composed of men with strength and skill in battle.... [I]n St. Bernard's view the soldier should also be the man of

> God, and his admiration for the Templars, half lay, half religious, mighty in war and fervent in prayer, knew no restraint.[13]

When Bernard championed the Templars' cause at the Council of Troyes in January 1129, everything changed for the original band of nine knights. They were formally recognized as an order—Christendom's very first military order—and given a religious rule of seventy-two clauses, the prologue of which exhorts recruits "who up until now have embraced a secular knighthood in favor of humans only, and in which Christ was not the cause, to hasten and associate yourselves in perpetuity with the order of those whom God has chosen from the mass of perdition and has assembled for the defense of the Holy Church."[14] The knights were also given a habit at Troyes, a white cloak or mantle symbolizing the purity they should strive after, and, later, under Pope Eugenius III, the red cross, a symbol of martyrdom and the knighthood of Christ.

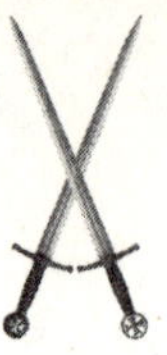

3

RISE OF THE TEMPLARS

Following their official recognition at Troyes in 1129, the Templars' fame exploded around Christendom: "Uniting in themselves the two most popular qualities of the age, devotion and valor, and exercising them in the most popular of all enterprises, the protection of pilgrims and of the road to the Holy Sepulchre, they speedily acquired a vast reputation and a splendid renown."[1] Many knights joined the new Order, and many great houses lavished the Poor Fellow-Soldiers of Christ with donations, changing their fortunes forever. Indeed, enthused by their noble purpose, nobles contributed land, income, and manpower on such a scale that, in two decades, the once impoverished Templars possessed a vast network of preceptories all across Europe. At their peak, these commanderies numbered nearly a thousand, and their commanders served their brethren in the Holy Land, including by raising money and recruits.

Attraction for the Templars was such that even before the Council of Troyes, whenever and wherever Europeans heard of this new band of knights' purpose and exploits, enthusiasm abounded. In 1128, King Baldwin II sent Hugh of Payns to Europe on a diplomatic mission. Naturally, the Templars' founding master (as Hugh and his successors were called) used this opportunity to raise support for his fledgling Order, and, according to the *Anglo-Saxon Chronicle*, "All good men gave him welcome and much treasure...and a great sum in gold and silver was given to him to take back to Jerusalem, and with him and after went as great a number as never before since the days of Pope Urban [II, meaning during the First Crusade]."[2]

That this was a martial age made the Templars all the more appealing: "Many Orders promised a heavenly reward through prayer or service to the poor and afflicted, but only the Temple held out the assurance of heaven through fighting, and it was an age in which every man of noble birth was trained for war."[3] As such, those who joined the Order did so when they were "not in their dotage or after [old] age or injury precluded further material activities—as was so often the case with traditional Benedictine orders—but while they were in their prime, willing and able to fight for what both they and Bernard saw as a just cause."[4]

This fusion between piety and masculinity, which epitomized the Temple, so permeated medieval society as to be evident in its highest echelons—beginning with King Baldwin II of Jerusalem, who generously supported them, including by housing them in the Temple (al-Aqsa Mosque). On the one hand, this Crusader king is described as having "had callouses on his hands and knees from frequent religious exercise and constant kneeling"; on the other hand, he was a wild man in battle: "The king," William of Tyre writes concerning a battle with the Muslims in 1126, "hurled himself like a lion against the serried ranks of the foe. Destruction on the right and on the left attended his progress, a massacre terrible even in the eyes of the conquerors. Our annals, even to the present time, contain no account of such a desperate and uncertain battle.... Finally...the infidels were put to flight. They had suffered a massacre which will be memorable forever."[5]

The observations of military historian and colonel E. J. King, concerning why the Templars and subsequent military orders were immensely popular, are especially germane and worth quoting at length:

> During the Middle Ages many military religious orders were founded, as is naturally to be expected, when we

> consider the ideals and the conditions that then prevailed. The Christian religion was still fighting for its very existence against the followers of Muhammad throughout all the Mediterranean lands. Religion was then a living force in man's every thought and word and deed, to an extent that is difficult now even to realize. The very ritual of knighthood had become clothed in such mystic and symbolic ceremonies that to the true knight even his sword seemed consecrated to the service of God.[6]

After indicating the various ways religious orders served God—devoting themselves to prayer and contemplation, teaching, preaching, helping the sick and needy, and undertaking "missions to the heathen," where they often met "their end in death by torture in its most hideous forms"[7]—King continues:

> Nothing could be more natural to the age than the foundation of yet other religious orders, in which the monks renouncing the things of this world and taking the same three solemn vows of chastity, obedience and poverty, should devote their lives to fighting against the heathen and the infidel in defense of the Christian faith. Religious orders of such a nature would appeal irresistibly to the noblest spirits of that hard-fighting military aristocracy then supreme throughout Europe. Gallant young gentlemen, filled with the spirit of adventure and burning with religious zeal, were ready enough to take the vows and renounce the things of this world, if it was to be accompanied by the congenial military life that they loved, and possibly by the most glorious of all ends, sword in hand, with their faces to the foe, fighting the battles of Christ. The foundation of the military religious orders was the natural outcome of the spirit of the age.[8]

All early recruits to the Temple were, in essence, echoing the words of the hero of the *Moniage Guillaume*, a twelfth-century chanson de geste (a type of Old French epic poem): "There is greater worth in the orders of knighthood, which fight against the Saracen race…[unlike] Monks [who] have no concern but to live in a monastery, to eat and to drink decanted wine, and to sleep when they have said compline."[9]

Why any knight would choose to join the Templars—that is, willingly give up all that he had, take vows of poverty, obedience, and chastity, and then devote his life to defending Christian pilgrims—is further reflected in several charters. Thus, according to the preamble of the charter of Hugh of Bourbouton, this lord in Provence gave all his possessions to and joined the Templars in 1139 "in direct response to Christ's injunction in Matthew 16:24: 'If anyone wishes to come after me, he should deny himself and bear his cross and quickly follow me.'"[10] In 1145, Hugh's son Nicholas also gave away his entire inheritance to the Temple, in order to "render myself to the same knighthood of God and the Temple to serve as servant and brother, although unworthy, all the days of my life."[11]

Perhaps most notable of all was Alfonso I of Aragon and Navarre (1074–1134), better known among contemporaries as "the Battler" due to his many exploits against the Muslims of Spain. After divorcing Princess Urraca, whom sources present as a vain and capricious wife, this "quintessential crusader devoted to the destruction of Islam until his dying day"[12] liberated Zaragoza from Islamic control in 1118, then a major watershed moment for the Reconquista—the centuries-long reconquest and reclamation of Spain from Islam—and regularly raided deep into Muslim territory. He "surprised several fortresses bordering upon his dominions, and carried fire and sword into the very heart of Muslim territory," often returning with thousands of free Christian captives in his train, to quote from one Muslim source.[13]

A warrior-king who essentially led the life of a warrior-monk, and thus sired no heirs, Alfonso's appreciation for those who shared his piously militant ideals—namely, the military orders—was unparalleled, as evidenced by his unprecedented will:

> For the salvation of my soul and of those of my mother and father, and of all my kin, I make this will before God, and our Lord, Jesus Christ and all his saints...[that] after my death I leave as heir and successor to me the Sepulchre of the Lord, which is in Jerusalem, and those who observe and guard it and serve God there [meaning the knights attached to it], and the Hospital of the poor which is in Jerusalem [which was then becoming militarized], and the Temple of the Lord with its knights who strive to defend the name of Christianity there.[14]

These three orders were "to have and to hold in three fair and equal parts" the "whole of my kingdom."[15] As might be expected, on his death, the nobles refused to honor his will, though a compromise was eventually reached, whereby the Templars and orders received and held various frontier castles and territories against Islam.

Alfonso's deep appreciation for that which was both pious and militant was reflective of the Iberian Peninsula's overall appreciation for the military orders—and for good reason. As one historian explains, after the Muslim conquest of nearly the whole of Spain in 711:

> By the eleventh century five Christian kingdoms had appeared [in the north]: Galicia (with Portugal), León, Castile, Navarre and Aragon, whose people lived in dread of razzias [jihadist raids]. Every year the Christian territories were devastated, crops burnt, fruit trees cut down, buildings razed, livestock driven off and the inhabitants herded back to the slave-markets. Those who escaped were cowed by ingenious atrocities, the victims' heads being salted as trophies to impress the caliph's unruly subjects. Yet the barbarous [Christian] princes with their puny kingdoms never forgot they were the rightful lords of Spain. The Reconquista was a holy war.[16]

Accordingly, for centuries, that peninsula became a theater of jihad and crusade and, therefore, its people appreciated the need for military orders more than those in any other Christian region save the Holy Land itself.* As such, it is unsurprising that the earliest donations to the Temple, which began as early as 1128, before the Council of Troyes, came from the Iberian Peninsula. The founder of Portugal, Count Afonso Henriques, confirmed a castle donation to the Temple, "for the love which I have in my heart for you and since I am a brother in your fraternity."[17]

Similarly, months after the Council of Troyes in 1130, Ramon Berenguer III, count of Barcelona, gave them the castle of Granyena "for the defense of Christianity according to the purpose for which the order was founded."[18] He then abdicated his throne, took Templar vows, sent vast sums of money to the Temple in Jerusalem, and immured himself in a small cell in the Templar house in Barcelona, where he engaged in constant spiritual exercises until his death.

His son, Ramon Berenguer IV, was no less devoted to the Temple. In 1143, out of "divine inspiration and a sense of piety," he granted

---

* Indeed, second only to the Holy Land, the Iberian Peninsula—as seen, particularly the Crown of Aragon—hosted a significant concentration of the Templars and Hospitallers, who played notable roles in the Christian military effort against Islam. Their presence, however, was unevenly distributed across the peninsula. While they established important commanderies and fortresses in Aragon and Catalonia (such as Monzón for the Templars and Amposta for the Hospitallers), their influence in Castile and León was much more limited, owing in part to the rise of powerful native orders that more directly aligned with local monarchs and Reconquista politics. Among these indigenous Spanish military orders were the Order of Calatrava (founded 1158), the Order of Santiago (also known as the Order of St. James of the Sword, founded 1170), the Order of Alcántara (1176), and, later, the Order of Montesa (1317), created to absorb the former Templar properties within the Crown of Aragon. In Portugal, the Order of Avis (1166) and especially the Order of Christ (1319) played parallel roles—the latter directly succeeding the Templars. Like the Templars and Hospitallers, these Iberian orders were religious-military institutions with vows of poverty, chastity, and obedience, and they were explicitly founded to wage war against Islam and defend Christian territories. All engaged in the ideology and practice of holy war, administered fortified frontiers, and combined martial, religious, and economic functions. That said, the Spanish orders were more closely integrated into local feudal and dynastic structures. And, just as their recruitment was largely regional, so too were their priorities territorially focused on the Reconquista rather than the broader defense of Christendom.

them several castles "to defend the Western Church in Spain, to crush, defeat and drive out the race of the Moors [Muslims], to exalt the faith and religion of Holy Christendom, after the fashion of the knighthood of the Temple of Solomon in Jerusalem which protects the Eastern Church."[19]

In short, and because it shared the same circumstances that gave rise to the Temple in the Holy Land—pious warfare against Islam—there was no end to the admirers and benefactors of the Temple in Spain. Another was Armengold VI, count of Urgel, who in 1132 gave the Temple his castle of Barbera, "in the Saracen March," meaning along the Muslim frontier.[20]

Due to the Templars' popularity with and great support from Christians throughout Europe, William of Tyre, writing some four decades after the Council of Troyes, says,

> They began to increase, and their possessions multiplied.... The Templars prospered so greatly that today there are in the order about three hundred knights who wear the white mantle and, in addition, an almost countless number of lesser brothers [sergeants, turcopoles, auxiliaries, etc.]. They are said to have vast possessions, both on this side of the sea and beyond [meaning in the Holy Land and Europe]. There is not a province in the Christian world today which does not bestow some part of its possessions upon these brethren, and their property is reported to be equal to the riches of kings.[21]

"They were also endowed," James of Vitry wrote some years after William, "with farms, towns, and villages, to an immense extent both in the East and in the West, out of the revenues of which they send yearly a certain sum of money for the defense of the Holy Land to their head Master at the chief house of their order in Jerusalem."[22]

Despite their popularity, the Templars themselves, who it may be supposed were willing to accept less than pious recruits simply to augment their ranks, were the first to stress the spiritual side of their vocation. During their admission ceremony, recruits were told that their service had three aspects: "the first is to abandon and leave behind the evils of this world; the second is to serve our Lord; the third is to be poor and to do penance in this life, for the salvation of the soul."[23] So serious was the Order that

> many illustrious knights of the best families in Europe aspired to the habit and the vows, but however exalted their rank, they were not received within the bosom of the fraternity until they had proved themselves by their conduct worthy of such a fellowship. Thus, when Hugh d'Amboise, who had harassed and oppressed the people of Marmontier [in France] by unjust exactions, and had refused to submit to the judicial decision of the Count of Anjou, desired to enter the order, Hugh of Payns refused to admit him to the vows, until he had humbled himself, renounced his pretentions, and given perfect satisfaction to those whom he had injured.[24]

Another important development occurred in the decade between the Temple's founding around 1119 and universal recognition at Troyes in 1129: From being exclusively devoted to the protection of pilgrims, "warfare against the Muslims had come to be regarded as its principal function."[25]

> As the hostile tribes of Muslims, which everywhere surrounded the Latin kingdom, were gradually recovering from the stupefying terror…of the First Crusaders, and were assuming an aggressive and threatening attitude, it was determined that the holy warriors of the Temple should, in addition to the protection of pilgrims, make the defense of the Christian kingdom of Jerusalem, of the Eastern Church, and of all the holy places, a part of their particular profession.[26]

As such, "they undertook to battle against the infidel, whether or not pilgrims were threatened, and the brethren became the nucleus of a standing army vowed to a perpetual struggle with Islam."[27] This expansion appears to have been inevitable and the next logical step in the evolution of the Temple. If it was axiomatic that Muslims would always and everywhere prey on Christians, pilgrims and otherwise—and it was—and if the Temple's entire purpose was to protect Christians, then by default the Temple was at war with surrounding Islam.

The reader is left with a final pertinent quote summarizing the Templars, written by Anselm, bishop of Havelberg, in 1145:

> Having left their own property they live a common life, and fight under [a vow of] obedience to one master. They cut themselves off from superfluity and costly clothes, prepared to defend the glorious Sepulchre of the Lord against the incursions of the Saracens. At home peaceful, out of doors strenuous warriors; at home obedient to the discipline of a religious rule, out of doors conforming to military discipline; at home instructed in holy silence, out of doors undaunted by the clash and attack of battle; and, to sum up briefly, they perform everything they are ordered to do, indoors and out of doors, in simple obedience (brackets in original).[28]

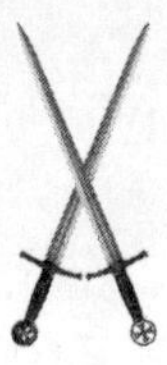

4

HUGH THE SINNER

Despite the Knights Templars' explosion in popularity, then as now, there were the naysayers and scoffers who criticized the fledgling brotherhood for taking up arms, instead of behaving like "true Christians"—that is, forsaking the world and leading purely contemplative lives praying, fasting, and meditating. In 1145, for instance, Henry the archbishop of Huntingdon described Henry the bishop of Winchester as "a certain new monster composed from purity and corruption, namely a monk and a knight." Though he was not talking about the Templars, clearly his thinking suggests that knights and monks were antithetical to one another.[1]

Others were more explicit. Safe from his monastery near Poitiers, the Cistercian monk, Isaac of Etoile, could scoff: "There has sprung up a new monster, a certain new knighthood [Templars], whose Order... is set up to force unbelievers into the Christian faith by lances and cudgels, and may freely despoil those who are not Christians, and butcher them religiously; but if any of them fall in such ravaging, they are called martyrs of Christ."[2] This, of course, was a straw man argument: Not only was the forcible conversion of Muslims never one of the Templars' functions; if anything, and as we shall soon see, they were often criticized for being *indifferent* to Muslim conversions. Still, others in Europe had heard tell that "the Templars did not want peace or to convert Muslims; they only wanted to fight."[3]

All such criticisms floating in the air prompted the writing of a letter addressed to the "Knights of Christ in the Temple at Jerusalem," presumably the original band of nine. Authored by a man who simply referred to himself as "Hugh the Sinner," the latest scholarship suggests that it was penned by the first master of the Order himself, Hugh of Payns, while he was away in Europe around 1128, in an effort to reinvigorate his demoralized fellow knights. In Hugh's own words,

> We have heard that some of you have been alarmed by certain indiscreet persons, as if your profession—in which you dedicate your life to bearing weapons against the enemies of the faith and of the peace and for the defense of Christians—as if that profession was illicit or harmful, a sin or an obstacle to greater progress![4]

The true source behind these seeds of doubt was the one "who does not sleep"—Satan:

> For he knows that if he tries to persuade you to sin, you will not listen and will not consent. So he does not say to you, "Get drunk, sleep around, get into fights, slander." You have nullified his first aim by rejecting sin. You have also destroyed your adversary's second aim: for in peacetime you fight your own body with fasts and abstinence so that when he suggests you should feel pride in your virtuous work, you resist and overcome him just as you fight with weapons in battle against the enemies of peace who injure you or wish to injure you. So he, the invisible enemy who is always tempting you and cruelly pursuing you, strives to spoil the good work which you are performing with proper and rational zeal.... [H]is aim is to spoil the action by corrupting your intentions.[5]

Even if Satan whispers directly in the overly conscientious knights' ears in an effort to convince them that they are *really* fighting and killing out of anger and hatred and taking spoils for reasons of cupidity, the brothers must not succumb to his wiles but remain clear in their purpose, insisted Hugh: They do not hate, fight, and kill *Muslims*; rather, they hate, fight, and kill the Muslims' *sins* (persecuting Christians, destroying churches, and so on), and they take spoils as just recompense for their sacrifices, in keeping with the normal rules of war, and because "'the workman deserves his wages.' [Luke 10:7; 1 Timothy 5:18]."[6]

"Oh deception of the enemy," a vexed Hugh continues, "when will you cease?"

> How does the angel Satan transform into an angel of light? [II Corinthians 11:14]. If the devil tried to persuade them [Templars] to reach out for worldly ostentation, his deception would be easily recognized; but now he tells the knights of Christ to lay down their weapons, not to wage wars, to run away from uproar, to seek the secret place—so that he can take away their true humility while pretending to offer an appearance of humility. For what is pride, if it is not refusing to obey what God has commanded you?[7]

As for the claim that true Christians must never resist evil but rather abandon the world and its problems and dedicate themselves to prayer, fasting, and contemplation—all of which the Templars *also* did when not fighting in defense of the faith—Hugh argued that different segments of Christian society had different but equally important functions, including both the praying monk and the fighting warrior. All of them, moreover, must do their share of work, just as the apostles of Christ did:

> [You] must not run away from work, and anyone seeking a crown must not avoid fighting. Christ Himself, whose example you ought to follow, before he ascended securely to Heaven to the right hand of the Father,

> labored on earth fighting godless and evil people. Look, brothers: if you were supposed to seek rest and quiet... there would be no religious orders left in God's Church. Even the desert hermits were not able to escape work altogether; they had to work for food, clothing, and the other necessities of this mortal life. If there was no one ploughing and sowing, harvesting and preparing food, what would the contemplatives do? If the Apostles had said to Christ: "We want to be free and contemplate, not run about or work; we want to be far from people's objections and disputes," if the Apostles had said this to Christ, where would the Christians be now?[8]

The idea that the truly pious man sets his hands to work rather than keeps them clasped in prayer was certainly not new and is reflected in many medieval texts. In the *Song of Roland* (c. 1040), while watching Roland "slicing" a Muslim "in two," an archbishop observed, "You act very well. A knight should have such valor, who bears arms and sits astride a good horse. In battle he should be strong and fierce, or else he is not worth four pence. He ought rather to be a monk in one of those monasteries and pray all day long for our sins!"[9]

Nor was the idea that Christian society consisted of different segments, each with its particular vocation, new or peculiar to Hugh. Indeed, in a letter addressed to "Hugh, master of the knights of the Temple and all fighting religiously under him," Simon the bishop of Noyon made that very distinction in 1130, thanking God for resuscitating the order of *defenders*:

> We give thanks to God, because through his mercy he has recovered the order which had perished. For we know that three orders have been instituted by God in the Church, the order of prayers, of defenders, and of workers. The other orders were in decline while the order of defenders had almost completely perished. But God the Father and our Lord Jesus Christ, God's Son, had mercy on his Church. Through the infusion of the

> Holy Spirit in our hearts, in these most recent times he deigned to repair the lost order. So in the holy city where once the Church originated, there the lost order of the Church began to be repaired...[10]

"Under the guise of piety," concludes the Temple's first master, "the enemy is striving to lead you into error's trap. Men should not flee from virtues, but from sin. You should not avoid physical activity, but mental confusion."[11]

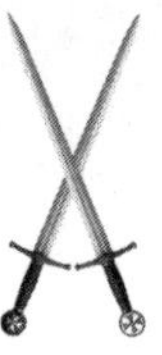

5

TWO SWORDS ARE "ENOUGH"

As part of Hugh of Payns's efforts to boost the Templars' morale, he had on three occasions implored Bernard of Clairvaux to lend his influential voice in support. The saint finally responded in a treatise titled *In Praise of the New Knighthood.* Published sometime shortly after the Council of Troyes in 1129, it is a valuable document that sheds much light on the nature and purpose of the Templars and all subsequent military orders.

Bernard's treatise was addressed to "Hugh, Knight of Christ, and Master of Christ's Militia" and is laden with allusions to and direct quotes from scriptures. It begins by showing that the Templars do indeed represent an entirely, but also much needed, new animal—the fusion of monk and knight—so that the two realms of Christian warfare that had hitherto been separated, the incorporeal and corporeal, or spiritual and secular, could be confronted by the selfsame warrior-monk: "This…is a new kind of knighthood and one unknown in ages past. It indefatigably wages a twofold combat, against flesh and blood and against spiritual hosts of evil in the heavens [Ephesians 6:12]."[1]

Nothing, Bernard continues, is new or shocking about warriors who fight their foes with might and main or of monks who combat demons through prayer and fasting:

> But for a man to powerfully gird himself with both swords [spiritual and secular] and nobly mark his belt [with the cross]—who would not consider this worthy of great admiration, even more so since it has hitherto been unknown? Truly, a fearless knight and secure on every side is he whose soul is protected by the armor of faith just as his body is protected by armor of steel. Doubly armed, surely, he need fear neither demons nor men. Not that he fears death—no, he desires it. Why should he fear to live or to die when for him to live is Christ, and to die is gain?... March forth confidently then, you knights, and with a stalwart heart repel the foes of the cross of Christ. Be sure that neither death nor life can separate you from the love of God, which is in Jesus Christ.[2]

Such an idea is logically consistent: If it is acceptable to fend off Satan's fiery darts against the soul, why is it not acceptable to fight off the enemies of Christianity, who harried Christians, not just with fiery darts but with swords, spears, and cruelty unbounded? Indeed, although forgotten today, "both swords" mentioned by Bernard are a reference to Luke 22:38 where Christ told his disciples that "two swords" are "enough." For premodern theologians, this was Christ's way of legitimizing two forms of warfare—one with a spiritual sword against spiritual enemies and one with a physical sword against physical enemies. Thus, nearly a century after Bernard, James of Vitry (1160–1240), the bishop of Acre, told of how

> Saracens and pagans undermine the peace of Christendom, tyrants and evil Christians attack the liberty of the Church, and false brothers undermine love.... Against the violence of the pagans and Saracens it [the Church] uses the physical sword [hence the Crusades]. Against tyrants and false brothers it uses a spiritual sword.... Since the Church has two swords, which the Lord said "is enough,"

> [Luke 22:38], one is to be exercised in a spiritual sense by the prelates, the other by princes and military Christians.[3]

James of Vitry went on to assert that only "heretics argue that it is not Christian to fight and cite scripture to prove this":

> They, lying, assert that it is not permissible for you to take up a physical sword, nor to fight bodily against the enemies of the Church. They abuse the authority of the Scriptures and present petty reasons.... And if we did not resist the Church's enemies, the Saracens and heretics would have already devastated the whole Church.... In fact knighthood was set up in order to repel violence, repulse injuries and exercise justice on evildoers.[4]

Returning to Bernard, this important spokesman for the Templars went on to argue in his *In Praise* that fighting, even killing, are not intrinsically evil; rather, it is the intention and motivation of the fighter that decides the matter: "Indeed, danger or victory for the Christian are weighed by the focus of the heart, not the fortunes of war. If he fights for a good cause, the outcome of the battle can never be evil; and likewise the result can never be considered good if the cause is evil and the intention unrighteous."[5] The new knights were engaged in *male*cide, not *hom*icide; their purpose was to exterminate evil, not evildoers (who, in this context, were seen as collateral damage):

> Surely, if he kills an evil doer, he is not a man-killer, but, if I may so put it, an evil-killer. Clearly he is reckoned the avenger of Christ against evildoers, and the defender of Christians. Should he be killed himself, we know he has not perished, but has come safely home.[6]

From here, Bernard compares and contrasts the new knighthood with the secular, and by then quite ostentatious, knighthood. Not only do the latter fight and kill for vain, un-Christian reasons—for fame, gain, vengeance, or wrath—but they dress in "effeminate tresses" and ornament themselves and their horses with baubles befitting the "trinkets of a woman."[7]

In stark contrast, the Templars had a decidedly manly look and austere outlook. Along with going against Frankish custom by refusing to shave and letting their beards grow long (in keeping with God's design and therefore will), "they cut their hair short, cognizant that, according to the Apostle, it is shameful for a man to cultivate flowing locks. They never dress, and seldom wash, their hair—content to let it appear tousled and dusty, darkened by chain mail and heat." Bernard continues:

> When battle is imminent, they protect themselves inwardly by their faith and outwardly by iron, not gold, so that, armed and not adorned, they strike fear into the enemy rather than arousing his greed [to plunder them of their rich trinkets]. They seek to have strong and swift horses, not ones decked out in many colors. They are intent on fighting, not pomp; victory, not glory; and they strive to inspire terror, not admiration.[8]

Worse, for the secular knighthood, because they fight and kill for "slight and frivolous" reasons—including "irrational anger," "empty glory," and "earthly possessions"—it is, for them, "not safe to kill or be killed," as hell would be a possible consequence.[9] In contrast, the new "knights of Christ may safely do battle in the battles of their Lord, fearing neither the sin of smiting the enemy nor the danger of their own downfall, inasmuch as death for Christ, inflicted or endured, bears no taint of sin, but deserves abundant glory."[10]

It bears repeating: The idea that those Christians who die fighting for the faith are martyrs far predates Bernard, goes back to at least the mid-ninth century, under popes Leo IV and John VIII, and was widely accepted by most European theologians. In the words of William of Tyre, "We believe, indeed, that those who fall in the ranks of the faithful, fighting with the warriors of the cross for the name of Christ, deserve that not only disgrace but all derelictions and sins whatsoever be erased from their records."[11]

None of this, of course, was seen as a *license* to kill. Bernard insisted that Muslims should not be "slaughtered when there is any other way of preventing them from harassing and persecuting the faithful."[12] However, because Muslims had—for centuries—proven themselves existential and intractable enemies to Christians, "now it seems better to destroy them than to allow the rod of sinners to continue to be raised over the lot of the righteous, lest perchance the righteous set their hand to iniquity," a reference to the well-known fact that, to escape persecution, millions of Christians had converted to Islam over the centuries.[13]

If, as Bernard continues to argue, Christians are not forbidden from fighting, provided it is for a just cause—he cites how John the Baptist, rather than banning military service, told soldiers to be content with their pay (Luke 3:14)—then they must certainly stand up to Muslims, who from the start had waged, and continued to wage, a wholly *unjust* war on Christendom. No room for cheek-turning here:

> Surely then the nations who choose warfare should be scattered, those who molest us should be cut away, and all the workers of iniquity should be dispersed from the City of the Lord—those who busy themselves carrying off the incalculable riches placed in Jerusalem by Christian people, profaning holy things, and possessing the sanctuary of God as their heritage. Let both swords of the faithful fall upon the necks of the foe [who represent both secular *and* spiritual evil, Luke 22:38] to the destruction of every lofty thing lifting itself up against the knowledge of God, which is the Christian faith, lest the Gentiles should then say, "Where is their God?"[14]

Even the Templars' residence, Solomon's Temple, underscored the muscular, no-nonsense side of Christianity. For was it not at the Temple that Christ himself engaged in righteous violence, argued the Cistercian:

> The facade of this temple is adorned…but with weapons rather than jewels, and in place of the ancient golden crowns, its walls are hung round with shields. In place

> of candlesticks, censers, and ewers, this house is well furnished with saddles, bridles, and lances. By all these signs the knights clearly show that they are animated by the same zeal for the house of God which of old vehemently inflamed the Leader of knighthood himself [Christ], who, having his most sacred hands armed, not with a weapon, but with a whip which he had fashioned from lengths of cord, entered the temple, ousted the merchants, scattered the coins of the money changers, and overturned the chairs of the pigeon vendors, considering it totally unfitting to defile this house of prayer by such traffic. Moved therefore by their King's example, his devoted soldiery [Templars], considering it far more unfitting and infinitely more intolerable for a holy place to be polluted by unbelievers [Muslims] than to be crowded with merchants, have installed themselves in this holy house with their horses and their armor. Having expunged it and the other holy places of every infidel stain and the tyrannical horde, they occupy themselves day and night with work as distinguished as it is practical. They honor the temple of God earnestly with fervent and sincere worship, in their devotion offering up, not the flesh of animals according to the ancient rites, but true peace offerings, brotherly love, devoted obedience, and voluntary poverty.[15]

For Bernard, the lifestyle of the Knights of the Temple, both in peace and war, is "an exemplar, or at least an embarrassment, for those of our knights who are apparently fighting not for God, but for the devil."[16] Abiding in perfect "discipline" and "obedience," the Templars, who followed a rule patterned after the Cistercians,

> live in cheerful community and sober company, without wives and without children. So that their evangelical perfection will lack nothing, they dwell united in one family with no personal property whatever, careful to

> keep the unity of the Spirit in the bond of peace.... They never sit in idleness or wander about aimlessly, but on the rare occasions when they are not on duty, they are always careful to earn their bread.... There is little distinction of persons among them, and deference is shown to ability, not to nobility. They rival one another in mutual consideration, and they carry one another's burdens, thus fulfilling the law of Christ. No arrogant word, no idle deed, no unrestrained laugh, not even the slightest whisper or murmur, is left uncorrected once it has been detected.[17]

Once the call to battle is heard, however, these seeming saints turned into raging demons, or in the more restrained words of Bernard:

> Yet once in the thick of battle, they set aside this earlier gentleness, as if to say, "Do I not hate those who hate you, O Lord; am I not disgusted with your enemies?" [Psalm 138:21]. These men charge the enemy, regarding the foe as sheep, never—no matter how outnumbered they are—as ruthless barbarians or as awesome hordes. Nor do they presume on their own strength, but trust for victory in the Lord of Sabaoth. They are mindful of the words of Maccabees, "It is simple enough for a multitude to be vanquished by a handful. It makes no difference in the sight of the God of heaven whether he grants deliverance by the hands of few or of many; for victory in war does not depend on a big army, but bravery is the gift from heaven." As they had on numerous occasions experienced, one man may pursue a thousand, and two put ten thousand to flight [Deuteronomy 32:30].[18]

This, then, was the "riddle" of the Templars:

> They appear gentler than lambs, yet fiercer than lions. Consequently, I do not know if it would be more

appropriate to refer to them as monks or as soldiers, or whether it would perhaps be better to recognize them as being both, for they lack neither monastic meekness nor military might. What can we say about this, except that this is the Lord's doing, and it is marvelous in our eyes.[19]

6

A TEMPLAR TEMPLATE

If *In Praise of the New Knighthood* explained *why* the Templars were needed, the so-called *Primitive Rule* (which was subsequently augmented) specified *how* they were to accomplish their purpose, that is, how they were to live.

The *Rule* was the result of deliberations at the Council of Troyes in 1129, and like *In Praise,* was largely written by Bernard of Clairvaux. As such, it was heavily influenced by the Cistercian rule (which was fortuitous, since "No religious body was more thoroughly masculine in its temper and discipline than the Cistercians"[1]). But it also contained practices that had been organic to the Templars since their founding under Hugh of Payns one decade earlier.

Not only was this the first rule written for a Christian military order—and essentially the founding document of the Templars—but many subsequent military orders based their rules or constitutions on it. Some, such as the Teutonic Knights and the Livonian Brothers of the Sword, adopted it in its entirety, with few modifications. Accordingly, because it provides a window into the lifestyle of all military orders, a closer examination into the *Rule* is in order.

The *Rule* literally offered *rules*—seventy-two originally, though these burgeoned to 686 by 1260 due to evolving circumstances—to govern the day-to-day living of history's first chivalric order.[2] Among other things, it addressed everyday life in the convent, social conduct, penances, hierarchy and military structure, clothing and equipment, and reception into the Order.

As with *In Praise*, its prologue condemns secular knighthood, which it depicted as little better than Saracens: "This knighthood despised the love of justice that constitutes its duties and did not do what it should, that is, defend the poor, widows, orphans and churches, but strove to plunder, despoil, or kill."[3] The rest of the document spells out how the true knight—the knight of Christ—lives and behaves.

Before all else, such knights, the Templars, were to lead a pious and blameless life and were to follow the same schedule of prayers (which began at 4 a.m. and continued throughout the day) as the Cistercians. In the words of the *Rule*,

> You who renounce your own wills...must with a pure heart ever strive to hear matins and all the services according to the canonical laws and the usage of the regular canons of the Holy City of Jerusalem. Venerable brethren—you who have for ever surrendered the attractions of this world and have despised the torments of your body out of your love for God—this must you do, so that, refreshed and satisfied with the heavenly food, instructed and fortified with heavenly teaching, none of you may, after the consummation of the divine mysteries, be afraid of the battle but be eager to win the crown (of martyrdom).[4]

Indeed, because "the practice of their faith was central to their life," the Knights of the Temple attended mass and offered prayers even on the battlefield, where "the tents of the knights were placed in a circle around the tent that served as a chapel—and the chapel tent was the rallying point in case of a surprise attack."[5]

In day-to-day living, unless there was something meaningful to say or a word of edification, they were to maintain silence: "For it is written...to talk too much is not without sin...Life and death are in the power of the tongue.... We altogether prohibit idle words and wicked bursts of laughter,"[6] and "Always, at the convent's dinner and supper, let the Holy Scripture be read, if possible."[7] In short, "all vile words are forbidden us, and all courtesies are permitted and good."[8]

No talk that could provoke temptation, even if expressed in the context of repentance or regret, was allowed. Thus, any Templar who heard someone reminiscing over, say, the carnal knowledge he once had "with immoral women" was "to leave that place and not give his heart's ear to the pedlar of filth."[9]

While relentlessly pruning out their own sins, Templars were to exercise prudence for others' sins: "When a brother knows for certain that his fellow brother has sinned, quietly and with fraternal mercy let him be chastised privately between the two of them."[10]

After all their spiritual and secular duties had been met, they were expected to remain busy and productive: "Each brother should ensure that the Enemy does not find him lazy, for the Enemy assails more boldly and more willingly with evil desires and vain thoughts and mean words, a lazy man than he does one whom he finds busy in good work." Sick and ailing brethren were naturally exempt and to be treated as though they "were Christ himself, remembering the words of the Gospel, 'I was sick, and ye visited me.'"[11]

Chastity is repeatedly stressed in the *Rule*:

> Henceforth the Knighthood of Jesus Christ should avoid at all costs the embraces of women, by which men have perished many times, so that they may remain eternally before the face of God with a pure conscience and sure life.[12]

While chastity was always a regular component of monastic life, more than other orders, the Cistercian rule "shunned female contact with greater determination" and "raised more formidable barriers against the intrusion of women."[13] Thus, according to the Templar rule,

> We believe it to be a dangerous thing for any religious to look too much upon the face of woman. For this reason

> none of you may presume to kiss a woman, be it widow, young girl, mother, sister, aunt or any other.[14]

Penalties for the unchaste were severe: "If a brother...enters an evil place, or a house of iniquity, with a sinful woman, alone or in bad company; he may not keep his habit, and he may be put in irons...and this has been done several times." (The *Rule* was eventually modified to "If a brother is *proven* to have lain with a woman, he should not keep his habit and should be put in irons.")[15]

While there were infractions if not defections against the demands of chastity—one knight quit the Order because "he was young and could not bear to abstain from women"—on the whole, "the history of the Order produced no public sexual scandals, unlike other religious Orders.... For the most part the Templars kept their Rule. Many contemporaries considered them to be pious."[16]

For all the talk of religion, the Templars' ultimate purpose—"that is, the union of war and religion"—was underscored by the *Rule*, "so that religion might be defended by war and the enemy may be struck down without sin."[17] As such, the Temple's religiosity never overshadowed its overarching purpose. Nor should its brethren be mistaken for mere monks bearing arms: "They were still knights and, as knights, their fundamental skills in fighting with the sword or lance would have been learnt from childhood, charging with practice lances against a target, which was often built in the shape of a Saracen."[18]

The Templars (and most subsequent military orders) consisted of two main classes: knights of noble birth and sergeants at arms (a third category, chaplains, who served the Templars' spiritual needs, were added later in 1139). The knights formed the nucleus of the Order and were never more than a few hundred at any given time (the number three hundred is generally given, though some sources suggest that at its peak, in the early thirteenth century, the Temple had as many as one thousand, possibly more, brother-knights, though this cannot be substantiated[19]). Although most initiates became lifelong members of the Temple, it was also acceptable for a knight to pledge a certain amount of time in the Order (as did Fulk, king of Jerusalem, r. 1131–1143).

The sergeants at arms, or "serving brethren" ("sergeant" is an Old French word meaning "servant"), were freemen of considerable standing, held various important offices, fought side by side with the knights, and made up the bulk of the Templar military force, far outnumbering the knights. Many of them were born of mixed marriages between Latins and Mideast Christians (such as Armenians and Syrians).[20]

Another subcategory, nonmilitary sergeants, was attached to and served the Order in various practical ways, for example as blacksmiths, carpenters, and domestics.

Despite differences in rank, both knights and sergeants were seen as and called "brothers" (until much later when rank became more rigid).

There were, finally, also a large number of native troops, turcopiles (or turcopoles), mounted and unmounted, who regarded it an honor to be connected to and fight under the banner of the Temple.

Needless to say, although women were admitted into other military orders as nuns and nurses, no sisters were admitted entry into the Temple, "since the ancient enemy expelled many from the right road to Paradise by the society of women."[21]

Above them all was the master, who ruled from the Order's headquarters, the Temple in Jerusalem. Elected for life, the master was both the spiritual and supreme leader of the Order and led his men in battle whenever present (approximately a quarter of all masters died either in battle against Muslims or in Muslim captivity; all but two died in office). Even so, the master was never to forget his humility, and "every Maundy Thursday he washed the feet of thirteen paupers."[22]

Other important offices included the seneschal, the master's deputy and standard-bearer; the marshal, in charge of military affairs; the turcopiler, in charge of mercenary and hired troops; and the draper, in charge of clothing.

The discipline and obedience of conventual life were especially evident on and complementary to the battlefield. This was one of the main reasons that the military orders tended to be much more effective and formidable than regular Crusader armies, which consisted of secular knights who, as criticized in Bernard's *In Praise*, often let their personal honor and glory come before discipline and prudence. Ever concerned for the welfare of fellow Christians, even these reckless ones were not to be forfeited. According to the *Rule*, "If it happens by chance that any Christian acts foolishly," for example, by breaking rank and rushing the enemy for death and glory, "and any Turk attacks him in order to kill him, and he is in peril of death, and anyone who is in that area wishes to leave his squadron to help him, and his conscience tells him that he can assist him, he may do so without permission, and then return to his squadron quietly and in silence."[23]

The Templar war flag (also known as the "piebald," "gonfanon," and "beauséant") played an important role in battle. Half black and half white, it symbolized the two contrasting faces of the Templars: ferocity to their enemies, friendship to their allies. As James of Vitry, who regularly accompanied the knights, observed, "When summoned to arms they never demand the number of the enemy, but where are they?... They carry before them to battle, a banner, half black and white, which they call beauséant...because they are fair and favorable to the friends of Christ, but black and terrible to his enemies."[24] Historian Malcolm Barber further discusses its importance in the context of the Templar cavalry charge:

> Once the time for cavalry charge drew near, the Marshal took up the banner, which was vital to the Templars' battle order especially during the melee which usually followed a charge. So important was the banner that a special guard of ten knights was placed around it and the precaution was taken of carrying a second folded banner, which could be raised if anything happened to the first one.... No Templar should ever leave the field while the piebald banner was still to be seen, whatever the overall military situation.[25]

Indeed, so long as the slightest chance of victory was possible, no Templar was ever to retreat from battle. Even if all "the Christians are defeated, from which God save them, no brother should leave the field to return to the garrison, while there is a piebald banner [Templar war flag] raised aloft; for if he leaves, he will be expelled from the house for ever."[26]

Even if their banner was laid low, Templars were required to rally to whichever Christian banner was still aloft (ideally that of another military order, such as the Hospitallers, though any Christian order would do). Only when no more Christian banners stood could the Templar honorably withdraw from the field of battle.[27] As we shall see, such tenacity further cemented their reputation among their Muslim enemies as fierce, relentless, and uncompromising warriors.

Even the Templar dress code was strict and austere. It differentiated between knights, who were to wear white mantles, and sergeants and other servants, who were to wear black or brown ones. (Because the Knights Hospitaller initially wore black (though later red), they were regularly confused—including on the battlefield—with Templar sergeants.) No ostentation or ornamentation was allowed: "And if any brother out of a feeling of pride or arrogance wishes to have as his due a better and finer habit," the *Rule* warns, "let him be given the worst. And those who receive new robes must immediately return the old ones, to be given to the squires and sergeants and often to the poor, according to what seems good to the one who holds that office [the draper]." To always be ready for the call of battle, "They will at all times sleep dressed in shirt and breeches and shoes and belts."[28]

Hair was to be worn short—possibly shaved altogether—and "all Templar knights wore beards," often long, to the point that, by 1240, Alberic of Trois-Fontaines described them as the "order of bearded brethren."[29]

Their diet was frugal, but not as mortifying as for some other orders. Though they followed all the (many) fasts of the liturgical calendar, it was understood that they, of all monks, needed their strength. Accordingly, they were allowed meat three times per week, with eggs, cheese, and milk being staples for the remainder of the week. This did not prevent some Templars from overly mortifying their flesh. Writing in the early thirteenth century, James of Vitry noted:

> We have encountered some knights of your order who were so intent on fasting and afflicting their bodies that

> in warfare and battles against the Saracens they easily succumbed because of excessive weakness. We heard of one who was very devout, but not wisely so, since in battle against Saracens he fell from his horse at the first blow of a lance; another brother, at great danger to himself, helped him to remount, but he immediately fell again to another blow.[30]

Acceptance into the Temple appears to have been more difficult than into other, nonmilitary religious orders. Unlike the Benedictines, for instance, parents could not pledge their sons but had to wait till they were of an age at which they could be assessed for their sincerity and commitment—not to mention were physically "able to bear arms with vigor, and rid the land of the enemies of Jesus Christ.... For it is better not to take vows in boyhood than to commit the enormity of retracting when one has reached manhood."[31]

The average age of those accepted into the Temple was 27.5 years—the prime of manhood and strength: "A knight was expected to be adept at mounted combat before he joined the Order. Given the weight of the accoutrements of combat, each must have been immensely strong."[32] In short, "Most knights were trained in individual fighting skills and many were very experienced warriors when they joined the Order..." It is precisely due to the warlike background of most Templar initiates that "Bernard and the Council fathers seemed more anxious to make monks out of knights than knights out of monks."[33]

While being inducted, the initiate had to demonstrate serious intent and not lie to any question. He was repeatedly asked if he had a wife or fiancée that had any claims on him. If a woman later appeared and he was found to have lied about being single, the rule was clear: "The habit will be taken from you and you will be put in heavy irons, and so you will be made to work with the slaves. And when you have been put to shame enough, you will be taken by the hand and delivered over to the woman, and you will be expelled from the house forever."[34] (Although the penances imposed on erring brethren seem extreme and cruel—including whippings and being forced to eat off the floor like a dog—they were similar to those of other orders and quite standard for the time.[35])

Because the Temple did not want to waste time on lukewarm men who might quit once they experienced the draconian lifestyle they had embraced, it went to great lengths to dissuade would-be entrants from joining. Initiates were repeatedly warned that taking the vow of obedience was no easy matter, "for it is a painful thing for you, who are your own master, to make yourself a serf to others."[36] According to Michael the Syrian, "Whoever comes to be a brother is tested for one year. The rules are read to him seven times, and each time he is asked: 'Well, have you perhaps any misgivings? Perhaps you won't be able to assume these rules right to the end? (If so), praise God and return home.'"[37]

Whoever could accept all this became a brother Knight of the Temple—no easy task which would in coming years demand much if not all of him.

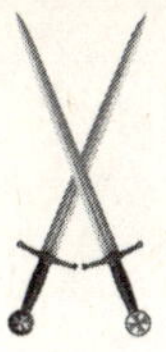

7

JIHAD REAWAKENS

For some forty-four years following the Christian recapture of Jerusalem and other cities in the Holy Land, the Crusaders ruled with little fear of confronting a united Islamic front. This began to change with the rise of Imad al-Din Zengi (r. 1127–1146), a particularly ruthless Turkish warlord and atabeg of Mosul and Aleppo who is credited as the first major Muslim leader to resuscitate and direct the ideology of jihad against the Christian states of the Holy Land. A Muslim inscription from 1142 described Zengi as the "tamer of infidels" and "leader of those who fight the jihad," while William of Tyre presents him as "a very wicked man and a most cruel persecutor of the Christians," at one point even calling him the "greatest persecutor of the Christian faith."[1]

Such unflattering epithets came to roost once Zengi set his sights on the oldest Crusader state, the northern county of Edessa. Mostly populated by native Christians, Armenians and Syrians, Edessa had welcomed the Crusaders as liberators in 1098 and took Baldwin I and his successors as their lords. To this small county, Zengi sent hordes of Turcomans "in fulfillment of their obligations in the jihad."

> Large numbers answered his appeal and they completely surrounded the city, intercepting all supplies and

> reinforcements. It was said that even the birds dared not fly near, so absolute was the desolation made by the besiegers' weapons and so unwinking their vigilance. Catapults drawn up against the wall's battered at them ceaselessly, and nothing interrupted the remorseless struggle.[2]

After four months of this nonstop bombardment, on Christmas Eve 1144, Edessa fell. Swarms of Muslims "rushed together from all directions, entered the city, and put to the sword all whom they encountered," writes William of Tyre. They slaughtered some thirty thousand Christians in the initial frenzy. "Neither age, condition, nor sex was spared."[3]

Historian Joseph-François Michaud elaborates on the nightmare that next unfolded based on a close reading of the sources:

> Neither the weakness of a timid sex, nor age on the brink of the tomb; neither the cries of infants, nor the screams of young girls who sought safety in the arms, or beneath the garments of their parents, could abate the rage of the Saracens. They whom the sword had not yet reached, looked for nothing but death; some crept to the churches to await it, and died embracing the altars of Christ; whilst others, yielding to their despair, remained motionless in their houses, where they were massacred with their families.[4]

To mark their victory, Muslim sheikhs ascended the steeples of the churches of Edessa, hollering "Allahu Akbar" and other triumphal ejaculations, including "Oh Muhammad! prophet of heaven, we have gained a great victory in your name; we have destroyed the people that worshipped stone [on the Muslim belief that Christians are idolaters], and torrents of blood have been shed to make your law triumph." Michaud continues,

> After this proclamation, the Saracens redoubled their excesses. The Gazis or conquerors satiated themselves

> with blood; the dead bodies were mutilated, and their heads sent to Bagdad; and even to Khorasan. All who remained alive in the city of Edessa were treated as a flock of animals, and sold in the public places. The Christians, loaded with chains, after having lost their property, their country, and their liberty, had the still further grief of seeing their religion, which was all they had left to console them in their misfortunes, made a subject of ridicule by the infidels. The churches were plundered of their ornaments, and the sanctuary became the scene of the most shocking debaucheries. Many of the faithful whom the horrors of war had spared, could not support the sight of such profanations, and died with despair.[5]

Sixteen thousand women and children were stripped naked, had their hands tied behind their backs, and, to the whip, made to run barefoot behind their horseback-riding escorts to the Islamic slave markets. Whoever could not keep up with the galloping hordes was instantly cut down. As visible representatives of Christianity, the clergymen who survived were especially targeted for torture and mockery within the city. The Armenian patriarch was stripped naked, dragged by his beard through the streets before the jeering Muslims, slapped, kicked, and beaten with rods. Matthew of Edessa, the great historian who bequeathed us an important history of the First Crusade in which he regularly bemoaned "the savage nation of infidels called Turks,"[6] who "mercilessly slaughtered the Christian faithful with the sword," was himself slaughtered.[7]

The fall of Edessa was a major and traumatic shock to Christendom. Before it, both Europeans and Muslims were convinced of the Crusaders' superior might. The conquest of Edessa shattered this decades-old image and helped "exalt the pride of the Saracens." Greatly impressed by Zengi, the caliph in Baghdad ordered that this mighty "annihilator of crosses" should "be named in the public prayers of the Fridays, and that the whole Muslim people should offer up thanks to Heaven for his victories."[8] For Muslim historians, the fall of Edessa would mark the formal start of the jihad against the Crusaders.

Meanwhile, in Christendom, Pope Eugenius III called for what would become the Second Crusade. "He dispatched throughout the various regions of the West religious men, eloquent in exhortation, powerful both in word and deed, to inform princes and people, tribes and tongues everywhere of the intolerable sufferings of their brethren in the East and to rouse them to go forth to avenge these terrible wrongs."[9] Among these was the pope's former spiritual advisor from his days at the monastery of Clairvaux, that staunch articulator of militant Christianity, Bernard of Clairvaux, now aged fifty-three.

Although he appeared emaciated and sickly from overfasting to the point of starvation, on Palm Sunday, March 31, 1146, Bernard spoke atop a large platform erected on a hill outside of Vézelay, France, where a vast host—peasants, monks, and priests, knights and nobles, and the Frankish king himself, Louis VII—assembled to listen. From the outset, Bernard made clear that it was Christians—not Armenians, Syrians, or Franks—that were suffering and, as such, required succor from their Western coreligionists. In the words of William of Tyre,

> With all due care he described the affliction of the people of the East and the woes by which they were continually oppressed. He set forth clearly that the cities of the faithful, once devoted to the Christian profession, were now suffering the direst servitude under the persecutors of the name of Christ. Bound with chains and shackles, consumed by hunger, confined in horrible prisons, in filth and squalor, clothed with bitterness, those brethren for whom also Christ was willing to die were sitting in beggary and irons. To the task of liberating their oppressed brethren he invited them and stirred their hearts.[10]

Satan, argued Bernard, was once again raging, using his Muslim minions to persecute the faithful: "The enemy of mankind has caused the breath of corruption to fly over all regions; we behold nothing but unpunished wickedness. Neither the laws of men nor the laws of religion have sufficient power to check the depravity of customs and the triumph of the wicked." The solution was not lamentation, the wearing of sackcloth and ashes, but war and the wearing of "impenetrable bucklers. The din of arms, the dangers, the labors, the fatigues of war are the penances that God now imposes on you."

Bernard invoked the same Christian logic that gave rise to the Templars, that is, the need to love one's neighbor as oneself:

> If it were announced to you that the enemy had invaded your cities, your castles, and your lands, had ravished your wives and your daughters and profaned your temples, who among you would not fly to arms? Well, then, all these calamities—and calamities greater still—have fallen upon your brethren, upon the family of Jesus Christ, which is yours. Why do you hesitate to repair so many evils—to revenge so many outrages? Will you allow the infidels to contemplate in peace the ravages they have committed on Christian peoples?... Fly then to arms! Let a holy rage animate you in the fight; and let the Christian world resound with these words of the prophet, "Cursed be he who does not stain his sword with blood!" [Jeremiah 48:10].

Bernard, it bears recalling, was talking to men of a fighting age—to professional warriors—who, if not fighting Muslims, would inevitably fall to fighting one another. As such, he reminded them to channel their energies where it was most needed:

> Christian warriors.... These are combats worthy of you, combats in which it is glorious to conquer and advantageous to die. Illustrious knights, generous defenders of the Cross, remember the example of your fathers, who conquered Jerusalem, and whose names are inscribed in Heaven.[11]

Wild applause and cries of *"Deus vult!"*—"God wills it!"—followed Bernard's exhortation. Although he had already vowed himself to the crusade, the twenty-six-year-old king, Louis VII, was so moved that he cast himself at the feet of the saint, demanding the cross. Multitudes of knights, barons, magnates, clergymen, and peasants followed his example. When Bernard and his assistants ran out of cloth to make crosses, the Cistercian flung off his own robe and vestments and cut them into small crosses for distribution. Others followed his example; well into nightfall were they still making and handing out crosses to men of resolve.

Soon after that fateful day, a song was written in Old French and sung by troubadours to rally people to follow their young king, Louis, into the fray. A portion of "Chevalier, mult estes guariz" ("Knights, you are under sure protection"), which nearly a millennium later is still performed, follows:

> Knights, you are under sure protection, since it is to you that God makes his outcry against the Turks and the Almoravids* who have committed such outrages against him, for they have wrongfully seized his fiefs!... Edessa is taken, you know this well, and Christians are dismayed at this, the monasteries burned and abandoned; the Eucharist is celebrated no longer. Knights, why are you still thinking about this? You who are prized for deeds of arms, offer yourselves to the One who was raised on the Cross for your sake! Follow Louis's example, who has more [to lose] than you have: he is a rich and powerful king, he has been crowned above all others. He has abandoned furs and sables, castles and villages and cities, and he has turned to the One who was tormented on the Cross for our sake.[12]

* The Almoravids were a Muslim jihadist dynasty originating in North Africa that was committing similar atrocities against the Christians of Spain during this time.

Before long, the call to arms became contagious and, along with France, the whole of Germany was aflame with ardor:

> A war-cry was heard from the Rhine to the Danube; Germany, although so long agitated by its own troubles, found in all parts warriors for the holy expedition. Men of all conditions obeyed the voice of the preacher of the holy war, and followed the example of kings and princes: a thing to be wondered at.... [Before long] All the provinces of France and Germany were in motion. The same motives which had armed the companions of Godfrey in the first expedition, inflamed the courage of the new Crusaders.[13]

Prior to departure, Louis "went to St. Denis, to take the famous Oriflamme,* which was borne before the kings of France in battle." At that time, the church of St. Denis held portraits of the great heroes (Godfrey of Bouillon, Raymond IV of Toulouse, Tancred of Hauteville) and battle scenes (Dorylaeum, Antioch, Ascalon) of the First Crusade, all of which "must have attracted the eyes and fixed the attention of Louis and his companions in arms."[14]

As for the Templars, whose first few decades of existence were largely limited to disputing the highways with Muslims, on April 27, 1147, their strength was such that not only did they have an active presence in the Holy Land but they also managed to assemble an additional 130 knights (and an unknown but much greater number of sergeants) from their commandery in Paris. They were led by the master of that preceptory, Everard of Barres. A close and trusted confidant of Louis, he and his Templars joined the king's train.

Prior to their departure, during a general council in the Templar headquarters in Paris attended by Louis and Pope Eugenius III, as well

* The Oriflamme, which derives its name from the Latin for "golden flame," was a bright red banner with streaming points resembling tongues of flame. It was used by the Frankish kings of old, stretching back to Charlemagne's wars with the Muslims of Spain, and signified that battle was holy, divinely sanctioned, and that no quarter would be given. Enemies were to be fought to the death.

as many prelates, princes, and nobles from all parts of Christendom, the Templars, with the pope's sanction, assumed the blood red cross as a symbol of their commitment to martyrdom.* It would forever become their distinguishing badge, worn on the left side of their white habits and mantles and over their hearts (giving them the alternate names of "Red Friars" and "Red Cross Knights"[15]).

Conrad III of Germany, at the head of a vast army, set out before the Franks. On October 25, 1147, when the Germans had reached Dorylaeum—the site of a major and bloody victory of the First Crusade fifty years earlier—hordes of galloping Turks appeared:

> With loud cries, they surrounded the camp and with their usual agility fell furiously upon our soldiers, who were retarded by their heavy armor. The Christians were superior to the foe in strength and practice in arms, yet, weighed down as they were with breastplates, greaves, and shields, they could not combat the Turks, nor could they pursue them very far from the camp. Their horses also, emaciated by hunger and the long marches, were utterly unable to gallop hither and yon. The Turks, on the contrary, charged en masse; while still at a distance they let fly countless showers of arrows which fell like hail upon the horses and their riders and brought death and wounds from afar.[16]

Although the battle raged for days, the Turks' typical hit-and-run tactics and avoidance of hand-to-hand combat decimated the

* Some seventy years after this council, James of Vitry described the Templars in his *Historia Hierosolymitana* as follows: "They wear white mantles, in token of their pure lives; they bear the red cross on their breasts to signify that they are ever ready to shed their blood for Christ." (The red cross on white is depicted in the pommel of the sword appearing on the left side of this book's cover.)

Christians, killing thousands.* Thus the army that had come to avenge Edessa suffered a similar fate:

> The rout became general; the country was covered with fugitives, who wandered about at hazard, and found no asylum against the conquerors. Some perished with want, others fell beneath the swords of the Muslims; the women and children were carried off with the baggage, and formed a part of the enemy's booty. Conrad, who had scarcely saved the tenth part of his army, was himself wounded by two arrows, and only escaped the pursuit of the Saracens by a kind of miracle.[17]

As for the Frankish army, it finally reached Ephesus in December 1147. Despite terrible winter conditions and failing food supplies, Louis pressed on. On reaching the river Meander, at the frontiers of Phrygia, "here for the first time, the longing of the Franks to see their foe was gratified."[18] The whole might of the Turkish army—the same that had decimated the Germans—was there, waiting to dispute passage over the river, which was already inundated from winter rains and difficult to traverse.

> Animated by the speeches and the example of their king [Louis], no obstacle could stop the French. In vain the Turks showered their arrows upon them, or formed their

---

* The rest of William's entry concerning this second Battle of Dorylaeum perfectly captured the Turkic way of war, which often (as at the Battle of Hattin, 1187) discomfited the Crusaders: "When the Christians tried to pursue, however, the Turks turned and led upon their swift horses and thus escaped the sword of their foes. Our army, hemmed in on all sides, was in mortal danger from the constant showers of darts and arrows. They had no chance to retaliate or to engage the foe at close quarters, nor could they lay hold of the enemy. As often as they tried to make a counterattack, the Turks broke ranks, eluded all their attempts, and galloped off in different directions. Then, when the Christians returned to their camp, the Turks reconstructed their lines, again surrounded our forces, and attacked even more furiously, as if they were besieging a town" (William of Tyre, *A History of Deeds*, vol. 2, 171).

> battle-array on the banks; the French army crossed the river, broke through the ranks of the barbarians, slaughtered vast numbers of them, and pursued them to the foot of the mountains.[19]

The Turks would be avenged a few days later. While traveling through the high and narrow region around Mount Cadmus, Louis's army was stretched thin and became disunited. On January 6, 1148, once the Crusaders had reached an especially long and narrow defile surrounded on all sides by chasms and steep precipices, the watchful Turks, who had been perfectly motionless, pounced forward from their hiding places to loud and frightful cries of "Allahu Akbar!" In such

> battle array, they fell upon our forces, and before the latter could seize arms the Turks had broken up their lines by force. No longer was the fight carried on with bows and arrows; it was fought at close quarters with the sword and brought death and destruction to the Christians. All who tried to flee were most cruelly pursued. Our people were hindered by the narrow defiles, and their horses were exhausted by the long marches and the difficulty of the roads.[20]

Caught in such dire straits, where maneuver was impossible, hundreds of Crusaders and their horses fell into the abyss—even as large boulders from the avalanche of war came crashing down upon and after them: "The cries of the wounded and the dying mingled with the confused roar of the torrents, the hissing of the arrows, and the neighing of the terrified horses."[21] It was the Battle of Yarmuk all over again.*

---

* The Battle of Yarmuk (636), arguably history's most consequential battle, opening as it did the way to the Muslim conquests of the seventh century, featured similar dynamics, including Christians trapped in passes and falling into defiles. Chapter 1 of my *Sword and Scimitar* is devoted to this pivotal battle, on which historian Francesco Gabrieli writes, "the battle of the Yarmuk had, without doubt, more important consequences than almost any other in all world history" (*Muhammad and the Conquests of Islam*, 1968, 100).

Those Crusaders in the van, who had already emerged from the narrow path in question, and those in the rear, who had not yet reached it, were also attacked, though, being able to maneuver, they managed to repulse the Turks. Louis himself, who, alongside the Templars, was in the rear guarding most of the baggage and pilgrims, nearly lost his life. At one point during the ensuing chaos, several knights rallied to the king and hacked their way to the summit of the mountain. There, thirty perished fighting alongside and protecting Louis.

In the end, he stood alone. Taking refuge upon a large boulder, with his back to a tree for cover, he singly resisted the Muslims with his sword. Before long, they—not knowing that he was the king and taking him for a simple soldier—abandoned Louis to his fate and turned to plunder, lest their share of booty be appropriated by their comrades. It was only after nightfall, when Louis heard the voices of some Franks who had escaped the carnage, that he quit his refuge, "mounted a stray horse, and, after a thousand perils, rejoined his vanguard, where all were lamenting his death."[22]

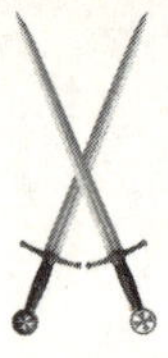

8

THE TEMPLE ASCENDANT

If the fall of Edessa had disgraced the Franks of the Holy Land, the January 6, 1148 defeat of Mount Cadmus called into question the very flower of France's chivalry. As William of Tyre writes, "That day the glorious reputation of the Franks was lost through a misfortune most fatal and disastrous for the Christians; their valor, up to this time formidable to the nations, was crushed to earth. Henceforward it was as a mockery in the eyes of those unclean races to whom formerly it had been a terror."[1]

It is precisely at this point, when all hope seemed lost, that the Templars emerged from the morass of Crusaders and showed their quality. After what remained of the Christian army had regrouped and rallied around Louis in the Mount Cadmus region, the Turks, "like a beast which becomes more savage after tasting blood," redoubled their attacks on the traumatized Christians, writes Odo of Deuil, the chaplain of Louis and his constant attendant during the Second Crusade. As a direct result, "the king handed over responsibility for the defense of the army to the Templars," writes Barber.[2] Not only did this make perfect sense—who but the Templars knew how best to escort and protect Christian pilgrimages, which, after all, is what every crusade was?—but from the moment when the Crusader army first left France, the pious king was continuously being impressed by the Templars. Odo "informs us that the king loved to see the frugality and simplicity of the Templars, and to imitate it; he praised their union and disinterestedness, admired above all things the attention they paid to their accoutrements, and their care in husbanding and preserving their equipage and munitions of war."[3]

All the talk of discipline found in their constitutions was clearly not just talk. Writing some twenty or thirty years later, an eyewitness offers a more detailed account of the strict movements of the Templars, which were no doubt also evident during the Second Crusade:

> They were always foremost in the fight and the last in the retreat; that they proceeded to battle with the greatest order, silence, and circumspection, and carefully attended to the commands of their Master. When the signal to engage had been given by their chief, and the trumpets of the order sounded to the charge,...then they humbly sing the psalm of David,...'Not unto us, not unto us, O Lord, but unto thy name give the praise'; and placing their lances in rest, they either break the enemy's line or die.[4]

Little wonder that Louis, who despaired of losing all his men in the desolate mountains, turned over the reins of leadership to Templar commander Everard of Barres, who had already earned a reputation as a man "of great religious character and a model of valor to the knights," continues Odo. And so "it was unanimously resolved, that all would unite with the brotherhood of the Temple, rich and poor promising on their faith...to obey in everything the commands that he gave them."[5] Thus, under the Poor Fellow-Soldiers of Christ, "whom the king himself obeyed, the Crusaders continued their march, and avenged their defeat several times upon the Muslims."[6]

Once in charge, Everard "organized the army into units of fifty, each under an individual Templar, in turn responsible to an overall commander, a Templar knight called Gilbert. These units were intended to provide a focal point for the various sections of the army within the column, as well as acting as a body when any manoeuver was undertaken."[7]

Under such strict military formation, the bedraggled Crusader army finally emerged out of Muslim-controlled territory, reaching the Byzantine port of Attalia with a few more victorious encounters against the Turks and no more misfortune.[8]

Even so, Louis's army was by now a tiny fraction of what it once was; all were dejected and dispirited, wanting to return home. Not the king. Louis—who never let a single day pass "without hearing mass, and without invoking the God of the Christians," according to Odo—continued to encourage them. When his counts pled that there were not enough men, horses, food, or morale, he countered by saying that all unarmed pilgrims should indeed return home. "As for us, we will redouble our courage, and we will follow the route which our fathers, who conquered Antioch and Jerusalem, followed. Whilst anything remains to me, I will share it with my companions; and when I shall have nothing left, which of you will not undergo with me poverty and misery?" Moved by his words, his barons swore to fight and die by his side.[9]

Louis and his men (a mere 10 percent of those who had first set out) finally arrived in Antioch in March 1148. By now the king was nearly penniless, having spent most of his money on supplies and shipping. Once again, it was the Templars who came to the rescue: On May 10, Everard left Antioch for Acre, where he secured the necessary funds, either directly from the Order's resources or by borrowing against the Order's possessions, bringing it near bankruptcy.

On June 24, 1148, a high council of European leaders was held in Acre. There, against Louis's wish to liberate Edessa, which was the original purpose of the crusade, a majority decision concluded that the best course of action was to travel south under the leadership of the three kings—Louis, a recovered Conrad, and Baldwin III of Jerusalem—and attack Damascus, then seen as the closest threat to Jerusalem. (Though an erstwhile ally, Damascus, it was feared, would soon fall to Zengi's son and successor, Nur al-Din, thereby uniting a Muslim Syria against Jerusalem.)

The Crusader army, now augmented with the full might of the Templars, arrived at and laid siege to Damascus on July 24, 1148. The Christians initially held a position on the west side of the city, whence they made some progress; but then, for some unclear reason that in later days would give rise to all sorts of accusations and conspiracy theories, they decided to quit this position and create another one on the east side. It soon became clear that that was an inferior position and, before long, both a protesting Louis and Conrad submitted to the will of the native Crusaders (known as the "Syrian Franks"), who insisted that the siege was futile. It was lifted and the Crusaders left, counting their losses.

Because the Second Crusade was the mirror opposite of the First Crusade—that is, an abject failure—accusatory fingers were pointed everywhere. No one was spared—the Eastern Roman Empire, the young king of Jerusalem, and even Bernard of Clairvaux, whose prestige, along with Louis and Conrad, plummeted. German chroniclers suggested that the local Franks had been bribed with Muslim gold to lift the siege by giving bad advice to the Western kings, whom they were envious of seeing take Damascus, which they themselves wanted.

Even the Templars, who were in the thick of the siege, were accused of being bought off by the Damascenes. In the words of one German annalist, the siege would have succeeded had it not been for the "greed, deceit, and envy" of the Templars.[10]

Needless to say, there is no actual or contemporary evidence of any wrongdoing on the part of the Temple. Louis, for instance, "was deeply disappointed with the result of the expedition and disgusted with the lack of support given to him by the Syrian Franks, but he was loud in his praise of the Temple."[11] In a letter to Suger, the abbot of St. Denis and regent of France, the king further extolled the Templars for always being there for him:

> I cannot imagine how we could have subsisted for even the smallest space of time in these parts, had it not been for their (the Templars') support and assistance, which have never failed me from the first day I set foot in these lands up to the time of my despatching this letter—a succor ably afforded and generously persevered in. I therefore earnestly beseech you that as these brothers of

> the Temple have hitherto been blessed with the love of God, so now they may be gladdened and sustained by our love and favor. I have to inform you that they have lent me a considerable sum of money, which must be repaid to them quickly, that their house may not suffer, and that I may keep my word.[12]

John of Salisbury states that, although Louis had been "betrayed and deceived," the king himself "always endeavored to exonerate the brothers of the Temple." Even Conrad, the emperor of Germany—whence accusations of treachery first emerged against the Templars—was of the same opinion and "denounced the charge [against the Templars] as wholly without foundation."[13]

Certainly, the main points of history—that the Knights Templars supported and sponsored the Second Crusade from start to finish—contradict and make accusations of betrayal seem illogical. Writing a generation later, William of Tyre said that he had spoken with many men who were involved in the siege of Damascus, and there was no agreement over what went wrong.[14] William, as shall be seen, was often critical of the Templars; yet he never mentioned them in his list of those accused, which speaks much to their innocence.

So, who did betray the Second Crusade? The modern scholarly consensus is that no one—not the Greeks, nor the indigenous Franks—betrayed anyone. Rather, poor planning and strategizing, and perhaps not a little overconfidence, a sort of piggybacking on the legacy of the First Crusade, were the chief culprits.

That the Templars, who only came into being some three decades earlier, were deemed relevant enough to be singled out for accusation was, paradoxically, a form of praise, as it underscored their significance to any crusading endeavor. As Malcolm Barber writes, "In a remarkably short time the Order of the Temple had come to epitomize the struggle with the infidel and while this brought widespread interest and support, equally, when money and lives seemed to have been wasted, as in the Second Crusade, this could sometimes rebound against it."[15]

Such was the double-edged sword that would henceforth pursue the Temple—to its very grave.

At any rate, with the departure of the Western Crusaders, things went from bad to worse. Sometime around 1151–1152, the treasurer of the Templars in Jerusalem described the sorry state of affairs in a letter to Everard, who, though elected master of the Order in 1149, had accompanied Louis back to Paris and, for some unknown reason, not returned:

> Since we have been deprived of your beloved presence, we have had the misfortune to lose in battle the prince of Antioch [whose head and right hand were cut off by Nur al-Din and sent to the caliph in Baghdad] and all his nobility. To this catastrophe has succeeded another. The infidels invaded the territory of Antioch; they drove all before them, and threw garrisons into several strong places. On the first intelligence of this disaster, our brethren assembled in arms, and in concert with the king of Jerusalem went to the succor of the desolated province. We could only get together for this expedition one hundred and twenty knights and one thousand serving brothers and hired soldiers, for whose equipment we expended seven thousand crowns at Acre, and one thousand at Jerusalem. Your paternity knows on what condition we assented to your departure, and our extreme want of money, of cavalry, and of infantry. We earnestly implore you to rejoin us as soon as possible, with all the necessary succors for the Eastern Church, our common mother.... We conjure you to bring with you from beyond sea all our knights and serving brothers capable of bearing arms. Perchance, alas! with all your diligence, you may not find one of us alive. Use, therefore, all imaginable celerity; pray forget not the necessities of our house: they are such that no tongue can express them. It is also of the last importance to announce to the Pope,

> to the King of France, and to all the princes and prelates of Europe, the approaching desolation of the Holy Land, to the intent that they succor us in person, or send us subsidies. Whatever obstacles may be opposed to your departure, we trust to your zeal to surmount them, for now hath arrived the time for perfectly accomplishing our vows in sacrificing ourselves for our brethren, for the defense of the Eastern Church, and the Holy Sepulchre.[16]

The pressure and pleas were too much for Everard. On receipt of this letter, the master of the Temple "abdicated his authority, and entered the monastery of Clairvaux where he devoted the remainder of his days"—that is, some twenty-five years, for he died aged sixty-one—"to the most rigorous penance and mortification."[17]

Even so, although the Second Crusade was a fiasco, the fledgling Order of the Temple had proven its worth—from taking charge to spending liberally on the cause. "Perhaps the most famous example of the value of Templar expertise was on the Second Crusade," observes one historian, before uncharitably elaborating: "Only when an inept Louis VII allowed the Templar Master to reorganize his column of march, were the undisciplined French Crusaders saved from certain annihilation."[18]

9

NUR AL-DIN: "A MIGHTY PERSECUTOR OF CHRISTIANS"

After the Second Crusade, and throughout the 1150s, Nur al-Din Zengi succeeded his father, the dreaded Imad al-Din Zengi, as the chief scourge and disseminator of jihadist propaganda against the Crusaders. As old as Islam and originating with its prophet, jihadist propaganda had never gone away, though it was rather dormant during and after the First Crusade. The Islamic world was disunited then, with the Shia Fatimids (centered in Cairo) and Sunni Abbasids (centered in Baghdad)—the latter effectively ruled by semi-savage Turks—at constant war. That petty chieftains with no allegiance and less religion sought everywhere to carve their own kingdoms did not help matters. As Ibn al-Athir wrote, rather disgustedly, in his history: "While the Franks—Allah damn them!—were conquering and settling in a part of the territories of Islam, the rulers and armies of Islam were fighting among themselves, causing discord and disunity among their people and weakening their power to combat the enemy."[1] In this context, the pure doctrine of jihad—warfare against non-Muslims, *infidels*—was lost on the average Muslim, who watched and suffered as empires, sects, and principalities collided, each claiming to be the legitimate successors and emulators of Muhammad.

There were, of course, some calls to jihad following the First Crusade. In 1105, cleric Ali bin Tahrir argued that if Muslims are obligated to go on regular jihads "to plunder the wealth, the women, and the property of the unbelievers," how much more duty bound are they to respond when the infidels themselves take the offensive against Islam? Instead, it was the newly arrived Crusaders who had "zealously practiced jihad against Muslims," complained the cleric, while Muslims "brought only listlessness and disunity to war, each striving to leave this duty to others." Ali's conclusion? "Devote yourselves to the duty of jihad!"[2]

As seen, such early calls fell on deaf ears until the rise of Imad al-Din Zengi (1085–1146). Thanks to that adroit atabeg, jihadist ideology slowly began to resuscitate—hence the especially savage, ideologically driven, and distinctly anti-Christian atrocities committed during the fall of Edessa.

But it was his son and successor, Nur al-Din Zengi (1118–1174), who became atabeg of Aleppo in 1146 and Mosul soon thereafter, who took holy war against the Crusaders to a new level. Indeed, nearly half of the thirty-eight preserved inscriptions of his name refer to him as a "jihadist" (or *mujahid*).[3] A Muslim ruler who "held the sharia in the deepest respect and applied its precepts," he founded numerous madrasas, mosques, and Sufi orders, all devoted to propagandizing the virtues of jihad and martyrdom.[4] Islamic zeal (today: "radicalization") reached a fever pitch during his reign.

As one example, Nur al-Din commissioned Ibn 'Asakir, a Muslim sheikh celebrated in his own time, to author a concise manual on jihad for wide distribution. His book, *The Forty Hadiths for Inciting Jihad*, reinforced all the old themes: "Lining up for battle in the path of Allah is worthier than 60 years of worship," to quote Muhammad.[5] If the *mujahid* "dies or is killed, all his sins are forgiven.... He will also be wedded to the virgins of Paradise [*houris*] and the crown of dignity will be placed on his head."[6] Those who shirk the duty of jihad "will be tortured like no other sinful human," and so forth.[7]

Even the Crusaders noted Nur al-Din's piety and Islamic bona fides: He was "a wise and prudent man," William of Tyre tells us, "and, according to the superstitious traditions of his people, one who feared God. He was fortunate also in that he greatly increased the heritage which was left him by his father."[8] As both father and son shared an abundance of Islamic zeal, so too did both share something else: "Nur al-Din, like his father," continues William, "was a mighty persecutor of the Christian name and faith."[9]

As the Crusaders had long dreaded, Nur al-Din finally took Damascus in 1154—thanks to the treachery of that ancient city's Muslims against their ruler, a sometime ally of the Christians. This posed a great threat for the Crusader states, as now all of Muslim Syria was united under jihadist rule. In a letter sent in the late 1150s to the French king, Louis VII—who, despite his failed Second Crusade, still closely followed events in the Holy Land—Templar master, Bertrand of Blanchefort, described the growing unity of Islam under Nur al-Din: "The persecutors of the church hasten to…gather themselves together from the ends of the earth, and come forth as one man against the sanctuary of God."[10]

Despite this dire development—and despite the fact that "the fear felt by the Christians made him [Nur al-Din] still bolder"[11]—"the Templars continued to be the foremost in every encounter with the Muslims, and the Monkish writers exult in the number of infidels they sent to hell. A proportionate number of the fraternity must at the same time have ascended to heaven, for the slaughter amongst them was terrific."[12]

Examples of this tit for tat are many. On June 19, 1156, the Knights of the Temple were ambushed while marching with King Baldwin III near Tiberias. A full three hundred Templars were slaughtered by Nur al-Din's forces and another eighty-seven captured. They were avenged soon thereafter, when "thirty Knights Templars put to flight, slaughtered, and captured, two hundred infidels; and in a night attack on the camp of Nur al-Din, they compelled that famous chieftain to fly, without arms and half-naked, from the field of battle."[13]

Thus, at a time when Europe was sending little help—the disastrous Second Crusade was still a living memory—the warrior-monks took it upon themselves to spearhead the counterthrust against Nur al-Din and his minions, "and the courage and devotion of the Temple... in the struggle against hordes of Muslims were praised all throughout Christendom. The Pope (Alexander III) held up the fighting monks as an example to all Christians," referring to them as "the stout champions of Jesus Christ."[14]

Indeed, during the turbulent years ushered in by Nur al-Din, the efficacy of the Temple was such that there was no end to those who endorsed and praised it. If the knights came into their own during the Second Crusade, they truly began to shine during the following decade. Thus, Alexander III's predecessor, Pope Adrian IV, referred to them as the "New Maccabees, far famed and most valiant champions of the Lord":

> The assistance rendered by those holy warriors to all Christendom, their zeal and valor, and untiring exertions in defending from the persecution and subtlety of the filthy Pagans, those sacred places which have been enlightened by the corporal presence of our Savior, we doubt not have been spread abroad throughout the world, and are known, not only to the neighboring nations, but to all those who dwell at the remotest corners of the earth.[15]

In a letter written around 1164, King Amalric of Jerusalem praised the Templars before King Louis VII, "his dear friend and father"—to the point of placing their importance to the Holy Land second only to God Himself:

> Above all, we earnestly entreat your Majesty constantly to extend to the utmost your favor and regard to the Brothers of the Temple, who continually render up their lives for God and the faith, and through whom we do the little that we are able to effect, for in them indeed, after God, is placed the entire reliance of all those [Christians] in the eastern regions who tread in the right path.[16]

By the mid-twelfth century, the Templars (and, as we shall see, the other main military order, the Hospitallers) came to hold a number of important castles and fortresses, especially along the dangerous frontier zones with Islam, from the Amanus Mountains (now Nur Mountains) in the north to south-central Turkey (such as Baghras and Darbsak) to Gaza, near Egypt, in the south. Many of these were donated by kings, princes, and counts who did not have the manpower—nor, perhaps, the will or nerve—to hold onto these dangerous outposts. (Maldoim—the "blood castle"—was one such outpost. Perched above the desolate road from Jericho to Jerusalem, this Templar castle guarded a treacherous pass long feared for its bandits and bloodshed. Austere and exposed, it stood like a stone sentinel over the valley.) Once staffed by the most committed fighters of Christ, these chains of fortresses essentially formed the backbone of the Crusader states, further underscoring the importance of the military orders.

All this time, and despite their expanding roles, "the Templars did not forget their original mandate to protect pilgrims, especially along the crucial routes from the ports of Jaffa, Haifa, and Acre to the holy places, and from Jerusalem to the Jordan."[17] Based on the records of Theoderich, a German pilgrim visiting the Holy Land in 1170,

> The Templars had a castle near the Jordan at the place of Christ's baptism, not only to protect pilgrims, but also to prevent a repetition of the massacre by Zengi of the six monks who had lived at a church which had been erected there. One of the duties of the Templar commander of Jerusalem was to keep ten knights on standby to protect pilgrims going to and from the Jordan, as well as a string of pack animals to carry food and exhausted travelers.[18]

Many of these earliest castles were built around the Muslim fortress of Ascalon, in order to keep it in check. With 150 towers, this monstrous stronghold was the bane of the Crusader states, especially Christian pilgrims. It was primarily from this coastal fortress, which was forever being supplied with resources and manpower from Fatimid

Egypt, that hordes of Muslims would issue forth to massacre and enslave pilgrims and other Christians.

The Muslim fortress of Ascalon first entered the Crusaders' consciousness days after they conquered Jerusalem on July 15, 1099. Word reached them that a mammoth army, assembled in Egypt and made up of various Muslim races, had reached the port of Ascalon. In the words of a contemporary Christian, who tended to see temporal conflicts as reflective of eternal ones, that "writhing serpent" Satan had "in his venom" stirred up the "whole of the Orient." Rather than barricading his vastly outnumbered and exhausted men in the Holy City, Godfrey, the first king of Jerusalem—though he rejected that title, adamantly refusing to wear a crown of gold where his Savior had worn a crown of thorns—decided to issue forth and intercept the Muslims at Ascalon. On August 11, 1099, the Christians overtook the much larger Muslim force unawares, scoring a magnificent victory—prompting the Fatimid vizier and general of the Muslims, al-Afdal, to cry out, "O Muhammad, our Master and protector, where is your strength?"[19]

Despite this Crusader victory, the impregnable fortress of Ascalon remained in Muslim hands and continued to serve as a base for countless devastating raids on the Christians, including, as seen, against newly arrived pilgrims.

As such, the Templars' first major castle, situated ten miles south of Ascalon, near the border of Fatimid Egypt, was devoted to checking these constant raids. Built by the Crusaders atop the ruins of the ancient city of Gaza, where Samson had been imprisoned and blinded by the Philistines, this forlorn fortress stood atop a hill overlooking the vast plain. Once complete in 1150, it was "committed by general consent to the care of the Knights of the Temple, to be held by them in perpetuity together with all the adjacent district."[20] From their Gazan fortress, the Templars terrorized the terrorists. Writing some two decades later, even William of Tyre—never a great friend to the Templars—had nothing but praise concerning how they upheld their mandate:

> These men, brave and vigorous in arms, have kept the commission prudently and faithfully up to the present

> day. They have struck hard against the aforesaid town [Ascalon] with frequent attacks both secretly and openly, so that those [Muslims] who previously terrorized us by overrunning and plundering the whole region, now regard themselves as most happy if, through prayers or payment, they are permitted to live in peace within the walls and quietly go about their business, temporarily untroubled.[21]

So terrifying was the reputation of the Templars that "the Egyptian army, also, which, as we have said, had so often brought aid to the now afflicted city, presently began to come by sea only. They feared the ambuscades arising from the fortress lying on the way and stood in great awe of the knights."[22]

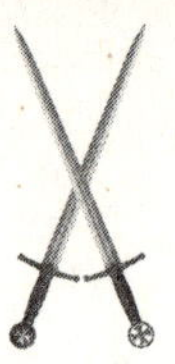

10

ASCALON: "SEIZED WITH A MAD FURY FOR EXTERMINATION"

Due to the Templars' effectiveness against Ascalon, King Baldwin III of Jerusalem felt the time was right to neutralize and take the long-held Muslim fortress. "For fifty years and more," writes William of Tyre, "after the Lord had given the rest of the Land of Promise into the hands of the Christian people, Ascalon had resisted all our attempts and shown itself a formidable rival to us. The Christians finally resolved to besiege the place."[1] On January 25, 1153, Baldwin, at the head of a large Crusader army, which included a strong host of Templars, put Ascalon to siege. William summarizes the importance of Ascalon to, and the great reinforcements it continued to receive from, Fatimid Egypt:

> There was a large population in that city, even the least of whom—and, indeed, according to the general report, even the youngest babes—received pay from the treasury of the caliph of Egypt. That monarch and his princes felt the utmost solicitude for Ascalon, realizing that if

> it should fall and come into the power of the Christians there would be nothing to prevent our leaders from invading Egypt without let or hindrance and seizing that kingdom by force. They regarded Ascalon as a bulwark, therefore, and four times a year with lavish munificence they furnished assistance to the city, both by land and by sea.[2]

Once the siege commenced, battle was fierce, and for months "rivers of blood flowed before its walls...both Muslims and Christians fighting with fury, neither giving nor receiving quarter."[3] Great feats of valor took place during the "incessant fighting," especially "along the walls,"[4] writes William:

> Almost daily our people, now the knights and again the foot soldiers, made attacks upon the city.... Scarcely a day passed without carnage, to say nothing of the great number of wounded on both sides. We have heard stories of memorable deeds wrought at that siege by certain individuals and of the remarkable valor shown both by the enemy and the Christians.[5]

Despite the initial bombardment, the siege stalled, "for Ascalon was well defended by walls and barbicans, towers and embankments, and equipped with an incredible amount of arms and provisions. In addition, it had a large population well trained and thoroughly versed in the practice of arms. In fact, from the very beginning of the siege even unto the end the number of defenders was double that of the besieging host." Worse, while the Christians controlled the land surrounding Ascalon, the Muslims still had mastery over the sea, and Egypt continuously supplied them "with everything needful and at regular intervals sent arms, food, and fresh troops." Nor was this mere Muslim altruism; "for while the Christians were occupied with Ascalon the Egyptians felt less anxiety over our" ability to attack Egypt itself.[6]

Four grueling months later, and after much Christian blood and treasure had been spilled, Baldwin decided to lift the siege in response to the desperate pleas of his dejected men—all, that is, except for one group: "The Templars opposed withdrawal. They assured the king that Ascalon would yet be taken, and, inspired by their faith, Baldwin countermanded his orders."[7]

Among the siege engines and catapults that Baldwin had brought was a huge wooden tower, positioned in the sector manned by the Templars. On the night of August 15 into 16, a detachment of Muslims stealthily issued from the fortress and set this tower, which had long harried them, aflame. Almost immediately, a strong easterly wind blew the flames back onto the walls of Ascalon, which themselves caught fire. Some of the masonry cracked and crumbled, causing one of the walls to collapse. Seeing this opportunity, forty Templars, led by Bernard of Tremelay, who became Templar master after Everard's resignation, instantly charged inside the city. Although the knights of Christ made a valiant stand, they were utterly outnumbered, overwhelmed, slaughtered and ritually beheaded—no other Crusader had followed them—by the throngs of Muslims holed inside the fortress.

In the words of a contemporary account based on an anonymous participant of the siege,

> It was brought about that the falling wall furnished a wide entrance to our men. The chief leader and commander of that army, which serves from the Temple under the profession of fraternal fellowship, rushed in with his troop, and, reaching an open space in the city surrounded by his band of men, he established a position; there, limited by the narrowness of the streets, closed in by walls and the overhanging roofs of the buildings, and beset from every side by a growing crowd, he was overwhelmed and slain with the entire body of his men. The heads of whom were gathered in one heap so they might be displayed to the king of Babylon [the Fatimid caliph of Egypt] as a sign of victory; they hung the bodies on the walls, taunting us and provoking the army of God with words of blasphemy.[8]

William of Tyre offers a vastly different account as to why the rest of the Crusaders failed to follow the Templars into the lion's den:

> Roused at the sound of the crash [of the wall], the entire army seized arms and rushed to the place, eager to enter at once as if an entrance had been opened from on high. But Bernard of Tremelay, the master of the Templars, and his brethren had reached there much before the rest; he held the opening and allowed none but his own men to enter. It was charged that he kept the rest back in order that his own people, being the first to enter, might obtain the greater and richer portion of the spoils and plunder.... Through cupidity, they refused to allow their comrades to share in the booty, therefore they alone justly suffered peril of death. About forty entered, but the rest were not able to follow.[9]

What to make of this odd rendering? The first fact to acknowledge is simple: As a member of the higher clergy, William, the archbishop of Tyre, had an axe to grind against the Templars and other military orders and was apparently always ready to believe, and record, the worst about them. The papal privileges bestowed on the military orders—followed by their meteoric rise in popularity, wealth, and influence—were always a double-edged sword, causing much resentment among those clergymen who did not enjoy the same privileges and among those higher clergymen who could not presume to control or treat the Templars as subordinates. William of Tyre appears to have been in this latter category and often complained—at one point even going to Rome to complain—about the military orders' ability to keep their churches open, ring their bells, and administer the eucharist to excommunicated

Christians, or during times when a bishop (such as himself) had issued a regional interdict.*

This makes William's chronicle, as authoritative as it is, somewhat suspect when it comes to the military orders, whose doings he not infrequently puts a negative spin on (thus making his occasional praise that much more impressive). That said, to his credit, while he mentions the worst interpretation, he seldom accepts it at face value and always leaves the door open to the possibility that it is incorrect. The current account is a perfect example; for William is still objective enough to write that "it was *charged*"[10] that the Templars prevented the others from entering, indicating that this accusation was made later—apparently much later—and as a pretext.

In fact, while William's account was written some twenty-five years after the siege of Ascalon, the two earliest known accounts—one of which is based on eyewitness testimony and was quoted above—say absolutely nothing about the Templars preventing the rest of the army from following them into Ascalon. After emphasizing this point, historian Helen Nicholson offers a more plausible reconstruction:

> What really happened at Ascalon was that the Templars succeeded into breaking into the city through the breach in the wall, but the other Christian attackers either did not realize that they had broken through or were reluctant to follow them in to probable death. The Templars were killed and the king [Baldwin III] was angry. His generals excused themselves by saying that the Templars

* William's complaints against the military orders even make it into his chronicle. As one example, he wrote, "The Hospitallers were in the habit of receiving to the celebration of the holy sacrament, without discrimination or question, those who had been excommunicated by their own bishops or interdicted by name and who, thus, in punishment for their sins, were cut off from the church. Neither did they refuse the viaticum and extreme unction to these same persons when sick, or deny them burial. When, because of crimes committed, silence was imposed upon all the churches or upon those of a certain city or castle, the Hospitallers were wont to ring their bells and call more loudly than usual, to summon those under interdict to divine service" (William of Tyre, *A History of Deeds*, vol. 2, 239).

> had prevented them from following them into the city—and this was the account which they and their children gave to William of Tyre.[11]

Nicholson is not the only historian to discount William's uncharitable interpretation. According to Emily A. Babcock and A. C. Krey, the translators and annotators of William's chronicle, "This charge of cupidity against the Templars is…a reflection of William's prejudice against the order, and unjustified by the facts."[12]

One can also add that it beggars the imagination to believe that a small group of forty Templars would forcibly prevent their much-needed reinforcements from helping them against what was likely a garrison of one thousand Muslim fighters—and all for gold.

Be that as it may, on August 19, 1153, a mere three days after the charge and subsequent slaughter of the Templars, the city surrendered to the Crusaders and was given until August 22 to evacuate. Now "cries of praise not unaccompanied by tears rose to heaven as from one voice, saying, 'Blessed be the God of our fathers who has not deserted those who trusted in Him; and blessed be the Name of His Majesty which is holy, because today we have seen wondrous things.'"[13]

This itself is an interesting development that further questions William's version. He initially presented the slaughter of the Templars as boosting Muslim morale, and shattering Christian morale, to no end. After hanging the headless bodies of the Templars from their ramparts, William portrayed the Muslims as jeering, mocking, and animated with a "renewed strength" and "courage reborn," so that they "girded themselves for the combat and renewed the fight…. The Christians, on the contrary, were prostrated in mind and heart. Overcome by grief, in bitterness of spirit, they became faint-hearted and lost all hope of ultimate victory."[14]

Why then did the city, which had withstood four months of continual bombardment, capitulate three days after the slaughter of the Templars? Could it be that the opposite had occurred? Could the Templars' bold charge have caused a tingle to run up the Muslims' spines? Could the knights of Christ's sacrificial act of martyrdom have inspired and inflamed the rest of the Crusaders to a holy fury? In fact, that is what the contemporaneous accounts suggest:

> They hung the bodies [of the Templars] on the walls, taunting us and provoking the army of God with words of blasphemy. Finally, our men much strengthened in the Lord, committing themselves to the Lord with most devout prayers and making vows to the holy mother of God, attacked the wall on the third day; standing firm in faith, they moved forward warlike implements, machines and balistas [missile-hurling siege machines]. Truly, the True Cross went before the army in the hands of the patriarch.... Finally, hard pressed, they delivered the city into the hand of the king, and from that time Ascalon was made ours and possessed by our people.[15]

Indeed, William himself eventually goes on to give this very reasoning—that a strong desire to avenge the sacrifice of the Temple prompted the rest of the Crusaders, now "seized with a mad fury," to greater feats of arms:

> Accordingly, with unanimity of purpose, all seized their arms and, returning to the task in hand, ordered the trumpets to sound the signal. The clarion's call and the voice of the herald soon summoned the whole people to battle. Eager to avenge the wrongs of their murdered brethren, the people gathered before the city with unusual fervor and with avidity challenged the foe to battle.... Seized with a mad fury for extermination, they rushed upon the enemy and attacked them so fiercely that the foe marvelled and stood dumbfounded before the evidence of our insuperable strength and indomitable perseverance. Although they made desperate efforts to retaliate with equal fury, it was all in vain, for they could not stand against the shock of our troops or avoid their swords. The battle that day was waged between

> far from equal forces, yet knights and foot soldiers alike won the palm of victory everywhere and triumphed at every point over the foe. Thus great slaughter was wrought upon the enemy, and the injury suffered by the Christians three days before [i.e., the slaughter of the Templars] was returned in overwhelming measure.[16]

There is no denying that the Templars played a decisive role in the conquest of Ascalon—arguably the greatest Christian achievement in the nearly seventy years between the Crusader capture of Tyre in 1124 and the Third Crusade. First, after every other Crusader had lost heart and was urging Baldwin to lift the siege, it was they alone who, through brave words and stalwart deeds, convinced him to persevere; second, their heroic charge terrified the Muslims of worse to come and emboldened the Christians to emulate, and ultimately avenge, the Templars. Ascalon's capitulation three days later was no coincidence.

With the capture of Ascalon, not only did the Egyptians lose their forward base to launch attacks on the southern border of the Crusader states, but the entire Palestinian coast was finally brought under Crusader rule. From being the bane of Christian pilgrims, Ascalon became a great succor—thanks to the sacrifice of the Templars who had vowed to fight and die in defense of fellow Christians:

> For fifty years, through fear of hostilities, the fields around Ascalon had lain without cultivation. But during the years following its [Christian] capture, the land was under the care of the farmer, and the people of that district, relieved from fear of the enemy, could freely cultivate the ground. Hence the entire kingdom enjoyed such abundance that all former years, in comparison with the present, might with justice be called sterile and fruitless.[17]

Worse for the Fatimids, the tables had turned, and now Ascalon would serve as a forward base for the Crusaders to launch attacks on Egypt, long seen as a prerequisite to secure the Holy Land.

11

THE ASSASSIN CONTROVERSY

Less than a year following the Crusader conquest of Ascalon, another interesting incident occurred in 1154. As with Ascalon, it too was used to present the Templars as cynical and greedy pragmatists, though in reality it would seem to underscore the depth of their prudence and learning concerning the enemy and his deceptive ways.

In April 1154, the twenty-one-year-old Fatimid caliph "was murdered by his homosexual favorite, Nasr [al-Din], who fled to Syria and was captured by the Templars." During his captivity, he insisted that he wanted to become Christian, but the brethren opted instead to accept Cairo's offer of 60,000 dinars for him, "and Nasr was taken home by the Egyptians in an iron cage, to be first horribly mutilated by the caliph's four widows, and then, still living, crucified at the Zawila Gate, where his rotting corpse hung for two years."[1]

Once again, William of Tyre gives the most unflattering rendering of this account:

> The brothers of the Temple held this man a prisoner for a long time. He professed an ardent desire to be reborn in Christ and had already learned the Roman letters and been instructed in the rudiments of the Christian faith when he was sold by the Templars for sixty thousand

> pieces of gold to the Egyptians, who demanded him for the death penalty. Heavily chained hand and foot, he was placed in an iron cage upon the back of a camel and carried to Egypt, where, to satisfy their savage passions, the people literally tore him to pieces bit by bit with their teeth.[2]

The implication is obvious: Rather than accept a new brother in Christ, the callous and greedy Templars preferred to profit by his agonizing death (and subsequent damnation). As Malcolm Barber argues, however,

> The Templars were not an Order dedicated to conversion nor...did they readily believe in changes of heart among Muslims. Certainly, Nasr had strong reason to affect an interest in Christianity [namely, to gain sanctuary among the crusaders].... There does seem to have been some exaggeration on William's part...[and] it seems unlikely that Nasr had advanced very far with his Christian studies during the time he was imprisoned by the Templars.[3]

Another very similar, though much more controversial, incident truly homes in on this question of Muslim conversions and Templar suspicions—and it concerns the dreaded "Assassins."

The Hashashin (whose named reached the West as "Assassins") were, as Shias of the Ismaili variety, committed to the deeper, more esoteric teachings of Islam. Since their founding in 1090 till late into the thirteenth century, this shadowy sect lived in the mountainous regions of modern-day Syria, Iraq, and Iran. From their eagles' nests, they engaged "in the most extensive system of murder and assassination known in the history of the world. Both Christian and Muslim writers enumerate with horror the many illustrious victims that fell beneath their daggers."[4] (As a Shia sect, they primarily targeted Sunnis and Christians.)

The Assassins were, first and foremost, highly committed Muslims—indeed "radicals," to use a familiar if anachronistic term. Even William of Tyre, who, as shall be seen, exhibited a bit of naivety concerning Assassin sincerity, confirmed that they were the most fanatical devotees of sharia law: "For about four hundred years they have followed the law and traditions of the Saracens so strictly that by comparison all other [Muslim] peoples seem as prevaricators and they alone the complete observers of the law." Elsewhere in his chronicle, he denounces their "worthless traditions, hateful to God," before adding, "they are a people very much distrusted and justly feared by the Christians."[5]

They were known to their contemporaries as "Hashashin" due to their use of hashish, a hallucinogenic cannabis plant that they drugged their young male recruits with as part of their indoctrination process. Once fully committed, these young Assassins would carefully and secretly track down their targets until the opportune moment arrived, at which point they would pounce on and ideally stab their target to death—preferably in public, for a maximum show of terror. Then they would just stand there, waiting to be mowed down by their target's guard and thus translated into Islamic paradise.

While these general facts are recounted in many modern history books, what is seldom mentioned is the distinctly Islamic origins of the Assassins. For example, the hallucinogenic cannabinoids which they were named after were employed precisely to trick recruits into thinking they had received a taste of Muslim paradise. The head of the Order, known to contemporaries as the "Sheikh (or Old Man) of the Mountain," would get young male recruits thoroughly "stoned," and then, while they were in a confused state of euphoria, lead them into a beautiful garden, "where every species of sensual gratification should be found" in the company of scantily clad and "amorous" women,[6] to quote Marco Polo, a contemporary of the Assassins, who left us one of the best and most extant descriptions of the group.

The purpose of this hashish-induced orgy was to convince the recruit that if he fulfilled his master's wishes—assassinating whomever the Sheikh ordered him to assassinate and then getting killed afterward—the paradise he had already experienced temporarily (while drugged and deluded) would be his forever.

All of this is, of course, based on the direct teachings of Muhammad, the prophet of Islam. "We have the assurances of our prophet," the Sheikh regularly reminded his young Assassins, "that he who defends his lord [by obeying him unto death] shall inherit Paradise, and if you show yourselves devoted to the obedience of my orders, that happy lot awaits you."[7]

In fact, not only did the prophet of Islam make use of and call for the stealthy assassination of his enemies, including those who merely mocked him—such as a mother who was stabbed to death while suckling her babe*—but he promised a decidedly carnal paradise to those men who died fighting in the name of Islam. This included seventy-two *houris*: supernatural, celestial women ("wide-eyed" and "big-bosomed," says the Koran 56:22; 78:33) created by Allah for the express purpose of sexually gratifying his favorites in perpetuity. The damsels in the gardens were dressed and behaved in a manner that would make the drug-addled recruits believe them to be *houris*—thus whetting their appetite for more. (It remains unclear whether the English word "whore" is etymologically based on the Arabic *houri* (pronounced hoo-ri) in the same way "assassin" is based on *hashashin*.)

We now reach the aforementioned controversy concerning the Templars. With the fall of the Fatimid Empire in 1171—a traumatic event for the Shia world to be highlighted later—the Assassins, themselves an offshoot of the now defunct Shia empire, were much alarmed

* After Muhammad learned that Asma bint Marwan, an Arab poetess, was writing verses that portrayed him as nothing more than a murdering bandit, he called for her assassination, exclaiming: "Will no one rid me of this woman?" That very night, Umayr, a zealous Muslim, crept into Asma's home while she lay sleeping surrounded by her young children. After removing one of her suckling babes from her breast, Umayr plunged his sword into the poetess. The next morning at mosque, Muhammad, who was aware of the assassination, said, "You have helped Allah and his Apostle." Apparently feeling some remorse, Umayr responded, "She had five sons; should I feel guilty?" "No," the prophet answered. "Killing her was as meaningless as two goats butting heads." From Muhammad's earliest biography, *Sirat Rasul Allah* by Ibn Ishaq, 676.

and decided to ingratiate themselves with the Crusaders. In 1173, their leader, Rashid al-Din Sinan, sent an embassy, led by one Abdullah, to King Amalric of Jerusalem. His message was that the "Old Man of the Mountain" and all of his Assassins were willing to embrace Christianity—on one condition: that the tribute they had been paying to the Templars be canceled. In William of Tyre's words, Abdullah the envoy pled,

> If the brethren of the Temple, who held certain fortresses adjacent to the lands of the Assassins, would remit the tribute of two thousand gold pieces which was paid to them yearly by his [Sinan's] people and would thereafter observe brotherly kindness toward them, the race of the Assassins would embrace the faith of Christ and receive baptism.[8]

Two decades earlier, sometime in the 1150s, on learning that the Assassins had assassinated a Christian as he knelt in prayer, the Templars had flown to arms, penetrated the mountain strongholds of the Assassins, and refused to let up their frenzied assault until the Sheikh, this terror of the region, submitted to paying them tribute in exchange for peace.[9] In the words of Oliver of Paderborn, a Crusader and chronicler,

> For the Assassins and their chief, the Old Man of the Mountain, had the custom of casting knives against the Christians to cut off the lives of those who care for the business of Christianity. For at the time of the truce they wantonly killed the son of the Count of Tripoli, a fine young man [Raymond, son of Bohemond the One-Eyed], who was prostrate before the altar in the church of the Blessed Virgin at Tortosa; wherefore the army of the Temple did not cease to pursue them for such a violation of religious liberty, until they were humiliated to the servitude of paying a tribute of three thousand bezants annually to the Templars.[10]

Although he had no authority over the Templars, who as a military order were ultimately only answerable to the pope, King Amalric agreed to the terms; peace with the Assassins and use of their vast network were definite assets. As for the Templars, even if they refused to exempt the Assassins, he, Amalric, was prepared to pay the owed tribute (2,000 dinars annually) in their stead.

However, as the Assassin envoys were traveling home with the good news to their master, "they were the victims of a sudden and unexpected attack by the Templars, who came at them with drawn swords," says William. Led by Walter of Mesnil—a restless, one-eyed knight who likely lost his light fighting Muslims—the Templars massacred the Assassin emissaries.[11]

Frothing at the mouth and saying that such a "treasonous" act undermined his royal authority, Amalric ordered the Templar master, Odo of St. Amand, to hand over the one-eyed knight for punishment. Odo refused. Instead, he offered to send Walter off to Rome, as no one—not even the king—had legal jurisdiction over the military orders; only the pope did. But Amalric would have none of it. He burst into the master's quarters in Sidon, seized Walter of Mesnil, and flung him into a dungeon in Tyre.

To the chroniclers of the time, there was no excuse for the Templars' actions, and various sordid motives were ascribed to them. Walter Map's rendering of this episode, written nearly a decade later in 1182, is especially sinister. The Templars killed the Assassin envoy, not because they were wild, reckless, or refused to release them from tribute, but because they were committed to preventing Christians and Muslims from ever attaining peace, thereby ensuring the necessity of their Order to the Crusader states. In the words of Walter Map,

> This pagan was ambushed en route by the Templars of the city and killed, it is alleged, so that peace and harmony would not come about through the disappearance of the Muslim religion, for they say that the Assassins are the prime movers of the Muslims' lack of Christian beliefs. When the Old Man learnt about the ambush,

> under the influence of the devil, he put a stop to his new Christian devotion.[12]

For the Templars' chief critic, William of Tyre, who, as seen, was always ready to report the worst motives attributed to them, this entire episode showed once again that the Templars were a menace—loose cannons answerable to no one. His entire case, however, is marred by the fact that, as in the previous case with Nasr, the homosexual assassin of the Fatimid caliph, William seems to accept the Assassins' claims of wanting to convert to Christianity on face value. Thus, after describing the current Old Man of the Mountain as "a very eloquent man, of subtle and brilliant intelligence," William waxes rather naively:

> Contrary to the habits of his ancestors, this man possessed the books of the Evangels and the apostolic law [the Bible]. Over these he pored continually and for some time had with much labor tried to follow the marvelous precepts of Christ and also the apostolic doctrine. The gentle and noble doctrine of Christ and His followers, when compared with that which the miserable seducer Muhammad had transmitted to his accomplices and deluded followers, caused him to despise the beliefs which he had absorbed with his mother's milk and to abominate the unclean tenets of that deceiver. He instructed his people also in the same way and made them cease observing the superstition of the prophet. He tore down the places of prayer which they had been accustomed to use, absolved them from fasting, and permitted the use of wine and pork. At length, desirous of advancing into a fuller understanding of the mysteries of God's law, he sent an envoy to the king.[13]

As we shall see in the following chapter, William's uncritical acceptance of such claims is reflective of his own biases and hopes rather than the complex realities of the Assassins, or the Templars' knowledge of the Muslims.

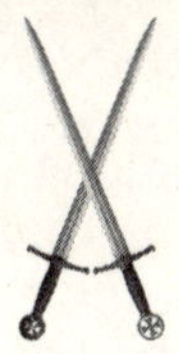

12

TAQIYYA: "SMILE TO THEIR FACE, HATE THEM IN YOUR HEART"

What to make of the preceding chapter? Did the Templars prefer cold cash over the conversion of Muslims to Christianity, as in the case with Nasr? Did they kill the Assassin envoys due to avarice, reckless hate, or a cynical desire to ensure a permanent state of war between Muslims and Christians?

Or did the knights of Christ perhaps know something that the "armchair chroniclers" of their time did not?

Evidence supports the third possibility: Up-close-and-personal contact with Muslims provided the Templars with a more intimate understanding of the inner workings and stratagems of Islam. If William of Tyre and Walter Map were naïve enough* to believe that the Assassins, arguably the most duplicitous Muslim group of the time (which is

* Whatever William of Tyre thought about the shadowy Assassins, his thoughts on Islam and its founder were clear and representative of the typical Christian of his time and place: He regularly lambasts "the seducer Muhammad" for misleading Muslims, and writes things like, "Muhammad, their [the Muslims'] prophet, or rather their destroyer" (William of Tyre, *A History of Deeds*, vol. 2, 323–325).

saying something), were on the verge of converting to Christianity en masse, the Templars were not—and for very good reason.

Unlike Christianity, which condemns all forms of deceit—a position which Christians, then and now, inadvertently project onto Muslims—Islam takes a rather lenient approach. Indeed, entire doctrines are dedicated to articulating the various ways Muslims may deceive others (with more "stringent" requirements for lies directed at fellow Muslims, e.g., through the employment of *tawriya*, or double entendre). Most of these teachings, however, tend to be conflated and placed under the umbrella term of Islam's most notorious doctrine of deception: *taqiyya**: "Let believers," the Koran (3:28) declares, "not take for friends and allies infidels [*al-kafirin*, non-Muslims] instead of believers. Whoever does this shall have no relationship left with Allah—*unless you but guard yourselves against them, taking precautions*." The Arabic words translated here as "guard yourselves" and "taking precautions" are derived from the triliteral root, *t-q-y*, whence the word "taqiyya" (see also Koran 2:173, 2:185, 4:29, 22:78, and 40:28).

Sheikh al-Tabari (d. 923), author of a standard and widely referenced Koran commentary, offered the following exegesis of 3:28: "If you [Muslims] are under their [non-Muslims'] authority, fearing for yourselves, behave loyally to them with your tongue while harboring inner animosity for them.... [Know that] Allah has forbidden believers from being friendly or on intimate terms with the infidels rather than other believers—except when infidels are above them [in authority].

* The best scholarly work on *taqiyya* is the Arabic language volume *Al Taqiyya f'il Islam* (*Taqiyya in Islam*). Written by the late Dr. Sami Makarem, a former Islamic studies professor at the American University of Beirut and author of some twenty-five books on Islam, the book demonstrates the ubiquity and broad applicability of *taqiyya* in its opening pages: "*Taqiyya* [deception] is of fundamental importance in Islam. Practically every Islamic sect agrees to it and practices it.... We can go so far as to say that the practice of *taqiyya* is mainstream in Islam, and that those few sects not practicing it diverge from the mainstream.... *Taqiyya* is very prevalent in Islamic politics, especially in the modern era." Translated excerpts from it and other Arabic sources can be found in my article, "How Taqiyya Alters Islam's Rules of War": https://www.raymondibrahim.com/2010/01/10/how-taqiyya-alters-islams-rules-of-war/.

Should that be the case, *let them act friendly towards them while preserving their religion.*"[1] Similarly, another mainstream authority on the Koran, Ibn Kathir (d. 1373) explains Koran 3:28 as follows: "Whoever at any time or place fears…evil [from non-Muslims] may protect himself through outward show." As proof, he quotes Muhammad's close companion Abu Darda: "We grin to the faces of some peoples, while our hearts curse them."[2]

None of this should be surprising considering that Muhammad himself, whose example as the "most perfect human" is to be tenaciously followed, regularly employed deceit, and generally permitted lying in three cases: in war (which applies to the entire Crusading era), to one's wife, and to reconcile two quarreling parties. He also permitted his followers to pretend to have apostatized from Islam in order to win the confidences of, and get near enough to murder, the enemy.

Thus, after a Jewish poet, Ka'b ibn al-Ashraf, had offended Muhammad with his verse, the latter exclaimed, "Who will kill this man who has hurt Allah and his prophet?" A young Muslim named Muhammad Ibn Maslama volunteered on condition that in order to get close enough to assassinate Ka'b, he be given permission to lie to the poet. The prophet consented. Ibn Maslama traveled to meet Ka'b and began to complain about Muhammad until his disaffection from Islam became so convincing that Ka'b eventually dropped his guard and befriended him. After behaving as his friend for some time, Ibn Maslama eventually appeared with another crypto-Muslim. Then, while a trusting Ka'b's guard was down, they attacked and slaughtered him, bringing his head to Muhammad to triumphant cries of "Allahu Akbar!"[3]

In another example, after Muhammad and his followers had attacked, plundered, and massacred a number of non-Muslim Arabs and Jews, the latter assembled and were poised to defeat the Muslims at the Battle of the Trench, 627. But then Naim Bin Mas'ud, one of the leaders of these non-Muslim "confederates," as they came to be known in history, secretly absconded to Muhammad and joined the Islamic team. The prophet asked him to return to his tribesmen and allies—without revealing that he had joined the Muslim camp—and try to get them to abandon the siege. "For," the prophet assured him, "war is deceit." Mas'ud returned, pretending to be loyal to his former kinsmen and allies, all while giving them poisoned advice. He also subtly instigated quarrels between the various tribes until, no longer trusting each other, they disbanded—thereby allowing a nascent Islam to grow and making Mas'ud a celebrated hero in Muslim tradition.[4]

Needless to say, then, false Muslim conversions, whenever advantageous to Muslims, have always been permissible. Although there are many past (and present*) examples, one of the most noteworthy occurred some three centuries following the Templar massacre of Assassins, on the other end of the Muslim-Christian theater of war: Spain.

In 1492, Granada, the final Muslim bastion of Spain that had long terrorized the Christians, was reconquered, bringing to a close the centuries-long Reconquista. Its Muslims were initially granted lenient terms, including the right to travel abroad and practice Islam freely. However, whenever the opportunity arose, they launched many hard-to-quell uprisings—several "involving the stoning, dismembering, beheading, impaling, and burning alive of Christians"[5]—and regularly colluded with foreign Muslim powers (e.g., Ottoman Turks and Barbary pirates) in an effort to subvert Spain back to Islam.

The Spanish crown eventually issued an edict that Muslims had to either convert to Christianity—and therefore slough off their animus for Christians—or return to Africa, whence their ancestors first invaded and conquered the Iberian Peninsula in the eighth century. In response, the entire population of Granada—hundreds of thousands of Muslims—openly embraced Christianity but remained crypto-Muslims. Publicly, they went to church and baptized their children; at home, they recited the Koran and preached undying hate for the infidel and the

---

* In 2013, an assassination plot against a Christian pastor in Turkey was exposed. Fourteen Muslim suspects, including at least three women, were arrested. According to the pastor in question, Emre Karaali, "Two of them attended our church for over a year and they were like family." One was even baptized. In reality, "These people had infiltrated our church and collected information about me, my family and the church and were preparing an attack against us." In this case, then, Muslims converted to Christianity, devoutly attended church, and behaved like "family" to the pastor and other Christians—all so they could get close enough to kill them. (*Christianity Today,* "Turkish Police Foil.")

Muslim obligation to resubjugate Spain. Such taqiyya was legitimized by the fatwas of leading Islamic clerics. One historian explains the great lengths to which these "Moriscos"—that is, Muslim converts to Christianity who were still "Moorish"—went to deceive the Christians:

> For a Morisco to pass as a good Christian took more than a simple statement to that effect. It required a sustained performance involving hundreds of individual statements and actions of different types, many of which might have little to do with expressions of belief or ritual per se. Dissimulation [taqiyya] was an institutionalized practice in Morisco communities that involved regular patterns of behaviour passed on from one generation to the next.[6]

Despite this elaborate masquerade, Christians increasingly caught on: "With the permission and license that their accursed sect [Islam] accorded them," a frustrated Spaniard remarked as late as the seventeenth century, "they could feign any religion outwardly and without sinning, as long as they kept their hearts nevertheless devoted to their false impostor of a prophet. We saw so many of them who died while worshipping the Cross and speaking well of our Catholic Religion yet who were inwardly excellent Muslims." For no matter how much the Moriscos "might present the appearance of the most peaceful submission," a nineteenth century historian wrote, "they remained nevertheless fundamentally Muslims, watching for a favorable opportunity and patiently awaiting the hour of revenge, promised by their prophecies."[7]

In short, generation after generation of Muslims pretended to be, and lived as, model Christians in Spain—even as they had nothing but hatred for Christians—all to remain and eventually reconquer Spain for Islam. Such are the overlooked origins of the Spanish Inquisition (which, contrary to popular belief, targeted many more Muslims than Jews). "Such of the Muslims as still remained in Andalus," writes a contemporary Muslim, "although Christians in appearance, were not so in their hearts; for they worshipped Allah in secret.... The Christians watched over them with the greatest vigilance, and many were discovered and burnt."[8]

If Muslims could never be loyal to non-Muslim authority—forever colluding and subverting, including with foreign Muslims—and if conversion to Christianity was no solution due to the dispensation of taqiyya, then only one solution remained: Between 1609 and 1614, all Moriscos were expelled from Spain to Africa, at which point the nearly one-thousand-year-long war for Spain was truly at an end.

Spain, of course, is just one example: "Sunni Muslims had invoked taqiyya to justify dissimulation under Christian domination in other periods and regions, including Sicily after the Norman conquest in 1061–91 and the Byzantine Marches."[9]

Returning to the aforementioned Templar-Assassin controversy, it is worth noting that William of Tyre himself was familiar with and denounced Muslim "fifth columns." After explaining how a major battle had drawn away many Crusaders from their castles in 1113, he writes:

> The infidels, well aware that the kingdom had been stripped of defenders, sent out bands of soldiers in every direction and overran the whole country. They wrought fearful carnage everywhere along the highways; they set fires, ransacked villages, seized farmers, and treated the entire region as if it had already been brought under their power. *During these days, our [Muslim] domestics deserted us and also the Saracen dwellers in our villages.... These joined the cohorts of the foe and instructed them how to destroy us. This they were well able to do, inasmuch as they possessed full information about our situation.* "For there is no more deadly and effective pest than an enemy within one's own doors." Thus the foe, guided by these people and rendered more efficient by their help, continued to go about among the towns and fortresses, carrying off booty and slaves. In short, they reduced the whole realm to such a state of terror that no one dared to venture outside the fortifications [emphasis added].[10]

In this context, then, and seeing the extremely deceptive lengths to which Muslims were permitted to feign conversion to Christianity, how realistic is it to believe that the duplicitous Assassin order—which more than any other Muslim sect thrived on deception, beginning with its very own members—was, after a supposed reading of the Bible, so moved as to be on the verge of renouncing Islam and embracing Christianity en masse? And all on one, rather temporal, condition: being relieved from paying tribute to the Templars.

This question becomes more pressing upon realizing that the Shias—which the Assassins were—took to and internalized taqiyya in ways that even the Sunnis (of Spain, Sicily, the Byzantine Marches, etc.) did not. Unlike their Sunni enemies, the Shias were an often-weakened minority and therefore had more reason and occasion to employ taqiyya in their struggle for mastery of the Muslim world. Deception became second nature to them (which is saying something, considering how adroitly the Sunnis also applied it, as in the Spain example). As Bernard Lewis writes, "Taqiyya is by no means peculiar to the Shia; it was they, however, who were most frequently exposed to the dangers of persecution and repression [by the Sunni majority], and by them therefore that the principle was most frequently invoked. It was used to justify concealment of beliefs."[11]

In short, the Shias were the Muslim world's dissimulation experts par excellence; and the Assassins were the dissimulation experts among the Shias. There are, in fact, numerous examples of the Assassins worming their way among the Crusaders, including by pretending to want to convert to Christianity and even getting baptized—only to turn around and murder their Christian target.[12]

Based on this lengthy excursus into the inner workings of Islam, it would seem that the Templars—unlike the chroniclers—were not fooled and slew the Assassin envoys before they could finalize their deception with the Crusaders, the consequences of which could have been far reaching and detrimental to the Christians. Something in William of Tyre's history would seem to lend support to this interpretation. He writes that, while defending the Templar attack on the Assassins before

King Amalric, Master Odo "issued other remarks with the arrogance that characterized him, but it is hardly necessary to list them here."[13]

Could it be that Odo was precisely arguing that the king was naively falling for an old Muslim trick—a rebuttal that, no doubt, would have been deemed insolent to Amalric and unworthy of mention by William? It is also telling that, despite Amalric's initial outrage at the slaying of the Assassin envoys—described as a "frenzied" and "violent anger"[14]—he went on to brush the whole matter under the rug, suggesting, perhaps, that he quietly came to appreciate the Templars' actions. As William writes,

> This outrage against the envoy came near plunging the whole kingdom into irreparable ruin. By declaring his innocence, however, to the master of the Assassins, whose representative had perished in so unfortunate a manner, the king was able to clear his own honor. In dealing with the brethren of the Temple he exercised such moderation that the matter remained in abeyance even to the day of his death.[15]

Incidentally, is it not odd that the Old Man of the Mountain, whom William presented as being so utterly convicted by and thus eager to convert to the Gospel, would altogether forget about converting due the actions of a single, one-eyed knight, who was anyway denounced and punished by the king—the same king who profusely apologized to the Old Man?

The debate concerning this episode, among both past and present historians, has hitherto centered around two views: those who see the Templars as loose cannons and ruthless cut throats, and those (their defenders) who see them as pragmatists, who preferred gold over converts. In fact, as should be evident by now, a third possibility exists: Decades of up-close-and-personal contact with Muslims had provided the taciturn Templars with a much more intimate understanding of the inner workings and machinations of Islam. As historian Jonathan Riley-Smith writes, "the Orders embodied as corporations an experience and knowledge of the Saracens that was shared by few...[and] some of the brothers could speak Arabic.... They were, moreover, well informed about the politics of the Arab world."[16]

They were especially, it seems, cognizant of the stratagems of Islam's founder. After all, "Some Christian writers identified Muhammad with Antichrist. Therefore, the Templars, champions of Christendom against the Muslims, were in the frontline of the war against Antichrist and needed to be well informed on the subject."[17]

In short, a strong case can be, and has now been, made that the Templars saw the Assassins' overture to the Christians for what it was—an old Islamic trick to be immediately nipped in the bud lest it bear fruit against Christendom.

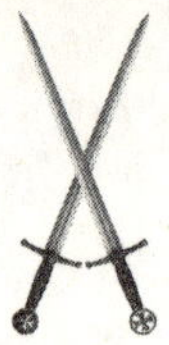

13

THE "POOR OF CHRIST"

We must now take a brief segue and travel back in time to introduce the second warriors of the Lord that make this history, for chronologically, they were both older and newer than the Templars: the Knights of the Hospital of St. John of Jerusalem.

As previously discussed, even after it was conquered by Islam in 637, Jerusalem remained important to Christendom. From the farthest reaches of Europe, Christians continued pilgrimaging to it despite the great costs and threats involved both on the road to and in the Muslim-controlled Holy Land itself.

After marching for thousands of miles, often on foot (from France to Jerusalem is about 2,700 miles), by the time European pilgrims had reached the Holy Land, they were in tatters—exhausted, starved, and often penniless. Moreover, because the region was controlled and populated by (often hostile, definitely unfriendly) Muslims, they could expect to receive little succor or hospitality both on the long road to and at their destination. (Although Muslims are expected to engage in charitable activities—one of Islam's Five Pillars is zakat ("charity")—sharia mandates that charity only be shown to fellow Muslims, never non-Muslims (unless by way of cajoling them to Islam).

It became, accordingly, imperative that there be Christian hospices to receive and refresh weary pilgrims. Under various Muslim rulers of Jerusalem, these were allowed to exist, so long as they paid whatever extra taxes this or that ruler demanded for their operation. Around the same time he was crowned the first Holy Roman emperor in 800, Charlemagne (Charles the Great) purchased and endowed one such hospice to welcome and host Christian pilgrims—most of whom were "devout men and women from Egypt and other lands by then under Muslim rule."[1] It is, in fact, in this context of helping poor Christian pilgrims that the Frankish emperor, as is often recounted, "befriended" Muslim leaders, such as the Abbasid caliph, Harun al-Rashid. As explained by Einhard, Charles the Great's biographer and a confidant,

> He was very enthusiastic in supporting the poor, and in that spontaneous generosity which the Greeks call alms, so much so that he made a point of not only giving in his own country and his own kingdom, but even overseas when he discovered that there were Christians living in poverty in Syria, Egypt and Africa; and at Jerusalem, Alexandria and Carthage he had compassion on their wants, and used to send money. *The reason that he zealously strove to make friends with the [Muslim] kings beyond seas was that he might get some help and relief to the poor Christians living under their rule* [emphasis added].[2]

Everything changed with the rise of Egyptian Fatimid caliph, al-Hakim bi-Amr Allah; Charlemagne's hospice in Jerusalem—and virtually every other Christian holy site, including the Holy Sepulchre—was destroyed. Later Fatimid caliphs, making a virtue out of a vice, magnanimously allowed Christians to rebuild and revisit their holy sites, including the Church of the Resurrection—so long as they paid a high extortion tax for the honor. As the anonymous Rothelin chronicler who continued William of Tyre's history explained, although Muslims routinely destroyed and desecrated Christian churches, they were often careful to spare the most sacred sites "not out of love for Christians, but for the sake of the heavy taxes, the extensive business and rich offerings the

Christians provided when they made their pilgrimages. They refrained from demolishing these buildings because of the great wealth they got from them every day."[3]

However, by 1073, the Seljuk Turks, who, as seen, had been running amok and staining all of Anatolia with Christian blood, took Jerusalem from the Fatimids, where they, once again, ushered in a new round of persecution. As already mentioned, when "the Turks were ruling the lands of Syria and Palestine," writes Michael the Syrian, "they inflicted injuries on Christians who went to pray in Jerusalem, beat them, pillaged them, [and] levied the poll tax [jizya]." Moreover, "every time they saw a caravan of Christians, particularly of those from Rome and the lands of Italy, they made every effort to cause their death in diverse ways."[4]

For example, "some years before" the First Crusade, Peter the Hermit went pilgrimaging, and when he finally reached Jerusalem "he saw many forbidden and wicked things occurring there," writes Albert of Aachen. So "he sought out the patriarch of the holy church of Jerusalem and asked why gentiles and evil men [Muslims] were able to pollute holy places and steal away offerings from the faithful, using the church as if a stable, beating up Christians, despoiling pilgrims through unjust fees, and inflicting on them many sufferings." The frustrated patriarch threw up his hands in exasperation: "Why do you reprimand me and disturb me in the midst of my fatherly cares?" cried he. "I have but the strength and power of a tiny ant when compared to those proud men. We have to redeem our lives here by regular tribute payments [jizya] or else face death-dealing punishment."[5] (A similar exchange continues to this day whenever Western observers chastise Mideast Christian minorities for not "standing up for themselves.")

In this backdrop, the seeds of what would become the great Hospital of St. John in Jerusalem were planted by Italian merchants from the maritime state of Amalfi (they also played a role in helping Rome thwart an Arab invasion in 849).

Sometime in the 1050s, in the quieter years before the Seljuk Turks burst onto the scene, Amalfi merchants purchased from the Fatimids a piece of ground "before the door of the church of the Resurrection of the Lord, barely a stone's throw away, [where] they built a monastery."[6] On learning that there was a sanctuary for them, Christians from Amalfi and other regions in Italy began to pilgrimage to Jerusalem. Some of these pilgrims, however, were women, who had no place in the monasteries of celibate men devoted to God. This led to the development of the first, original hospital—for women. William of Tyre explains:

> Even in those days it often happened that chaste and holy widows came to Jerusalem to kiss the revered places. Regardless of natural timidity, they had met without fear the numberless dangers of the way. Since there was no place within the portals of the monastery where such pilgrims might be honorably received, the same pious men who had founded the monastery made a suitable provision for these people also, that when devout women came they might not lack a chapel, a house, and separate quarters of their own. A little convent was finally established there, by divine mercy, in honor of that pious sinner, Mary Magdalene, and a regular number of sisters placed there to minister to women pilgrims.[7]

Due to an influx of European pilgrims between 1065 and 1070, and because the original monastery could no longer house such a large number of visitors, the Amalfians built another convent for male pilgrims around 1080. Dedicated to John the Baptist, it was named the Hospital of St. John in Jerusalem. William offers a snapshot of the circumstances that led to it becoming a great hospital for all Christian (and even non-Christian) peoples:

> During these same perilous times there also flocked thither [to Jerusalem] people of other nations [not just Italy], both nobles and those of the middle class. As there was no approach to the Holy City except through hostile lands, pilgrims had usually exhausted their travelling money by the time they reached Jerusalem. Wretched and helpless, a prey to all the hardships of hunger, thirst,

and nakedness, such pilgrims were forced to wait before the city gates until they had paid a gold coin [to the Muslims], when they were permitted to enter the city. Even after they finally gained admission and had visited the holy places one after another, they had no means of resting even for a single day, except as it was offered in a fraternal spirit by the brothers of this monastery. All the other dwellers in Jerusalem were Saracens and infidels with the exception of the patriarch, the clergy and the miserable Syrian people. These latter [indigenous Eastern Christians] were so overburdened by daily exactions of manifold corvees [jizya tribute and forced, unpaid labor] and extra services, and by work of the most menial nature, that they could scarcely breathe. They lived in the direst poverty and in continual fear of death.

Since there was no one to offer shelter to the wretched pilgrims of our faith, thus afflicted and needy to the last degree, the holy men who dwelt in the monastery of the Latins in pity took from their own means and, within the space allotted to them, built a hospital for the relief of such pilgrims. There they received these people, whether sick or well, lest they be found strangled by night on the streets. In addition to offering shelter in the hospital, they arranged that the fragments remaining from the food supplies of the two monasteries, namely, of the monks and of the nuns, should be spared for the daily sustenance of such people....

This venerable foundation which thus stretched out the hand of charity to its fellow men had neither revenues nor possessions; but each year the citizens of Amalfi, both those at home and those who followed the business of trading abroad, collected money from their own number as a voluntary offering. This they sent to the abbot of the hospital, whoever he might be at the time, by the hands of those who were going to Jerusalem. From this

> money food and shelter were provided for the brethren and sisters and the remainder was used to extend some assistance to the Christian pilgrims who came to the hospital.[8]

Although referred to as a hospital, it was more akin to what would today be called a hospice—a place to offer food, rest, shelter, and basic medical services to weary (and traumatized) pilgrims. There is, moreover, reason to believe that the aforementioned horrific attack on a German pilgrimage in 1064—when the Muslim Turks publicly gang-raped to death a "noble abbess of graceful body and religious outlook"—directly led to the rise of this institution.[9]

Itself oppressed, the Hospital continued to offer succor to whichever Christians managed to reach Jerusalem during these times, until "there came at last a Christian people, led by chiefs under the protection of God, to whom the Savior willed that the kingdom be surrendered"[10]—that is, until the First Crusaders had come and liberated Jerusalem in 1099.

After taking the city, they "found one Gerald, a man of upright life who, under the orders of the abbot and monks, had long rendered devoted service to the poor in that place during the supremacy of the enemy."[11] This same Gerald (or Gerard) Sasso (c. 1040–1120), who was appointed by the abbot of the Amalfian monastery as rector of the hospice built for men around 1080, would eventually come to be seen as the founder of the Order of the Hospital of St. John in Jerusalem. For nearly twenty years before the Crusaders arrived before the walls of Jerusalem in 1099, he and his brethren faithfully served all and sundry. After describing Gerald as "a certain man of consecrated life, renowned for his piety," William wrote that "he was in charge of the hospital, mentioned above, where the poor were lodged who came to Jerusalem for the sake of prayer and where they received refreshment suited to the conditions of time and place."[12] Nor did Gerald make any distinctions according to religion. Under his authority, the Hospital in Jerusalem,

> knowing that the Lord, who calls all to salvation, does not want anyone to perish, mercifully admits men of

> the Pagan faith [Muslims] and Jews...because the Lord prayed for those afflicting him, saying, "Father, forgive them for they know not what they do." In this blessed house is powerfully fulfilled the heavenly doctrine: "Love your enemies and do good to those who hate you"; and elsewhere: "Friends should be loved in God and enemies on account of God."[13]

It was precisely because the Hospital, unlike Muslim institutions, did not discriminate that, prior to the Crusader besiegement of Jerusalem in June 1099, when the Muslim governor (Iftikhar al-Dawla*) expelled all native Christian men (lest they become a fifth column), Gerald and a few of his serving brothers were allowed to remain in the Hospital and render their services—tending to the sick and wounded, most of whom were non-Christian. Before long, however, Muslim paranoia targeted Gerald for torture. "The infidels," according to William,

> believed that this man had a secret fund laid aside and feared that he might be able to injure them when our army [the First Crusaders] arrived. They therefore beat him and cast him into prison. There he was subjected to torture so terrible that the joints of both his hands and feet were wrenched apart and his limbs became practically useless.[14]

Another story, now dismissed as legend due to its miraculous nature, became popular some thirty years after Gerald's death. Because the besieging Crusaders were suffering from immense hardships, including starvation, Gerald, knowing this, made it a point to visit the walls of Jerusalem three times a day. There, he would mingle with the Muslims detailed to hurl stones and other missiles on the Christians; but instead of hurling stones, he hurled loaves of bread from his basket. Suspicions were eventually aroused, and he was taken to the Muslim governor. But

---

* A Fatimid: Egypt had only recently recovered Jerusalem from the Seljuks.

when his basket was inspected, no loaves were found, only stones. So he was released and permitted to continue as before.[15]

Once under Crusader rule, the Hospital began to flourish and grow. The earliest known donation—an entire *casal* (or "village") called Hessilia—came from the first Christian ruler of Jerusalem, Godfrey, duke of Lorraine. Subsequent kings of Jerusalem offered similar donations, as did many Crusaders who settled in the Holy Land. As with the Templars, once people in Europe heard of the pious and altruistic efforts of the Hospital, despite the oppression it had periodically experienced under Muslim rule, gifts of lands and houses, particularly from and in Italy, Spain, Portugal, and southern France, poured in. They were all made out to the Hospital, then known as the "poor of Christ."[16]

With all these new funds, Gerald dramatically expanded the Hospital's operations, establishing other hospitals, both in the Holy Land and in Europe, particularly along the pilgrim routes connecting the two. In 1113, Pope Paschal II confirmed the Hospital of St. John in Jerusalem as an independent religious order. From then on, its serving brothers were formally recognized as the Hospitallers of St. John.

14

RISE OF THE HOSPITALLERS

No matter how strong or wealthy they became, the Hospitallers never forgot their original mandate: "Their prime commitment was to the service of the 'holy poor.'" Even their clothing was reflective of this truism. According to their rule, composed around 1130, they should be humble "because the poor of Our Lord, whose serfs we acknowledge ourselves to be, go about naked and meanly dressed. And it would be wrong and improper for the serf to be proud and his lord humble." Thus, when the Hospital was overflowing beyond capacity, the brothers gave up their dormitory beds to the pilgrims and slept on the floor.[1]

Few, if any, Christian orders were as devoted to Christ's famous parable, which follows, as the Hospital:

> Then the King will say to those on his right, "Come, you who are blessed by my Father; take your inheritance, the kingdom prepared for you since the creation of the world. For I was hungry and you gave me something to eat, I was thirsty and you gave me something to drink, I was a stranger and you invited me in, I needed clothes and you clothed me, I was sick and you looked after me, I was in prison and you came to visit me." Then the

> righteous will answer him, "Lord, when did we see you hungry and feed you, or thirsty and give you something to drink? When did we see you a stranger and invite you in, or needing clothes and clothe you? When did we see you sick or in prison and go to visit you?" The King will reply, "Truly I tell you, whatever you did for one of the least of these brothers and sisters of mine, you did for me." [Matthew 25:34–40, NIV].

As Jonathan Riley-Smith put it, "A feature of Hospitaller nursing was this: Because every poor man and woman *was* Christ, he or she should have not just good treatment but the best and most luxurious treatment possible. This was a religious imperative; it was also the application of the basic nursing principle that patients should be comfortable and contented."[2]

The histories offer many anecdotes of the Hospitallers providing such lavish hospitality to all and sundry. In the mid-thirteenth century, the so-called Minstrel of Reims recounted a legend concerning how even the famous Saladin (who will soon figure prominently in this history) had confirmed their limitless hospitality in Acre. "Historically there is a certain slight foundation for this story," writes historian E. J. King, who summarizes it as follows:

> Saladin, having heard of the boundless charity of the brethren of the Hospital, went to Acre disguised as a sick pilgrim to test their charity for himself. Pretending to be unable to eat the food provided, he at last told the distressed knight in charge that he had one impossible caprice, which alone could satisfy him. The knight urged him to make his request saying, "A sick man here is given whatsoever he fancies, if gold can buy it; ask what you will and you shall have it." So Saladin made his request, "It is the foot of the Master's famous horse Moriel that I desire to eat, and unless it be cut off in my presence, I can never touch food again." When the Master of the Hospital heard the story of the knight, he ordered that

> the caprice of the sick man should be granted, "Since it be so, take my horse; better that all my horses should perish than one sick man." But as they were about to strike off the foot of Moriel in his presence Saladin suddenly announced that the desire had passed away, and that he would be content with the ordinary food supplied. And when he had returned to his own country, he sent the brethren of the Hospital a charter, sealed with his own seal, which is said to have read as follows: "Let all men know that I Saladin, Sultan of Babylon, give and bequeath to the Hospital of Acre a thousand besants of gold, to be paid every year in peace or war, unto the Master be he who he may, in gratitude for the wonderful charity of himself and his Order."[3]

At any rate, by the time of Gerald's death in 1120, when he was about eighty years of age, the Hospital had grown to become a powerful organization, both in and out of the Holy Land. And on his epitaph was written,

> Here lies Gerard, the most humble man in the East and the servant of the poor. He was hospitable to all strangers, a gentle man with a courageous heart. One can judge within these walls just how good he was. Provident and active in every kind of way, he stretched out his arms to many lands in order to obtain whatever was needed to feed his people.[4]

It is only under the forty-year rule of Gerald's successor, Raymond of Puy (1083–1160), a French knight, that the slow process of the Hospital's militarization began. Summarizing the oldest surviving accounts, King writes that

> The older historians loved to dwell on the story of how Raymond du Puy, the first of the great heroes of their Order, deeply moved by the constant dangers to body

> and soul in which the Christian population passed their lives, formed the design to add to the duties of his Order the defense of the Christian faith. How it long formed the subject of his earnest meditations and prayers, until at last the divine call came to him, and he summoned his monks together, and proposed that they should take up in defense of their fellow Christians those swords, which they had flung aside when they entered the service of the Hospital. The brethren accepted with alacrity the proposals of their revered Master and it was agreed that whilst they must in no way relinquish their original vows, or relax their care of the sick and the poor, a part of the monks should always be in readiness to take up arms against the attacks of the infidels. The new proposals were placed before the Patriarch of Jerusalem and received his blessing, and Raymond du Puy at the head of his monks, all armed and mounted, placed their services at the disposal of King Baldwin II.[5]

The logic was simple: Rather than treat the symptom, the Hospitallers were finally in a position to preemptively fight the cause:

> As one major need of pilgrims of the Holy Land was protection from Muslim bandits, any organization which claimed to care for pilgrims needed to meet this need as well as their more mundane requirements for food and beds. Rather than caring for wounded and dying pilgrims after they had been attacked on the road, it seemed much more advantageous to protect them against being attacked in the first place. The militarization of the Hospital did not reflect rivalry with the Templars; it reflected the desperate need of the kingdom of Jerusalem for military forces, which the Templars also tried to supply.[6]

That the Hospitallers were not abandoning their original mandate is further reflected in that it was also under Raymond that the Hospital was expanded into an infirmary. It was, moreover, always in connection to the poor that any justification for militancy was found. Thus, "the first reference in the Hospitaller statutes to the brothers-at-arms lists their function among other charitable acts performed by the order; in other words, as an extension of the care of the poor."[7]

The exact process of the Hospital's militarization is unclear and appears to have been very gradual. The first indication occured sixteen years into Raymond of Puy's rule. In 1136, King Fulk bequeathed the newly built fortress of Bethgibelin (Bayt Jibrīn) to the Hospitallers. Consisting of a ring of castles, it encircled the then Muslim-held fortress of Ascalon, which, as seen, had long harried the Christians: "It was a moment of the utmost importance in the history of the Order of St. John, for it marks the beginning of their great and noble career as the defenders of the outposts of Christendom against Islam." A few years later, around 1140, Pope Innocent II issued a papal bull stating that the Hospital was retaining, at its own expense, "servientes" to ensure that pilgrims could advance to the holy places safely. This word could mean "sergeants"—that is, non-knightly fighting men, hired to protect pilgrims, which would further confirm a militant wing to the Hospital—or it could simply mean "servants" who helped escort pilgrims.[8]

Like Fulk before him, in 1143, Raymond II, count of Tripoli, donated five castles, including the famous Krak des Chevaliers, on the frontiers of Tripoli, to the Hospitallers, thereby making them wardens on the marches of Tripoli. Other castles kept coming in, most of them on the northern and southern frontiers of Islam.

Based on these inferences, the best that can be surmised is that, between the late 1130s and throughout the 1150s, the Hospital was, at most, *defending* against Muslim attacks. Although it had not yet become an offensive force to campaign against Muslims, as the Templars had some decades earlier, the Hospital, nonetheless, clearly played an "advisory role in the military affairs of the kingdom of Jerusalem."[9] During the Second Crusade, for example, although the Hospital lent money to the war effort and Raymond of Puy was present at the council of Acre offering military advice, nowhere do the Hospitallers appear as campaigning.[10] Similarly, after the Templars were slaughtered during the siege of Ascalon in 1153, "old Raymond of Puy, by far the most experienced officer of the army, brought all the weight of his great influence to bear upon the king." Even so, there is no indication that the Hospitallers actually fought at Ascalon.[11]

At any rate, in 1160, the Hospital's second master, Raymond of Puy, died, like his predecessor, also at the age of eighty.

> For forty years he had ruled over the Hospital, and during that period it had grown and prospered to a degree almost inconceivable. From a local charitable society it had developed into one of the greatest and most powerful institutions in Christendom. In the East its influence and wealth were wellnigh incalculable, and in the West from England to Hungary, from Scandinavia to Sicily, all Europe had combined to shower gifts and grants of lands and privileges upon a society which represented so completely the spirit of the age. If the Blessed Gerard was the founder of the Order of St. John, Raymond du Puy was its real maker, and the first and greatest of the military Masters of the Hospital.[12]

In the same year of Raymond's death, in 1160, the German pilgrim John of Wurzburg, who was in Jerusalem, described the Hospital as follows:

> Over against the Church of the Holy Sepulchre on the opposite side of the way towards the south is a beautiful church built in honor of John the Baptist, annexed to which is a Hospital, wherein in various rooms is collected together an enormous multitude of sick people, both men and women, who are tended and restored to health daily at very great expense. When I was there I learned that the whole number of these sick people amounted to two thousand, of whom sometimes in the course of one

> day and night more than fifty are carried out dead, while many other fresh ones keep continually arriving.[13]

A few years after John's pilgrimage, one Theoderich, another pilgrim, wrote the following:

> Here on the south side of the church of the Holy Sepulchre stands the Church and Hospital of John the Baptist, no one can credibly tell another how beautiful its buildings are, how abundantly it is supplied with rooms and beds and other material for the use of the poor and sick people, how rich it is in the means of refreshing the poor, and how devotedly it labors to maintain the needy, unless he has had the opportunity of seeing it with his own eyes. Indeed, we passed through this palace and were unable to discover the number of sick people lying there, but saw that the beds numbered more than one thousand.[14]

Raymond was likely buried in the Conventual Church of the Hospitallers in Jerusalem and, shortly after his death, was venerated and referred to as "Blessed," much like his predecessor. Based on a reading of contemporary records, René-Aubert Vertot, one of the Order's premier historians, summarizes Raymond's final days thus:

> The venerable old man, covered with wounds and worn out with years, had withdrawn himself to the House of the Hospitallers of St. John at Jerusalem. There in a profound retirement, amidst serious reflections, and in continual exercises of piety, this genuine soldier of Jesus Christ prepared himself for the great day that is so terrible, even to the holiest monks. He saw at last that dreadful moment arrive, which decides the fate of an eternity; but if he saw its approaches with a wholesome fear, it was also with the filial confidence of a true Christian, who had exposed his life a thousand times in defense of

> the Holy Places, where the Author of life Himself vouchsafed to die for the salvation of man. Thus Raymond du Puy ended his days in the arms of his brethren, the first of the military great Masters, much greater by his solid piety and rare valor, than by his dignity.[15]

Eight years after Raymond's death, in 1168, the Hospital finally appears in the histories as an offensive, military force campaigning against Muslims alongside the Templars.

Concerning the organization, hierarchy, administration, and rules of the Knights of the Hospital of St. John, these were very similar to those of the Knights Templars. Like them, the Hospital had three categories: knights, serving brothers ("sergeants," militant and nonmilitant), and chaplains.

It was not long, however, before "the knights were the most important and numerous class, almost the whole of the power was in their hands, practically the whole of the great executive and administrative offices were reserved for them, and they so entirely overshadowed the other two classes, that the Order of St. John is generally spoken of in history as if it consisted of knights only."[16]

During his solemn induction ceremony, a knight took an oath to live and die according to the monastic vows of poverty, chastity, and obedience, and as a slave to his "lords the sick." After the officiating priest blessed and returned the initiate's sword to him, the former said, "Receive this holy sword in the name of the Father, and of the Son, and of the Holy Ghost, amen; and use it for thy own defense, and that of the Church of God, to the confusion of the enemies of Jesus Christ and of the Christian faith, and take heed that no human frailty move thee to strike any man with it unjustly." The priest was also quick to tell the initiate to "remember that it is not with the sword, but with faith, that the saints have conquered kingdoms." Then, as the new knight of Christ held the blessed blade aloft, "Let the brilliancy of this sword," his brother knights in attendance cried out, "represent to you the brightness of faith; let its point signify hope, and its hilt charity. Use it for justice, and for the consolation of widows and orphans: for this is the true faith and justification of a Christian knight."[17] Finally, his new habit was thrown over him—a black mantle with a white cross in the center, shaped like an eight-pointed star.*

When not fighting, the day-to-day routine of all Hospitallers was no less monastic and disciplined than the Templars (though the Hospitallers likely followed the Augustinian rule), including on the battlefield. As one example, during the Third Crusade,

> A certain knight of the Hospital named Robert de Bruges rode out of the ranks of his brethren, contrary to the rules of the Order, to challenge to single combat a Saracen champion, whom he ran through with his lance and slew. [Master] Garnier de Nablus thereupon sternly ordered him to dismount from his horse, and to return to his tent under arrest, and there to await the punishment that his conduct deserved. It was only at the urgent request of the leaders of the crusading army that the Master of the Hospital consented to pardon this breach of discipline.[18]

Also like the Templars, at no point in time did they seem to have more than three hundred brother-knights in the Holy Land, though they had many sergeants, turcopoles, and mercenaries.

The only major difference between the two orders is that, whereas the Templar rule strongly forbad any contact with women, the Hospital always had and continued to have sisters in its service. Along with all the other general labors they were involved in for their "lords the sick," these good sisters always took in, educated, and raised any child whose

---

* Concerning this eight-pointed white cross on black background (which appears in the pommel of the sword on the right side of this book's cover), the initiate's fellow knights also informed him that "We wear this white cross as a sign of purity; wear it also within thy heart as well as outwardly, and keep it without soil or stain. The eight points are the signs of the eight beatitudes, which thou must ever preserve: 1. spiritual joy; 2. to live without malice; 3. to weep over thy sins; 4. to humble thyself to those who injure thee; 5. to love justice; 6. to be merciful; 7. to be sincere and pure of heart; and 8. to suffer persecution" (Drane, *Knights of St. John*, 3).

mother, whether from sickness or poverty, had abandoned. These were known as "the children of St. John," and many of the boys no doubt grew up to become fighting men and sergeants for the Order.[19]

Due to the overall nature of the Knights of St. John's work, some historians argue that "nursing made the Hospitallers more humane [than the Templars], while the presence of women within the Order must also have had a softening influence."[20]

The following history will put this theory to the test.

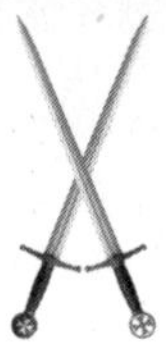

15

SALADIN: THE "OPPRESSOR OF THE CROSS"

Following the Crusader high point of the 1150s (the capture of Ascalon) and despite the lack of succor from Europe, the Templars continued to hold their own against Nur al-Din's forces. As late as 1163, they scored an especially decisive victory against him. Under the command of Gilbert of Lacy, "an experienced warrior and commander of the Knights Templars," the Christians, writes William of Tyre,

> made a sudden attack upon his army. Nur al-Din was taken by surprise; many of his men were made prisoners, and still more perished by the sword; in fact, his army was almost annihilated. The prince himself, in despair of his very life, fled in utter confusion. All the baggage and even his sword were abandoned. Barefooted and mounted on a beast of burden, he barely escaped capture at the hands of our forces.[1]

This humiliating defeat had a profound impact on the sultan: So "filled with confusion and fear," "overwhelmed with dismay," and "anxious to wipe out the disgrace and to avenge his own injuries," Nur al-Din called for aid from every corner of the Muslim world, and "there was scarcely a prince in the East on whom he did not call as a suppliant, now entreating assistance by prayers and again by promise of reward. Meanwhile, he recruited his own strength and collected military reinforcements from all sides."[2]

One year later, in 1164, Geoffrey Fulcher, an old Templar who had been with the Order for over twenty years, sent a letter to King Louis VII describing how Nur al-Din, after recruiting "hordes" of Muslims of every nation from "the ends of the earth to avenge his disgrace," had managed to terrorize and slaughter Christians throughout the Holy Land:

> The very small number of us in Jerusalem are now not safe from a military assault, such is the size of the Turkish horde, or more to the truth, whored.... Unless you bring aid before the remnants of Christendom are destroyed, it is feared that you will not be able to when you finally choose to do so. Let those who belong to God and are counted among the Christians take up their arms and come to liberate the kingdom of their Father and the land of our freedom, so that what has been courageously earned by the blood of our fathers shall not be lost in an ignoble and irremediable fashion by the hands of their sons.[3]

Worse, in Nur al-Din's effort to unite all Muslims into a jihadist war machine that could be directed against and annihilate the Christians, the sultan sent, also in 1164, one of his warlords, the Kurd Shirkuh—"a man bent on destroying the Christians"[4]—to bring Fatimid Egypt under his rule. As a united Syrian and Egyptian front was a terrifying prospect for the Crusaders, they, under King Amalric, did all they could to prevent such a union, including by trying to take Egypt for themselves.

At one point—in 1168, when the Hospitallers at last appear as a full-fledged fighting force of knights—they put Cairo to siege. Of the master of the Knights of St. John, Gilbert of Assailly, and his activities during this campaign, Lambert Wattrelos, a contemporary, writes,

> He was sharp and confident in his natural ability as a warrior, a strong and bold knight in battle. At last he came, with the Lord God's help, to a certain very strongly fortified city named Bilbais. The prince did not fear the strength or audacity of its inhabitants and boldly attacked the city with his men, broke the walls and brought it swiftly to the ground, killing those who came out to meet him.[5]

When not campaigning, the knights of the military orders continued to perform their first function. Theoderich, a pilgrim who visited the Holy Land also in the 1160s, describes the "Templars and Hospitallers escorting bands of pilgrims down to the Jordan to bathe in the holy river, watching over them while they stayed the night there, and protecting pilgrims on the Jordan plains."[6]

During these turbulent times, Shawar, the vizier of Egypt, made and broke alliances, first with Shirkuh against the Crusaders, then with Amalric against the Turks. His dangerous game could only last so long. In 1169, his then ally Shirkuh had his nephew, Salah al-Din—history's famous Saladin—treacherously slaughter and bring him the vizier's head. "Thus," writes William, "strong through the power of the sword, Shirkuh became master of all Egypt."[7] Two months later, Egypt's new vizier—who was "small of stature, very stout and fat and already advanced in years"—died from overeating. His nephew, Saladin, succeeded him as vizier and effective ruler of Egypt.[8]

This Saladin (c. 1137–1193) was no less a devotee of jihad than his nominal master, Nur al-Din. He, too, was devoted to unifying Islam and directing its full might against the Crusader states. According to Baha' al-Din, a contemporary of Saladin, the latter was a highly observant Sunni Muslim—he loved hearing Koran recitals, prayed punctually, and "hated philosophers, heretics, and materialists and all opponents of the sharia."

> The sacred works [Koran and hadith] are full of passages referring to the jihad. Saladin was more assiduous and zealous in this than in anything else.... Jihad and the suffering involved in it weighed heavily on his heart and his whole being in every limb; he spoke of nothing else, thought only about equipment for the fight, was interested only in those who had taken up arms, had little sympathy with anyone who spoke of anything else or encouraged any other activity.[9]

He regularly made it a point to inflame his men with jihadist rhetoric and ordered sections of the hadith read to his men in camp or even while riding, "hadith that had to do specifically with jihad and the rewards of martyrdom in the path of Allah."[10]

Lesser known, but no less reflective of his animosity toward Christianity, is that upon becoming vizier of Egypt, Saladin severely persecuted that ancient nation's indigenous Christians, the Copts—including by crucifying or hanging many thousands of them, smearing black tar on their churches, and breaking their crosses off—even though the Copts, who refer to Saladin in their chronicles as "the Oppressor of the Cross Worshippers," had nothing to do with the Franks or the crusades.[11] Nor was his mind merely set on expelling the Crusaders from the Middle East. Afterward, it was his dream to "then set sail on this [Mediterranean] sea for their far-off lands [in Western Europe] and pursue the Franks there, so as to free the earth of anyone who does not believe in Allah, or die in the attempt."[12]

For all that, Saladin was also shrewd, calculating, and pragmatic. He knew when and how to curry the favor of the common Muslim man. Speaking of the Kurd's rise to power, the contemporary author of the *Itinerarium Peregrinorum et Gesta Regis Ricardi** states,

> Saladin collected illgotten gains for himself from a levy on the girls of Damascus: they were not allowed to practice as prostitutes unless they had obtained, at a price, a

* "The Journey of the Pilgrims and the Deeds of King Richard."

> license from him for carrying on the profession of lust. However, whatever he gained by pimping like this he paid back generously by funding plays. So through lavish giving to all their desires he won the mercenary favor of all the common people.[13]

In 1171, Saladin put an end to the Fatimid caliphate—by murdering its last caliph, according to William of Tyre—and realigned Egypt under the Sunni Abbasid caliphate, with Nur al-Din as his nominal lord. No sooner did he do this when he launched, that same year, a massive raid on the nearest Christian outpost along the Egyptian frontier: the fortress of Gaza, which had been entrusted to the Templars since 1149:

> At the head of forty thousand horse and foot, he crossed the desert and ravaged the borders of Palestine; the wild Bedouins and the enthusiastic Arabians of the far south were gathered together under his standard, and hastened with holy zeal to obtain the crown of martyrdom in defense of the faith. The long remembered and greatly dreaded Arab shout of onset, *Allahu Akbar* ["Allah is greater"], again resounded through the plains and the mountains of Palestine, and the grand religious struggle for the possession of the holy city of Jerusalem, equally reverenced by Muslims and by Christians, was once more vigorously commenced. Saladin besieged the fortified city of Gaza, which belonged to the Knights Templars, and was considered to be the key of Palestine towards Egypt. The luxuriant gardens, the palm and olive groves of this city of the wilderness, were destroyed by the wild cavalry of the desert, and the innumerable tents of the Arab host were thickly clustered on the neighboring sand-hills. The warlike monks of the Temple fasted and prayed, and invoked the aid of the God of battles; the gates of the city were thrown open, and in an unexpected sally upon the enemy's camp they performed such prodigies of valor, that Saladin, despairing of being

> able to take the place, abandoned the siege, and retired into Egypt.[14]

Although a resounding victory for the Temple, the toll exacted was heavy nonetheless: One in five of all brethren were slain, along with two thousand Christians.[15] Pope Alexander III responded by exhorting them to continue the good fight, reminding them that "inflamed with true charity, you fulfill by your works the word of the Gospel which says, 'Greater love has no man than this, that a man lay down his life for his friends.'"

> In obedience to the voice of the great Shepherd, ye in no wise fear to lay down your lives for your brethren, and to defend them from the inroads of the pagans; and ye may well be termed holy warriors, since you have been appointed by the Lord as defenders of the Catholic Church and combatants of the enemies of Christ.[16]

But what kind of "friends" and "brethren" were the Templars constantly laying down their lives for? In 1171, the same year Saladin attacked Gaza, Amalric held a council with his leading men and barons to discuss yet a new, though internal, crisis. On the one hand, "the enemies of the Christian faith were constantly increasing not only in number and valor but in power and riches as well," writes William:

> On the other hand, our realm was completely without wise and discreet leaders. The younger generation which was taking the places of their elders were growing up in wickedness; without purpose or result they were occupying the places of illustrious men and squandering in disgraceful ways the inheritance received from their fathers. As a result, the realm had deteriorated so greatly that its weakness was apparent even to the dullest. The king therefore requested the advice of his nobles as to how these evil conditions could be remedied and the kingdom saved.[17]

They concluded that they would appeal to Europe for help. Nothing came of it. Indeed, a couple of years earlier in 1167, during the triangular conflict between the Christians, Turks, and Egyptians, Philip of Naplous, the master of the Temple, "reported in letters to Europe how the Templars had been slaughtered by great Muslim armies and he begged earnestly for succor. His appeals were ignored, and, weary of leading an Order which received so little support in its work, he resigned in 1170."[18] In his stead came the proud and fiery warrior, Odo of St. Amand—the same who would refuse to relinquish the one-eyed knight for killing the Assassins—a man "in whose nostrils dwelt the spirit of fury," to quote the ever-critical William, "one who neither feared God nor revered man."[19]

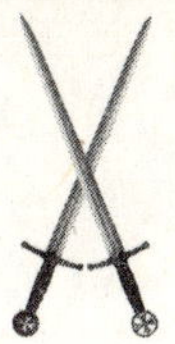

16

MONTGISARD: "TWO PUT TEN THOUSAND TO FLIGHT"

In 1174, the two heads of the crusade and the jihad—Amalric and Nur al-Din—died. This opened the way for Saladin to begin appropriating Nur al-Din's Syrian domains. Meanwhile, Amalric was succeeded by one of the most tragic figures of the entire crusading venture, Baldwin IV (1161–1185)—the so-called "Leper King." His malady was only discovered after he had ascended his father's throne at age thirteen, says William of Tyre, who tutored the lad:

> It is impossible to refrain from tears while speaking of this great misfortune. For, as he began to reach years of maturity, it was evident that he was suffering from the terrible disease of leprosy. Day by day his condition became worse. The extremities and the face were especially attacked, so that his faithful followers were moved with compassion when they looked at him. Nevertheless, he continued to make progress in the pursuit of letters and gave ever-increasing promise of developing a lovable disposition. He was comely of appearance for his age, and far beyond the custom of his forefathers he was

> an excellent horseman and understood the handling of horses.[1]

Despite the cross that he bore, this young Crusader king—disparagingly referred to in Muslim sources as a "blue-eyed, freckled, leprous evil-doer"—would come to demonstrate a level of long-suffering, courage, and wisdom rarely paralleled among his race.[2]

One of the first clashes between the new Christian and Muslim masters occurred in the winter of 1177. On learning that most of the Crusaders had issued out of Jerusalem to do battle against one of his relatives who was harrying the north, Saladin, concluding that "he could safely invade a land thus stripped of its troops," put together a massive army of twenty-six thousand Muslims—Turks, Arabs, Kurds, Sudanese, and Mamluks, all of them "equipped even better than usual with arms and all manner of things commonly used in warfare."[3] On November 18, Saladin led this destructive force across the frontier and into Crusader territory with the express purpose of raiding and devastating the Christian realms.

> The first troops to react to the invasion were the Knights Templars, under Master of the Temple Odo of St. Amand. The sexagenarian was stubborn, dogmatic and unflappable. He had been elected to serve as the order's eighth master in 1171. When he learned that a force of thousands of Muslims was pouring across the border, he ordered the 80 knights under his command to seek protection at the order's hilltop castle at Gaza. When Saladin realized that the castle was garrisoned, he detached a small force to besiege it and continued on to Ascalon.[4]

Cognizant of Saladin's invasion, and in an effort to intercept the Muslim army, young King Baldwin IV, with a much smaller force of under five hundred mounted knights and sergeants and several thousand feudal levies, galloped to, and garrisoned, Ascalon. Considering Baldwin's failing condition, "Everyone despaired of the life of the sick king, already half dead, but he drew upon his courage and rode to meet Saladin," says the *Chronicle of 1234*.[5]

By November 22, Saladin had reached and surrounded Ascalon. After Baldwin, who "had but few with him," confronted the Muslims in a few scrimmages, "the Christians prudently retired to the city again, for in view of the enemy's superior numbers it seemed hazardous to trust their modest forces to a camp for the night. This act roused Saladin and his men to such a pitch of arrogance that they no longer remained in close array but paraded about in admiration of their own prowess."[6]

Indeed, so sure that he had cowed the Christians and their diseased king, Saladin repeated what he had done at Gaza. He left a small detachment to blockade Baldwin and his smaller force in Ascalon, while he and his army, divided now in smaller squadrons for maximum damage, went off in all directions to wreak havoc among the now largely defenseless Christian lands. One of Saladin's commanders, the Armenian Jevelino, "abandoning the faith of the Mediator [Christ] between God and man," had converted to Islam "and was following devious ways," writes William. He torched Ramla to the ground, and "with showers of arrows and weapons of all kinds," he unleashed hell on the Christians "and harried them without intermission."

Meanwhile, "Great terror descended not only upon the people in the plains, where the enemy was roving about freely without opposition, but even upon those living in the mountains." The Christians of the kingdom of Jerusalem were also on the verge of fleeing, as the Muslim "marauders…had spread over almost the entire surface of the plain…. Now was the appearance of this region desolate and overwhelmed with bitterness."[7]

On learning of the devastation Saladin was causing throughout his realm, Baldwin, trapped in Ascalon and vastly outnumbered, decided "to try the dubious chances of battle with the enemy than to suffer his people to be exposed to rapine, fire, and massacre."[8] With his men, he broke through the blockade. Before that, he sent word to Odo, who himself was holed up with eighty Templars in Gaza, to also break through their blockade and meet him, which the master did.

Although William says the Christian army "including all ranks and conditions, were barely three hundred and seventy-five"[9]—versus twenty-six thousand Muslim fighters—the king likely had an additional three thousand infantrymen and auxiliaries. Now, "reinforced by a band of ultra-zealous Knights Templars, Baldwin pursued the plundering raiders."[10] Everywhere they were met with devastated towns set aflame.

On November 25, they tracked down a large Muslim force near Montgisard, between Ramla and Yimla. It happened to be the very one led by Saladin himself. The Christians advanced, "intent on the one purpose of avenging their wrongs, the sight of the fires on every side and the reports of the massacre of their people inspired them with divine courage, and they hastened on as one man."[11] Saladin immediately recalled the rest of his marauding troops, and "the enemy's forces who had ventured some distance away to seek booty and spread conflagration began to arrive from different directions, a circumstance which greatly increased Saladin's strength."[12] Then, "by the sound of the trumpet and the roll of the drums," the sultan "sought to encourage his men for the conflict and to rouse them by his words," laden as they were with jihadist and anti-Christian rhetoric.[13]

Over at the Christian camp, something both similar and different was happening: Wrapped in bandages and supporting his frail weight on a staff, the wearied king and his men were on their knees imploring God before the True Cross, which Albert the bishop of Bethlehem, had brought at their head. This ritual concluded, and despite their vastly outnumbered status, the Christians arose with a renewed spirit, says William:

> Had not the Lord, who never fails those who put their trust in Him, graciously inspired our men with inward courage, the Christians would have been driven to despair, not only of victory, but of liberty and safety as well [due to the overwhelming numbers of the enemy]. However, they nonetheless drew up their forces in battle array and arranged their lines according to military rules, disposing in proper order those who were to make

> the first attack and the reserves who were to come to their aid.[14]

First listed in William's battle array were Christendom's crack troops: "Odo of St. Amand, the master of the Knights Templars, and eighty of his brethren." Surrounded by the flames of consumed Christian towns, the Leper King led the Christians into the fray. The battle was initially indecisive, but before long, the Templars, followed by other heavy horsemen behind them, especially the Hospitallers, "began to press on with ever-increasing boldness," writes William.[15] In the words of one modern historian,

> The valley filled with the sounds of battle: weapons clanged, men shouted, and the wounded and dying cried out in agony. The Frankish foot, which advanced in the wake of the successful cavalry attack, entered the fight to capitalize on the successful charge of the Knights Templar and Franks. Crusader crossbowmen fired bolts that shattered enemy shields and armor, inflicting fatal wounds, and Frankish spearmen thrust their spears with great force into unhorsed Ayyubid horsemen.[16]

Before long, "Saladin's lines were broken," continues William of Tyre, "and, after a terrible slaughter, were forced to flee."[17] One by one, the Muslim squadrons fled the field of carnage—all except Saladin's hardy Mamluks, a thousand slave-soldiers who must fight to the death. From William's vantage point, they were

> slaves captured in war, [while] others are bought or perhaps born of slave mothers. These youths are instructed in military science [as well as, according to Muslim sources, the Koran and hadith[18]].... To them is entrusted the duty of protecting the person of their lord in the vicissitudes of battle, and upon them in no slight degree depends the hope of obtaining the victory. Always surrounding their lord, they endeavor with one accord

> to protect him from harm, and they cling to him even unto death. As one man, they continue to fight until he has fled. Consequently it often happens that while the rest make good their escape by flight, nearly all the Mamluks fall.[19]

And that is precisely what happened:

> The only unit in Saladin's army that did not try to flee the battlefield at that point was his 1,000-strong mounted Mamluk Guard, which had been held in reserve. The Mamluks, who were clad in yellow silk tunics, entered the fray. A swirling melee occurred in the middle of the valley floor. Crusaders and Mamluks slashed and thrust with their swords and swung their battle axes in close combat. What unfolded was a fight to the finish in which neither side gave nor received quarter. The Crusaders, who had the advantage of momentum and were supported by the infantry, carried the day. Although none of the Mamluks survived, they had done their duty.[20]

In fact, it was Odo, at the head of his eighty Templars, who "broke through the guard of Mamluks, slew their commander, and penetrated to the imperial tent, from whence the sultan escaped with great difficulty, almost naked."[21] The mighty Saladin, who only hours before was confidently terrorizing the Christians, barely managed to mount a racing camel and beat a swift retreat back to Egypt through the desert, where he rejoined the remnants of his army. For twelve miles, the Crusaders chased the Muslims deep into the stormy night and "mercilessly slaughtered" many more before halting at the Egyptian frontier.[22] The bedraggled and exhausted sultan finally reached Cairo on December 8, with a tenth of his original army of twenty-six thousand.

And so it was that God "scattered a great multitude and thus made it plain that it was He alone," the archbishop of Tyre reminded, "and not another, by whose aid one could 'chase a thousand, and two put ten thousand to flight.'"[23]

In the annals of Crusader lore, the Battle of Montgisard would be celebrated as "the most glorious victory that the Christians had ever gained over the infidels, since Godfrey's victory at Ascalon in 1099."[24] Though wildly exaggerating the number of Muslim invaders, one contemporary chronicler emphasized the role of the military orders:

> The Templars and Hospitallers and knights of the king of Jerusalem went forth to meet the pagans. Making a bold attack upon the pagans they forced them to give way, and O, supreme bounty of the Most High! the Christians, who were not in number more than ten thousand fighting men, gained the victory over five hundred thousand pagans, and that by the aid of the Most High.[25]

Exaggerations aside, Montgisard was certainly a shocking reverse—so much so that Saladin sent forth propagandists and criers throughout Egypt to trumpet *his* "victory" in order to deceive the Muslim populace. Although a glorious Crusader victory, it was nonetheless costly: Of the 3,000–4,000 Christians believed to have participated, 1,100 were killed and nearly 1,000 seriously wounded. And although 90 percent of Saladin's army was destroyed, the pool of men he could draw from was bottomless.

17

BLOODY VALLEYS AND SPRINGS

Just as Saladin's former master, Nur al-Din, had been humiliated by the Templars in 1163 only to avenge himself soon thereafter, so too would Saladin be avenged in less than two years after Montgisard. In 1179, the bitter sultan launched several wild incursions—"laying waste the fields of Sidon while slaughtering, burning, and pillaging" to quote William of Tyre.[1] So, the weary Leper King once again "took up the wood of the cross of our Lord and assembled what troops he could," before rushing to intercept Saladin.[2]

On the morning of June 10, the Crusaders came across and ambushed a large Muslim raiding party, commanded by a nephew of Saladin, at Marj Ayun, also known as the Valley of the Springs. The Crusaders, making quick work of the Muslims and believing the battle won, let their guard down to rest—only to be ambushed by Saladin and his entire army. Standing on a small hillock and undaunted by the Muslim onrush, five hundred mounted Knights of the Temple and Hospital, augmented by the forces of Count Raymond of Tripoli, rushed into battle on the orders of Templar Master Odo.[3]

A savage battle ensued; but despite their headlong courage, the vastly outnumbered military orders were swallowed up and butchered by the Muslims: "The count of Tripoli at last cut his way through the infidels, and fled to Tyre; the Master of the Hospital, after seeing most of his brethren slain, swam across the Jordan, and fled, covered with wounds, to the castle of Beaufort; and the Templars, after fighting with their customary zeal and fanaticism around the red-cross banner, which waved to the last over the field of blood, were all killed or taken prisoners."[4] The fiery Templar master, Odo, was among those captured alive and loaded with chains. King Baldwin barely escaped the same fate. Unable to mount and flee due to his crippling condition, a knight hoisted the emaciated Leper King onto his saddle as he galloped away from the carnage.

Even though this was a spectacular victory for Saladin, the wily sultan did not try to push his advantage. He knew that he could never achieve his ultimate goal—the elimination of the Crusader Kingdom of Jerusalem—until he held and could direct every last Muslim city and fortress in the region. So he made various truces with the Crusaders and spent his energies over the next few years conquering and bringing the few remaining independent Muslim cities under his rule—the most significant being Aleppo in 1183 and Mosul in 1185. By then, the circle was complete; all of Syria and Egypt were united under Saladin—the caliph in Baghdad gave his formal blessing, acknowledging him as the uncontested "Sultan of Egypt and Syria"—and the tiny Crusader kingdoms were surrounded. The time was finally right: "We should confront all the enemy's forces," Saladin proclaimed to his leading men, "with all the forces of Islam."[5]

Following the unification of Islam under Saladin in 1185, that young tragic hero, Baldwin IV, finally died of his leprosy, aged twenty-four. The crown went to his eight-year-old nephew, Baldwin V, with Raymond, the powerful count of Tripoli and Baldwin IV's cousin, acting as regent. When young Baldwin V died less than a year later, the crown, somewhat controversially, went to Guy of Lusignan, husband of Baldwin IV's sister, Sibylla. This decision "led to endless discord and dissension; Raymond, Count of Tripoli, withdrew from court; many of the barons refused to do homage, and the state was torn by faction and dissension at a time when all the energies of the population were required to defend the country from the Muslims."[6]

The situation was exacerbated by the rise of what several historians consider to be one of the worst masters of the Temple, Gérard of Ridefort. Elected in 1184, he is often portrayed as an impulsive, hotheaded knight—or so the sources, which may not be altogether unbiased, indicate—who may have joined the Order for less-than-sincere motives. Desmond Seward offers the worst—but also most popular—rendering:

> The sinister Gerard de Ridefort became Master of the Temple in 1185. A penniless noble from Flanders, he had taken service with Raymond III [of Tripoli] on condition that he be given the hand of the heiress of Botrun. Raymond did not keep his promise and the embittered Gerard joined the Templars. His driving ambition and aggressive self-confidence soon took him to the top, but he embodied all his Order's worst faults [that is, pride and arrogance, following William of Tyre's (not unbiased) accusations].[7]

Apparently as part of his vengeance against Raymond, Gérard staunchly supported Guy's claim to the throne. (Raymond had earlier been told that, if both Baldwin IV and his heir (Baldwin V) ended up dying, the next king—whom many expected would be Raymond himself—would be decided by the kings of England and France, the Holy Roman emperor, and the pope in Rome, but that did not happen.)

Contentions reached the point that, holed up in his castle in Tripoli and refusing to acknowledge Guy as king, Raymond was now even begging Saladin, whom he had a truce with, for military aid. (The two apparently became so allied that, if Imad al-Din is to be believed, Raymond's "sincere intentions towards the Muslims strengthened to such an extent that were it not for fear of his [Christian] co-religionists he would have become a Muslim."[8])

Guy, eager to secure a reconciliation, sent a delegation of noteworthy personages to speak reason with Raymond. Among them were the masters of the Temple and Hospital, the latter being Roger of Moulins. It was too late; Saladin and his men, having already been given the green light by Raymond, were on the warpath. While the sultan besieged the great castle of Kerak—where Raynald of Châtillon was holed up—Saladin sent an army under al-Malik al-Afdal, one of his seventeen sons, to raid and pillage the land surrounding Acre, which the Muslims were able to access because Raymond had given them free passage.

On April 30, Guy's delegation to Raymond temporarily divided near Nazareth, with the masters of the Temple and Hospital traveling to the Templar castle of La Fève. Once "the two Masters heard the news that a party of Saracens was over the border, their delicate mission of peace was entirely forgotten, and their fighting instincts took complete control. If infidels had had the effrontery to enter Christian lands, there was only one course open to the knights of the military Orders," that is, nonnegotiable war.[9]

On the very next day, May 1, 1187, the two masters mustered all the knights they could—140 in all, with the majority, about ninety, being Templars and perhaps also a few hundred sergeants and auxiliaries—and gave chase. They tracked down the Muslims watering their mounts at the Springs of Cresson, in the environs of Nazareth—all seven thousand of them. Against such hopeless odds, both the marshal of the Temple, Robert Fraisnel, and the master of the Hospital advised retreat. The Templar master, Ridefort, would have none of it, accusing both men of cowardice. "You love your blond head too well to want to lose it!" he scoffed at the marshal, to which the wounded captain of the army coolly replied, "I shall die in battle like a brave man. It is you who will flee as a traitor."[10]

Outraged by his subordinate's cheek, Ridefort instantly ordered the trumpets blasted; the cry to battle was heard, and the knights—outnumbered by as much as forty to one—charged to certain death. At first, the very sight of these madmen stupefied their enemies. According to an Arab eyewitness, among the Muslims, "even the blackest head of hair went white with fright as the Frankish horsemen hurtled towards them."[11]

As a reflection of what ensued, consider Michaud's words on this and other desperate Crusader charges:

> Old chronicles, whilst celebrating the bravery of the Christian knights, relate prodigies which we have now great difficulty in believing. These indomitable heroes, after having exhausted their arrows, plucked from their own bodies such as had pierced them, and launched them back upon the enemy; pressed by fatigue and heat, they drank their own blood, and revived their strength by the very means which must weaken it; at length, after having broken their lances and swords, they rushed upon their enemies, fought body to body, rolling in the dust with the Muslim warriors, and died threatening their conquerors.[12]

Numbers being what they were, however, it was impossible for the Christians to maintain the tempo of this berserker frenzy, and a general massacre inevitably ensued. In the end, only three Christians survived the carnage; many notable knights fell on that day, including the master of the Hospital, Roger of Moulins, whose body was found riddled with arrows and (finally) run through with a lance. A true representative of the Hospital, this warrior "never allowed himself to forget the original charitable objects for which his Order had been founded," and he was eulogized by the Order's official chronicler as "a man of great wisdom, and vigorous in battle, a good man and pious and very high-minded, and he loved much his brethren, and our lords the sick."[13]

Interestingly, as Templar Marshal Robert Fraisnel, who also died fighting, had foretold, one of the three Christians to escape the carnage was Gérard of Ridefort: Badly wounded and bruised, he and two other knights fled the battlefield, even as the Muslim victors methodically decapitated the bodies of the slain, placing their heads on the tips of spears to triumphant cries of "Allahu akbar!"[14]

After asserting that "the Templars and Hospitallers were the backbone of the Frankish armies," Ibn al-Athir boasts that "the joyful news [of Cresson] spread far and wide"[15] among the Muslims, including the fact that "among the dead was the Master of the Hospital...who had done much harm to the cause of Islam."[16]

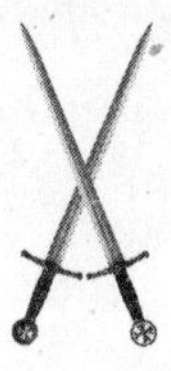

18

"ONE CHASED A THOUSAND"

Last chapter's wild charge at Cresson is a reminder that St. Bernard's inspirational words concerning what it meant to be a knight of Christ were still being taken to heart in 1187. As Malcolm Barber writes, the "charge against impossible odds at the Springs of Cresson bore more relation to St. Bernard's claim that 'one chases a thousand, two put to flight ten thousand' than to the pragmatic and often devious ploys used by most other contemporary warriors," especially Muslims, who not infrequently prioritized stratagems and missile warfare over bravery and hand-to-hand combat.[1] Indeed, a closer look at the preserved exploits of one particular Knight Templar at Cresson underscores what it meant to be a holy warrior—that the pious militancy delineated in their founding documents was not just mere talk and rhetoric but truly informed their conduct. According to the author of the contemporary *Itinerarium Peregrinorum*,

> In this conflict, in which a handful of our people were surrounded by an immense army, a remarkable and memorable event occurred. A certain Templar—a knight by profession, of Touraine by nation, Jakelin de Mailly by name—brought all the enemy assault on himself through his outstanding courage. While the rest

> of his fellow knights (estimated to number 500) had either been captured or killed, he bore all the force of the battle alone and shone out as a glorious champion for the law of his God. He was surrounded by enemy troops and almost abandoned by human aid, but when he saw so many thousands running towards him from all directions he strengthened his resolve and courageously undertook the battle, one man against all. His commendable courage won him his enemies' approval. Many were sorry for him and affectionately urged him to surrender, but he ignored their urgings, for he was not afraid to die for Christ. At long last, crushed rather than conquered by spears, stones and lances, he sank to the ground and joyfully passed to heaven with the martyr's crown, triumphant.[2]

The medieval chronicler proceeds to wax reverent over this act of heroism:

> It was indeed a gentle death with no place for sorrow, when one man's sword had constructed such a great crown for himself from the [enemy] crowd laid all around him. Death is sweet when the victor lies encircled by the impious people he has slain with his victorious right hand. And because it so happened that the warrior had been riding a white horse and had white armor and weapons, the Gentiles [Muslims], who knew that St. George had this appearance in battle, boasted that they had killed the Knight of Shining Armor, the protector of the Christians.[3]

Despite its surreal nature, especially to modern-day sensibilities, the above account is a rare glimpse into what so many of these battles consisted of—men sacrificing every ounce of their being for an unshakable cause. Though these episodes are often left out of modern-day histories, which affect a "scientific" approach by fixating only on dry data—years, numbers, outcomes, and other statistics of conflict—they do, in fact, permeate the contemporary chronicles. Such was the passion, faith, and glory that animated the men of old.

Nor were such feats of self-sacrifice uncommon. Three months after Cresson, in another assault on the Templar fortress of Chastelet (near Jacob's Ford) in August 1187, Saladin, unable to overcome the stalwart resistance of its garrison, ordered it set on fire and then taken by storm. Although the sultan took seven hundred Christian prisoners, rather than be captured, "the Templars," relays Abu Shama, a Damascene chronicler, "flung themselves, some into the fire, where they were burned, some cast themselves into the Jordan, some jumped down from the walls on to the rocks, and were dashed to pieces." As for the Templar commander of the fort, "when the flames arrived at his side, he threw himself into a hole full of fire without fearing the flames," writes another Muslim chronicler, Qadi al-Fadil, predictably adding, "In burning, he was soon thrown into the other furnace [i.e., Hell]."[4] Such sacrifices, and the total destruction of the fortress that he had hoped to preserve for his own use, so dampened Saladin's victory that the enraged sultan ordered any Templar found or captured alive to be sawn in two.[5]

Incidentally, that only Muslim sources mention this act of self-immolation is a reminder of why we know very little about the feats of individual knights from the Temple and Hospital (even the exploits of Jakelin of Mailly at Cresson were recorded by a non-Templar historian). As Helen Nicholson explains, discipline and humility were more important than heroics:

> The Templar emphasis on the community of Brothers acting together was probably the reason why no individual Templars were recognized by the Catholic Church as saints. Because the whole Order had to work together in Christ's service, the Order would have tried to discourage its members from venerating individual Brothers. If individuals were singled out in this way it would encourage Brothers to "go it alone" in the search for martyrdom

> and glory, which would destroy the vital cooperation and discipline on the battlefield.[6]

Even the Temple's previous master, the implacable Odo of St. Amand, who was captured during that other disaster at Marj Ayun in 1179, can be said to have taken the way of ignoble anonymity:

> Saladin offered Odo de St. Amand his liberty in exchange for the freedom of his own nephew, who was a prisoner in the hands of the Templars; but the Master of the Temple haughtily replied, that he would never, by his example, encourage any of his knights to be mean enough to surrender, that a Templar ought either to vanquish or die, and that he had nothing to give for his ransom but his girdle and his knife. The proud spirit of Odo de St. Amand could but ill brook confinement; he languished and died in the dungeons of Damascus.[7]

In fact, Odo was selflessly upholding the Templar rule, which forbad the ransoming of brothers. Yet even this noble move provoked William of Tyre, that archbishop hostile to the military orders for their independence, to further anti-Templar acrimony: Odo, he writes, "died in chains in the squalor of a prison in the same year he was captured, mourned by no one."[8]

19
THE DEVIL'S HORNS

The Battle of Cresson was a prelude to war between the Crusader states and the united forces of Islam. "Saladin," writes the contemporary author of the *Itinerarium Peregrinorum*, "was greatly exhilarated by his troops' victory" over the Templars and Hospitallers, "and his mind was kindled with the desire of seizing the Kingdom of Jerusalem. And so he turned his mind to greater things."[1]

Meanwhile, as might be imagined, both Christian and Muslim sources indicate that the slaughter of the military orders at Cresson cast Raymond of Tripoli in a dim light. His erstwhile alliance with Saladin was seen by the Crusaders as both a political and religious betrayal—one that had cost many Christian lives. The count promptly severed ties with Saladin and returned to Jerusalem where he bent the knee to King Guy.

Saladin responded by lifting the siege of Kerak, ordering more men to augment his forces (approximately twenty thousand), and marching to and laying siege to his former ally Raymond's castle in Tiberias. The Crusaders mustered their forces and held council in Acre. Templar Master Gérard Ridefort, having recovered from his wounds at Cresson, was there and contributed funds to the forthcoming war effort "to avenge the shame and damage which they [Muslims] had done to him, and to Christianity," to quote a chronicler.[2]

The council agreed to march to the relief of Tiberias—all except for the lord of Tiberias himself, Raymond, who suggested a sit-and-wait approach. Considering that his "dealings" with Saladin had led to a Christian bloodbath two months earlier, not a few Crusaders doubted his motives. "You have tried hard to make us afraid of the Muslims," scoffed Raynald of Châtillon, whose own castle, Kerak, Saladin had just besieged. "Clearly you take their side and your sympathies are with them, otherwise you would not have spoken this way. As for the size of their army, a large load of fuel will be good for the fires of Hell!"[3] In the end, Guy conceded to Raymond's sit-and-wait approach. Later that night, however, the Templar master held a private conference with the king. He insisted that the Christians go out and meet the Muslims head on, and Guy agreed.

On the following day, July 3, the king set out for Tiberias with a large Crusader force, consisting of over twenty thousand fighters. The True Cross was carried at the van by the bishops of Acre and Lydda. To the relic's right marched 300 Knights of the Temple, to its left, 250 Knights of the Hospital—all making strange sounds of war: "The Templars were humming like bees," wrote one bewildered Muslim, "the Hospitallers bellowing like the wind." Almost immediately, light Muslim cavalry harried the marching Crusaders, prompting them to make camp near Hattin—meaning the "two horns," a reference to twin peaks of an extinct volcano in Lower Galilee—where all night long arrows rained down on them. On the following day, July 4, battle commenced.[4]

There are various accounts concerning what happened during the Battle of Hattin.[5] According to one, something similar to what happened at Ascalon in 1153—when the Templars rushed in alone and got slaughtered—occurred:

> At their entreaty [King Guy] gave the honor of striking the first blow to the Master and Knights of the Temple. Upon this, the brethren of the Temple, rushing upon the foe with the bravery of lions, put some to the sword and

> forced others to take flight. The rest (of the Christians), however, neglecting the king's command, did not join the battle or give them any succor whatever; in consequence of which the knights of the Temple were hemmed in and slaughtered.[6]

Muslim sources confirm that the military orders fought with a feral fury. After describing the Crusaders as "mountains in movement," one Arab eyewitness account tells of how the Knights Templars—"horrible in arms, having their whole bodies cased with triple mail"—were arrayed at the front lines at the break of dawn, all of them animated with "a flaming desire of vengeance."[7]

Once battle commenced, in the words of Baha' al-Din, one of Saladin's secretaries, "Terrible encounters took place on that day; never in the history of generations that have gone have such feats of arms been told."[8] The fighting knights, especially the Templars and Hospitallers, "burned and glowed in a frenzied ferment."[9] Knowing that "the only way to save their lives was to defy death they made a series of charges that almost dislodged the Muslims from their position in spite of their numbers, had not the grace of Allah been with them. As each wave of attackers fell back they left their dead behind them; their numbers diminished rapidly, while the Muslims were all around them like a circle about its diameter."[10]

After piecing together the several Christian and Muslim accounts of the Battle of Hattin, Charles G. Addison offers the following summary, with an emphasis on how Muslim contemporaries saw it:

> Saladin set fire to the dry grass and dwarf shrubs which lay between both armies, and the wind blew the smoke and the flames directly into the faces of the military friars and their horses. The fire, the noise, the gleaming weapons, and all the accompaniments of the horrid scene, have given full scope to the descriptive powers of the oriental writers. They compare it to the last judgment; the dust and the smoke obscured the face of the sun, and the day was turned into night. Sometimes gleams

> of light darted like the rapid lightning amid the throng of combatants; then you might see the dense columns of armed warriors, now immovable as mountains, and now sweeping swiftly across the landscape like the rainy clouds over the face of heaven. "The sons of paradise and the children of fire," say they, "then decided their terrible quarrel; the arrows rustled through the air like the wings of innumerable sparrows, the sparks flew from the coats of mail and the glancing sabres, and the blood spurting forth from the bosom of the throng deluged the earth like the rains of heaven."... The avenging sword of the true believers was drawn forth against the infidels; the faith of the Unity [Islamic tawhid] was opposed to the faith of the Trinity, and speedy ruin, desolation, and destruction, overtook the miserable sons of baptism![11]

As more and more Crusaders fled the field of battle, Guy and about 150 knights—mostly Templars, Hospitallers, and his own guard—made a final stand around the True Cross, which they had thrust into "the hill of Kurn-Hattin, on the very spot where more than eleven hundred years before Our Savior had preached the Sermon on the Mount."[12]

But the Muslim onrush would not be stayed: Charge after charge of horsemen and volley after volley of arrows fell on the Crusaders. With arms raised high and eyes blinded with tears, the Christians implored the Cross for deliverance—only to see Muslims hack their way to, and seize, Christendom's most precious relic: "Its capture was," writes a Muslim chronicler, "the gravest blow that they sustained in that battle.... It seemed as if, once they knew of the capture of the Cross, none of them would survive that day of ill-omen."[13] Encircled by an ever-shrinking ring of fire and Islamic horsemen, tormented by arrows and thirst, the Crusaders finally succumbed.

"The many and great calamities" they experienced, wrote Templar Brother Terric, preceptor of Jerusalem, a few days later to the Temple in London, "we cannot for grief unfold to you, neither by letters nor by our sobbing speech.... The enemy having hemmed us in among barren rocks, fiercely attacked us; the holy cross and the king himself fell into the hands of the infidels, the whole army was cut to pieces, two hundred and thirty of our knights were beheaded, without reckoning the sixty who were killed on the 1st of May [at Cresson]."[14]

Walking through the carnage later, Imad al-Din confirmed that, win or lose, the Crusaders had given it their all:

> I passed by them and saw the limbs of the fallen cast naked on the field of battle, scattered in pieces over the site of the encounter, lacerated and disjointed, with heads cracked open, throats split, spines broken, necks shattered, feet in pieces, noses mutilated, extremities torn off, members dismembered, parts shredded, eyes gouged out, stomachs disemboweled.... [T]he faces of the infernal Templars [were] ground in the dust, skulls trampled underfoot.[15]

Great was the gloating now: "This defeat of the enemy," announced the Muslim herald, "this our victory occurred on a Saturday, and the humiliation proper to the men of Saturday [Jews] was inflicted on the men of Sunday [Christians], who had been lions and now were reduced to the level of miserable sheep."[16] In the end, single Muslim soldiers were seen dragging as many as thirty Crusaders with one rope, any of whom would once have terrified the same—so maddened with thirst and reduced to delirium were the Christians. Saladin "dismounted and prostrated himself in thanks to Allah, weeping for joy."[17]

Once the dust had settled, as had happened following the Second Crusade, accusatory fingers were pointed everywhere to explain away the disaster at Hattin—with a great many of them pointing at the master of the Temple, Gérard Ridefort. As seen, after King Guy had agreed to Count Raymond's advice not to go out and meet Saladin head on, it was Gérard who, later that evening, convinced the king otherwise. During their private conference, the master had threatened that "the Templars would put aside their white mantles" unless his Order was avenged against the Muslims for Cresson. Not wanting to go against Gérard's advice—"for he loved and feared him," writes Ernoul the chronicler, "because he had made him king, and had handed over to him the treasure of the king of England"*—it was then that Guy agreed and decided to set out on the following morning for Tiberias and Saladin.[18] The problem with this rendering is that Ernoul was not as objective a chronicler as might be hoped, and, as historians have shown, was likely writing an apologia for his faction (which sided with Raymond and the Ibelins). "Somebody had to take the blame," Malcolm Barber writes,

> for the fall of the kingdom; the Ibelins and Ernoul wanted to make sure that it was [King] Guy of Lusignan and Gérard of Ridefort, leaving the historian with a problem in interpretation no easier to solve than that presented by William of Tyre's [negative] stories about the Temple.[19]

The master's overall behavior and counsel, continues Barber, would likely have been the same even if he did not have a vendetta against Raymond:

> Gérard's nature showed itself most dramatically in the war with Islam.... There is, moreover, a consistency about Ridefort's actions which...are clearly shown to be based upon the French chivalric code which held in contempt any compromise with the Muslims. His personal grudge against Raymond of Tripoli therefore reinforced his conviction that the count shared the values of *vilains* [base men who compromise], which he despised, *but it is likely that Ridefort would have given the king the same advice whatever position the count had taken* [emphasis added]."[20]

* Gérard, as seen, was one of the primary supporters of Guy's candidacy to the throne. The "treasure" Gérard gave to Guy is a reference to the penance money Henry II had donated to the Temple for the murder of Thomas Becket.

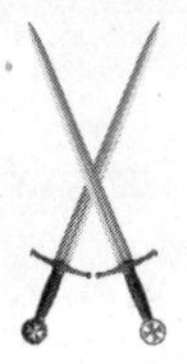

20

THE GREAT MARTYRDOM

Immediately following the routing of the Crusaders at Hattin, King Guy, Gérard, and other captured nobles were hauled off to Saladin's tent to await their doom. The sultan was magnanimous to Guy, explaining that "a king does not slay a king," and saved his invective for the Arabic-speaking count of Châtillon, Raynald (whose sixteen years in Nur al-Din's dungeons had transformed him into the "most dangerous enemy of Islam," as Arabic chroniclers frequently refer to him). "Your Christ has deceived you," Saladin began his taunt. "If you do not deny him, he will not be able to free you this day from my hand!"

"Christ deceives no man," retorted Raynald, "but that man is deceived who does not believe in him." Then, knowing his fate was sealed, the lord of Kerak made public confession: "I adore him, I confess him, I declare his name to you! If you believed in him, you would be able to escape the punishment of eternal damnation, which—doubt not!—has been prepared for you. But why are you delaying what you are about to do? I know that you thirst for nothing other than Christian blood!" Saladin instantly drew out his scimitar and struck the defiant infidel—before his henchmen pounced on, decapitated, and triumphantly paraded Raynald's head around the Muslim camp.*

He was only the first; all other dedicated foes of Islam—namely the Knights of the Temple and Hospital—were consigned to slaughter (minus the Templar master, Gérard, whom Saladin held for ransom, and William Borrel, the interim master of the Hospital since Roger of Moulins was killed at Cresson two months earlier; this temporary master clove through the carnage at Hattin and gained sanctuary at a nearby castle, but died the following day from his wounds). Nor was it enough for Saladin to kill all those captured monkish warriors; the sultan took the additional step of "ransoming" any Templar or Hospitaller from their Muslim captors for fifty dinars each—simply so he could have the pleasure of watching them all sheared like sheep.

Like Raynald, the knights of the military orders were given the choice of Islam or death. All night long during their captivity, in the midst of wild cries and hoots from their would-be executioners, the brethren of the Temple and Hospital, rather than panic, despair, or beg for mercy, reconfirmed their calling as knights of Christ and prepared for their doom, or as they saw it, their martyrdom. According to the contemporary *Itinerarium Peregrinorum*, "a certain Templar named Nicholas had been so successful in persuading the rest to undergo death willingly that the others struggled to go in front of him and he only just

---

* Peter of Blois (b. 1135) is the source of this little-known dialogue. He preceded it by saying, "I am changing absolutely nothing of the words of Raynald," but recording them as "they were related and written down to the lord pope and many then present," including Aimery of Lusignan. Special thanks go to historian Paul F. Crawford, an expert on the apparently much misunderstood Raynald. (Peter of Blois, *Passio Raginaldi*, unpublished translation-in-progress by Paul F. Crawford and Sarah J. Downey, all rights reserved by the translators, used here by express permission.) Baha' al-Din recorded a similar exchange, though without giving voice to the defiant Christian: "'Here I [Saladin] am, having asked victory through Muhammad, and God [Allah] has given me victory over you.' He offered him [Raynald] Islam but he refused. The sultan then drew his scimitar and struck him, severing his arm at his shoulder. Those present finished him off and God [Allah] speedily sent his soul to Hell-fire" (Din ibn Shaddad, *Rare and Excellent*, 75).

succeeded in obtaining the glory of martyrdom first—which was an honor he very much strove for."[1]

Again, having pieced the various sources together, Charles G. Addison recounts the final passion of these warriors of the Lord:

> The warlike monks of the Temple and of the Hospital, the bravest and most zealous defenders of the Christian faith, were, of all the warriors of the cross, the most obnoxious to zealous Muslims, and it was determined that death or conversion to Mahometanism should be the portion of every captive of either order, excepting the Master of the Temple, for whom it was expected a heavy ransom would be given. Accordingly, on the Christian Sabbath, at the hour of sunset, the appointed time of prayer, the Muslims were drawn up in battle array under their respective leaders. The Mamluk emirs stood in two ranks clothed in yellow, and, at the sound of the holy trumpet, all the captive knights of the Temple and of the Hospital were led on to the eminence above Tiberias, in full view of the beautiful lake of Gennesareth, whose bold and mountainous shores had been the scene of so many of their Savior's miracles. There, as the last rays of the sun were fading away from the mountain tops, they were called upon to deny him who had been crucified, to choose Allah for their Lord, Islam for their faith, Mecca for their temple, the Muslims for their brethren, and Muhammad for their prophet. To a man they refused, and were all decapitated in the presence of Saladin by the devout zealots of his army, and the doctors and expounders of the law.[2]

Both Muslim and Christian sources underscore and are in agreement as to why Saladin sought to exterminate the military orders, both on the fields of Hattin and wherever they could be found. According to the *Itinerarium Peregrinorum*, Saladin "decided to have them utterly exterminated because he knew that they surpassed all others in battle."[3]

Similarly, according to Ibn al-Athir's account,

> These two groups were especially selected for execution because they had the greatest valor of all the Franks; so Saladin saved the [Muslim] people from their evil. He wrote to his deputy in Damascus ordering him to kill all of them who fell into his hands, and it was done.... It was Saladin's custom to execute the Templars and Hospitallers because of their fierce enmity towards the Muslims and their great courage....[4]

Eyewitness Imad al-Din offers the most comprehensive rendering. He heard Saladin boast that "I will purify the earth of these two filthy races [Templars and Hospitallers]," for "they will certainly not desist from aggression and they will not serve in capacity [meaning submit to slavery]."[5] So the sultan "ordered that they should be beheaded, choosing to have them dead rather than in prison." Many of Saladin's men, especially among the expounders of sharia, "begged to be allowed to kill one of them, and drew his scimitar and rolled back his sleeve. Saladin, his face joyful, was sitting on his dais." Thereafter, Imad describes the grisly ritual: how some men "slashed and cut cleanly," while others made a mess of things. After indicating that, before long, some of these once-eager executioners could no longer stomach the work of shearing off Christian heads, Imad extolled one—possibly Saladin himself—who "killed unbelief [*kufr*] to give life to Islam":

> I saw there the man who laughed scornfully and slaughtered, who spoke and acted; how many promises he fulfilled, how much praise he won, the eternal rewards he secured with the blood he shed, the pious works added to his account with a neck severed by him.[6]

Although this scene, which is copiously recorded in both Christian and Muslim accounts, has—for some odd reason—never made it in any of the big budget Hollywood films that otherwise revolve around Saladin's "magnanimity," it continues to inspire modern-day jihadist organizations. The Islamic State of Iraq and Syria (ISIS) has made several films intentionally modeled after Saladin's beheading of the knights of the military orders, the most notorious being ISIS's decapitation of twenty-one Christians (twenty Copts and one Ghanaian) in Sirte, Libya, 2015.

At any rate, if the slaughter of the military orders was a crowning victory for the Muslims, so too did it impart the laurels of martyrdom to the Templars and Hospitallers; and ransomed Crusaders spoke ever after of strange and celestial lights that had danced about the corpses of the warrior monks as they lay unburied for three days in evidence of heaven's approval.[7]

As for the rest of the Crusaders captured at Hattin who could not purchase freedom—which included the overwhelming majority of the thousands captured—following the execution ritual of the crack troops of Christendom, the rank and file were all sold into slavery, and "that night was spent by our people in the most complete joy and perfect delight," writes Baha' al-Din, "with cries of 'Allahu Akbar' and 'There is no god but Allah,' until daybreak on Sunday."[8]

Not one to let a major victory go unheralded, Saladin had news of his triumph widely proclaimed throughout the lands of Islam. "Allah and his angels," he wrote directly to the caliph in Baghdad, "have mercifully succored Islam. The infidels have been sent to feed the fires of hell! The cross is fallen into our hands, around which they fluttered like the moth round a light."[9] Saladin ordered the True Cross sent to Damascus, where it was dragged upside down in the dirt to Muslim spits and jeers, at which point it disappears from history and enters legend.

Jubilations over the capture of the True Cross did not hamper Saladin's jihad. In his letter written just days after Hattin, Templar Brother Terric underscored the great speed with which the indefatigable sultan recommenced his war against the Crusader kingdoms, now left vulnerable and unguarded, as most of its fighting men had either been killed or captured at Hattin. After summarizing "the many and great calamities" to have befallen the Christians at Hattin, he wrote,

> The Pagans, drunk with the blood of our Christians, then marched with their whole army against the city of Acre, and took it by storm. The city of Tyre is at present fiercely besieged, and neither by night nor by day do the infidels discontinue their furious assaults. So great is the multitude of them, that they cover like ants the whole face of the country from Tyre to Jerusalem, and even unto Gaza.[10]

Indeed, days after his letter was sent, many more Christian kingdoms and castles fell—Ascalon, Beirut, Jaffa, Sidon, Tiberias—culminating with Jerusalem. After being in Christian hands for some eighty-eight years, it surrendered to Saladin on October 2, 1187, at which point "a great cry went up from the city and from outside the walls," writes Ibn al-Kathir, "the Muslims crying the Allah akbar in their joy, the Franks groaning in consternation and grief. So loud and piercing was the cry that the earth shook."[11]

Once the gates of Jerusalem opened to Saladin's hordes on October 2, they rushed in by the thousands. Abbot Coggeshall, who was present and nursing an injury he had incurred during the siege, wrote,

> The imams and the doctors and expounders of the wicked errors of Mahomet first ascended to the Temple of the Lord.... With horrible bellowings they proclaimed the law of Mahomet, and vociferated, with polluted lips, "Allah Acbar!—Allah Acbar!" They defiled all the places that are contained within the Temple.... And as a disgrace to the Christians, with vast clamor, with laughter and mockery, they hurled down the golden cross from the pinnacle of the building, and dragged it with ropes throughout the city, amid the exulting shouts of the infidels and the tears and lamentations of the followers of Christ.[12]

For two days, Saladin—"who vanquished the adorers of the cross," in the words of a contemporary panegyric[13]—had this large, gilded cross dragged in the dirt, kicked, and spat upon by the riotous and unrestrained Muslims, now drunk with victory. Saladin eventually sent it as a trophy to the caliph in Baghdad, where it was "buried beneath the Nubian gate" to be forever "trodden upon" by Muslim feet. Churches throughout Jerusalem were desecrated, their bells silenced, their icons and crosses destroyed.[14]

The *Itinerarium Peregrinorum* records a similar account concerning a Hospitaller church:

> When the city had been surrendered, a crier of the law of Muhammad ascended the rock of Calvary and there loudly proclaimed their filthy law. The terrible enemy also undertook another unspeakable action. There was a cross fixed on top of the spier of the Hospitallers' church. They tied ropes around it and threw it down, spat contemptuously on it, hacked it into pieces, then dragged it through the city dung-pits, as an insult to our faith.[15]

Although such anti-Christian animus is nowadays portrayed as a bit of triumphalism against those who had long humiliated Islam—namely, the Crusaders—Saladin's intrinsic contempt for Christians far transcended his wars with the Franks. For example, once they came under his sway around 1170, the sultan severely persecuted Egypt's indigenous Coptic Christians, even though the Copts, for whom Saladin was "the Oppressor of the Cross Worshippers,"[16] were an already oppressed minority that had nothing to do with the Franks or the Crusades.

In keeping with Jerusalem's surrender terms, Saladin allowed its Christians to ransom themselves and quit the city, and "the Temple exhausted its treasury to pay the ransom of the poor inhabitants and guarded them on their journey from the Holy City to Tripoli."[17] But because the Temple's and Hospital's coffers were not enough to ransom everyone, fifteen thousand Christians were enslaved. "Women and children together came to eight thousand and were quickly divided up among us, bringing a smile to Muslim faces at their lamentation," wrote Imad al-Din, who was present at Jerusalem's capitulation, before launching into a sadomasochistic tirade extolling the sexual debasement of European women at the hands of Muslim men:

> How many well-guarded women were profaned...and miserly women forced to yield themselves, and women who had been kept hidden [nuns] stripped of their modesty...and free women occupied [meaning "penetrated"], and precious ones used for hard work, and pretty things put to the test, and virgins dishonored and proud women deflowered...and happy ones made to weep! How many [Muslim] noblemen took them as concubines, how many ardent men blazed for one of them, and celibates were satisfied by them, and thirsty men sated by them, and turbulent men able to give vent to their passion.[18]

Saladin allowed the Hospital to remain, though it was henceforth known among the Muslims as a *muristan*, a word of Persian origin meaning "mad house." Either Saladin transformed it into an asylum, or it was called that in derision, much like the Church of the Resurrection (in Arabic, *qiyama*) was always punned among Muslims as (*qumama*), the church of "garbage."

21

HOLDING THE LINE

After the fall of Jerusalem, it was Saladin's nemeses—the stubborn Knights of the Temple and Hospital—who did more than anyone else to prevent the sultan from achieving his ultimate goal and victory: the complete defeat and ejection of the Crusaders from the Holy Land. Although the military orders established their new headquarters in Antioch, they still garrisoned many frontier castles. As these strongholds interrupted the Muslims' movements and supply lines, Saladin first needed to take them before fully investing the few kingdoms remaining to the Christian name: Antioch, Tripoli, and Tyre, being the main ones. Saladin's forces put Tyre to siege in November 1187 and it soon became the focal point of the war. Because "the brethren realized that resistance would help the coastal towns," the vastly outnumbered and holed up Templars and Hospitallers committed themselves to draining the sultan's manpower.[1]

The most heroic defense occurred at the Hospitaller fortress of Belvoir, which was manned by the surviving Knights of St. John, "determined men whom the war had so far spared."[2] The Templar Terric wrote to King Henry II in a letter: "The brothers of the Hospital of Belvoir as yet bravely resist the Saracens; they have captured two convoys, and have valiantly possessed themselves of the munitions of war and provisions which were being conveyed by the Saracens." Terric went on to mention several other castles—including the Templars' Safed as well as the Hospitallers' Krak des Chevaliers, Margat, and Castel Blanc—all of which as yet "resist Saladin."[3]

It was, however, due to their fierce defense of Belvoir that "the Hospitallers did much to reinforce their image in the eyes of the Muslims as doughty and fearless warriors." Never at a loss for words, Imad al-Din, Saladin's florid secretary, described the fortress of Belvoir as "an inaccessible citadel, an inaccessible refuge, an unattainable summit, an unstrikeable flint, an inviolable woman."[4]

In January 1188, Saladin ordered his general Sayf al-Din Mahmud, a pious Muslim who sought to demonstrate the "strength and power of Allah," to take over the siege of Belvoir. Late one storm-swept night—"a night fertile with terrors, dark, obscure, shadowy, pitch-black, deep, cold...a night abundant in rain which fell in torrents"—the Knights of St. John, like phantoms from the deep, fell upon the Muslim camp and "the noble Mahmud and his drowsy companions came to themselves only when the Franks [Hospitallers] had entered and placed their knees on their chests. They were then incapable of defending themselves, they could not resist; supreme blessing came to them, for martyrdom took them by surprise. The emir defended himself until he died, surrounded by his enemies; Allah's order is a judgement fixed in advance."[5]

When word of this unexpected reverse reached Saladin, he was "shaken by it, and furious," and redoubled his efforts, further draining his time and resources. In the end, he wasted a year on both Belvoir and Safed, ceaselessly bombarding the two castles with catapults and battering rams, mining their foundations, and mounting one assault after another. Having reached their final extremities, Safed surrendered in December 1188 and Belvoir in January 1189. Several other castles—including the Templars' Tortosa and the Hospitallers' Krak des Chevaliers—had also done their part to waste the increasingly frustrated sultan's time and manpower. The knights further discomfited their besiegers, and we encounter strange anecdotes, including how "the Templars astonished the Muslims by standing motionless and silent in the breach" during the siege of their castle of Darsak far to the north.[6]

Arab chroniclers further confirm that it was the military orders' stubborn defense that prevented Saladin from a complete takeover. "Belvoir, with Safed and Kerak," wrote Ibn al-Athir, "were for the Sultan a great source of trouble and agitation, seeing that the coastal region from Acre to the south had been entirely conquered with the exception of these fortresses; and that he could not leave in the middle of the country places that troubled his spirit, dividing his attention and forcing him to watch them for fear that they would inflict great damage on the Muslims and travelers."[7]

In short, Saladin's efforts against the fortresses of the Hospitallers and Templars "had taken too long," writes Jonathan Riley-Smith, "and the Military Orders must take much of the credit for the survival of Latin Syria." It is, incidentally, from this point on that the Hospitallers appear in the sources—especially the Muslim sources—as no less formidable than their Templar counterparts. Riley-Smith continues,

> The perils threatening Latin Syria and the important part played by the Hospitallers in the defense of the settlement after 1187 had exercised an inexorable influence. The Franks in the East could not survive without the Order's military commitment, and that was recognized by the papacy in 1191. "Who could not admire how God's might powerfully flowers and perseveres in the said Order and brethren; where each day so many are sustained in arms, so many of the poor are cherished, so many are received into the hospice."[8]

The dogged perseverance of the military orders especially helped prevent Saladin from applying his full might against the kingdom of Tyre, which the sultan had put to siege early on in November 1187. Conrad of Montferrat, the uncrowned king-elect of Jerusalem, took charge of Tyre's defense. Muslim sources confirm—that is, lament—his capable leadership. For Ibn al-Athir, Conrad "was a devil incarnate in his ability to govern and defend a town, and a man of extraordinary courage." At one point, Saladin brought Conrad's father, William the Elder, who had been captured at Hattin, to the walls of Tyre, demanding that

Conrad surrender Tyre or watch his father be cruelly tortured to death. Conrad responded by shooting a crossbow in the general direction of his hostage-father: It was either a sign that he would continue to hold regardless of what was done to his father; or else it was a missed shot to take out and end the sufferings of his father. "This man is an infidel and very cruel," a disgusted Saladin was reportedly heard to mutter.[9]

Unsurprisingly, the Knights of the Temple and Hospital cooperated with such a determined kindred spirit. In his letter to Henry II, after Terric describes how "Saladin has besieged Tyre incessantly, by night and by day, throwing into it immense stones from thirteen military engines," he closes with how Conrad

> with the assistance of the house of the Hospital and the brethren of the Temple, engaged the galleys of Saladin, and vanquishing them, he captured eleven, and took as prisoners the great admiral of Alexandria and eight other admirals, a multitude of the infidels being slain. The rest of the Muslim galleys, escaping the hands of the Christians, fled to the army of Saladin, and being run aground by his command, were set on fire and burnt to ashes. Saladin himself, overwhelmed with grief, having cut off the ears and the tail of his horse, rode that same horse through his whole army in the sight of all. Farewell![10]

After ordering the torching of all his ships and engines of war, the shamed sultan returned to Damascus in early 1188, but not before consoling himself by destroying a church in Tortosa—"one of the largest of its kind"—as well as another in Lydda.[11]

As time slipped away, so too did Saladin's chance of evicting the Crusaders from the Holy Land. Not only were many secular knights now arriving from Europe, but the Temple and Hospital had ordered their Western commanderies to pour forth all their manpower and resources to the East; from all the preceptories, knights rushed to the Holy Land aboard vessels from Genoa, Pisa, and Venice. That they drove themselves more vigorously than the average Crusader is seen in the fact that a disproportionate number of Templars and Hospitallers died fighting in comparison to the secular knighthood during this time.

> Many minor engagements were fought, and both the Christians and Muslims suffered heavily. The losses among the Temple and the Hospital were especially severe. Most of their members were newcomers to the East, and these recruits were eager to show their valor and prove themselves worthy successors of the brethren who had so long preserved the Holy Land for Christendom against tremendous odds.[12]

By the spring of 1189, even the notorious master of the Temple, the infamous Gérard of Ridefort, having been ransomed, appears again—now issuing out of the gates of Tyre at the head of all the newly arrived Templars, as well as a large army of Crusaders, including Guy and Conrad, to reclaim Acre, which had fallen to Saladin soon after Hattin. The sultan—the "victorious defender of the faith, tamer of the followers of the cross"—rushed to its defense with a large army. What happened next contrasts the austere discipline of the Temple with the impetuous cupidity of the secular knights that Bernard of Clairvaux had warned against nearly sixty years earlier:

> On the 4th of October, the newly-arrived warriors from Europe, eager to signalize their prowess against the infidels, marched out to attack Saladin's camp. The Master of the Temple, at the head of his knights and the forces of the order, and a large body of European chivalry who had ranged themselves under the banner of the Templars, formed a reserve. The Muslim array was broken by the impetuous charge of the soldiers of the cross, who penetrated to the imperial tent, and then abandoned themselves to pillage. The infidels rallied, they were led on by Saladin in person; and the Christian army would have been annihilated but for the Templars. Firm and immovable, they presented, for the space of an hour,

> an unbroken front to the advancing Muslims, and gave time for the discomfited and panic-stricken crusaders to recover from their terror and confusion; but ere they had been rallied, and had returned to the charge, the Master of the Temple was slain; he fell pierced with arrows at the head of his knights; the seneschal of the order shared the same fate, and more than half the Templars were numbered with the dead.[13]

So ended Gérard of Ridefort, and "in his death, he atoned, so far as it was possible to do so, for the grave misfortunes that his own turbulent nature had brought upon the Holy Land."[14] During the onslaught against the Templars, as the master had witnessed the butchery of his brethren, his companions urged him to flee, to which he responded in typical fashion: "Never! It would be shame and scandal for the Templars. I would be said to have saved my life by running away and leaving my fellow-knights to be slaughtered."[15]

The *Itinerarium Peregrinorum's* account of this same disastrous assault on Muslim-held Acre is worth quoting at length as it suggests that, once again, something similar to what happened at Ascalon in 1153 and Hattin in 1187—that is, a vanguard of Templars rushing in without support from the rest of the Crusaders, resulting in their annihilation—had occurred:

> The knights of the Temple, who are second to none and devoted to slaughter, had already charged through the enemy lines. If the rest of the Christians had pressed on after them and pursued the enemy with equal enthusiasm, that day they would have won a happy victory over the city and war. But the Templars went on too far.... The [Muslim] townspeople suddenly rushed down on them. Yet although they were innumerable numbers crushing just a few, they only triumphed after much slaughter of their own forces. There the master of the Temple, Gérard de Ridefort...fell slain. Happy man! The Lord conferred such great glory on him, giving him

the laurel wreath which he had earned in so many battles and making him a fellow of the college of martyrs.... He could indeed have escaped had he wished, but he fell slain with the slain.[16]

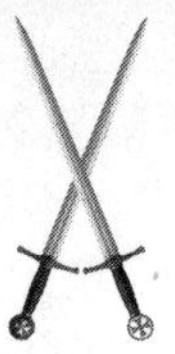

22

IN THE LION'S SERVICE

Following the fall of Jerusalem, Christians from all across Europe traveled to the Holy Land "to avenge the injuries inflicted on the Cross" in what became history's Third Crusade.[1] Because the Templars' reputation had long preceded them, and their ongoing tenacity against the overwhelming forces of Saladin had been proclaimed throughout Christendom, the "proudest of the nobility, and the most valiant of the chivalry of Europe, on their arrival in Palestine, manifested an eager desire to fight under the banner of the Temple." The new master, Robert of Sable, permitted "many secular knights…to take their station by the side of the military friars, and even to wear the red cross on their breasts whilst fighting in the ranks." It was because "the Templars performed prodigies of valor" that newcomers sought the privilege to fight alongside them. According to James of Vitry, bishop of Acre,

> The name of their reputation, and the fame of their sanctity…was diffused throughout the entire world, and all the congregation of the saints will recount their battles and glorious triumph over the enemies of Christ, knights indeed from all parts of the earth, dukes, and princes, after their example, casting off the shackles of the world, and renouncing the pomps and vanities of

> this life and all the lusts of the flesh for Christ's sake, hastened to join them, and to participate in their holy profession and religion.[2]

The Third Crusaders began pouring in as the Christian siege of Muslim-held Acre raged on. In one of the most grueling sieges of the entire crusading era, famine and pestilence ravaged the Christians' ranks, and many thousands died "from the foul air, polluted with the stink of corpses, worn out by anxious nights spent on guard, and shattered by other hardships and needs," to quote from the *Itinerarium Peregrinorum*. "There was no rest, not even time to breathe."[3]

Things took an upturn once the kings of the West—Richard I (the Lionheart) of England and Philip II of France—arrived, bringing renewed fervor to the siege of Acre. Although Philip's (short-lived) stay was helpful, it was Richard who would truly spearhead the Third Crusade. As Muslim chronicler Ibn al-Athir observed, once the Lionheart arrived, "The damage they [Crusaders] did to the Muslims increased greatly."[4]

After the kings arrived with much needed succor, all the engines of war rained down death-dealing destruction on the Muslim defenders of Acre—even as they continued to defy and taunt the Christians. The chroniclers tell of one Muslim soldier who stood atop the wall mocking a crucifix and waving it around "with obscene movements, with filthy and sinful miming actions and blasphemously shouting impious words against our religion." This diabolical ritual culminated with him urinating on the crucifix—only to be shot in the groin by a Crusader crossbow and falling to his death.[5]

Massive boulders—some aflame and setting anything inside the city not built of stone ablaze—rocked the Muslim-held fortress. Even here, the military orders made their presence felt: "The Templar's stonethrower wreaked impressive devastation," writes the author of the *Itinerarium Peregrinorum* (the best account of the Third Crusade, hence referred to as the "chronicle"), "while the Hospitallers' also never ceased hurling, to the terror of the Turks. Besides these, there was a stonethrower which had been constructed at general expense, which they called 'God's Stonethrower.'"[6]

On July 12, 1191, Acre, for long the focal point of the Crusade and jihad, finally capitulated to the Christians. A month later, the Crusaders, under Richard's leadership, left Acre and began their long march south (Philip had seen enough and returned to France). Although Jerusalem was the goal, it was imperative to first recapture its nearest port, Jaffa. During the Crusaders' seventy-five-mile march from Acre to Jaffa, Saladin and his forces sought every opportunity to annihilate the Christians. His horsemen repeatedly "harassed the Franks on their march and loosed arrows at them which well nigh veiled the sun," writes Ibn al-Athir.[7]

From the start, Richard tried to safeguard against Muslim attacks by keeping the army in remarkably tight formation. As King Louis VII had done half a century earlier during the Second Crusade, so now did Richard entrust the most vulnerable sides of the marching men to the most veteran guardians of Christians: "The Templars formed the vanguard and the Hospitallers the rearguard," writes the chronicler. "Both of them acted energetically and displayed an image of great valor."[8] Richard was especially close to and "relied heavily on the Templars," to whom he was a longtime benefactor.[9]

During the army's long trek, the Knights of the Temple and Hospital often traded sides; whether at the van or rear, they were both exposed to the brunt of jihad. Thus, one day, after the army had marched "through an empty waste land" and had reached a mountainous region choked by much overgrowth, "the Templars were in command of the rearguard. They lost so many horses that day as the Turks charged them from behind [letting loose countless volleys of arrows] that they almost despaired." Ibn al-Athir may have been referring to this same attack when he wrote about how Muslims "fell on the Frankish rearguard, killed several and captured several others."[10] Richard himself, who was never far from the military orders, was pierced with an arrow that same day.

And so it continued for weeks: "The Turks raged in their stubborn wickedness," writes the chronicler, "keeping alongside our army as it advanced, struggling to inflict what injury they could on us, firing darts and arrows which flew very densely, like rain." It reached the point that wherever "the army passed through you could not have found a space of four feet of ground free of darts."[11]

Despite the casualties from arrows, sunstroke, starvation, and disease; despite the wounds, snake bites, and overall misery, the Christian warriors, led and protected by the military orders, remained undaunted. Saladin's own biographer, Baha' al-Din, expressed his dismay at these relentless men who behaved more like tanks of war: "I saw various individuals amongst the Franks with ten arrows fixed in their backs, pressing on in this fashion quite unconcerned.... Consider the endurance of these people, bearing exhausting tasks without any pay or material gain."[12]

Finally, on September 6, 1191, as the Crusaders emerged from a dense wood, there on the vast plains of Arsuf, they saw "all the forces" of Islam marshaled before them, "from Damascus and Persia, from the Mediterranean Sea to the East." There was not a single, warlike Muslim people "whom Saladin had not summoned to aid him in crushing the Christian people," for he "hoped to wipe the Christians completely off the face of the earth." Prior to the commencement of battle on the morning of September 7, a wild din erupted from the Muslim camp—drums, horns, and cymbals banged and brayed to reverberant cries of "Allahu Akbar" and other "horrible yells" and "harsh cries"—even as the Christians were kneeling in prayer and assuming battle formation.[13]

Once these preliminaries were over, the Muslims "fell on our army from all sides.... There was not a space for two miles around, not even a fistful, which was not covered with the hostile Turkish race.... As they kept up their persistent assaults they inflicted very grave losses on our people."[14] One of the Muslim contingents, led by a nephew of Saladin, Taqi al-Din, was especially fierce in its assault, which is unsurprising considering that "this same Taqi al-Din," the chronicler writes, "always persecuted Christians very savagely with an obstinate hatred."[15] The already exhausted Crusaders fought back against the better-rested and better-provisioned Muslims as best they could. Unhorsed knights were seen "walking on foot" and "returning blow for blow as far as means and strength allowed," even as the Turks galloped about and continued to rain darts on them.[16]

The situation was exacerbated by Richard's order that the army remain on the defensive and not break rank until the time was right. Before long, however, a "very fierce race of people," one "proud and insolent, rendered unyielding by demonic instigation," pummeled the Christian rearguard held by the Hospitallers. The latter's attempt to hold the line only prompted the Muslims to "rage with even worse barbarity." Even so—and although they were burning to do so—the Knights of St. John refrained from charging the enemy, in keeping with Richard's command to hold the line until he gave the order. In the words of the chronicler,

> More than 20,000 Turks made a sudden massed charge, wielding clubs and swords in hand-to-hand combat. They redoubled their blows on the Hospitallers, crushing and striking them and piling on the pressure in various ways. Almost overcome by their barbarity, one of them named Brother Garnier of Nablus [master of the Hospital] cried out in a loud voice: "St. George, unique among knights, surely you aren't going to leave us to be defeated? Christianity is perishing because she is not fighting back against this unspeakable race!"[17]

"Lord king," the Hospitaller master turned to and implored Richard, "we are being violently attacked. We will be stained with eternal dishonor as if we did not dare to fight back. Each of us is losing his mount at no cost to the enemy. What more must we bear?"

"Good master," coolly replied the Lionheart, "you must sustain their attack; no one can be everywhere."[18] The king's plan was sound: Only when the entire Muslim army had gotten close enough, and their horses had tired, would he give the signal for the countercharge.

"As the [Hospitaller] master returned to his troops," continues the chronicler, "the Turks bore down on them again, hewing at them from behind." It was more than human nature—even that of the stoic military orders—could bear. Invariably, "two knights who could not bear to wait" any longer—one being the marshal of the Hospital—"burst out of the line," whereupon "everything was thrown into confusion."[19]

Unburdening their pent-up rage, they charged into the midst of, and began slaughtering, their enemies.

> The rest of the Christians heard these two calling with loud voices for St. George's aid* as they charged boldly on the Turks. In the name of Christ the Savior they spun their horses round and followed those two, charging as one into the relentlessly attacking enemy. Despite being under great pressure, the Hospitallers and their detachments had kept ranks all that day as they rode; but now they immediately urged their horses to a gallop and charged manfully into the enemy. Likewise, each troop turned their horse around and charged the enemy, still keeping to their original order so that those who had been in the vanguard [Templars] while they marched became the rearguard in the attack. So the Hospitallers, who had been placed at the rear of the army, became the first to attack.... Brave and doughty as they were, every one of them gave each approaching Turk a bold reception, transfixing them with their lances and throwing them from their horses. The air grew black with dust.... The Turks who had deliberately dismounted from their horses to fire darts and arrows more easily at our people all lost their heads at once in that military engagement; the knights knocked them down and our foot-soldiers beheaded them.[20]

Once Richard understood what was happening, the warrior-king signaled for the general assault, and sped to where the fighting was thickest—crashing with thunderous violence into the Hospitaller/Muslim melee. "Stunned by the strength of the blows he and his force

---

* St. George was and remains the patron saint of military men (with the exception of St. James Matamoros, the "Moor Slayer" and patron saint of Spain). The Templars venerated him no less than the Hospitallers did: "George, like the Templars, had been an active warrior; he had patiently suffered a horrible martyrdom at the hands of pagans because of his Christian faith. His life was an obvious model for the Templars to follow" (Nicholson, *Knights Templar*, 149).

inflicted on them," Saladin's men "fell back to the right and the left," and a "great number were but headless corpses trodden underfoot by friend and foe regardless."[21] Driven into a battle frenzy, in the words of the chronicler,

> King Richard pursued the Turks with singular ferocity, fell upon them and scattered them across the ground. No one escaped when his sword made contact with them; wherever he went his brandished sword cleared a wide path on all sides. Continuing his advance with untiring sword strokes, he cut down that unspeakable race as if he was reaping the harvest with a sickle, so that the corpses of Turks he had killed covered the ground everywhere for the space of half a mile.[22]

With this inspiring sight of the Lionheart's entrance into the fray, the battle reached a fever pitch: "Constantly slaying and hammering away with their swords, the Christians wore down the terrified Turks, but for a long time the battle was in the balance. Each struck each other, each struggled to overcome; one drew back stained with blood, the other fell slain. How many banners and multiform flags, pennons and innumerable standards you would have seen fall to the ground!"[23]

In the end, the Christians prevailed; the Knights of St. John had initiated the battle, but Richard's prowess saw it through, and the "rout of the enemy was so complete that for two miles there was nothing to see except for people running away, although they had previously been so persistent, swollen with pride and very fierce."[24] Arabic sources confirm the magnitude of this defeat: "The Muslims were routed, a great number of them were killed," writes Ibn al-Athir, before indicating how terror-stricken his coreligionists had become: "When the Franks made camp, the Muslims did so too—though keeping their horses' reins in their hands."[25]

Arsuf was a Christian victory of the first order: "It settled the question as to whether Saladin was strong enough to drive the Crusaders out of Syria, and he never ventured to engage them in another pitched battle"[26] It did, however, come at great cost; many Christians died there. One of Richard's men in particular, James of Avesnes—"the most outstanding knight, the renowned warrior," who fought with distinction at the siege of Acre[27]—was particularly missed, and a search mission was sent for him. It was led by those knights most concerned about the welfare of Christian pilgrims:

> So the Hospitallers and the Knights Templar armed themselves.... When they came to the battlefield they searched carefully and at last found the body [of James of Avesnes], with its face so smeared with congealed blood that they could hardly recognize it until it had been washed with water; it was all bloodied and swollen from wounds and very unlike what it was when he was alive. They wrapped up the body decently and, carrying it with them, returned to Arsuf.[28]

Before succumbing to the vast forces of Islam, James had put up a fight worthy of a knight of the Temple or Hospital: "According to those who were sent to seek and bring back his body, before his strength failed he had beheaded around fifteen Turks who were found lying dead around him."[29]

Following Arsuf, Saladin's lofty stature as an invincible jihadist leader extraordinaire virtually collapsed overnight. Despite his magnificent victories—with Jerusalem at their pinnacle—he had lost Acre, and now there was the ignominy of Arsuf. As for Jaffa, the ultimate destination of the Crusaders, after seventy-five miles of warfare and travails, they marched onto it without impediment, for the scared sultan had ordered its fortifications destroyed.

Before fleeing, Saladin also ordered a Muslim contingent to hold Ascalon, which—because it was the most important coastal fortress for whoever would be master of Jerusalem—was next on the Crusaders' route. According to Ibn al-Athir, they told him "If you wish to hold the place, then come in with us yourself and one of your older sons. Otherwise none of us will enter lest we suffer what the men at Acre suffered."[30]As with Jaffa, Saladin destroyed Ascalon and withdrew to, and holed himself up in, Jerusalem.

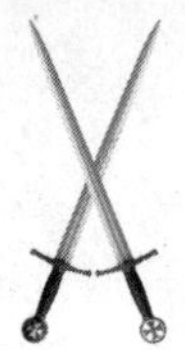

23

"WE OUGHT TO FOLLOW… THE TEMPLARS AND THE HOSPITALLERS"

By late October 1191, the Crusaders, with Richard at their head, were finally in a position to set off for Jerusalem. During the early stages of this journey, and because it was nearby, they also sought, on the advice of the military orders, "to restore the Casal of the Plains, for it was thought that this was absolutely essential for the safety of the pilgrim traffic, which passed through at that point."[1] This tower was originally built by Duke Godfrey of Bouillon, the original defender of the Holy Sepulchre, to secure the pilgrimage route from Jaffa to Jerusalem. During his swift conquests following Hattin, Saladin had destroyed it in 1187. On October 30, the army reached their destination:

> They pitched their tents and encamped between the Casal of the Plains and Casal Mein. The Turkish army was then at Ramula, from where they often launched sudden raids, harassing us. Our army remained for fifteen days or more between the two aforesaid casals,

> while the king repaired Casal Maen to perfection. What was more, the Templars built the Casal of the Plains; while the Turks constantly threatened them and harassed them however they could.[2]

Although Muslim archers continued to harass the men once they resumed their march to Jerusalem, no major encounters ensued until November 6. After setting up camp, the squires and men-at-arms went out to forage for grass and fodder for the army's horses and pack animals. "The Templars were responsible for protecting the squires as they dispersed and wandered through the valleys to look for grassy places."[3] Suddenly, four thousand howling Turks appeared "and charged arrogantly down on the Templars."

> At once they had them shut in and surrounded and were pressing down on them relentlessly, intending to crush or capture them [not least as Saladin always paid top dinar for Templar heads].... As the threatening enemy compressed them, the Templars realized that they must exercise their valor. They quickly dismounted from their horses, and standing with backs firmly against their comrades' backs and faces to the enemy they began to defend themselves manfully. But the Turks charged and immediately killed three Templars. Then the bitterest fight ensued. There were powerful blows, helmets rang and sparks flew as striking swords collided; armor jangled, and there was a great noise of shouts and yells from the combatants. The Turks hurled themselves forward manfully, the Templars resolutely threw them back; those on one side threaten while the other beat them back; the Turks made an excellent assault, while the Templars defend themselves strenuously. At last the crowd of Turks broke in and each reached out a hand to seize the Templars, who were all but crushed and shattered by the persistence of their many attackers.[4]

Hearing the cries of the squires, other Crusaders rushed to the aid of the Templars: "The conflict was growing very heated on both sides with everyone mixed up together in the confusion, when King Richard arrived, roaring."[5] Seeing the Christians' vastly outnumbered status, the king's leading men tried to dissuade him from joining in the fray: "We believe it would be less damaging if those who are surrounded by the enemy [the Templars] perish alone, rather than to allow the Turks to swallow you up with them, for then the hope of Christendom would perish and its confidence be destroyed. We judge that you would be better advised to remain in safety while it is possible to avoid danger."[6]

This was not the counsel to offer a king such as Richard. His face "changed color as his blood boiled," and he informed them that he would be no king were he to abandon Christians to their fate. "And without another word," continues the chronicler,

> he put spur to horse and with indescribable rage—I might almost say madness—he charged the Turks [with his lance], scattered their close-knit ranks with his powerful impact, passing through them like lightning and throwing down a great many with a single blow. Then, returning into them, brandishing his sword, he routed them all at once, charging back and forth this way and that, fearing none, just like a lion. Wherever he turned they fell back from him on all sides, as he cut off a hand here, there arms or head.[7]

Such was Richard.* Though the military orders were renowned for their ferocity and seen as the protectors of the average Crusader, this warrior-king, or pilgrim-lion, had now on two occasions been the one to provide them with succor: first at Arsuf, in defense of the Hospitallers, and now, in support of the Templars. It should be noted that Arabic sources also confirm Richard's prowess, which not a few modern readers dismiss as hyperbole from Christian sources. "He, the accursed

* For Richard's Crusade, see chapter 3 of *Defenders of the West,* which is dedicated to the Lionheart and his many exploits against the forces of Islam.

one," writes Baha' al-Din, who witnessed the English king in action, "was brave, valiant, and expert in battle." For Ibn al-Athir, "the king was the outstanding man of his time for bravery, cunning, steadfastness and endurance. In him the Muslims were tried by an unparalleled disaster."[8]

By January 1192, the Crusaders had at last reached the outskirts of Jerusalem, and the excitement of the exhausted men was palpable: "Everybody hurried to set out on the journey and no obstacle or hostile encounter could delay them. They made great boasts and looked forward to completing their pilgrimage as they had previously vowed, whether the Saracens liked it or not."[9] A council was held between Richard and the leading barons, as well as those who best knew the lay of the land and the mind of the enemy: the military orders. There, seasoned prudence won out over amateur enthusiasm:

> Wiser people were not of the opinion that they should acquiesce in the common people's rash desires [to attack Jerusalem]. For the Templars and Hospitallers and also the Poulains, [European] natives of that country [the Holy Land], who could see more clearly what needed to be done for the future, advised King Richard not to go towards Jerusalem at that juncture.[10]

Their reasoning was logical. Besieging Saladin and his men in heavily fortified Jerusalem would also mean fighting on another front, against those Turks—the majority—who were outside of and surrounding Jerusalem. The supply line back to Jaffa had, moreover, already been stretched thin and was under constant attack. Finally, even if they took Jerusalem, it would be an ephemeral victory; for, before long, all those who had come to liberate, and pilgrimage in, Jerusalem would, as they invariably always did, return to Europe. Left defenseless, Jerusalem would again fall to the Muslims.

Rather, the military veterans argued that the army should return to and travel south along the coast to take and rebuild the port of Ascalon, thereby disrupting communications between Saladin's Syrian and Egyptian domains, and so compromising his ability to bring supplies and reinforcements from the latter. The logic was simple: Ascalon must first be placed, if Jerusalem was ever to remain, in Christian hands.

The king agreed, prompting much outrage among the rank and file. They had gone through so much to get to where they were—standing before the gates of Jerusalem—and now they were to retreat. Many Crusaders, including most of the French who had remained after Philip left, broke away from Richard's command and returned to Acre. Not Richard; as the military orders had suggested, he returned to and, with great indefatigable labor and expense, rebuilt Ascalon and captured more castles from the Muslims.

On June 6, the Crusaders decided to give it another go; they mobilized and set off, once again, for the Holy City under Richard's leadership. On arriving, it quickly became clear that the situation had only worsened: Jerusalem's garrison was now swollen with Muslims. Saladin had mustered all his men around him and poisoned all the surrounding wells. If, as seemed likely, Jerusalem did not fall fast, the Crusaders would be trapped in a waterless desert in the summer—dehydrated sitting ducks for the hordes of roaming Turks that surrounded and patrolled the city.

Another council was held. Although everyone, including his own men, insisted on proceeding, Richard exhibited a level of patience and prudence antithetical to what modern histories assign him. "We and our people are foreigners and know absolutely nothing about this region," he argued, adding that

> it would be safer to act with the advice of the natives of the country, who wish to recover their former territories and inheritances, and do what most seems appropriate to them, because they have better knowledge of the terrain. It seems to me that we ought to follow whatever course of action the Templars and the Hospitallers honestly judge and decide that we should undertake: whether we should advance to besiege Jerusalem; whether we go to seize Babylonia [Cairo]; or to Beirut, or to Damascus.[11]

After deliberating, the council of seasoned military order members reached the same conclusion as before: Even if Jerusalem was captured, it could never be held onto without first subduing Egypt. The king agreed, the rank and file howled in protest, and the Crusade came to an end. Such was the inevitable clash between the average pilgrim-crusader, who held a myopic viewpoint—liberate Jerusalem and go home—and the military orders who always took the long view. As Jonathan Riley-Smith explains,

> The advice given on the Third Crusade foreshadows a common attitude of the Military Orders in the thirteenth century. They were usually cautious counsellors-of-war not only because of their experience of the Saracens, but also because of their experience of crusaders. Once the crusaders had gone, and they generally left too soon, it was doubtful if any newly conquered territory could be held with the power remaining.[12]

Before quitting the Holy Land, Richard managed to exact several concessions from Saladin. The sultan granted "free passage everywhere, and access to the Lord's Holy Sepulchre without any exactions."[13] Additionally, he agreed to leave all Crusader holdings from Tyre to Jaffa in peace, though the latter—being so close to Jerusalem and in Crusaders' hands again—especially vexed Saladin. For his part, the English king had to agree to the re-dismantling of Ascalon. As the chief port between the Holy Land and Egypt—which both he and Saladin knew was pivotal to whomever would permanently hold Jerusalem—Richard was loath to agree to this stipulation, not least due to all the hard labor and resources he had spent rebuilding it. But in the end, he, too, had little choice but to compromise.

Thus ended the Third Crusade, during which "the most intense conflicts of the two centuries [of the Crusading era, c.1096–1291] took place...when the opposing personalities were thrown into the highest relief, the fighting was more widespread and its implications more dramatic."[14]

Although it failed to meet its ultimate goal—the restoration of Jerusalem—the Third Crusade completely halted and even reversed many of Saladin's gains. Virtually all the coastal plain was returned to the Crusaders; and "by the valor and exertions of the lion-hearted king, the city of Gaza, the ancient fortress of the [Templar] order, which had been taken by Saladin soon after the Battle of Tiberias [Hattin], was recovered to the Christian arms, the fortifications were repaired, and the place was restored to the Knights Templars, who again garrisoned it with their soldiers."[15]

Nor should the influence of the Knights of the Temple and Hospital be underestimated. "Throughout Richard's campaign," Riley-Smith writes,

> the Military Orders formed an important part of his army, and they seem to have been willing to serve under him. He was, however, too great a general not to respect their advice. When he planned to leave for Europe in July 1192, it was with their "license and blessing." It was reported that when the news of Jaffa came through [which was delivered by Richard's personal valor], it was they who persuaded him to go to its relief. And the most convincing demonstration of their influence was to be seen in those councils-of-war that considered how best to capture Jerusalem.... Richard did little without their advice and nothing against it.[16]

The Third Crusade witnessed three other developments germane to our history. First, the Hospitallers—who, as seen, only emerge as an offensive, military force campaigning against Muslims in 1168—are, by the end of the Crusade in 1192, finally seen as on a par with the Templars. Aside from the fact that their targeting for extermination alongside the knights of the oldest military order following Hattin in 1187 underscored that the Muslims saw them as one with their fiercest enemy (the Templars), Nicholson offers a succinct summary of this evolution:

> During the Third Crusade (1189–1192), the Hospitallers played a major military role for the first time in a crusade. As well as advising on strategy [which they had done as early as the Second Crusade], they took part in attacks on the enemy, their ships assisted in the defense of Tyre (now Sur) in the winter of 1187–8; their siege-machines played a role in the siege of Acre, 1189–91; their forces took it in turns with the Templars to take command of the rearguard or the vanguard on the march to Jaffa in September 1191.... The Hospitallers' prominent military role during the Third Crusade established the Hospital in the minds of western European commentators as a military order. From this period onwards, the Hospitallers were usually named alongside the Templars in western accounts of military activity in the Holy Land. Regrettably for the Order, the military significance of the brothers in the East meant that they also received blame when the crusader states received military reversals.[17]

Although they were indeed henceforth "named alongside the Templars,"[18] the latter would still be seen as the premier military order for some years to come.

The second important development following the Third Crusade concerns the growing role of both the Templars and Hospitallers. As Ernle Bradford writes,

> What finally emerges from this turbulent period in the history of Outremer [Crusader states of the Holy Land] is the power and prosperity of the two great crusading Orders, the Templars and the Hospitallers. While all the other Franks were impoverished through loss of lands and revenue, being dependent on their resources in the Levant alone [which had been devastated following Hattin in 1187], the military Orders were secure. They had their firm bases in Europe, their lands and houses

> and income deriving from areas which were secure whatever disasters might befall in the East.[19]

Or, in the words of Charles G. Addison,

> To narrate all the exploits of the Templars, and all the incidents and events connected with the order, would be to write the history of the Latin Kingdom of Palestine, which was preserved and maintained for the period of ninety-nine years after the departure of Richard Coeur de Lion, solely by the exertions of the Templars and Hospitallers. No actions of importance were ever fought with the infidels, in which the Templars did not take an active and distinguished part, nor was the atabal of the Muslims ever sounded in defiance on the frontier, without the trumpets of the Templars receiving and answering the challenge.[20]

The third and final development concerns the rise of yet another military order, the Order of Brothers of the German House of St. Mary in Jerusalem, better known as the Teutonic Knights. Around 1190, at the height of the Crusader siege of Muslim-held Acre, a hospice of Germanic origin was founded to take care of the many sick and wounded Christians. Its original members were not fighting men, and its head was likely a priest. However, like the Hospitallers of St. John before them, it was not long before they concluded that fighting Muslims was the best way to care for fellow Christians, and by 1198, they became a formal military order, adopting the Templars' rule. Although the Teutonic Knights quickly became the third greatest military order in the Holy Land, they never really rivaled the Templars and Hospitallers, and before long, much of their attention and fighting skills were diverted to combat the pagans of their northern homelands.

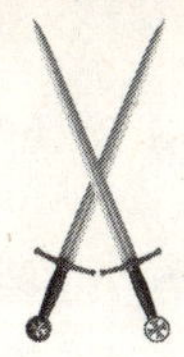

24

THE PASSION AND PAGEANTRY OF CRUSADING

Saladin died a few months after the Third Crusade in 1193, at which point the Ayyubid dynasty he had founded fractured. His many sons quarreled among each other, and by 1200, Saladin's brother Saphadin had usurped his nephews' inheritance and became sultan (all later Ayyubid sultans were his, not Saladin's, descendants).

Saphadin wasted no time in living up to the meaning of his name ("sword of the religion/Islam"). In 1202, Philip of Plessis, the master of the Temple, wrote a letter describing how the new sultan was "most cruelly" persecuting Christians "with all his troops from Egypt, Jerusalem and Damascus and even with a horde of pagans from beyond the Euphrates." The Christians were so surrounded by encroaching Muslims that, "if the enemies of the Christian cross left their castles in the evening they would be visible in front of our castles at the break of dawn."[1]

One of the military orders' responses was to create more, and refortify older, castles. Between 1217–1222, the Templars built the imposing castle of Atlit—also known as Pilgrim Castle (Château Pèlerin)[2]—which jutted out into the sea, just south of Haifa. Standing between Acre and

Jerusalem, it served its purpose: "From this new castle the infidels suffer considerable damage, and they are forced to abandon their cultivated lands as they flee in terror of God."[3]

During the construction of Atlit Castle, the Knights of the Temple and Hospital were back on the offensive, as chief participants of the next major venture for the sake of the Holy Land—history's Fifth Crusade (1217–1221).* The longtime belief championed by the military orders and other veterans that Egypt must first be conquered before Jerusalem can be secured was finally put into action.

A large crusading force of as many as thirty thousand men, including many newly arrived European pilgrims, assembled in Acre under the general leadership of John of Brienne (titular king of Jerusalem) and set sail for Egypt. On May 27, 1218, they cast anchor in the Nile Delta and quickly set up a fortified position outside the port city of Damietta. Long known among the Crusaders as "the key to all Egypt," Damietta was also immensely fortified, with three rings of walls, a moat between the first two walls, and twenty-eight strong towers.

The first task confronting the Crusaders was the massive chain stretched between the city walls and a fortified tower on an island in the Nile Delta garrisoned with three hundred Muslim fighters; it prevented access to the city's harbor. The assault began on June 24, when the Hospitallers, along with the forces of the duke of Austria, led a fierce charge against this chain tower. They sailed to the tower and, from their boats, set up ladders against its side, which they ascended one after the other. The attempt failed; the Muslims destroyed the ladders, thereby sending "to heaven soldiers who were vigorous and well-armed, wounded in body to the advantage of their souls, crowned with a glorious martyrdom," to quote an eyewitness. "The overjoyed Egyptians, mocking us violently, raised their voices, beating drums and sounding sackbuts; gloom and sadness invaded the Christians."[4]

* The Fourth Crusade is passed over because this book is not about the Crusades but rather the Templars and Hospitallers—and, to their credit, they played no part in that disastrous venture.

It is the Templars, however, whose martial exploits are repeatedly praised in the chronicles of eyewitness sources. For example, the bishop of Acre, James of Vitry, who accompanied the warrior monks on this expedition, "pays many tributes to the valor of the Templars at Damietta."[5] He likens them to those whom God "will encircle my house with" to "serve me in war." (Zechariah 9:8, CPDV).* Oliver of Paderborn, a participant and the chief source of the Fifth Crusade, especially singles them out for praise in his account. Thus, during an early and especially fierce Muslim sortie on the Crusader camp, Oliver reports that the Christians were overwhelmed and nearly routed—if not for "the courage of the Templars"[6]:

> On July 31 they [Muslims] brought forward all the power which they could muster, and after many assaults, finally crossed the ramparts against the army of the Temple [which, as usual, was stationed in the most vulnerable area]. Violently bursting the barriers, they put our foot soldiers to flight, to such an extent that the whole army of the Christians was then endangered. The knights and soldiery of France tried three times to drive them farther back beyond the rampart, but were unable to do so. The Saracens, when our wooden fortifications had been shattered, ranged lines of horsemen and foot soldiers within our walls; their shouts arose as they mocked us; the whole multitude prepared its retinue. Fear welled up in the Christians, but the spirit which came upon Gideon

* Even before Damietta, James of Vitry, as bishop of Acre, had nothing but praise for the Temple. A few excerpts follow from his sermon collection, *Sermones Vulgares*: "The brothers of a military order are appointed in order that they may defend Christ's Church with a physical sword, especially against those who are outside it, that is against the Saracens in Syria [and] against the Moors in Spain.... The Lord says of these, 'I will surround my house with those who will fight for me, going out and returning.' They go out in time of war and return in time of peace; they go out to action and return to contemplation. They go into war to fight, and return in peace to rest and to take time to pray: so that they are knights in battle, and like monks at home." (Jacques de Vitry, "Sermons to a Military Order.")

> animated the Templars. The Master of the Temple, with the Marshal and other brothers who were then present, made an attack through a narrow approach and manfully put the unbelievers to flight.[7]

Emboldened by the Templars, other Christians returned to or joined the fray, including the Teutonic Knights, slaughtering and scattering a great many Saracens:

> Thus on that day did God save those who hoped in Him through the courage of the Templars and of those who, having worked together with them, committed themselves to the conflict. A few of our men were killed or captured.[8]

The bitter assault on the chain tower continued for two months, until August 24, 1218, when the Crusaders finally managed to capture it thanks to various siege engines they had constructed, including a large wooden tower floating atop two ships lashed together. Oliver's eyewitness account of that day is a snapshot of the passion and pageantry that was medieval crusading:

> The Patriarch lay prostrate in the dust before the wood of the Cross; the clergy, standing barefoot, garbed in liturgical robes, cried out to heaven. The [Muslim] defenders of the tower with lances extended, smeared the front of the ladder with oil; next they added fire which caused it to burst into flames. And when the Christians who were on it ran to put out the fire, they pressed on the head of the ladder with their weight so much that the movable bridge placed near its edge was made to bend. The standard-bearer of the Duke of Austria fell from the ladder, and the Saracens captured the banner of the Duke. The Babylonians, thinking that they were victorious, shouted madly, disturbing the air with their clamor. The Christians, descending from their horses,

> threw themselves down in supplication, beating their hands; their faces streamed with tears of sorrow as they protested the pity they had for those who were enduring peril in the depth of the river, and the loss of all Christendom. In answer to this devotion of the people and the raising of their hands to heaven, divine kindness lifted the ladder, the tears of the faithful extinguished the fire; and thus our men, with renewed vigor, manfully fought with the defenders of the tower by means of swords, pikes, clubs, and other weapons. A certain young knight of the diocese of Liège was the first to ascend the tower; a certain young Frisian, holding a flail by which grain is usually threshed but which was prepared for fighting by an interweaving with chains, lashed out bravely to the right and to the left, knocked down a certain man holding the saffron standard of the Sultan and took the banner away from him. One came after another, vanquishing the enemy, who were known to be hard and cruel in their resistance. O ineffable kindness of God! O unexplainable joy of Christians! After lamentation and grief, after weeping and groaning, we saw joy and triumph. "We praise Thee, O God," "Blessed be the Lord God of Israel," and other canticles of thanksgiving to the heavens we sang for joy, our voices being mingled with tears and our praises repeated.[9]

Less than a week "after the tower had been captured…Saphadin, grown old with evil days and sickness," continues Oliver, "died and was buried in hell."[10] Once the chain was dropped, allowing access to Damietta, the real siege began. Saphadin's son al-Kamil, the new sultan of Egypt, took over its defense. The Muslims mounted several attempts to dislodge the encroaching Crusaders, to no avail. For example, on October 26, "the enemy at dawn invaded the camp of the Templars, and though causing us a slight loss, they were driven away by our alert horsemen, to the bridge which they had built a short distance from us in the upper part of the river; they were killed to the number of five hundred, as we learned from deserters."[11]

The Crusaders built many more vessels, along with floating towers and siege engines—including what was essentially an enormous floating fortress—for the assault on Damietta. During a sea storm one day in early November, a Templar ship, which was already closer to the city than most Christian ships, was "carried away by the violence of the current" and "cast over near the side of the city toward the enemy."[12] The Muslims did everything to seize or destroy it—grappling it with iron hooks and hurling Greek fire and other projectiles against it:

> Since they could not prevail on account of the bravery of the defenders, they eagerly climbed up the ship, and throwing themselves headlong into it, descended upon the Templars. When they had fought there for a long time, the ship at last was pierced (whether by the enemy or by our own men we do not know) and sought the depths, drowning Egyptians with Christians, so that the top of the mast scarcely appeared above the water. And as Samson "killed many more at his death than he had killed before in his life" [Judges 16:30, CPDV], so also those martyrs dragged into the abyss of the waters along with themselves more than they could have killed with swords.[13]

As should be evident by now, based on the many surviving anecdotes of the Templars' exploits, it appears that they were indeed "in the forefront of every fight, and on several occasions they saved the Christian army from destruction."[14] Thus, on February 5, 1219, the sultan, terrified of the encroachment of the Christians, fled his own camp near the city wall, which was quickly appropriated by the Christians—with the Templars, once again, in the van:

> But the land of the enemy was so muddy and so difficult to land upon because of the rather deep waters that the horses, being driven without saddles or riders, could

scarcely get up. The Templars, leaders in the ascent of the horses, having put up their banners, hurried to the city in a swift march, throwing down the wicked ones who came boldly from the gates to resist those who were advancing.[15]

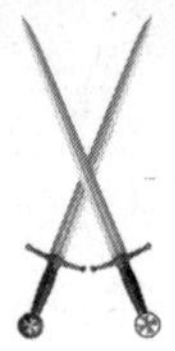

25

INTERFAITH DIALOGUE (MEDIEVAL STYLE)

Terrified by the aforementioned Templar-led advance against Damietta, on February 5, 1219, Sultan al-Kamil offered generous terms to the Crusaders: In exchange for their withdrawal from Egypt, he would restore Jerusalem to the Christians, establish a thirty-year truce, return all castles captured west of the Jordan River, and pay a tribute of between 15,000–30,000 gold bezants (sources differ).

John of Brienne was eager to accept this handsome offer, but the papal legate, Cardinal Pelagius, who by now shared leadership of the army with John, rejected it. In fact, "Pelagius might have consented had it not been for the opposition of the military orders. They claimed that it would be dishonorable to accept such a peace when all Egypt could be won by a little further effort, and they represented that the making of the proposal was a proof that al-Kamil feared the Christian might. Pelagius was convinced and he rejected the Sultan's offer."[1]

The military orders' reasoning was sound. Why would al-Kamil be so willing to relinquish what for a century had been the chief source of contention between Muslims and Christians—Jerusalem—if not because he believed that he was on the verge of defeat? But there was another reason why those Crusaders who had long lived with, and intimately knew, the enemy rejected this Muslim olive branch. In the words of James of Vitry,

> Many of our pilgrims judged these offers [by al-Kamil] important and proper to satisfy us, but those who knew by experience the fraud of these men [Muslims] who change unceasingly, and principally the Templars, the Hospitallers, and the Teutonic Knights, the legate, the Patriarch, the archbishops, the bishops, all the clergy and some of the pilgrims, made nothing of their false words, thinking that the Saracens had no other intention than, under the veil of a simulated peace, to disperse the army of Christ as soon as the pilgrims had retired.[2]

It is interesting to note that all those who mistrusted the Muslim offer as a ruse were of a distinctly Christian station—either brothers of an order or clergymen—whereas those who took the offer at face value, such as John of Brienne, were seculars. (Clearly, if Christians today are as "innocent as doves," their medieval counterparts were as "wise as snakes" [Matthew 10:16].)

Even if al-Kamil was sincere, from a long-term point of view—which is what the military orders ultimately cared for, unlike their myopic secular counterparts who would quit the Crusade once a particular goal had been reached, in this case, the (temporary) restoration of Jerusalem—having the Holy City without first subduing Egypt was pointless:

> The Orders had consistently maintained that Jerusalem could only safely be held by the Christians provided that the Muslim power was utterly broken, and for many years their declared policy had been the capture of Cairo. The Holy City might be ceded to the Christians [by al-Kamil for instance], but the Franks must rule in Cairo as well before Jerusalem would be secure from the aggression of Islam.[3]

So, the Crusade continued, though the Christians made little headway even as disease and dysentery, which had plagued their ranks from the start—killing the original Templar master, William of Chartres, soon after the siege began—continued to harry and reduce their numbers.

On August 29, 1219—now fourteen months since they anchored at Damietta—the Franks suffered a serious setback. After making a desperate attempt to storm a key fortress, some of the Crusaders "showed their timidity to the Saracens"[4] and fled, even as "the Patriarch, who was carrying the Cross, begged them earnestly to stand their ground, but in vain."[5] Chaos ensued as the emboldened Muslims pursued those who broke rank. Those Christians "who defended themselves as they stood their ground" were "wiped out" by the sudden and unexpected onrush of Muslims:

> But the King, with the Templars, and the House of the Teutons, and the Hospitallers of Saint John...sustained the attack of the pursuers. The King was almost burned with Greek fire; these men all served as a protection for those who were fleeing. As often as they showed their faces to the enemy, so often did the enemy flee, but as they gradually returned, these men had to sustain the blows and weapons of the enemy.[6]

In the end, many Christians—especially among the military orders that stood their ground—were massacred and beheaded:

> Thirty-three Templars were captured or killed with the Marshal of the Hospital of Saint John, and certain other brothers of the same House. Nor did the House of the Teutons escape without loss. The army of the Temple, which is usually first to assemble, was last to retreat. Therefore, when it arrived last at our ramparts, it stayed without, so that it might bring those who were before it back within the walls as soon as it was possible. Our persecutors finally returned to lead off the captives and to gather their spoils, presenting, as we afterward

> learned from a Saracen, five hundred heads of Christians to the Sultan. Gloom took possession of our men, but not despair.[7]

John the Baptist, it was said, received many companions on that day: "This great Saint," observed one chronicler, "who was decapitated because of his love for God, was joined by scores of fallen Crusaders, whose own faith in Christ had led them to the same fate."[8]

Although the Muslims certainly appeared to be holding their own, the sultan surprisingly reoffered his generous terms, this time adding a promise of funds to rebuild Jerusalem's fortifications, which had been dismantled earlier that year by his brother, al-Mu'azzam Isa, the emir of Damascus. Once again, John of Brienne was eager to accept, and once again Pelagius, backed by the military orders, refused. Not only did all their logic still hold, but now everyone was clinging to the hope that the future Emperor Frederick II—who had taken the cross as far back as July 15, 1215, in Aachen—was, as he had repeatedly promised, on his way with a massive army of fresh troops.

It was during this downtime that one of history's most memorable "interfaith dialogues" took place: Francis of Assisi, a mystic, ascetic, and itinerant preacher, whose pious exploits would go on to earn him sainthood, had arrived at Crusader-held Damietta in early August 1219 with the express purpose of converting the Muslims to Christ, both to save their souls and end the war: "Francis, like the crusaders," writes Christoph Maier, an expert on the saint, "wanted to liberate the holy places in Palestine from Muslim rule. What was different was his strategy.... He wanted their total submission to the Christian faith."[9]

Although the Crusaders warned Francis that the Saracens were "a mean people who thirst for Christian blood and attempt even the most brazen atrocities," the friar was determined to gain an audience with and convince al-Kamil of the truths of Christianity. On reaching the Muslim side, he and a companion were seized, beaten, mocked, and loaded with chains. Nonetheless, once dragged before the sultan, they professed Christ and urged al-Kamil to do the same; otherwise, "if you die while holding to your law [sharia], you will be lost; God will not accept your soul. For this reason we have come to you." Intrigued, "the Sultan called in his religious advisers, the imams. However, they refused to dispute with the Christians and instead insisted that they be killed [by beheading], in accordance with Islamic law."[10]

Al-Kamil rejected his religious advisers' demands—he was impressed by the cheek of these friars—and kept them around for some time, theologically debating them. At one point, the sultan tried to trap them with their own logic: If Jesus, he inquired, had taught Christians to "turn the other cheek" and "repay evil with good," why were "Crusaders…invading the lands of the Muslims?"

Francis quipped by also quoting Christ: "If your right eye causes you to stumble, gouge it out and throw it away. It is better for you to lose one part of your body than for your whole body to be thrown into hell." Francis then explained: "That is why it is just that Christians invade the land you inhabit, for you blaspheme the name of Christ and alienate everyone you can from His worship." In other words, the Christians had chosen the lesser of two evils: Fight Muslims rather than allow Muslims to persecute Christians.

In the end, the sultan, while not converting—one early source has him protest that "I could never do that. My people would stone me"—allowed Francis and his companion to return to Crusader-held Damietta unmolested, which itself was seen as a miracle.[11]

It is, of course, notable that even St. Francis, who nowadays is seen and even epitomized as some sort of passive "hippie," was both sympathetic to crusading and "made it clear during his discourse with the Sultan that he believed the Crusade itself was justified." As Maier writes, "Francis accepted the crusade as both legitimate and ordained by God, and he was quite obviously not opposed to the use of violence when it came to the struggle between Christians and Muslims."[12]

Indeed, Francis went so far as to believe that "it could be deduced from the Gospel [as opposed to just the Old Testament] that the crusade was a legitimate act of retribution for the Saracens' forcible conquest of Christian territory and their blasphemies against Christ."[13] As for the rewards of those who died fighting for Christ, Francis, who was fond of chansons such as the *Song of Roland*, once remarked that "paladins and valiant knights who were mighty in battle pursued the infidels even to death," and, as such, were "holy martyrs [who] died fighting for the Faith of Christ."[14]

In short, there would seem to be more in common between St. Francis and the military orders than between St. Francis and his contemporary namesake, the late Pope Francis.

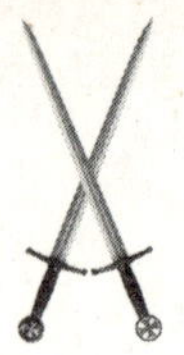

26

FROM VICTORY TO DEFEAT

Several more months passed without Frederick's arrival; the Crusaders continued to exert themselves, and, on November 5, 1219, finally managed to storm and take Damietta. On entering the city, it became clear why al-Kamil had been so generous in his offers: The city was a graveyard, littered with corpses.

> As we were entering it [Damietta], there met us an intolerable odor, a wretched sight. The dead killed the living. Man and wife, father and son, master and slave, killed each other by their odor. Not only were the streets full of the dead, but in the houses, in the bedrooms, and on the beds lay the corpses.... Almost eighty thousand, as we learned from the report of captives, perished in the city from the beginning of the siege to its end; all except those whom we found, healthy or ill, about three thousand in number. Three hundred of these, the more notable ones of both sexes, were kept for the ransom of our captives; some died after the victory, others were sold for a great price, and others were baptized and given to Christ.[1]

Although it took seventeen months of grueling warfare—not to mention the sufferings caused by constant pestilence and plague—the conquest of Damietta, "the key to all Egypt,"[2] was a great victory. And although many contributed to it, no one seems to have played a greater role than the military orders, especially the Templars, who "were of major importance in the encirclement of Damietta which led to its fall," and who are repeatedly singled out in Oliver of Paderborn's eyewitness account.[3] Even so, the Knights of St. John also played an important role, as evidenced by the words of the pope at the time, Honorius III:

> Our beloved sons the brothers of the Hospital and the knighthood of the Temple have been outstanding among all the Christians in the world, standing as defenders of the orthodox Christian faith, their hearts inflamed with the fire of the Holy Spirit, because they continually fight the Lord's battles to receive the martyr's crown; and because they also become for Christ's sake the servants of the poor, pressing on with the service of hospitality and unwearyingly exercising works of piety.[4]

Following the capture of Damietta, the exhausted Crusaders took a respite, waiting for the imminent arrival of Frederick and fresh troops—already more than a third of the original Crusaders had died from fighting or disease—before moving on to the next step: taking Cairo and becoming masters of Egypt.

No such respite awaited the military orders. If many of the Crusaders now became "lazy and effeminate,"[5] as Oliver charges, the restless Templars immediately raided the coastal town of Burlus and brought back a large quantity of spoils, including many pack animals, goats, and household utensils, to better accommodate the Crusaders.[6]

The Crusaders waited for months, but in all that time, Frederick never came. The master of the Temple, Peter of Montagut, sent a letter to England expressing how "we have long expected the arrival of the emperor and other nobles by whom we hope to be relieved, and on their arrival we hope to bring this business, which has commenced by the hands of many, to a happy termination." But, continued the prescient master more ominously, "if we are deceived in our hope of this assistance in the ensuing summer, which I hope will not happen, both countries, namely Syria and Egypt, and that which we have lately gained possession of as well as that which we have held for a long time, will be placed in a doubtful position."[7]

Finally, in May 1221—one-and-a-half years after the Crusaders had captured Damietta—Frederick, who had been crowned Holy Roman emperor on November 22, 1220, sent an army under the leadership of Duke Ludwig of Bavaria to join the Crusaders. It was far from the massive imperial army the Crusaders were expecting, but, because they had already wasted too much time holed up in Damietta, the Crusade resumed and the men were ready to march by mid-July 1221. According to Oliver, the army consisted of 1,200 knights (not counting sergeants and turcopoles), 4,000 archers, most being mercenaries, and an infantry force of unknown numbers.[8] Large numbers of noncombatants and women also followed the army. They all marched toward Cairo, along the eastern bank of the Nile, which was guarded and supplied by over six hundred Christian vessels.

By the end of July 1221, the Crusaders had reached a narrow triangle of land bounded by two branches of the Nile, just opposite the fortified city of Mansoura. As the army began to enter this precarious bottleneck, two of al-Kamil's brothers appeared at the heads of thousands of Muslim fighters from the east. Supported by the sultan's own navy coming down the Nile, they surrounded and harried the Crusaders. Trapped and cut off from their supplies, the Christians tried to manage but to no avail; on August 26, the command to retreat back to Damietta was given. As usual, last to leave were those original defenders of Christian pilgrims:

> The Templars, bringing up the rear at their own great risk, stayed constantly together as a protection for those who went ahead, as they were prepared with weapons. But those who went ahead, going into different roads, wandered through the darkness of the night like sheep astray. The Egyptians were informed of our flight by

> the fire and smoke and promptly followed after us. They reached us even more quickly and inflicted on the Christians losses which we cannot describe.[9]

On the following day, August 27, the surrounding Muslims unleashed all hell on the retreating army, which was already hampered by its many sick, wounded, and noncombatants. Surrounded from every corner, the army was nearly routed—if not for the Knights of the Temple and Hospital:

> Now there appeared the great and fearful cavalry of the Turks harassing us at the right; annoying galleys went up and down at the left; a phalanx of Negroes [black Ethiopians] going on foot and using the marshy places for a camp pressed upon us savagely from the rear; and also a wedge-shaped formation of enemies, coming from the front, denied us rest. In this contingency King John made an attack on the Turks who were opposite him, and returned to his own battle line. The Templars, with the Hospitallers of Saint John who at that time were united with them, did not tolerate the insolence of the Ethiopians. As they massacred them they made them jump onto the bank like frogs, and even drove them back when they wished to approach the bank on our side. Thus about a thousand of the great multitude, swimming away or suffering wounds, perished. On account of this [Muslim] misfortune our opponents retreated a little.[10]

Vexed and desperate to finish off the Christians, on the following night, August 28,

> the Egyptians broke open the floodgates and made the waters pour in upon the heads of those who were sleeping. Before daybreak, when darkness still covered the earth, the Ethiopian foot soldiers came...desiring to avenge

> their losses; they swarmed like locusts, and although for the greater part they were naked, they attacked our rear lines. You could see that our knights and their attendants were attempting flight in a closely packed throng; and the common people, being unarmed, displayed manifest timidity, but being blocked on all sides by the waters and the enemy, they had nowhere to flee. However, the Marshal of the Temple with his battle line which he was leading, raised his banner, turned upon those who were pursuing, and forced them to halt and retreat.[11]

Fight as they might, the chaos caused by inundating the Nile, which was already in full flood, and the sultan's and his brothers' full might, proved too much. As the master of the Temple, Peter of Montagut, later explained in a letter to England,

> At night we commenced our march, but the infidels cut through the embankments of the Nile, the water rushed along several unknown passages and ancient canals, and encompassed us on all sides. We lost all our provisions, many of our men were swept into the stream, and the further progress of our Christian warriors was forthwith arrested. The waters continued to increase upon us, and in this terrible inundation we lost all our horses and saddles, our carriages, baggage, furniture, and moveables, and everything that we had. We ourselves could neither advance nor retreat, and knew not whither to turn. We could not attack the Egyptians on account of the great lake which extended itself between them and us; we were without food, and being caught and pent up like fish in a net, there was nothing left for us but to treat with the sultan.[12]

Al-Kamil, eager to be rid of them, agreed: In exchange for the Crusader surrender of Damietta, the sultan would provide the Christians with much-needed food, safe withdrawal from Egypt, an eight-year truce, and the return of the True Cross. As proof of his sincerity, he swore that, if he did not observe everything agreed to, "may I be separated from…the society of Muhammad, and may I acknowledge the Father, the Son, and the Holy Ghost"—just as St. Francis had wanted.[13]

The Crusaders accepted, even as the military orders gnashed their teeth in rage and frustration. Giving up Damietta, their hard-won foothold in Egypt, was especially bitter for them. As Templar Master Peter expressed in his letter, "Had there been any reasonable chance of success" in defending Damietta, "we would rather have been thrust into perpetual imprisonment than have surrendered, to the shame of Christendom, this conquest to the infidels."[14]

And so, "on September 8, 1221, al-Kamil entered Damietta in triumph and the dispirited Crusaders went home. The Fifth Crusade had repeatedly been on the brink of fantastic success, yet it ended in humiliating failure. The one apparent minor victory, the return of the True Cross, never occurred. The Templars, it appears, were right: Al-Kamil did not have it."[15]

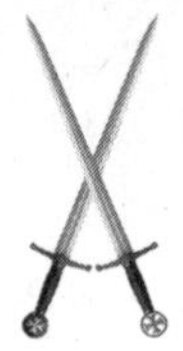

27

A MUSLIM-LOVING, ATHEISTIC EMPEROR

In 1229, that reluctant Crusader, Emperor Frederick II—who for years had vowed to go crusading until he was formally excommunicated—signed a ten-year truce with al-Kamil.* The sultan was again having problems with his relatives, especially his brother, al-Mu'azzam Isa, and temporarily restored Jerusalem's holy sites to the Christians in exchange for Frederick's allegiance. While on the surface it seemed like a great victory for Christendom, the truce was racked with problems.

For starters, the all-important Temple Mount—where the Templars' original and much-missed home was headquartered—was to remain under Muslim control. Frederick also pledged to support the Egyptian sultan in all his wars, including against those Christians outside the truce, such as those in Antioch and Tripoli. Worst of all, the Christians were forbidden from rebuilding the fortifications and walls of Jerusalem, which had been utterly razed by al-Mu'azzam, leaving them like sitting ducks. In short, "the agreement between the emperor and the

---

* Frederick's crusade is technically considered history's Sixth Crusade, though some historians, including the present one, deign not give it that appellation as it was primarily diplomatic and self-serving in nature and featured no fighting.

sultan represented the prostitution of the crusade and the Holy Land.... a legalistic victory achieved by a clever excommunicate [Frederick], not the rescue of Jerusalem from the stain of Islam. The Templars and Hospitallers solidly opposed the deal. They considered it a political sham, not a military victory. Unfortified Jerusalem would remain in Christian hands only as long as Muslim leaders wished it to be."[1]

Christian concerns were not unwarranted. "We have only conceded to them some churches and ruined houses," al-Kamil privately explained to fellow Muslims. "The sacred precincts, the venerated Rock and all the other sanctuaries to which we make our pilgrimages remain ours as they were; Muslim rites continue to flourish as they did before, and the Muslims have their own governor of the rural provinces and districts." Once the truce expired, by which time he hoped to be in a better position, al-Kamil further vowed to "purify Jerusalem of the Franks and chase them out."[2] After all, "He could seize the concessions back from them later," adds Ibn Wasil, a Cairo-based contemporary, "when he chose."[3]

Frederick's conduct in this affair, along with his many broken Crusader vows and promises—which continued to manifest for two decades *after* the Fifth Crusade*—were such that Christians widely saw him as being secretly allied with and aiding Muslims. Thus, after writing that "Frederick did not rebuild the churches of the holy places, nor did he strengthen the holy city [Jerusalem]," the anonymous Rothelin chronicler, who continued William of Tyre's chronicle, adds, "Such was his fondness for the unbelievers, so close his intimacy and friendship with them." The anonymous author went on to enumerate various

---

* During the Barons' Crusade (1239–1241), Frederick repeatedly promised to join the Crusaders if they postponed their war efforts. It was not long, however, before they concluded that his promise was, in the words of the Rothelin chronicler, "nothing but guile, trickery and deceit, sent because he was determined that the pilgrims should not cross the sea with his support to make war on the unbelieving Muslims who were his dear, close and intimate friends." (Shirley, *Crusader Syria*, 39). Even Muslims saw him as a "friend to Muslims," wrote Ibn Wasil (Gabrieli, *Arab Historians*, 268). "It was clear" to them, Ibn al-Jawzi added, that Frederick "was a materialist and that his Christianity was simply a game to him" (Alfred, *Encyclopedia of the Crusades*, 302).

examples—all of Frederick's closest servants and confidants were Muslim; he constantly showered Muslims with love, gifts, and praise, and in many ways followed Saracen customs and manners—before asserting, "for this reason the pope and all Christians who knew of this were very much afraid he had fallen in the unbelief of Muhammad's law."

In fact, Frederick's problem was that he was not a man of his, but rather our, times—indeed, something of what is referred to today as a "globalist elite." As the chronicler continues,

> Others, however, maintained that he believed none of it, and that whenever he felt like it he would say privately that he had not yet decided which faith to destroy and which to keep as the best. He also said, they alleged, that Moses had fooled the Jews, Jesus Christ the Christians, and Muhammad the Saracens.[4]

At any rate, no sooner was the truce enacted than roaming bands of Muslims—"lone wolves" reportedly acting against al-Kamil's wishes—attacked Jerusalem's Christians, as the Knights of the Temple and Hospital who strongly opposed Frederick's agreement with al-Kamil had warned. In the words of the Rothelin chronicler,

> Great was the danger in which Frederick left the Christians of the Holy Land in Jerusalem, for the city was completely open and unprotected. The Saracens had demolished all the fortifications.... Neither the emperor Frederick nor his deputy did anything to repair the city's defenses. The Saracens in neighbouring towns saw this clearly, and one morning [in 1229] crowds of villainous Saracens gathered and entered Jerusalem, intending to kill the Christians. The Christians defended themselves vigorously, killing more than 500 and losing only one man, an Englishman.[5]

Moreover, because they adamantly "refused to accept the Christian dominion," roaming bands of Muslims regularly "swept down on pilgrims on the way from the coast to Jerusalem. On one occasion ten thousand Christians were trapped and slaughtered by these marauders. At the same time, the Prince of Damascus invaded the Christian lands. The succession of minor engagements was a constant drain on the military orders."[6]

Needless to say, it was business as usual in those regions of the Holy Land unaffected by the ten-year truce. Thus, in 1237, William of Montferrat, Templar preceptor of Antioch, being "desirous of extending the Christian territories, to the honor and glory of Jesus Christ, besieged a fortress of the infidels" that was too close for comfort. "He refused to retreat before a superior force, and was surrounded and overwhelmed; a hundred knights of the Temple and three hundred cross-bowmen were slain, together with many secular warriors, and a large number of foot soldiers."[7]

Even so, the old warrior code continued to animate the warriors of the Lord to great feats, and "the Preceptor of Antioch, before he was slain, sent sixteen infidels to hell." Similarly, the standard-bearer, an English Templar named Reginald, "performed prodigies of valor. He was disabled and covered with wounds, yet he unflinchingly bore the beauséant, or war-banner, aloft with his bleeding arms into the thickest of the fight, until he at last fell dead upon a heap of his slaughtered comrades." Once news of this disaster reached England, "the Templars and the Hospitallers, eagerly prepared to avenge the blood of their brethren so gallantly poured forth in the cause of Christ," writes Matthew Paris, and sent men and money "to the succor of the Holy Land."[8]

The facts speak for themselves: Frederick, who technically "restored" portions of a dilapidated and defenseless Jerusalem to the Christians, was widely hated for his duplicitous and cynical behavior—to the point of being pelted with dung by the people of Acre as he fled the Holy Land—whereas the more honest but unsuccessful military orders continued to be widely honored and respected. Thus, when, in 1231, Frederick tried to avenge himself on the military orders by confiscating their estates in Sicily, Pope Gregory IX chided him in a letter that ultimately underscores their worth: "You must not worry the Hospitallers and Templars, molesting those through whom the [Holy] Land has up to this time been governed among many difficulties, and without whom it is believed that it would be in no way governable."[9]

The usual hostilities and internecine raids were actually exacerbated by the recovery of Jerusalem, as it led to a resumption of mass Christian pilgrimages from Europe, which in turn forced the military orders to resume their original duties—the Templars protecting and the Hospitallers serving Christian pilgrims traveling through hostile territory.

It was in this context that the mighty Templar castle of Safed was rebuilt. Its story, which sheds much light on the overall value and function of these Templar and Hospitaller castles that once dotted the holy landscape, is worth recounting.

A smaller castle originally stood in its place in Upper Galilee. In 1168, King Amalric gave it to the Templars for the express purpose of protecting pilgrims from Turkic raids, that is, "to shield the Christians against the Saracens,"[10] to quote an account written around 1260, which adds, "to the protection of the faithful and destruction and routing of the infidels...this castle of Safed was intended principally."[11]

Twenty years later, as a result of Hattin, the castle fell to Saladin's armies in 1188. In 1219, while the Crusaders were besieging Damietta, al-Mu'azzam resorted to his usual policy of razing the walls and fortifications of those cities and castles under his jurisdiction to prevent their potential capture and reuse by future Crusaders. In 1240, as part of negotiations, Safed—now in complete ruins—passed back into Crusader hands.

That same year, Benedict of Alignan, bishop of Marseille, visited the site. He was surprised to discover a few destitute Templars still living, whether from devotion or homelessness, within the castle's ruins. Later, during his travels, he discovered that local Muslims were still haunted by the shadow of Safed and lived in dread that it might one day be resurrected and manned by the Knights of the Temple. "In short," continues the anonymous author who was probably in Benedict's entourage, "he discovered from common gossip that there existed no other fortress in that land from which so much damage could be inflicted on the Saracens, so much help brought to Christians, and Christendom so enlarged."[12]

So while in Acre, Benedict paid a visit to the Templar master, Armand of Périgord, who was then sick in bed. The bishop implored him to rebuild Safed, stressing "what he had seen and heard in Damascus.... Namely...how great was the fear and trembling of the Saracens" in regard to Safed. With much sighing and groaning, the weary master patiently explained to the good bishop what an immense cost and laborious project it would be to rebuild the castle. "Master, you rest in your bed,"[13] Benedict continued, and asked simply for an opportunity to speak before a council of the brethren, which Armand granted for the following day. Once standing before the Knights of the Temple, the bishop began by reminding them of their original function, as well as the uncompromising indefatigability of the great men who founded their order:

> Lords, I understand that your Order was founded for a specific purpose by holy knights [Hugh of Payns, Godfrey of St. Omer, et al.] who devoted themselves entirely to the protection of the Christians and the attacking of the Saracens. Because they showed themselves energetic and faithful in these aims, the Lord has exalted and enhanced your Order in the eyes of the Apostolic See, kings and princes. Today your Order is extremely famous and reputed with God and men. It seems to me that you ought to do now what was done then by those holy knights, since, when I was at Damascus, several Saracens told me that there was nothing they feared as much as the building of Safed, because they consider that once that has been done the gates of Damascus will be closed. I myself have seen and inspected the environs of the place, and it is public knowledge that no castle or fortress can be built in this land to defend Christendom and harry the Saracen infidels in the way that Safed would. Consequently, as your faithful friend, mindful of the glory of God, the salvation of souls and the promotion of your Order, I ask, advise and request

> that as strong knights, devoted and faithful to God, you look back at the example of those holy knights who first founded your Order, and following the example of your predecessors you devote yourselves and your goods to the building of Safed, which will always be such a great threat to the infidel and such a great protection for the faithful.[14]

Inspired by this exhortation to emulate their forbears, the Templars agreed; and, because "the decision to build the castle of Safed brought enormous joy to the house of the Temple, the city of Acre, and to the people of the Holy Land," before long, everyone could be found digging and building at Safed—including Benedict, his monks, and a great many pilgrims.[15] Atop these many volunteers were over a thousand dedicated workers. Three years and 40,000 bezants later—a considerable sum—the massive castle of Safed was complete in 1243. It was significantly larger than the original and could house 2,200 soldiers in time of war. To this day, the "ruins of this famous castle crowning the summit of a lofty mountain, torn and shattered by earthquakes, still present a stupendous appearance."[16]

Writing some twenty years later, Bishop Benedict's secretary confirmed that it was proving its worth—to both Christian bodies and souls:

> Those people who know that before the construction of the castle, the Saracens, Bedouins, Khwarazmians and Turcomans frequently launched attacks as far as Acre and through other Christian territories, now know by experience just how useful and necessary it is for the whole of Christendom and how dangerous it is for the infidels. But with its construction, Safed has become a bulwark, an obstacle that dissuades people from making attacks from the River Jordan to Acre except in enormous numbers. It is now safe for pack-animals and carts to travel from Acre to Safed while agriculture and cultivation of land can be pursued in peace. However, from

> the River Jordan to Damascus the land remains uncultivated like a desert because the Saracens are in fear of the castle of Safed, from which the knights of the Temple make important sorties as far as Damascus, causing destruction and havoc. There they have achieved many miraculous victories over the enemies of the faith.... But the one usefulness that transcends all others, and hence should not be forgotten, is that now the faith of our Lord Jesus Christ can be preached without hindrance in all the above-named places; the blasphemy of Muhammad can be publicly disproved and annihilated, something that was impossible before the building of Safed. The Saracens do not dare openly proclaim the blasphemies of Muhammad as they used to before against the faith of our Lord Jesus Christ. Now, too, it is possible to visit such famous places in the jurisdiction of Safed as the cistern of Joseph.[17]

Even Muslims confirmed Safed's impact; for the fourteenth century Egyptian chronicler Ibn al-Furat, the castle was "an obstruction in the throat of Syria and a blockage in the chest of Islam."[18]

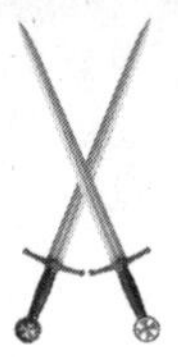

28

"ENORMITIES TOO HORRIBLE TO RELATE"

In 1244, the sultan of Egypt, al-Salih Ayyub, the offspring of al-Kamil and a Nubian concubine, hired the Khwarazmians—a particularly savage and sadistic Muslim Turcoman tribe notorious for torturing captives and mutilating the dead—to assault Jerusalem. The Crusaders were then allied with the Ayyubids of Syria, enemies of the Egyptian sultan, their cousin. However, because the defenseless city was in no shape to withstand an attack from a horde of Khwarazmians, about six thousand Christians (men, women, and children) fled the Holy City to the coast.[1]

Although they had to pass through Muslim territory, the Christians "relied confidently on the truce" they had "with the unbelievers." But when the Muslims saw them, "they kept no faith, no oath, no truce they had made with the Christians, but gathered from all sides and attacked them. Some they killed and others they took away, bound, and sold them in markets and towns." Those Christians who managed to elude their allies-in-name-only "escaped one danger only to run into another, for the Khwarazmians encountered them on the Ramla plain where they attacked and massacred them. In this way, all those [six thousand] men and women who left Jerusalem were lost, for no more than 300 reached Christendom, and these were in a pitiable condition."[2]

Meanwhile, more atrocities were being committed in Jerusalem, which the Khwarazmians easily captured on August 11, 1244. "In the church of the Sepulchre," the Rothelin chronicle continues, "they found Christians which had refused to leave with the others. These they disemboweled before the Sepulchre of Our Lord, and they beheaded the priests who were vested and singing mass at the altars." To further "disgrace and dishonor [the] Christians," the Khwarazmians desecrated the Sepulchre, destroying much of it, and, underscoring the religious hostility animating them, sent its marble columns "to Muhammad at Mecca as a sign of victory." They even exhumed the bones and remains of Christian kings "and scattered them about. In different ways they soiled and made filthy...all the holy places of the city and in all the Holy Land itself, where they committed far more acts of shame, filth, and destruction against Jesus Christ and the holy places and Christendom than all the unbelievers who had been in the land had ever done in peace or war."[3]

In short, the atrocities that had led up to and precipitated the First Crusade 150 years earlier* were being reenacted—this time inside Jerusalem itself.

Delighted by this development and seeing his opportunity, the Egyptian sultan, al-Salih Ayyub, sent his own army to augment the Khwarazmians in an effort to further annihilate the Christians. The

---

* Compare the following recounting of Pope Urban II at the Council of Clermont, 1095: "They [Muslim Turks] have completely destroyed some of God's churches and they have converted others to the uses of their own cult [mosques]. They ruin the altars with filth and defilement. They circumcise Christians and smear the blood from the circumcision over the altars or throw it into the baptismal fonts. They are pleased to kill others by cutting open their bellies, extracting the end of their intestines, and tying it to a stake. Then, with flogging, they drive their victims around the stake until, when their viscera have spilled out, they fall dead on the ground. They tie others, again, to stakes and shoot arrows at them; they seize others, stretch out their necks, and try to see whether they can cut off their heads with a single blow of a naked sword. And what shall I say about the shocking rape of women?" (Brundage, *Crusades*, 18–19).

two forces met somewhere near the village of Forbie in northeast Gaza, where the vastly outnumbered Crusaders prepared to make a final stand against the Islamic horde. The Christian army's center was primarily made up of Templars; its left of Hospitallers, Teutonic Knights, and the knights of St. Lazarus; and its right of their Muslim allies. Once battle commenced on the morning of October 17, 1244, the Muslim right only "faintly opposed" the first onslaught, writes the Egyptian chronicler al-Maqrizi, before they "instantly fled."[4] Although the battle lasted two days, "the main burden was borne by the Templars, the Hospitallers and the Teutonic Knights."[5] These men, "who had been enraged to extremity by the savage excesses" of these new Muslim invaders, "fought with desperate valor," only to be "overwhelmed by tenfold numbers, and almost annihilated."[6] In the words of the Rothelin chronicler,

> [The Christians] were very few compared with their enemies. Vigorously the two forces attacked each other; very sharp and cruel was the encounter. It was hard to believe that so few could fight so well against so many unbelievers. Then the Khwarazmians and the men of Babylon made a joint attack and at last ours could not stand against such overwhelming numbers.[7]

Some seven thousand Crusaders were slaughtered at Forbie. The sixty-six-year-old master of the Temple, Armand of Périgord, was killed in battle or died in captivity; the master of the Hospital was captured and imprisoned until being ransomed four years later; and every leper knight of St. Lazarus was slaughtered.[8] According to another contemporary chronicle, the Eracles, "more than 30,000 were killed" in total by the Khwarazmians, "men, women, and children…for these people took no prisoners, all they wanted to do was kill."[9]

Meanwhile, over in Cairo, the devastation wrought by the Turcomans was being acclaimed; Sultan al-Salih Ayyub himself led celebrations to the "sound of drums and trumpets," and the heads of the Christian slain were sent to adorn that city's gates.[10] As for the Muslims in Syria, "it was a calamitous day, the like of which had not happened in [early] Islam nor in the time of Nur al-Din and Saladin," lamented

Sibt ibn al-Jawzi[11]—not least as Muslims had deigned to fight under Christian banners with crosses "above their heads...as for the lord of Homs...he began to weep, saying, 'I knew when we departed under the crosses of the Franks that we would not prosper.'"[12]

The remaining, and now terrified, Christian forces holed themselves up in their fortresses along the coast and sent frantic letters to Europe begging for aid. Among these was a letter signed by the vice-master of the Temple, and patriarch Robert of Jerusalem, on November 5, 1244. It comprehensively describes what befell the Christians following the "sudden and unexpected arrival of the Khwarazmians"[13] and was read at a general council assembled by Pope Innocent IV at Lyons. Once "the cruel barbarian," the missive begins, had descended on the Holy Land, "we called in the assistance of the sultans of Damascus and Carac, who were bound to us by treaty...[and] they promised and solemnly swore to give us their entire aid, but the succor came slow and tardy; the Christian forces were few in number, and were obliged to abandon the defense of Jerusalem."[14] After describing the horrible slaughter of thousands of Christians—many of whom were women, children, monks, and nuns—the letter continues,

> The...perfidious savages having penetrated within the gates of the holy city of Israel, the small remnant of the faithful left therein, consisting of children, women, and old men, took refuge in the church of the sepulchre of our Lord. The Khwarazmians rushed to that holy sanctuary; they butchered them all before the very sepulchre itself, and cutting off the heads of the priests who were kneeling with uplifted hands before the altars, they said one to another, "Let us here shed the blood of the Christians on the very place where they offer up wine to their God, who they say was hanged here."... [They went on to destroy the Holy Sepulchre] utterly battering to pieces the marble shrine which was built around that holy sanctuary. They have defiled, with every abomination of which they were capable, Mount Calvary, where

> Christ was crucified, and the whole Church of the Resurrection. They have taken away, indeed, the sculptured columns which were placed as a decoration before the sepulchre of the Lord, and as a mark of victory, and as a taunt to the Christians, they have sent them to the sepulchre of the wicked Muhammad [in Mecca].[15]

The letter lists a number of other Christian holy sites—Mount Zion, the temple of the Lord, and the church of Bethlehem that was built atop the "place of the nativity of our Lord"—all of which "they have polluted with enormities too horrible to be related, far exceeding the iniquity of all the Saracens."[16]

That this letter is reminiscent of the aforementioned Rothelin chronicle's account is less a reflection of "scribal duplication" and more a reflection of the traumatic impact and deep imprint the Khwarazmian invasion had on Christians everywhere—for all of these atrocities and more were reported far and wide and remain extant in various contemporary documents. Indeed, even wholly independent Arabic sources recount the same devastation. After writing that the Khwarazmians "advanced to Jerusalem, took it by storm, and put all the Christians to the sword," the Muslim historian al-Maqrizi repeated the same tale of woe: "The women and girls, having suffered every insult from a brutal disorderly soldiery, were loaded with chains. They destroyed the church of the holy Sepulchre; and when they found nothing among the living, to glut their rage, they opened the tombs of the Christians, took out the bodies, and burnt them."[17]

The letter read at Lyons also recounts the mustering of the Crusaders, chief among them the Templars and Hospitallers, and gives more details concerning the Battle of Forbie:

> Those holy warriors, boldly rushed in upon the enemy, but the Saracens who had joined us, having lost many of their men, fled, and the warriors of the cross were left alone to withstand the united attack of the Egyptians and Khwarazmians. Like stout champions of the Lord, and true defenders of catholicity, whom the same faith

> and the same cross and passion make true brothers, they bravely resisted; but as they were few in number in comparison with the enemy, they at last succumbed, so that of the convents of the house of the chivalry of the Temple, and of the house of the Hospital of Saint John at Jerusalem, only thirty-three Templars and twenty-six Hospitallers escaped.[18]

Those able to escape, including the vice-master of the Temple himself, "fled half dead" until they reached Acre and "found that city and the adjoining province filled with sorrow and mourning, misery and death. There was not a house or a family that had not lost an inmate or a relation.... The Khwarazmians have now pitched their tents in the plain of Acre, about two miles from the city. The whole country, as far as Nazareth and Safed, is overrun by them, so that the churches of Jerusalem and the Christian kingdom have now no territory, except a few fortifications, which are defended with great difficulty and labor by the Templars and Hospitallers...."[19]

For Christians, this was a disaster of apocalyptic proportions, arguably worse than Hattin. If that battle directly led to the Muslim reconquest of Jerusalem, Forbie seemed to mark the total annihilation of Crusader power in the Holy Land.

As the death and destruction visited upon the Christians of the Holy Land by the Khwarazmians was unprecedented, a Crusade was immediately called for, and many in Europe (nominally) took the cross. But 1244 was not 1095; if the First Crusade witnessed the whole of Europe shake to the march of hundreds of thousands of pilgrims, the Crusade to redress these latest atrocities was only embraced by the most committed, namely, King Louis IX of France, better known today as St. Louis.* On hearing of Forbie, he took the cross—from his sickbed no less, where he lay dying and dreaming of Jerusalem—and began vast preparations, which took years to accomplish.

---

* For a more through treatment of Louis IX and his Crusades against Islam, see Chapter 5 of *Defenders of the West.*

Meanwhile, in the Holy Land, the new master of the Temple, William of Sonnac—"a discreet and circumspect man, who was also skilled and experienced in the affairs of war," [20] to quote Matthew Paris—ordered the commanderies in Europe to pour forth all their manpower and resources to the Holy Land; and "the Pope praises both the Templars and Hospitallers for the zeal and energy displayed by them in sending out the newly-admitted knights and novices with armed bands and a large amount of treasure to the succor of the holy territory."[21]

The immediate goal was to neutralize the savage Khwarazmians, who were still running amok in the Holy Land. Now regrouped and replenished with fresh manpower, the knights of the military orders set to work:

> [By 1247] the Khwarazmians were annihilated; they were cut up in detail by the Templars and Hospitallers, and were at last slain to a man. Their very name perished from the face of the earth, but the traces of their existence were long preserved in the ruin and desolation they had spread around them. The Holy Land, although happily freed from the destructive presence of these barbarians, had yet everything to fear from the powerful sultan of Egypt, with whom hostilities still continued.[22]

As for Louis IX, after much deliberation with the military orders, the French king decided to begin where the nearly successful Fifth Crusade had left off—Damietta—and on the same standard logic (before Jerusalem could be secured, Egypt must be subdued). Before he set off, the arrogant sultan of Egypt, still exulting over the devastation he had wrought among the Christians, sent a vain message warning Louis to forfend: "No one has ever attacked us without feeling our superiority," al-Salih boasted. "Recollect the conquests we have made from the Christians; we have driven them from the lands they possessed; their strongest towns have fallen under our blows."[23]

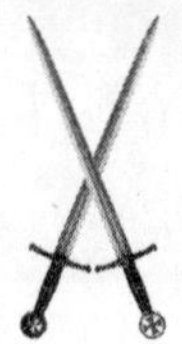

29

"COME, LET US GO TO OUR DEATHS" IN EGYPT

By June 4, 1249, King Louis IX's Christian fleet had reached and was anchored on the west bank of the Nile, across from Damietta. Before attempting the shore, all the men—who had already suffered from sea-storms, death, and disease during their seaborne trek—confessed their sins, made their wills, "and put their affairs in order for death, if Our Lord Jesus Christ so willed it."[1] On June 6, the Crusaders, to a loud battle cry, furiously stormed the shore. Waiting for them, the Muslims "attacked our men so furiously that it seemed they would all be killed and cut to pieces. But ours did not shift from the seashore but fought back with such vigor that they seemed to have lost nothing at sea, no danger, no trouble or distress, all was through the strength of Jesus Christ."[2] The Christians made quick work of and routed the Muslims.

Rather than fall back on and guard Damietta, the terrified Muslim soldiery galloped away. On seeing them flee and not wanting to face, in the words of Muslim chroniclers, "the fury of the Christians,"[3] the garrison in Damietta, followed by its entire citizenry, recalling the terrors they or their forbears had suffered thirty years earlier, fled the city under the cover of night—though not before cutting the throats or "dash[ing] out the brains" of most of their Christian slaves and prisoners, many of whom were captured during the Fifth Crusade.[4]

A few escaped captives and slaves, crying "blessed is he that cometh in the name of the Lord,"[5] intercepted the Crusaders on their march to Damietta, which the latter were astonished to find completely deserted: "In its prison were found fifty-three Christian slaves, who had been there, they said, thirty-two years. They were released and taken to the king. They said the Saracens had fled on the Saturday night, and that they were telling each other about the Christians, saying that 'the pigs had come.'"[6]

Considering that it had taken a year-and-a-half for the Fifth Crusaders to take Damietta, its collapse in just one day was deemed a miracle—certainly a good augur for the Crusade. In a brief note to the preceptor of England, William of Sonnac shared this "happy and joyful news" of how, after "having utterly put to flight the heathen host, Damietta…has been captured, not through our deserts, nor by armed might, but through the workings of God's power and grace. You should know in addition that the lord King plans with God's grace to head towards Alexandria or Babylonia, in order to liberate our brothers and several others who are kept in captivity and, with the Lord's aid, to return the entire country to Christian worship."[7]

This latter point about "return[ing] the entire country [of Egypt] to Christian worship" is noteworthy and underscores that the Crusaders saw not just the Holy Land but much of the "Muslim world" for what it was—long-conquered Christian territory also in need of liberating from Islam. Such knowledge was widespread and hardly limited to the Temple; similar remarks were made in letters written by other Europeans—including Louis's mother, Blanche, and the knight Gui—immediately following the capture of Damietta.

While the Christians exulted over Damietta, the Muslims of Egypt saw it as a "terrible disaster, the like of which had never happened," writes Ibn Wasil.[8] Fear gripped the Egyptian populace; the ease with which the Christians had conquered Damietta, the people lamented, may well result "in their conquest of Egypt and even (Allah forbid) of the whole of Islam."[9] And so, as often happened whenever Muslims suffered setbacks at the hands of Crusaders, and by way of "collective punishment," the followers of Muhammad proceeded to vent their anger on whichever Christians they could get a hold of, which in Egypt meant the indigenous Copts.

Indeed, once the Crusaders had reached the shores of Damietta, "Muslims throughout the region precipitated popular actions against native Egyptian Christians, including the desecration of Christian holy space."[10] (Needless to say, the same thing happened during the Fifth Crusade, which "had roused all the Muslim fanaticism from which the Copts suffered." Then, Muslim armies marching toward Damietta "destroyed every church by which they passed; even the church of St. Mark in the suburbs of Alexandria was leveled to the ground."[11])

On November 20, 1249, the Christian army left Damietta and marched south along the Nile's eastern bank for Mansoura; a convoy of supply-carrying boats sailed alongside it. Due to the many watercourses and canals, which were often guarded by the enemy, the journey was fraught with difficulties. As in the Fifth Crusade, the Templars were always in the van, confronting the brunt of whatever the Muslims had in store for them. At one point, they damned and created a waterway for the Crusaders to cross over; but just then, on December 6, the sultan sent five hundred of his best horsemen to prevent the crossing and hamper the Crusaders' march. Louis commanded his men not to engage the enemy but to brave the crossing—and the downpour of arrows—as best they could. According to Joinville, Louis's close confidant and best source for the Seventh Crusade,

> Now it happened that when the host began to move forward, and the Saracens saw that no attack was to be made upon them—and they knew by their spies that the king had forbidden it—they waxed bold and attacked the Templars who formed the van; and one of the Turks bore a knight of the Temple to the earth, right before the horse-hoofs of brother Renaud of Vichiers, who was then Marshal of the Temple. When the marshal saw this, he

> cried to his brother Templars: "Out on them for God's sake! I cannot brook this!" He struck his spurs into his horse, and all the [Templar] host with him.

The Templars so utterly tore up the Muslim horsemen that, of the five hundred, "not one of them escaped, but all perished. Many of them had got into the river, and were drowned."[12]

This incident was much extolled among the Crusaders, as evidenced by its inclusion in many of the contemporary accounts, one of which, the Eracles, puts the number of slain Muslims at one thousand.[13] In the Rothelin chronicle's rendering,

> Six hundred of the bravest and most experienced Turks, the best armed and mounted of all their army, were sent at daybreak to charge our vanguard. So fast and fiercely they came, it seemed they must defeat our whole host. But the Templars and the others of ours in the vanguard were not in the least startled or dismayed. Steadily they received them on the edges of their swords, fierce and sharp was the conflict while it lasted. Soon it was over, the defeated Turks fled back to their ambush and from there they fled all together to their host. Three hundred Turks were found killed, but only two Christians.[14]

So it went until the Crusaders reached the outskirts of Mansoura on December 21, 1249. There they found the same Muslim soldiery that had abandoned Damietta reinforced and encamped before the city, which was further blocked to the Crusaders by a tributary of the Nile. For over a month, the Christians tried to build causeways, but the enemy bombarded and burned them all. On January 20, the Muslims launched an especially savage sortie, during which the military orders again proved their mettle:

> The Saracens very suddenly and in great strength… attacked a section defended by the Hospitallers, and another by the brothers of Our Lady of the Germans

> [Teutonic Knights]. Both gave them a pitiless welcome. While it lasted it was a great and bitter conflict. Many heroic deeds, many fine blows and feats of courage were performed on both sides. In the end the Turks' double attack was beaten off. Very many were killed. Ours pursued them to the main branch of the Nile, overthrowing and cutting them down. In terror of death, they plunged into the water. Very many Saracens were slain and drowned on that day.... The Hospitallers lost eleven of their brothers in this battle. The Brothers of Our Lady of the Germans did not lose more than four, but were highly praised and commended that day throughout the host.[15]

It was only when "Saracen traitors" revealed,[16] in exchange for rich reward, a fordable area to Mansoura four miles downstream that the Crusade managed to progress. Under the cover of darkness in the early morning of February 8, 1250, Louis dispatched the Templars and a few Hospitallers with his younger brother Robert the count of Artois and his men; a small English contingent led by William Longespee, the earl of Salisbury, brought the rear. Their mission was to ford and secure the landing for the main army, which would follow later under Louis's command.

It was a difficult and slippery crossing, and many men drowned in the damp darkness; but the army, with the Templars in the van, managed to make it to the other side. Rather than wait for Louis, however, his younger brother decided to seize the initiative and attack the unsuspecting enemy camp. The Muslims were taken unawares and, after some resistance, routed.

Elated by this easy victory, Robert threw all caution to the wind and ordered the Crusaders to advance onto Mansoura itself. At this point, William of Sonnac, the more experienced Templar master, commended the young count for his daring but urged him to stick to the original plan and await Louis. The men and their horses were exhausted and still much too outnumbered to try an assault on Mansoura itself. The count became wroth and hurled what had become popular stock criticisms against the military orders since the one-eyed Templar had slaughtered the Assassin envoys in 1173:

> Oh ancient treachery of the Temple! Oh old sedition of the Hospitallers! Oh fraud long concealed, now you burst out openly in our midst. This is what we predicted and foreseen for a long time...that this whole eastern land would have been captured long ago if our forces had not been impeded by the fraud of the Temple and the Hospital and of others who claim to be religious. For the Templars fear, and the Hospitallers and their accomplices are afraid, that if the land is subdued to the Christian faith their dominion, which they feed with ample revenues, will expire.[17]

Dismayed and not a little wounded by these accusations, Knights of the Temple and Hospital responded:

> For what purpose, O noble count, did we receive the religious habit [meaning renounce the world and lead a life of asceticism, chastity, and war]? Surely not to overturn the Church of Christ and to lose our souls through plotting treachery? Far be it from us, far be it from us, no, far be it from every Christian![18]

Others of Robert's entourage jumped in, goading him on: "My lord," they cried, "don't you see that the Turks are beaten and running? Won't it be wicked and cowardly if we don't pursue our enemies?"[19] Now even William Longespee interjected, insisting that they listen to the Templar master, whose experience in Eastern affairs was much greater than their own. For his trouble, the Englishman was also treated to a volley of insults from Robert, who now in a paroxysm was "bellowing and swearing disgracefully, as is the French custom," to quote chronicler Matthew Paris.[20]

Such insults and accusations of cowardice—which culminated with Robert suggesting that the Templars stay behind while he and his men pursue the fleeing enemy—finally pushed the already irritated master over the edge, prompting him to cry to his brethren, "Lift up our banner, then—let us go to our death!"[21] After describing the master as "a good knight, valiant, hardy, wise in war and clear-sighted,"[22] the Rothelin chronicle ascribes to him a longer, more restrained response: "My lord, neither I nor my brothers are afraid. We shall not stay behind, we shall ride with you. But let me tell you that none of us expect to come back, neither you nor ourselves."[23]

So the outnumbered and exhausted Crusaders charged into the heart of heavily populated Mansoura, hacking and hewing at all and sundry. Although they persevered and managed to even reach the sultan's palace, they were confronted by the full might of the city's garrison of Mamluks. The narrow city streets further impeded fighting and maneuvering for the mounted knights, and Muslim citizens joined the fray by hurling missiles from the windows and porches of their homes. In short, "the Saracens could hardly believe our men engaged in so stupid a pursuit.... They had them at their mercy, as they clearly saw."[24]

The Christians were overwhelmed and annihilated. Louis's brother Robert and William Longespee were both killed. Of the original 280 Templars to charge Mansoura, only the master—who lost an eye fighting—and less than a handful of others, along with one Hospitaller, managed to cut their way back to Louis's army, which by now had crossed over the causeway near Mansoura.

Emboldened by their great victory, and now in a frenzied bloodlust, thousands of Muslim fighters poured forth out of Mansoura to attack the rest of the recently arrived Crusaders. Seeing this great horde descending upon them, the saint-king, sounding more like a Templar master, "exhorted them strongly, and told them they must not be afraid of this great number of unbelievers riding towards them, for Our Lord Jesus Christ, for whose sake they were here, was stronger and mightier than any other."[25] The Christians responded with valor:

> With swords and broadswords they killed and brought down many, but there were such multitudes of Turks that this seemed little or nothing. For every Turk killed, another at once appeared, fresh and vigorous.... It was amazing to hear and to see how closely they harassed our men on every side. Many of ours who fought in this battle said and affirmed afterwards that if the king had not behaved with such courage and energy, they all would have been taken and killed. Never in this battle did the king turn his face away or try to keep himself safe from the Turks. He exhorted and comforted our people and gave them fresh heart; fiercely did they defend themselves, overwhelmed as they were and subjected to wave after wave of Saracen attack.[26]

There was, incidentally, no rest for William of Sonnac. As the Templar master had reached the Christian host before Mansoura's outpouring Muslims, he instantly took command of a vanguard of brothers and hurled himself back into the fray—despite having lost an eye moments earlier in Mansoura—and continued fighting until evening, when Joinville mentions espying him repulse another Saracen camp raid.[27]

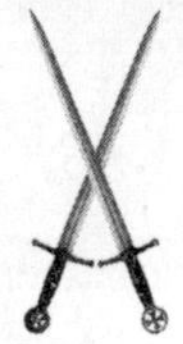

30

"WHO CAN TELL THIS STORY WITHOUT TEARS?"

Following the butchery of Christians inside Mansoura, the Muslims continued to launch sorties on Louis's newly established and nearby camp. One of the worst occurred on February 11, when the "Saracens gathered in from all sides, coming in such numbers as to cover the ground." The number of arrows and other missiles they launched were such that "some witnesses said they had never in their lives seen hail fall as heavily" (which, considering the preceding pages of this history, was certainly saying something). "So persistently, horribly and dreadfully did they attack" that many native Crusaders "said they had never seen such a bold and violent assault in any part of Outremer."

> They hardly seemed human, but like wild beasts, frantic with rage.... The Turks and our men hammered at each other with maces, lances, swords, Danish axes, with cutlasses, clubs, daggers and other weapons as if they were striking on rocks, timber or other inanimate objects. When the battle had lasted a long time and the Saracens were exhausted and had done and lost enough, they drew

> off and retired to their quarters. The Turks lost many more killed and wounded in this battle than we did.[1]

Aside from a few more raids and skirmishes, for the next few months, the two armies remained at a standstill, with the Muslims holed in Mansoura and the Christians camped outside. Time was on the Muslims' side. Pestilence and dysentery—aided by the Muslims polluting the rivers with hundreds of corpses—now plagued the Crusaders. Muslim fleets blocked the Nile, preventing Christian ships from bringing food and supplies from Damietta. Starvation set in. Because many sacrifices had been made to bring them to this point, the thought of abandoning the hard-won and strategically placed camp across Mansoura was intolerable, and Louis, who was himself suffering from dysentery and barely able to stand, urged his men to persevere as best they could. But try as they might, matters only worsened. The men, although long encouraged by their king, had reached their final extremity. One way or another, doom seemed inevitable, for "all the best of our host"—a reference to the Templars—"had been lost with the count of Artois," while weaker "Christians had deserted for lack of food and gone to join the Saracens, and these, they said, were doing most damage to our men."[2]

By the start of April 1250, only one-sixth of the original Crusader army was either alive or in fighting condition. There was nothing left but to "entrust themselves all to the two-edged judgment of war or death," wrote an anonymous Templar. Under the cover of night on April 5,

> [the Crusaders] retreated along the [Nile] river towards Damietta, weakened and in no state to fight, and as the enemy, who were positioned as guardians of the banks, hurled missiles and Greek fire, they were pierced or set alight, or were slaughtered by the warriors, or drowned. The remainder engaged in close fighting with the enemy for as long as they were able.[3]

After saying that "our men now expected nothing but death," the Rothelin chronicler adds that "their sole purpose was to sell their lives dearly." Because so few were still able to stand against the full might of Islam—the sources talk of tens and even hundreds of thousands of Egypt's Muslims chasing down the Crusaders[4]—the new sultan, Turanshah (al-Salih had died), who was also there, exhorted them in distinctly Islamic terms: "[What] a dishonor…that a handful of wretched, miserable Christians, hungry, sick, weak, enfeebled, ill-mounted and few in number, their footsoldiers completely exhausted, should hold out against us so long." In keeping with Islamic parlance, he further belittled the Christians as "the dogs and infidels they are, who call Muhammad and his law worthless and speak of it only to mock," and did his utmost to incite the Muslims to a fury, adding, "much danger, much harm, will come to Muhammad's law if they escape us now!"[5]

In the end, Muslim rage seems to have been superfluous; it was a question of numbers. As the anonymous Templar wrote,

> But what could a few achieve against such a great number of enemies, the hungry and starving against those who were alert and refreshed, those who did not know the terrain against natives? They stood their ground in the conflict, however, though the bloodshed was indescribable, until they were pitiably vanquished—alas!… But almost all fought on until they breathed their last.[6]

With the coming of dawn, thousands of Christians lay dead, many affixed to the ground with arrows. Among them was the hitherto resilient one-eyed Templar master, William of Sonnac. Although he had fought on like a man possessed, at the last even he was laid low: He lost his second eye, going completely blind; was burned with Greek fire and, finally, beheaded to resounding cries of "Allahu Akbar!" Joinville's account follows:

> When the Saracens came to attack him [William], they threw Greek fire onto the barrier he had made; and the fire caught easily.… And you should know that the Turks did not wait for the fire to burn itself out, but rushed upon the Templars among the scorching flames. And in

> this battle, Brother William, the Master of the Templars, lost an eye; and he had lost the other on the previous Shrove Tuesday [during the battle in Mansoura]; and that lord died as a consequence—may God absolve him! And you should know that there was at least an acre of land behind the Templars, which was so covered with arrows fired by the Saracens, that none of the ground could be seen.[7]

Seeing that all was lost, and in the interest of saving whomever he could, Louis surrendered. Vast numbers, including the French king himself, were taken captive. It was an Islamic victory of a magnitude unheard of: first Hattin, then Forbie, and now this. After writing "I saw the dead, and they covered the face of the earth in their profusion," one Egyptian added, "It was a day of the kind the Muslims had never seen before.... Of the Muslims, there were slain no more than a hundred."[8]

As with most Crusades, "the military Orders had relatively lost more heavily than the French in the Crusade. In every expedition, the Temple and the Hospital felt themselves bound to demand the most hazardous posts and outdo all others in battle, and their death-toll was always out of proportion to their numbers."[9]

The slain may have been more fortunate than the captured. In the prisons, the Muslims "blasphemed against Christ and ridiculed our men," who were "most vilely destroyed and treated with contempt," continues the anonymous Templar.[10] Aside from those few nobles who could fetch a high ransom price, such as Louis himself, the rank and file were subjected to an old ordeal: Renounce Christ, embrace Muhammad, or be put to death. Joinville, who was among the captives, offers a glimpse of this trial:

> Many of the knights and other people were kept by the Saracens in a court enclosed by mud walls. From this enclosed place they caused them to be taken, one after the other, and asked them, "Will you renounce your faith?" Those who would not renounce were set to

> one side, and their heads were cut off; and those who renounced were set on the other side.[11]

The Seventh Crusade was such an unmitigated disaster that even the anonymous Templar, member of an order that never questioned God's justice, could not restrain himself:

> O God...did not Thy faithful come to repulse Thine enemies and to liberate from them the land of Thy birth, Thine own land, and to worship there Thy footprints? But in this affair Thou hast clearly shown mortal men how precarious is the joy of this world.... Neither has to this day such an event been witnessed or reported.... Who can tell this story or recall it without tears, when... such prominent Franks were massacred, trodden down, or like thieves seized by base men and dragged off to imprisonment, subjected to the judgement and the grinning mockery of God's enemies. Here the oriflamme* was torn to pieces, the bauséant [Templar standard] trampled underfoot, a sight no one remembers having ever beheld. Over there the standards of magnates, since ancient times an object of dread to the infidel, were bespattered with the blood of men and horses and, spurned under the heels of a triumphant enemy who blasphemed against Christ and ridiculed our men, were most vilely destroyed and treated with contempt. How great are the rewards they deserve to expect who for the sake of Christ endured such trials to the point of death![12]

As had happened at the close of the Fifth Crusade, Louis eventually agreed to relinquish Damietta, as well as pay a king's ransom to liberate himself and all his men—including every Christian captured over the previous two years. Once they received their exorbitant ransom—much of which was raised by the Temple—the Muslims partially reneged:

* For more on the Oriflamme, see the footnote on page 51.

They released Louis and four hundred of his men but refused to release more than twelve thousand Christian prisoners who were part of the deal. "What is still more detestable," a betrayed Louis later wrote in a letter to France,

> is that having made and sworn a truce they picked out young men from among the Christian captives and, leading them like sheep to a sacrifice, they did their utmost, by putting swords to their throats, to force them to apostatize from the Catholic faith and to proclaim the religion of the wicked Muhammad. Many of them, in their enfeebled and vulnerable state, turned away from the faith and professed this loathsome religion. But the rest, like strong athletes, rooted in the faith and persisting most steadfastly in their firm resolve, could in no way be overcome by the enemy's threats and blows, but put up a proper resistance and obtained the bloodied crown of martyrdom.[13]

It may be safely assumed that the majority of surviving Knights of the Temple and Hospital who were dragged to the dungeons of Egypt were among "the rest" who refused to give in to Muslim "threats and blows." No doubt, as had happened following Hattin, the knights of Christ encouraged one another in their prison cells to defy the scimitar of Islam and vie over the "bloodied crown of martyrdom."

As for those Christians they had no use for, the many sick and infirm, the Muslim oath-breakers burned them alive. Finally, and in what should by now be a familiar scene, the Muslims "took the crosses and crucifixes found in Damietta, tied ropes to them and then, jeering and laughing, dragged them about in scorn and mockery. Then they would beat them and then smash them to pieces and villainously trample them under their feet."[14]

On being released, Louis continued on to the Holy Land, though the overwhelming majority of his men, whom he gave leave, chose to return home to France. With only a tiny force under his command, any thought of trying to regain Jerusalem was out of the question. With the help of the indefatigable Templars and Hospitallers, the king did, however, manage to recapture a few fortresses in the Holy Land, and, more importantly, help fortify those already in Christian possession.

Otherwise, promising that "he would live or die with them,"[15] the king spent most of his time trying to secure the release of the rest of those Christians whom the faithless Muslims had refused to release from Egypt. Louis made several more bargains, some of which required more concessions and money, only for the Muslims to renege time after time, to the point that "the king and those with him were so shocked, they could find no words to express it."[16]

*****

We close this chapter with an incident that occurred during Louis's time in the Holy Land—one that, yet again, reflected the formidable nature of the Temple and Hospital, and one that, yet again, concerns the Assassins.

The dreaded Hashashin, who were still paying tribute to not only the Templars but, since 1186, the Hospitallers as well, were back to their old games, trying to convince this or that king to remove the burden of tribute. So the Shia Muslim lord of the Assassins sent an embassy to Louis in Acre. The chief envoy began by asking Louis if he knew his master, the Sheikh, or Old Man of the Mountain. Louis responded that he did not, though he had heard tell of him. To this, the envoy replied,

> Seeing that you have heard tell of my lord, I marvel greatly that you have not sent him so much of your substance [monetary tribute] as would keep him for your friend—as the Emperor of Germany, the King of Hungary, the Sultan of Babylon, and the rest do year by year, because they know of a certainty that they can only keep their lives as long as my lord pleases. And if it does not suit you to do this, then cause him to be acquitted of the tribute that he owes to the Hospital and to the Temple, and he will cry quits with you.[17]

Louis asked the envoys to return in the afternoon to discuss this matter. When they did, the Muslims found, to their consternation, Louis sitting again at his table—but now with the masters of the Temple and of the Hospital standing behind him, one on each side, both with faces made of stone. Louis asked the envoy to repeat what he had said that morning, but the abashed Assassin messenger refused, saying that "he had no intention of repeating what he had said save in the presence of those who had been with the king in the morning." To this, both masters barked, "We command you to repeat what you said," and the hapless messenger gave in. He was then informed, in Arabic, to return the following day and speak with both masters at the Hospital.

When the Assassin envoys arrived, the two masters upbraided them, saying that the Old Man was "very rash in daring to address such rude" and threatening words to the king, and that, were it not for the fact that they were envoys under the protection of the king, the masters themselves would have personally drowned them in the sea of Acre. What's more, not only was the Assassin tribute to the military orders not going to be canceled, "We command you to return to your lord, and to come back here within fifteen days, bringing to the king, on the part of your lord, such letters, and such jewels, that the king may hold himself appeased."[18]

Joinville, who witnessed and recorded these interviews, went on to explain why the Assassins, who were notorious for assassinating whichever leader they targeted, did not bother eliminating, and knew not how to deal with, the masters of the Temple and Hospital, whom they were beholden to:

> Now at that time the Old Man of the Mountain paid a tribute to the Temple and to the Hospital, for the Templars and Hospitallers stood in no fear of the Assassins, seeing that the Old Man had nothing to gain by the death of the Master of the Temple or of the Hospital, inasmuch as he knew very well that if he caused one to be killed, another, equally good, would be put in his place. Wherefore he had no wish to sacrifice

> his Assassins in a service where there was nothing to be gained.[19]

Whereas individual kings, dukes, counts, and nobles could be cowed and blackmailed into saving their lives, the military orders—which were not about individuals but collectives—could not.

31

THE "DEMONS OF TARTARUS" COMETH

Not only was Louis's Seventh Crusade an unmitigated disaster, but on its tail came yet another catastrophe for the Christians of the Holy Land: the Mongols or "Tatars"—which, for Christians, became "Tartars" to indicate that they originated from the bowels of hell, or "Tartarus" (2 Peter 2:4)—had come from the farthest east to terrorize and conquer. The atrocities they committed against all who fell into their hands are mindboggling and not unlike those the Khwarazmians inflicted on the Christians of the Holy Land in 1244. (In fact, that Turcoman tribe first entered the region because it was fleeing the westward advance of the even more savage Mongols.) Smoke, ruins, and pyramids of human heads were all that remained wherever the hordes of Genghis Khan passed through.

The first Christian region to feel their rage, Russia, was reduced to ashes in 1241. "Thus," laments Bishop Serapion of Vladimir, "fell upon us a merciless people who devastated our land, took entire cities off to captivity, destroyed our holy churches, put our fathers and brothers to death, and defiled our mothers and sisters."[1] This Mongol monsoon continued westward and struck southern Poland, Hungary, and even Austria; victory was added to victory, and none could stay their onslaught. "The Latin world was darkened by this cloud of savage hostility," observed Edward Gibbon; even "the remote nations of the Baltic and the ocean trembled at the approach of the Tatars, whom their fear and ignorance were inclined to separate from the human species. Since the invasion of the Arabs in the eighth century Europe had never been exposed to a similar calamity."[2]

Like Russia, the eastern lands of Islam—particularly Persia and Mesopotamia—were devastated and Syria overrun. Baghdad, for half a millennium the opulent capital of the Abbasid caliphate, was torched in 1258, its population decimated, and the last caliph rolled up in a carpet and stomped to death by Mongol horsemen.

A year earlier, in 1257, the Mongols had begun to eye the Crusaders' few coastal possessions: "Advance as far as the coasts of the sea," Hulegu Khan, a grandson of Genghis, had ordered a commander, "and wrest those countries from the hands of the children of France and England." On being told to submit to Mongol rule or pay the ultimate price—meaning their heads on a stake—the military orders responded with customary defiance, adding, "Let therefore these Tartars—these demons of Tartarus—come on, and they will find the servants of Christ encamped and ready to do battle!"[3]

By 1260, the Mongol monsoon had reached and was battering Christendom's few possessions along the Palestinian coastline, most of which were manned by the military orders. Although they fought with customary valor, being so utterly outnumbered by the horde, many of them were cut to pieces. According to the Rothelin chronicle's entry for the years 1258–1260,

> There was scarcely a land in all the country, near or far, which they [Mongols] did not conquer, utterly destroy or hold in subjection through huge exactions of gold and silver, of men and women and many other forms of slavery, so that they would all have been better off dead. Only a very few Christians now remained free of Tartar dominion in the whole land of Syria. These few

> Christians took counsel together and said that never, please God, would they submit to the Tartars. As they were now so close, they said, almost the entire land was lost except for some strong castles, and they decided to put the strongest of these into a state of defense.

As the chronicler continues, it becomes clear—unsurprisingly so—who those "very few Christians" were that would never "submit to the Tartars":

> The Templars would garrison seven of their strongest castles, the Hospitallers two, the Hospitallers of Our Lady of the Germans [Teutons] one, and all would share in the defense of the cities of Acre and Tyre.[4]

More and more secular Franks fled the Holy Land, selling or donating their castles to the military orders, who, in their turn, built more strongholds and strengthened existing ones. The situation was so dire that a Templar messenger carrying letters from Thomas Berard, master of the Temple, made it from the Holy Land to London in just thirteen days—an amazing feat for travel by ship and horse. On June 16, he delivered the master's missives describing the situation to the English king and the Templars in London. According to the St. Albans chronicle,

> When they had read these letters, both the king and the Templars, as well as the others who heard them, gave way to lamentation and sadness, on a scale no one had ever seen before. For the news was that the Tartars, advancing with an innumerable force, had already occupied and devastated the Holy Land almost up to Acre.... Also, they have already killed almost all of the Templars and Hospitallers there, [and] unless help is quickly brought, God forbid, a horrible annihilation will swiftly be visited upon the world.[5]

In a separate letter to Brother Amadeus, preceptor of London's Temple, dated March 4, 1260, the master of the Temple elaborated on the "terrible and awesome arrival of the Tartars," who "are now here in front of our walls, knocking at our gates." Their "exploits...have shaken Christendom externally on this side of the sea and troubled and oppressed it internally with the weapons of great pain and fear," including the use of despicable tactics, such as using captive Christian women and children as their personal shields. "They rely on the power of their incredibly huge numbers and conquer provinces left and right with such great ease for their leader that none can resist their strength."[6]

No one was spared, continued the Templar master, Thomas Berard; the caliph in Baghdad, the Old Man of the Mountain—everyone was being killed. After mentioning the few castles still held by the Templars, Hospitallers, and Teutons, the master affirmed that "we intend to hold these with the help of God for the work of Christianity fighting until our last man falls."[7] Although the master repeatedly emphasized that "we and our honorable brotherhood remain fully committed to give up our lives in defense of the Christian faith,"[8] as a realist, he knew their fate was sealed unless their Western coreligionists acted fast:

> May you be in no doubt that unless help comes quickly to us from your countries, whatever our ability to resist the attack and onslaught of such a great horde, there is no doubt that the whole of Christendom this side of the sea will be subject to Tartar rule.... May God in His mercy spare our souls; we do not worry about temporal things.[9]

Happily for the Christians, after their initial invasions, the Mongols soon turned their full attention to the much more numerically powerful foe of the region, Islam, particularly in the guise of the rising Mamluk sultanate centered in Egypt. Even when King Louis IX was still captive in 1250, these slave-soldiers had risen against and torn the heart out of Egypt's last Ayyubid sultan, Turanshah. Although they governed over the next decade from behind the scenes and in the name of several puppet rulers, by 1259, they had openly proclaimed themselves masters of Egypt. A showdown between Mongol and Mamluk was brewing.

Needing all the help they could get, the Muslims went so far as to ask their traditional enemies—the Crusaders—to fight alongside them against the common foe. The Christians, who had already experienced and were eager to neutralize the Mongol storm, were on the verge of agreeing when, during a council meeting, the master of the Teutonic Knights reminded them of how "they had often discovered, and very recently too, that the Saracens never kept any truce or agreement with the Christians as they should, but frequently broke them."[10] He further pointed out that, if they fought alongside the Muslims and perchance were victorious against the Mongols, "any Christians who survived such a battle would be exhausted" and far outnumbered by their nominal "allies," who could easily turn on and butcher them to a man. "All agreed when they heard this, and they sent a reply to the [Mamluk] sultan [Qutuz] saying they would not join them in battle, but they could be quite certain that no harm would come to them from the Christians, who would on the contrary help and support them with food supplies and safe conduct."[11]

On September 3, 1260, after receiving safe passage from the Christians, a massive Mamluk army met and defeated the Mongols at Ayn Jalut in Syria. In the short term, such a development drew a sigh of relief among the Christians: better the Muslims they knew than the newly come demons from Tartarus.[12] On the other hand, as the Mongol threat began to slowly recede, the Mamluks filled the vacuum, reunifying Syria and Egypt under their control and thereby completely surrounding the few territories left to the Christian name: Acre, Antioch, and Tripoli.

One month after the Battle of Ayn Jalut, as its hero, Mamluk Sultan Qutuz, was making his triumphal entry into Cairo on October 24, 1260, one of his leading men, Baybars, stabbed him to death and ascended the throne. With the possible exceptions of Saladin and Nur al-Din, no Muslim leader would go on to be as committed to the ideals of relentless jihad against infidels as this slave-soldier-turned-sultan of Egypt and Syria. Both he and his propagandists were highly committed to presenting him before the Muslim world as "a mighty warrior of jihad"[13] and the "tamer of the worshippers of the cross."[14]

Indeed, to underscore that he was heir to the great jihad warriors of the past, when he passed through Homs, Syria, and came across the mausoleum of that jihadist extraordinaire, Khalid ibn al-Walid—the much revered "Sword of Allah" who led the Arabs to victory at the pivotal Battle of Yarmuk in 636—Baybars ordered his own name inscribed on the tomb, followed by an epithet: "The sultan of Islam and the Muslims, the killer of infidels and polytheists."[15]

Nor was this mere pretense; Baybars was a sincere and zealous Muslim, committed to all things Islamic, with jihad at its pinnacle.* This was especially evident in the vast armies he led against the Crusaders: Islamic ritual and prayers were strictly enforced in camp; and veritable throngs of religious scholars, ascetics, and indigent Sufis—in a word, fanatics—were unleashed in the camp to inspire and incite the men to fight and die for jihad.

Baybars was especially effective in that he seems to have imbibed the more fraudulent tactics recommended by his prophet, Muhammad—especially as captured by that famous dictum, "War is deceit." Truces were kept only as long as they served his purpose, again, in keeping with Muhammad's example (or *sunna*): "If I take an oath and later find something else better," the prophet said in a canonical hadith, "I do what is better and break my oath."[16†]

---

* Although many modern academics regularly disassociate Baybars from Islam and present him as cynically exploiting jihadist rhetoric for purely political and propagandistic purposes, according to historian R. Stephen Humphreys, an expert on Baybars, "that terrifying man...was [in his own mind] purifying the lands of Islam from the pollution of unbelief.... [He] also saw himself as a Muslim. We witness the public dimension of his commitment to the faith in his extensive program of public works and...in the quite puritanical public morality which he demanded.... [A]ll the evidence indicates that Baybars was personally and deeply engaged with Islam, and this inevitably colored the way he envisioned his strategic policy" (Humphreys, "Ayyubids," 10, 13–14).

† Muhammad also encouraged Muslims to do the same: "Whenever you take an oath to do something and later you find that something else is better than the first, then do the better one and make expiation for your oath" (*Sahih Bukhari* 8:78:618–619). The logic here is that, if the default status between Islam and infidels is one of hostility (and it is), and if the opportunity presents itself to (profitably) exercise this hostility, clearly that is "better" than maintaining a temporary peace treaty.

Baybars's jihadist bona fides were further confirmed in that his hate for the "cross worshippers" was intrinsic, as seen in his treatment of the already disenfranchised native Christians of Egypt, the Copts. Although they had no connection whatsoever to the Crusades, under Baybars's rule, churches and monasteries were desecrated, burned, or transformed into mosques; Christians were randomly executed in brutal ways, including by being sawn in half or thrown into pits and burned alive; others were forced to convert to Islam at the tip of the sword. The biblical warning—"Woe to you, O land, when your ruler is a slave!" (Ecclesiastes 10:16, BST)—proved all too true for the Copts.[17]

Finally, Baybars took stealth and dissembling to another level; even his most loyal men never knew his mind, goals, or intentions, and lived in paranoia. According to Ibn Shaddad, the Mamluk sultan's biographer, "Baybars forbade all gatherings, had everyone watched, and kept the spies in their turn under surveillance. Even at home, people feared the walls had ears. Those who disregarded his prohibitions were hanged, drowned, crucified, imprisoned, banished, and blinded at the sultan's orders."[18]

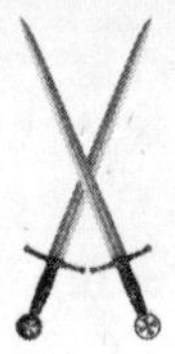

32

NOW THEY ALL FALL LIKE DOMINOES

Although Baybars's first two years of rule were focused on further neutralizing the Mongol threat to Syria and consolidating his own power, once he was able, he turned his full attention to the Christians, beginning in 1263. In keeping with his surprise tactics and unpredictability—and in an effort to unnerve and "strike terror in the heart of the infidels" (to quote Allah, Koran 8:12)—he began a series of abrupt campaigns. He would suddenly appear before this or that Christian possession, which included the Crusader headquarter, Acre; terrorize, besiege it, and massacre any Christians he could get a hold of—before just as suddenly leaving, appearing somewhere else, and repeating the cycle.

Such assaults were, as usual, tinged with religious fanaticism. As one example, that same year, 1263, Baybars "gave orders," his biographer, Ibn Abdul Zahir approvingly writes, "that the church of Nazareth should be demolished, this being the most important place of worship for them; it is said that the religion of the Christians had its origin there."[1]

In early 1265, Baybars, at the head of a vast army, easily conquered Caesarea—slaughtering every last Christian unable to flee—and, by late March, was besieging the great fortress of Arsuf, then manned by the Knights of St. John. Although the sultan had a treaty with them, he reneged. For over a month, the fortress's 260 Hospitallers took everything the sultan could hurl at them through siege engines, mangonels, battering rams, mining operations, and direct assaults. By April 26, much of Arsuf lay in ruins and the remaining knights—ninety had already died during the defense—were pushed to and holed in the fortress's citadel, where they continued to valiantly resist. As it was also filled with terrified civilians who had fled to Arsuf, and seeing how vastly outnumbered they were with no aid to come, the knights finally agreed to surrender on condition that they and every Christian they were protecting be allowed to withdraw unmolested to Acre.

Once they opened their gates, the treacherous sultan double-crossed them and had everyone shackled and enslaved. First, he put the Christians to immense labor, making them demolish the fortress (to prevent any future Crusaders from occupying it). Then, on May 29, Baybars made his triumphal entry through the streets of Cairo, with the Knights of St. John marching in his train. With large, broken crosses hanging around their necks, they were met with jeers, spits, and slaps.

These hapless Hospitallers were among the first of their kind to disappear in Mamluk dungeons: "During the final years of the Crusader States, large numbers of Hospitallers fell into Mamluk hands and those brethren who did become prisoners-of-war could expect to languish in bad conditions or to be worked hard on construction projects for many years. One English Hospitaller, Roger of Stangrave, was still in Mamluk hands in 1318 and was still seeking a huge ransom of 12,000 gold florins from his friends and family."[2]

As Baybars's prestige soared, "anger and grief" struck the Christians, as recorded in a dirge by the Templar Ricaut Bonomel following the fall of Arsuf:

> Anger and grief are so set in my heart that I all but kill myself at once; Or lay down the cross I took up in

> honour of Him Who was put on the Cross; For neither cross nor law helps nor guides me against the evil Turks, God curse them! Rather it seems to me, as far as one can tell, that God wishes to help them destroy us. At the first assault, they conquered Caesarea, and the strong castle of Arsuf was taken by force, alas! Lord God, and what was their end, all those knights, all those sergeants, all those townsfolk who were within the walls of Arsuf? Alas! the kingdom of Syria has lost so much, if one may speak the truth, it will never recover again.[3]

Like so many other Crusaders—recall the anonymous Templar who lamented the destruction of St. Louis's army in Egypt—the much-disillusioned Ricaut could not understand why the more Muslims raged and destroyed Christendom, the more God was nowhere to be found:

> Then whoever fights the Turks is a real fool since Jesus Christ certainly does not attack them; They have conquered and will conquer, it grieves me to say...and we are defeated every day for God sleeps, who used to stand watch, and Bafometz [Muhammad] acts with all his power and spurs on Melicadefer [Baybars]. Nor does it seem to me that he will ever retreat, No, he has sworn and said openly that no one who believes in Christ will remain in this country, if he has his way.... No, he will build a mosque out of the Church of St. Mary and since her Son, who ought to be grieved, wishes and is pleased with this, it must therefore please us.[4]

Despite this spirit of anti-theodicy, the Templar closed by acknowledging the more pragmatic reason that the Mamluks were overwhelming them: Neither the pope in Rome, nor the Christians of Europe, were supportive of another crusade to help their dying brethren in the Holy Land.

Next on Baybars's picking list was the Templar fortress of Safed, which, as seen, had long terrorized Muslims. He laid siege to it on June

13, 1266. Defended by as many as one hundred knights and two thousand sergeants, Turcopoles, and other fugitive Christians who had fled the Muslims' advance, for some six weeks Safed resisted. Like the Hospitallers of Arsuf, when the Templars had reached their final extremity and were holed up in the citadel and few remaining towers alongside terrified civilians, they too entertained Baybars's terms of surrender (being unaware of his betrayal of the Hospitallers):

> The knights accepted and opened the castle gates, whereupon the sultan offered them a choice of Islam or death. Next morning, when they were paraded outside the walls to give their answer, the castellan stepped forward, begging his brethren not to apostatize. Baybars had him skinned alive and the brethren decapitated, after which he decorated his new possession with their rotting heads.[5]

As for the Christian civilians holed up in Safed, Baybars ordered them all—as many as two thousand—ritually slaughtered. The contemporary chronicler known as the Templar of Tyre (who was likely not a Templar but associated with them) offers more details on this breach of trust:

> [Baybars] swore to conduct them in good faith to Acre, safe and secure, so they came out of the castle…[but] he had them all seized and conducted some distance from Safed, to a small hillock about half a league away, and there he put them to death, beheaded. Then he had a circular wall erected around them, and their bones and heads may still be seen.[6]

Always keen on having posterity appreciate his pious exploits, Baybars proceeded to boast in an inscription on the citadel of Safed that he had "delivered it from the hands of the accursed Franks…from the possession of the Templars to the possession of the Muslims." He had engaged in jihad—that is, "He made efforts and struggled [*jahada*, root

Roland sounds his olifant for aid at Roncesvalles (1873).

History's first armed pilgrimage (a.k.a. the First Crusade, c. 1840).

Templar emblem of two knights on one horse with their war flag (from Matthew Paris's chronicle, c. 1245).

Hugh of Payns (1841).

St. Bernard preaching the Second Crusade (1840

An assassin delivers a fatal strike (13th-century Arabic manuscript).

Templar Charge by Samuel McIntire (2025).

Raymond of Puy (1842).

Fatimid ink fragment depicting Muslim soldiers (12th century).

1148 siege of Damascus (13th century).

Hospitallers Defending Pilgrims by Samuel McIntire (2025).

A Templar knight (12th-century fresco from the Templars' chapel at Cressac, France).

nages of the Second Crusade and Louis VII (c. 1350).

Louis VII, back to a tree, defends himself at Mount Cadmus (1892).

Ruins of Baghras, a Templar fortress in the Amanus Mountains.

Templars playing chess (from a Castilian chronicle, c. 1283).

Partially paralyzed, Baldwin IV, the "Leper King," is carried into battle (1841).

One Against a Thousand: Templar knight Jakelin of Mailly's last stand at Cresson, 1187 (c. 1877).

Krak des Chevaliers, the Hospitaller's "mountain" fortress, cursed by Muslims as "a bone stuck in the throat."

Battle of Damietta, 1218 (Matthew Paris's chronicle, c. 1245).

Naval battle for the chain tower of Damietta (c. 1615).

Interfaith Dialogue: Saint Francis and Sultan al-Kamil (c. 1787).

Edward I fights off an assassin sent by Baybars (c. 1850).

The Sheikh's pretend "houris" seduce Assassin recruits (from *The Travels of Marco Polo,* c. 1310).

Decapitated by Baybars: Christian slave women search for and mourn their dead (c. 1850).

Diabolical Rite Imagined: Templar initiate tramples the crucified Christ (c. 1886).

The inquisition of Master James of Molay (19th century).

Matthew of Clermont, marshal of the Hospital, spearheads the defense of Acre in 1291 (c. 1840).

The Oriflamme (“golden flame”) symbolized holy, no-quarter warfare for the Frankish kings since Charlemagne.

mplars burned at the stake (German chronicle, c. 1384).

1314 execution of James of Molay and Geoffroi of Charney (1836).

Hospitaller castle of Rhodes (Master's palace and knights' headquarters).

Dieudonne of Gozon and his dogs slay the Dragon of Rhoc (c. 1850).

Siege of Rhodes (c. 1483).

Master Peter of Aubusson and the lifting of the 1480 siege of Rhodes (1841).

Reconstruction of Muslim (or Barbary) corsair flag.

Contemporary drawing of Hayreddin Barbarossa, a.k.a. "the King of Evil" (c. 1535).

Contemporary drawing of the slave market in Algiers (1684).

Knights of St. John galleys capturing an Ottoman vessel (1652).

The slave market of Constantinople (after it became Istanbul, c. 1838).

Contemporary German painting showing Charles V overseeing the liberation of 22,000 Christi
slaves following the 1535 conquest of Tunis (c. 1550).

St. James the Moor Slayer (c. 1660).

Fort St. Elmo today.

Turkish assault on Castile during the siege of Malta (c. 1575).

Doomed, elderly, and injured—but unbroken: the knights of St. Elmo hold the line (1878).

Master John of Valette praises God for the lifting of the 1565 siege of Malta (c. 1850).

The Last Crusader:
Betrayed, not bested (c. 1835).

form of jihad] until he exchanged unbelief [*kufr*] for faith, church bells for the call to prayer, and the Gospel for the Koran."[7]

Coming so close on the heels of Arsuf, the fall of Safed caused Pope Clement IV to despair that Christendom's two greatest military orders were on the verge of eradication: "By the death of so many knights of both orders, the noble college of the Hospitallers, and the illustrious chivalry of the Temple, are almost destroyed, and I know not how we shall be able, after this, to find gentlemen and persons of quality sufficient to supply the places of such as have perished."[8]

With the loss of Safed, the way was opened not only to Galilee but as far as Acre, Tyre, and Sidon, where Baybars increasingly pillaged and plundered, including by annually marching his troops to and terrorizing Acre, the best fortified Crusader stronghold. During one of these raids, on May 2, 1267, he again followed Muhammad's dictum that "war is deceit" by approaching Acre "with all his host...carrying banners from the Temple and the Hospital," which completely "surprised the poor ordinary folk of the plain of Acre, who had come out to work in the fields," and who had assumed the approaching army was led by the military orders. As a result, he "killed more than five hundred of the common people whom he had taken prisoner, and spilled the bile from every one of their bodies. And he sliced all the hair off their heads, to below their ears, and carried it back to Safed, where he strung the scalps on a cord and hung the cord around the great tower at Safed. It remained there as long as the cord lasted."[9]

Such ritualistic carnage was par for the course. A few pages later into his chronicle, the Templar of Tyre tells of the aftermath of another confrontation between the Crusaders and Muslims, where all the Christians were later found "headless, because the Saracens had struck off the heads of all those who had been killed in the battle, so that it was difficult for anyone to recognize even a relative from the features of his body."[10]

On March 8, 1268, Baybars stormed Jaffa "by treason and during a truce. He killed many of the common people," and, in a rare act of clemency, "let the rest go to Acre."[11] Less than two months later, Baybars boasted of his ongoing jihadist rampage in a letter detailing how wherever he passed through, "the churches themselves were razed from the face of the earth, every house met with disaster, the dead were piled up on the seashore like islands of corpses, the men were murdered, the children enslaved, the free women reduced to captivity."[12]

Next to fall—and terrible was its fall—was the ancient Christian city of Antioch, one of the oldest and best fortified Crusader kingdoms. In May 1268, after the Muslims had breached the city, which was swollen with some one hundred and twenty thousand Christian fugitives, many of whom were women and children, Baybars entered and ordered the city's gates shut behind him. An orgiastic bloodbath—the "single greatest massacre of the entire crusading era"—followed.[13]

Indeed, the scale of slaughters, atrocities, and rapes visited upon the Christians of Antioch was unprecedented. Seventeen thousand Christians were massacred inside the city, and more than one hundred thousand were enslaved. In the Mamluk train was such a surplus of human booty that the price of Frankish slave women and children plummeted on the Muslim slave markets to just a few silver pieces. That said, not all would consent to rape and slavery, and "amid the usual atrocities" during the sack of Antioch, "one incident shocked even the Turks. The canonesses of St. John had cut off their noses with scissors and gashed their cheeks in order to avoid rape. The appalled Muslims slaughtered them on the spot."[14]

Needless to say, Baybars, who was never at a loss for words, gloated over his latest handiwork in a letter to Bohemond VI, lord of Antioch, who was not present at the time of its fall:

> You would have seen your knights prostrated beneath the horses' hooves, your houses stormed by pillagers and ransacked by looters...your women sold four at a time and bought for a dinar of your own money! You would have seen the crosses in your churches smashed, the pages of the false Testaments scattered, the Patriarchs' tombs overturned. You would have seen your Muslim enemy trampling on the place where you celebrate the mass, cutting the throats of monks, priests and deacons

> upon the altars, bringing sudden death to the Patriarchs and slavery to the royal princes. You would have seen fire running through your palaces, your dead burned...your palace lying unrecognizable, the church of St. Paul and that of Qusyan [Cathedral of Saint Peter] pulled down and destroyed.[15]

The situation had reached a breaking point; in the same year that Antioch was sacked, 1268, Hugh Revel, the master of the Hospital, sent a letter to Europe describing how "the tiny number of Christians" remaining in the Holy Land "are unable to resist the indescribable power of the Saracens"; they "are so stupefied at the immense damage which they have received and which they are receiving every day, that they can provide no remedy of defense."[16]

Following his crowning achievement of Antioch, Baybars took a brief hiatus from terrorizing the Franks and turned his attention to their allies, the Armenian Kingdom of Cilicia, which he utterly destroyed, "killing in the process some 60,000 Christians and enslaving thousands more."[17]

In 1271, the sultan was back on the warpath, laying siege to the finest, most fortified castle in all of Christendom, Krak des Chevaliers, the "Fortress of the Knights," also known as "the Mountain." Sitting two thousand feet atop a hill in the Homs Gap, east of Tortosa, Syria, this vast and lonely fortress was "the key to Christian lands," and "the greatest and strongest of the castles of the Hospitallers, exceedingly injurious to the Saracens." The prophet's followers concurred and referred to it as "a bone stuck in the throat of Muslims."[18]

At its peak, Krak des Chevaliers could hold as many as two thousand fighters and exponentially more civilians, but when Baybars and his hordes arrived on March 3, it was garrisoned with a meager two hundred knights and an unknown number of sergeants, all under the authority of the Order's marshal. Once again, the Muslims unleashed all hell on the Mountain; day and night, siege engines hurled two-hundred-pound stones and catapults thundered against the walls of the fortress, while miners undermined it. Several sections of this once-impregnable stronghold came crashing down, crushing a number of knights to death.

On April 8, the defenders accepted Baybars's terms and surrendered; and, for whatever reason—perhaps he had finally been glutted on Christian blood, perhaps he was impressed by the Hospitallers' mettle—the hitherto treacherous Baybars kept his word and allowed the survivors to withdraw to Tyre, though not without his customary boasting. "You fortified this place," he exulted in a message to the Order's master, Hugh Revel, "entrusting its defense to the best of your men. All was in vain and you sent them only to their deaths." The sultan ordered the Hospitaller chapel transformed into a victory mosque.[19]

That same year, in 1271, Lord Edward of Wales (England's future King Edward I), one of history's last true Crusaders, came to the aid of the Holy Land. He helped refortify Acre and, with the aid of the military orders, even began to do what had not been done in years—take the fight to the Muslims.

Thus, according to the Templar of Tyre, in July, "Lord Edward mounted a raid" and "the Templars and Hospitallers went with him.... They destroyed the [Muslim] village and slew a great many Saracens." Then again, on November 24, Edward, "along with the Templars and Hospitallers," attacked a Mamluk fortification in Caesarea: "They did a good deal of damage...[and] slew many Saracens."[20]

In order to deal with this latest upstart, Baybars resorted to his more diabolical tactics. Sometime in 1272, he sent an assassin bearing gifts to worm his way into Edward's confidences.* The attempt nearly worked; the English prince was stabbed by the assassin's poisoned dagger and only survived because this future giant king ("Longshanks") fought off and killed his assailant and had the venom sucked from his wound, possibly by his wife, Eleanor. When the sultan's assassination attempt failed, and because he needed to turn his attention to a then-resurgent Mongol threat, he made a ten-year truce with the Crusaders.

* It is unclear if this assassin was an actual member of the Hashashin or just an everyday Muslim assassin. Sources only indicate that he was a "Saracen."

Five years later, on July 1, 1277, Baybars died—apparently by accidentally drinking a beverage that he had poisoned for a political rival.[21] Despite his ignominious end, in the history of the Crusades, Baybars would be seen as a sort of second Saladin: Both men were outsiders (the one a Kurd, the other a Turcoman slave); both managed to rule over a united Egypt and Syria; both championed and popularized the cause of jihad; both used their formidable powers and limitless resources against the Christians; and both came very close to completely ejecting the Crusaders from the Holy Land. And if Saladin's wish was to invade and wage jihad on Christian Europe, "so as to free the earth of anyone who does not believe in Allah, or I will die in the attempt," the slave-turned-sultan wished to wage jihad "until no more Franks remain on the surface of the earth."[22]

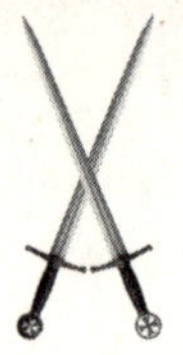

33

ACRE: "THE LAST STRONGHOLD OF THE CHRISTIAN FAITH"

Because jihadist zeal outlived Baybars death in 1277, becoming a hallmark of the Mamluk Sultanate, Muslim engines of war were soon pounding on the remaining Crusader holdings under one of Baybars's leading generals, al-Mansur Qalawun, who became Mamluk sultan in 1280.

One of the first Crusader possessions he targeted was the powerful Hospitaller castle, Margat (or Marqab). Situated atop a dead volcano, a mile from the sea and just south of Baniyas, it had long been a thorn in the side of both Baybars and Saladin, both of whom tried to but could not conquer it. Margat is also a reminder that, even as late as one decade before the final curtain call on the Crusaders, the military orders were still true to their calling. Thus, as late as 1280,

> the Saracens of the country round about assembled from all sides, in number about six thousand horsemen and many footmen, and they came intending to besiege Margat Castle. They assaulted the castle and ravaged

> all the land and did all the harm they could manage. Thereupon the brethren of the Hospital who were within Margat Castle came out against them, and took the battle into the Saracen host. They worked such feats of arms that, with the help of God, they defeated the Saracens and slew a great many.... In this host were a great many Turks, men of distinction and hardened in battle, who had come up to the castle. The others were Turcomans and Saracens. The Hospitallers had only six hundred horsemen, yet they lost only twelve sergeants and one brother, by the mercy of God.[1]

Indeed, despite their increasing isolation, the Hospitallers of Margat "showed an incredible insolence," writes Ibn 'Abd al-Rahman. "Their ravages and raids in the surrounding territories had spread such terror that the inhabitants of the neighboring fortresses were shut up as if in prison, or more as though in a tomb." As such, although "the knights had been relying on the fact that a ten-year truce had been agreed upon with the Sultan," which did not include the surrounding countryside they were raiding, when it came to keeping his word, "Baybars successor was no more to be relied upon than Baybars himself had been."[2]

In April 1285, Qalawun marched his formidable forces to and besieged the volcano castle, taking it on the following month. Rather than destroy the strategically placed fortress, the sultan had it repaired and garrisoned. "On this memorable day were avenged the evils caused by the house of the Hospitallers," wrote one contemporary Muslim, "and the brightness of day replaced the shadows." Once again Islam triumphed, and within the fortress "the call to prayer resounded with praise and thanks to Allah," to quote a contemporary Muslim, "for having cast down the adorers of the Messiah and freed our land of them."[3]

Next to fall in 1289 was Tripoli, which had been in Christian hands since 1102. This particular sacking and the atrocities that followed were described by Abu al-Fida, a Muslim eyewitness, who offers a snapshot of the hate-driven zeal that almost always accompanied Muslim conquests of Christian holdings:

> A great many Franks fled with their women to the island and the church [of Saint Thomas, a short distance by sea]. The Muslim troops flung themselves into the sea and swam with their horses to the island, where they killed all the men and took the women, children and possessions. After the looting I went by boat to this island, and found it heaped with putrefying corpses; it was impossible to land there because of the stench.[4]

Meanwhile, back in Tripoli, insult was, as usual, being added to injury: "Muslims put holy pictures [icons] to an insulting use, subjected images to various insults and dragged a crucifix through the streets at the tail of an ass.... Christian children who were captured...were made Muslim and taught to spit on the crucifixes." [5]

Following the Muslim sack of Tripoli in 1289, virtually every Frankish civilian still in the Holy Land fled to Acre, the largest, best fortified, and last remaining Crusader fortress city, which had also been serving as the de facto kingdom of Jerusalem since the Holy City fell to Saladin a century earlier. Except for the two years that Saladin held it, Acre had been in Christian possession for nearly two centuries, and the military orders' massive complexes dominated the city. Now it was swollen with some fifty thousand Christian fugitives from everywhere—a rich bounty for the coming jihad.

Although Acre and the Mamluks had signed a ten-year truce in 1283, with the conquest of Tripoli in 1289, the need for peace with this final Christian holdout became obsolete, and in August 1290, the perfect pretext presented itself for the Mamluk sultan Qalawun to go on the warpath. A group of unemployed Italian would-be Crusaders arrived in Acre and, in a violent spree—possibly started by rumors that a Muslim man had seduced a Frankish woman[6]—killed about nineteen Muslim merchants in the city.[7]

Many in Acre still hoped the truce would hold. After all, during the signing, Qalawun had sworn "By Allah, by Allah, by Allah; in the name of Allah, of Allah, of Allah; the witness being Allah, Allah, Allah...I bind myself to uphold this blessed truce agreed between myself and the

Commune of Acre and the Masters who live there."[8] Moreover, when Qalawun inquired of them, "many of the emirs believed that the terms had not been breached—that the incident was the result of accidental brawls—and that they were bound by sacred oath to uphold it."[9]

It did not matter; jihad was declared. While discussing these events, even the Templar of Tyre observed that "the sultan was planning to do grievous harm to the city of Acre anyway."[10]

As per Islam's modus operandi, the first to feel Muslim wrath, always the nearest and most vulnerable Christians (in Egypt, the Copts), were collectively punished. The sultan ordered the closure of virtually all their churches (which was apparently not enough as the "Muslims clamored for the destruction of all the Christian churches" and savagely beat and stoned any Christian they came across).[11]

Although he began mobilizing the vast Muslim army that would soon descend on Acre, Qalawun died in November 1290. From his deathbed, he had made his son and the new sultan, al-Ashraf Saladin al-Khalil, also swear to Allah to see the jihad through. Khalil accepted the honor and even announced it in a letter to the Templar master, William of Beaujeu, who had been, in vain, trying to placate the Muslims:

> Because you have been a true man, so we send you advance notice of our intentions, and give you to understand that we are coming into your parts to right the wrongs that have been done. Therefore, we do not want the community of Acre to send us any letters or presents, for we will by no means receive them.[12]

As we shall see, there was a reason why even his enemies respected the Templar master.

Like other Mamluk sultans, Khalil knew how to whip up religious fervor among the masses. Jihadist rhetoric from pulpits everywhere incited and summoned Muslims to "avenge" Muslim bloodshed in Acre; zeal for holy war spread like wildfire. Thus, when Baybars al-Mansuri, governor of Kerak, was ordered to provide men for the upcoming campaign, he did more than that: "My soul," he later explained, "had a strong desire for jihad, a desire for it like the earth thirsts for delivering rain!"[13] So he personally joined the expedition, though he was not expected to. The air was tinged with omens and prophecy, and Muslim elders dreamed dreams. In one, a sheikh heard the following words recited: "Already the Muslims have taken Acre and cut off the heads of the infidels."[14]

In the end, Sultan Khalil set out with an army of nearly a quarter of a million men, including more than 150,000 infantry and over 70,000 cavalry—the largest army ever assembled against the Crusaders. A great proportion of these men, some say the majority, were volunteers—all of whom were "thirsting for Christian blood," to quote from the *Excidium Acconis* ("The Destruction of Acre"), which is based on eyewitness accounts.[15]

On March 6, as Khalil and his army prepared to march out of Cairo, the Mamluk *qadi* (or judge), Muhyi al-Din, was heard to imprecate, "Oh you, sons of the blond one [Christ], soon will Allah's vengeance rain down on you, of whom nothing will remain! Already al-Malik al-Ashraf is descending on your shores. Prepare to receive at his hands unbearable blows!"[16]

Against the Muslim masses coming for their throats, all the Christians of Acre could muster were thirteen thousand infantry and eight hundred knights (most of whom were of the military orders, including many that had been called forth from the commanderies of Europe). The rest of the city's population of some thirty to forty thousand were noncombatants, including many women and children, the last of the descendants of the First Crusaders.[17]

Except for those few garrisoning remote outposts, all the men of the military orders—especially of the Temple and Hospital—were present. Even the last of the lepers of the Order of St. Lazarus—twenty-five knights, ghostly reminders of Baldwin IV, the Leper King—were there, as were nine knights of the tiny Order of St. Thomas. Each military order manned a section of Acre's walls and defenses.

Although there were other troops—a Cypriot contingent, Pisan and Venetian garrisons, and a sprinkling of French and English—everyone looked to the military orders for delivery; and the sixty-year-old Templar master, William of Beaujeu, "a veteran warrior of a hundred fights, took the command of the garrison." Master of the Order for nearly two decades (since 1273), this formidable man was also "great-hearted and liberal in all kinds of matters, and was very charitable," recalled the Templar of Tyre (who was in his employ and present during, and personally witnessed, the siege of Acre).[18]

John (or Jean) of Villiers, master of the Hospital, was also present, as was—for a surreal moment—the master of the Teutonic Knights, Burchard von Schwanden. If his arrival with forty knights and four hundred Crusaders heartened the people of Acre, his immediate resignation and quick departure demoralized them.

On April 5, 1291, Sultan Khalil surrounded and invested Acre. The Muslim camp stretched for miles. According to John of Villiers, the master of the Knights of the Hospital of St. John, the sultan "invested the city of Acre on all sides from one sea as far as the other," as far as the naked eye could see. "With all his battering-engines" and with so "great a host, he sat down before the city."[19]

Indeed, some six hundred siege engines of war, catapults, mangonels, towers, and every possible instrument of destruction, "such as never were collected against any other place," to quote Abu al-Fida, an eyewitness source, were set up along every strategic point, as Acre's barricaded Christians looked on aghast.[20] They were given creative names too, such as "the Victorious One," or "the Black Bull." One of the largest siege engines, surnamed "the Furious," was set up and would soon wreak havoc against the wall defended by the Templars.

By all accounts, it looked like all the lands of Islam had risen against them. The *Excidium Acconis* offers a glimpse of the days preceding the bombardment:

> An innumerable people of all nations and every tongue, thirsting for Christian blood, were assembled together from the deserts of the East and the South; the earth trembled beneath their footsteps, and the air was rent with the sound of their trumpets and cymbals. The sun's rays, reflected from their shields, gleamed on the distant mountains, and the points of their spears shone like the

> innumerable stars of heaven. When on the march, their lances presented the appearance of a vast forest rising from the earth, and covering all the landscape.... They wandered round about the walls, spying out their weaknesses and defects; some barked like dogs, some roared like lions, some lowed and bellowed like oxen, some struck drums with twisted sticks after their fashion, some threw darts, some cast stones, some shot arrows and bolts from cross-bows.[21]

At this point, seeing what must have seemed the futility of resistance, Acre could have capitulated to the sultan and its people withdrawn. Its harbor was still secure and full of relief vessels, many of which belonged to the military orders:

> Yet the two great monastic and military orders [of the Temple and Hospital] scorned to retire to the neighbouring and friendly island of Cyprus; they refused to desert, even in its last extremity, that cause which they had sworn to maintain with the last drop of their blood. For a hundred and seventy years their swords had been constantly employed in defending the Holy Land from the profane tread of the unbelieving Muslim; the sacred territory of Palestine had been everywhere moistened with the blood of the best and bravest of their knights, and, faithful to their vows and their chivalrous engagements, they now prepared to bury themselves in the ruins of the last stronghold of the Christian faith.[22]

34

NOW THE "BATTLE RAGED FURIOUSLY"

On April 6, 1291, the Muslim bombardment of Acre began, and, day and night, "the battle raged furiously," writes Abu al-Fida, adding, rather incredulously, that the "Franks did not close most of the gates; in fact, they left them wide open and fought in front of them in their defense." This was, after all, not just the last stand of Acre; it was the last stand of the Crusader presence in the Holy Land, and everyone knew it.[1]

So the Muslims turned to their usual tactics: Thaddeus of Naples, who was either there or based his account on eyewitnesses, reported "innumerable sharp arrows that came whistling through the air from all directions onto the defenders' heads like heavy rain. These continuous volleys not only dealt death, they poisoned the very air of heaven. Well-armored soldiers deployed along the ramparts to defend the city were being mortally wounded, while the unarmed were prevented from going to the walls at all."[2]

For over a month, siege and sally, attack and counterattack, were incessant, particularly from the Muslim side. "Neither by night nor by day did the shouts of the assailants and the noise of the military engines cease; the walls were battered from without, and the foundations were sapped by miners, who were incessantly laboring to advance their works." Part of the nonstop nature of the assault was psychological: "When the investment is underway," a Muslim military manual (by al-Ansari) advised, "there should be no pause in the discharge of the mangonels against them, and there should be no abating [of fire] in any hour of the day or night. To desist in attack against them is among that which cools fright and strengthens their heart."[3]

Indeed, the psychological toll created by the sights and sounds of such a massive and nonstop siege was beyond traumatic for the large civilian population: the careening and thundering missiles; the repeated creak and crash of catapults discharging, followed by the spectacle of monstrous beams rearing wildly in the sky; the anticipated crash, followed by the sounds of wood splintering and stone shattering; the nonstop and ominous drum beat; and the jihadist cries for Christian blood emanating from a hundred thousand throats. Surely all of these struck the inhabitants of Acre with terror and dread. Despite it all, "for a long time their utmost efforts were foiled by the valor of the besieged, who made constant sallies upon their works, burnt their towers and machines, and destroyed their miners."[4]

An example of these sorties occurred on the night of April 15. The Knights of the Temple, under the leadership of Master William, launched a midnight raid on the massive Muslim camp with but three hundred mounted knights, including a few secular ones. Their immediate goal was to destroy some of the nearest and most effective siege engines, especially the "Furious One," with Greek fire. Once the knights burst out of Acre, "the Saracens who were there were all killed, horsemen and footmen." In their zeal, however, "our men, both brethren and secular knights, went so far in among the tents that their horses got their legs tangled in the tent ropes and went sprawling, whereupon the Saracens slew them [for a total of eighteen Christians].... Then my lord and his men returned back to Acre. On the way, they ran into a number of Saracens lying in ambush, all of whom they killed, for the moonlight was bright as day and they could see them clearly."[5] Although "close to two thousand" Muslim horsemen intercepted the knights of Christ before they reentered Acre, "they dared not close with our men,"[6] even though they were "scarcely three hundred."[7]

With the coming of dawn, the city was greeted by the decapitated heads of the eighteen slain knights mounted atop poles facing the city. The Templars responded by displaying "a number of Saracen shields and bucklers and trumpets and drums" which they had seized during their sortie. According to one Muslim account, the sultan was so humiliated that he "started to call the emirs and rebuke them for prolonging the siege."[8]

Three days later, on April 18, the military orders led another nighttime raid: "It was decided that all the lords and the forces of Acre should make a sortie in the middle of the night from the Gate of St. Anthony, to fall suddenly on the Saracens. This was decided so secretly that no one knew of it until the command 'To horse!' was given." Even so, once the horsemen blitzed out the gates "the Saracens were forewarned, and illuminated the scene with torches so that it seemed to be day along their lines." Thousands of Muslims rushed "against our men and raked them so fiercely with javelins that it seemed to be raining. Our men could not endure this and so withdrew into the city, many of the horsemen being wounded."[9]

In fact, as the Crusaders had long suspected—hence why all the secrecy—traitors and crypto-Muslims were operating within the walls of Acre. One night before their failed sortie of April 18, an arrow had gone whizzing over the walls into the Muslim camp. Wrapped around it was a message in Arabic:

> In the name of Allah, the Merciful, the Compassionate. The blessings of Allah be upon our master Muhammad and his family. The only true faith in Allah's sight is Islam. Oh, sultan of the Muslims, preserve your military from the raid tonight, for the people of Akka [Acre]... intend to attack you, and take care also about your emirs, for they [the Christians] mentioned that some are corresponding against you.[10]

The chief problem facing Acre remained time and numbers: No matter how valiant the Christians' defense and sorties, and no matter how many Muslims they killed, "Day by day…the numbers of the garrison were thinned by the sword, whilst in the enemy's camp the places of the dead were constantly supplied by fresh warriors from the deserts of Arabia, animated with the same wild fanaticism in the cause of their religion as that which so eminently distinguished the military monks of the Temple."[11]

At one point, the military orders planned on one final all-out effort: They would entrust themselves to God and sally forth with their Muslim prisoners as shields, taking as many of the enemies' lives with them. In the words of the *Chronicle of Lanercost*,

> Those, then, who were in command upon the walls, perceiving that they could not hold the town for long against so many foes, determined by common counsel to make confession and receive the communion, penitently imploring help for their arms from the Lord, and that all should sally forth on the day of our common redemption [Easter Sunday, April 22], with ranks arrayed and the prisoners set in the van, and adventure their lives for the Author of life.

Deeming such an attempt overly suicidal, the elderly patriarch of Jerusalem, Nicolas of Hanapes, refused to bless such an enterprise, and it was dropped.[12]

On May 4, Henry II, the nominal king of the kingdom of Jerusalem, who, nonetheless, resided in Cyprus, arrived with the reinforcements of seven hundred men. Soon deeming the situation hopeless—the *turris maledicta*, or "Accursed Tower,"* which was key to Acre's defense, was finally thrown down on the same day he arrived[13]—the young monarch

* It is unclear why that tower was so named. Some said Jesus had cursed it and never entered the city; others that the thirty silver coins Judas betrayed Christ for were minted there. More probably it was so called because the Crusaders found it the hardest tower to take during their siege of Acre in 1190.

opened negotiations with the sultan and offered to pay tribute to retain Acre. Khalil refused, though he did entertain allowing the Christians to withdraw unmolested, at which point the Muslim rank and file, eager for their forthcoming share of the booty—animate and inanimate—howled in protestation and reminded him of his duty to jihad. "Only these infidels remain in all the lands of the coast!" cried they. "O our master, the sultan in the martyr's tomb [his father who made Khalil swear to obliterate Acre] would not come to an agreement with those cursed ones!"[14] The engines of war resumed their bombardment, as Christian ships frantically accelerated the evacuation of the tens of thousands of noncombatants—especially women, children, elderly, and infirm—to nearby Cyprus.

Finally, on the evening of May 15, Acre's outer wall and its towers, much of them now in rubble, were breached. Crying that all was lost, Henry II, along with his entourage, three thousand of Acre's wealthiest nobles, and several secular Crusaders, abandoned the city, prompting the indignant author of the *Excidium Acconis* to exclaim, "Would to God that a whirlwind had arisen, and had submerged these base fugitives, and that they had sunk like lead to the bottom of the sea!"[15]

No such luxury was available to the warriors of the Lord who had vowed to fight or die in the Holy Land.

35

"I BEG YOU...RETURN TO THE FIGHT!"

Early in the morning of May 16, the Muslims began to fill the moat between the outer and inner walls of now breached Acre with anything they could find to effect a makeshift bridge—corpses, carcasses, wood, stone, and earth; the Christians even "saw a band of fanatical Hajjis throw themselves into the ditch, in order that their troops might mount to the assault over their bodies"[1] Atop all this rubbish rushed a multitude of Muslims to a cacophony of horns and howls. Many of the Christian rank and file fled before their face, "but their victorious career and insulting shouts were there stopped by the mail-clad Knights of the Temple and the Hospital, who charged on horseback through the narrow streets, drove them back with immense carnage, and precipitated them headlong from the walls."[2]

The countercharge was led by Matthew of Clermont, the marshal of the Hospital—a man who, like a select few of his calling, had performed feats of valor that conformed to the biblical dictum that one man could "chase a thousand and two put ten thousand to flight" (Deuteronomy 32:30 KJV). As the Muslims flooded the defenses, Matthew rallied as many Knights of the Hospital and Temple as he could find, and the mounted men charged out of the Hospital "armed and plated," says the *Excidium Acconis*, "heads protected by polished helmets, gauntlets fitted round their arms and seated on their war horses with lances raised." Their progress was impeded by "terrified but not wounded" Christians fleeing the Muslim advance. "Are you mad?" cried Matthew at the panicked troops: "Fleeing with your armor intact, your helmets and shields unshattered, your bodies still unwounded? I beg you for the faith of the Church, return to the fight!"

Without another word, the marshal swung round and spurred his horse straight for the Muslim onrush near St. Anthony's Gate, which was pivotal for the Christians to hold and where the carnage was great. In the words of the chronicler,

> Rushing through the midst of the troops like a raging man…he crossed through St. Anthony's Gate beyond the whole army. By his blows he threw down many of the infidels dying to the ground. For they fled from him like sheep flee before the wolf, whither they knew not.[3]

Accounts note that Matthew wreaked havoc with his sword—slicing heads and extremities of the enemy in his berserker fury. Before long, a ring of dead Muslim bodies lay round his stomping steed, prompting the hitherto exulting Muslim chargers to retreat in terror.

The rest of the Hospitallers and Templars were no less valiant, and on Matthew's heels, the "heavy cavalry rode through and through the Saracen ranks, cutting them down by hundreds, until at last they drove them back in panic through the breaches they had so recently stormed." There, before the crumbling walls, "the military friars at last closed up the passage with their bodies… presenting a wall of steel to the advance of the enemy. Loud appeals to God and to Muhammad, to heaven and the saints, were to be heard on all sides; and after an obstinate engagement from sunrise to sunset, darkness put an end to the slaughter."[4]

Despite the bravery of the few, however, numbers again had the final say. Two thousand Christian warriors were killed on that day, leaving only seven thousand, most of them badly wounded, to hold the line; and although exponentially more Muslims were slain, the well of recruits whence the sultan could draw was bottomless. And although Matthew and his band of heroes had repulsed those Muslims attempting to take St. Anthony's Gate, the rest of the inner wall was now theirs as well.[5]

On the morning of May 17, a final war council was held in the Hospital, a massive compound that dominated Acre. The mood was grim, and the men started to bicker, at which point, Patriarch Nicolas of Hanapes "rose, motioned for silence with his hands, and delivered a mighty exhortation for faith, resistance, and courage in the name of Jesus Christ. To surrender now would be to put themselves in the hands of the infidel. And he stressed the likelihood of a wholesale rape and slavery of the women and children." "For you know," asserted the Patriarch, "that whoever of you was chosen by your Lord to defend his honor fighting against one or many, there is no doubt that we are all men tied to Jesus for the faith that we have in him through which we must be saved.... Confess your sins to one another, hoping that through the mercy of God you will be saved and obtain eternal life."[6]

His exhortation worked; the last standing defenders of Acre attended mass, confessed, partook of communion, and gave each other the holy kiss of peace before girding their loins and returning to their posts. Over at the Muslim camp, meanwhile, everything was eerily quiet; it was the calm before the storm.

"Before dawn on the next day, Friday," the Templar of Tyre picks up the narrative, as the city was shrouded in mist, "a drum began a powerful stroke, and at the sound of this drum, which had a horrible and mighty voice, the Saracens assailed the city of Acre upon all sides. The place where they entered first was by the Accursed Tower, which they had already taken.... They came on afoot, so many that they were without number."[7]

It was a repeat of the previous day—but with much more force and numbers. At their head again "came the fanatical dervishes and fakirs, shouting out the name of Allah as they ran wildly forward, impelled by holy zeal and visions of paradise to die at the foot of the wall and to provide a human bridge over which the soldiers might cross."[8]

The sights and sounds were apocalyptic. Fire and smoke rose everywhere, and thousands of Muslim warriors began to pour through the cracks and over the walls—even as a wild din created by three hundred camel riders pounding on drums and braying horns and the bloodcurdling jihadist cries emanating from tens of thousands of throats filled the air.

Yet another sound—much smaller, it is true—was heard from within the city. "Surround us with your impregnable wall, O Lord," cried the knights of Christ to the clang of church bells, "and protect us with your weapons!"[9]

Now all hell broke loose; all along the inner wall, men fought to the death as arrows and other projectiles fell on them "like rain."[10] The Templar of Tyre watched as an English knight was burned alive: He "was so badly hit by the Greek fire which the Saracens were hurling that his surcoat burst into flames...his face was burned, and then his whole body, and he burned as if he had been a cauldron of pitch, and he died there."[11]

The *Excidium Acconis* offers a snapshot of the assault, as the much-outnumbered Christians were engulfed by the Muslim onslaught:

> You could see many with heads severed from their necks, and from their shoulder blades, hands from arms, others split up to their breastbones, or run through with a spear or swords, or cut in two. Men were dying covered in blood or writhing in pain or with their eyes rolling in their heads, one with his head twisted back and another lying on his stomach, another with his tongue lolling, dying in great pain, and others again, though mortally wounded, making feeble attempts to get up again and fight. The slaughter on both sides was so great that it was impossible to step anywhere without treading on corpses.[12]

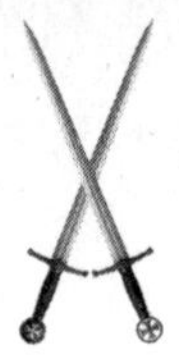

36

"MY LORDS, I CAN DO NO MORE FOR I AM KILLED"

Once the Muslims were inside Acre, and as if Heaven was showing its disapproval, a wild storm of rain and hail burst over the city on that fateful May 18, 1291. In the midst of this Armageddon, "the master [of the Temple] gathered ten or twelve brethren and his own household troops and headed for the St. Anthony Gate, right between the two walls." On the way, he saw and "summoned the master of the Hospital to join him. The Hospitaller master in turn collected some of his brethren."[1] The two mounted masters "stumbled grimly towards the Mamluks, forcing a path through fleeing soldiers and over piles of dead and wounded, many horribly burnt by Greek fire, amid screams, groans, triumphant yells from the Turks."[2] On reaching St. Anthony's Gate, "they counter-attacked" the enemy, continues the Templar of Tyre:

> But it was all to no effect…for there were too many Saracens. When the two masters of the Temple and the Hospital arrived there and went into combat, it seemed as if they hurled themselves against a stone wall. Those of the enemy hurling Greek fire hurled it so often and

> so thickly that there was so much smoke that one man could scarcely see another. Amongst the smoke, archers shot feathered arrows so densely that our men and mounts were terribly hurt.[3]

As he smote the enemy, and as his left arm was raised in a sword stroke, Templar Master William was run through with a javelin to his armpit: "It came through the gap where the plates of the armor were not joined." Being so "mortally wounded, he turned [his horse] to go." Seeing this, the standard-bearer quickly fell in behind, followed by many of the men—none of whom knew why the master was withdrawing. "Oh for God's sake, Sir, don't leave," one group of still-fighting knights cried out, "or the city will fall at once!" But Master William, crying out "to them in a loud voice, so that everyone could hear him," said, "My lords, I can do no more, for I am killed! See the wound here." Continues the Templar of Tyre,

> And then, we saw the javelin stuck in his body, and as he spoke he dropped the spear to the ground, and his head slumped to one side. He started to fall from his horse, but those of his household sprang down from their horses and supported him and took him off, and laid him on a shield that they found cast off there, a tall, broad buckler.[4]

They bore him away to the Temple fortress. The master of the Hospital, John of Villiers, was also gravely wounded in the fighting and was found stricken among the dead. Thanks only to his body servant, who was returning with a sergeant, he and seven other Knights of the Hospital were carried away to the harbor and onto a ship.[5]

As for the master of the Temple, William, "he lived all that day without saying a word, for since he had been taken down from his horse he had not spoken." He finally broke his silence "when he heard the clamor of men fleeing death," for "he wanted to know what was happening." They informed him that the battle was raging; he offered a feeble smile but also "commanded that they should leave him in peace.

He did not speak again." After some time, when his men turned back to look at him, they found the master slumped over, for he had "given up his soul to God."[6]

For many commentators at the time, this was by far the most demoralizing blow the Christians had thus suffered: "What great harm was caused by his death," reflected the Templar of Tyre. "As men learned what had happened, and saw the master carried off, they began one by one to abandon their posts and flee." Meanwhile, "the Saracens...had come through the Accursed Tower...and everyone they encountered they put to the sword."[7]

The master's death provoked different responses from different men. When that scourge of Islam and marshal of the Hospital, Matthew of Clermont, saw the limp body of his noble-hearted friend, William, he again gathered as many Hospitallers and Templars as would follow him, sallied forth out of the Temple to the blast of trumpets, and found a clearing where he and his brethren made what would become their final stand—hewing down countless enemies before finally being drowned in a sea of scimitars and spears. In the words of the Templar of Tyre, an eyewitness,

> Among those who fell back on the Temple that day was Brother Matthew of Clermont, Marshal of the Hospital of St. John. He saw the master of the Temple, who was dead as I have told you, and then returned to the battle, gathering around him all his brethren, for he would not abandon any of them, and some of the Templars went with him, and they came to a square of the Genoese quarter which was empty of houses, and there Matthew plunged into combat. He and his companions slew many Saracens, but in the end he was slain, him and the others, like true knights and valiant, and good Christians. May God preserve their souls![8]

Matthew of Clermont must have been a sight to behold; various eyewitness accounts tell of his final stand. According to one, it was only because he rode his horse to death that the Muslims were able to run him through:

> His war horse was utterly exhausted and was unable to charge any further. It resisted the spurs and stood in the middle of the street as if rooted to the spot where it was hit by a spear and fell prostrate on the ground. With his horse collapsed he was run through by spears. So the faithful warrior knight of Christ gave up his soul to his creator.[9]

He, and Master William before him, were only two of many noble hearts to fall on that day. Every knight of the orders of the Teutons, St. Thomas, and St. Lazarus were wiped out to a man. For "at last," says the *Excidium Acconis*, "the gates collapsed, and a suffocating multitude of infidels burst in beneath the arch, on horses with their lances, and ran the Christians through."[10]

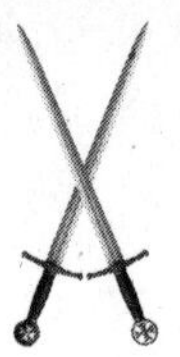

37

"THAT DAY WAS TERRIBLE TO BEHOLD!"

With tens of thousands of Muslims running amok and slaughtering any Christian they came across, mass chaos overtook Acre on that May 18, 1291. "The terrified ... men, women and children, deprived of the chance to flee," writes Thaddeus of Naples, "were trapped miserably or cornered in the squares, streets, houses and corners of the city." At the same time, the harbor "was a mass of screaming women and children, and panic-stricken soldiers, struggling to get into the boats, with the sailors haggling over the price of safety and trying to pick out those who could pay the most. Into this mob of helpless fugitives, mad with fear, rode the merciless Saracen horde, killing all whom they could reach and pursuing them into the waves of the sea."[1]

Adding to this nightmare were the darkling clouds and massive hailstorm that capsized a number of boats overflowing with fugitives—including the one containing the elderly Patriarch Nicolas of Hanapes. A good Christian to the last, he had "insisted upon holding back in order to rescue as many people as possible, with the result that his overloaded boat sank beneath the waves."[2] The Templar of Tyre, who was among those fortunate enough to escape by boat (which was especially fortunate for posterity) never forgot those last moments:

> Know that that day was terrible to behold. The ladies... and other lesser folk came fleeing through the streets, their children in their arms, weeping and despairing, and fleeing to the sailors to save them from death. And when the Saracens came across them, one seized the mother and another the child, and carried them away from place to place, and separated them from each other. Once there was a quarrel between two Saracens over a woman and she was killed by them; and another time a woman was led away captive, and the infant at her breast was thrown to the ground where the horses trampled on it, slaying it thus. There were some women who were pregnant and who were caught in the press of the flight and suffocated and died, and the life in her womb died with her. And there were some women whose husband or child was lying ill or wounded by an arrow at their lodging; they left them alone and fled, the Saracens slew them all.[3]

After describing some more carnage and atrocities silhouetted by smoke and flames, the Templar of Tyre confessed that "no one could adequately recount the tears and grief of that day. The pitiful sight of the little children, tumbled about and disemboweled as the horses trampled them...! There is no man in the world who has so very hard a heart that he would not have wept to see the slaughter."[4]

Despite it all, or perhaps because of it, small pockets of defiant knights and Christian warriors continued to resist. According to Thaddeus,

> Completely trapped inside the cities and squares and corners they offered armed resistance against the enemy entering and pushed them back...men from the religious orders and pious lay people of all social ranks persisted in this exhausting struggle for two days, their numbers

> slowly being whittled away, weighed down by their heavy armor and weakened by thirst, hunger and stress, until they were all killed in the name of Christ.[5]

Others were passively martyred. When those Muslims who were targeting and burning churches and monasteries "out of hatred for Christianity," barged into a monastery, they massacred dozens of Dominicans and Franciscans as they knelt before and prayed at the altar. Similarly, Dominican nuns were slaughtered while singing hymns in their church. Another group of nuns, the devoted Sisters of St. Clare, had refused to flee in order to tend the sick and wounded. "When the end came they followed the example of the sisters of the Hospital at the sack of Antioch, and by mutilating and disfiguring their countenances, provoked the indignant Muslim soldiery to slay them forthwith, and their dead bodies were seen flung into a heap in one of the streets."[6]

Once the smoke had cleared and the dust settled, only one monument to resistance continued to stand—the massive Temple compound, where some three hundred Templars, the last of the brethren, continued to defy the invading horde. It was, moreover, rather fitting that it was at the Temple—which from of old existed to guard Christian pilgrims in the Holy Land—that the remaining Christian civilians, more than ten thousand men, women, and children, sought sanctuary "for it was the strongest place in the city" and "occupied a large site on the sea, like a castle" at the very tip of the promontory.[7]

On May 20, the marshal of the Temple, Peter of Sevrey, who had assumed command following Master William's death, offered to surrender the Temple on condition that all Christians be allowed to withdraw to Cyprus unmolested. The sultan agreed. The gates were dropped, and four hundred Muslim horsemen entered the Temple complex, where they promptly hoisted the crescent flag of Islam in victory. Once inside, however, both Christian and Muslim accounts emphasize that, on seeing the potentially rich harvest of Frankish women and children they were supposed to grant safe passage, the Muslims immediately began laying hands on and trying to rape many of them—including the boys—in fact, any Christian "who pleased them," not least to "dishonor them."[8]

Outraged by this gross betrayal, Peter ordered the Temple's open gates slammed shut, thereby separating the four hundred Muslim oath breakers from their comrades outside the Temple. The flag of Islam was swiftly cast down and the Order's black and white standard—the dreaded beauséant, that ancient herald of implacable war—was again raised aloft, even as the "Christians [who] found this [Muslim] conduct intolerable, drew their weapons, and flung themselves upon the Saracens, slaying them all and beheading them, so that none escaped alive. Then the Christians set themselves determinedly to defend their [the women's and children's] bodies to the death."[9]

On the following morning, Sultan Khalil, who was both happy and angry—happy that victory was at hand, angry at the stubborn resistance that continued—sent a messenger saying that he knew that his own men were at fault and got what they deserved. As such, he was happy to reopen negotiations, provided that Peter came forth to discuss terms. Seeing the desperate situation of the moaning and groaning civilians, the marshal of the Temple decided he had no choice but to trust the sultan. He set out with a small delegation of Templars, but before they could even reach his tent, the sultan—proving he was a fine successor to that fork-tongued devil of aforetime, Baybars—ordered them all bound and beheaded.[10]

The remaining Knights of the Temple, some of whom were elderly, and all of whom were wounded, yet again girded their loins to resume the defense of the last heirs of the Christian pilgrims their order was founded to protect. And for eight long days, they fought off one assault after another until, at the last, throngs of Muslims rushed in through a breach made to the complex.

There, on May 28, amid the flames and shrieks of women and children, the last men of the Temple and Hospital fought as the final curtain drew on Acre. The tower of the Temple, where most of the clash took place and which was already weakened from undermining and now overburdened with the influx of hundreds of rushing men, came crashing down in a fiery inferno, killing everyone inside, swords still in hands. As usual, the Muslims, who always outnumbered the Christians, bore the brunt, for "when the tower collapsed, it fell outwards towards the street, and crushed more than two thousand mounted Turks" who were surrounding the complex.[11]

When all was said and done, approximately thirty thousand Christians were killed at Acre, and many thousands—primarily women and children—were sold into slavery.[12] Before leaving, Khalil ordered all the rest of Acre's fortifications razed and the entire city set ablaze, just as his predecessor, Baybars, had done to the traumatized remains of Antioch thirty-three years earlier.*

---

* It is significant to note that Muslim histories agree with the Christian eyewitness accounts concerning the fall of Acre—including that the Muslims broke their word by trying to rape the civilian population and that the sultan broke his word by slaughtering the Templars after they surrendered. Here, for example, is Egyptian chronicler Abu al-Mahasin's contemporary account: "There was fighting every day and a certain number of Muslims fell as martyrs for the Faith. At dawn on Friday 17 the Sultan and his troops, mounted on their horses, moved in to attack before sunrise. They beat their drums, creating a terrible, terrifying noise, and the army massed under the walls. The Franks fled and the city was taken by storm. Not three hours of the day had passed before the Muslims entered Acre and made themselves masters of it, while the Franks cast themselves into the sea, trampled on by the Muslim troops who killed and captured them. Only a few escaped. The Muslims took all the booty they could find, goods, treasure and arms, and the population was killed or taken prisoner. Templars, Hospitallers and Teutonic Hospitallers made a last stand in four lofty towers in the middle of the city, where they were besieged. On Saturday 19th of the month, two days after the fall of the city, regular troops and others attacked the house and tower where the Templars were. The Templars begged for their lives, which the Sultan granted them. He sent them a standard which they accepted and raised over the tower. The door was opened and a horde of regulars and others swarmed in. When they came face to face with the defenders some of the soldiers began to pillage and to lay hands on the women and children who were with them, whereupon the Franks shut the door and attacked them, killing a number of Muslims. They hauled down the standard and stiffened their resistance. The siege continued. On the same day the Teutonic Hospitallers asked for an amnesty and this was granted to them and their women by the Sultan, by the hand of the amīr Zain ad-Din Kitbughā al-Mansuri. The battle against the Templars' tower continued until Sunday 20 when they and the defenders of the other two towers sued for their lives. The Sultan granted them permission to go where they liked, but when they came out he killed more than 2,000 of them, took an equal number prisoners and sent the women and children as slaves to the gate of the Sultan's pavilion" (Gabrieli, *Arab Historians of the Crusades*, 347–348).

With the fall of Acre, for a century the headquarters of the kingdom of Jerusalem, so too came the end of the Crusader presence in the Holy Land. Over the next few weeks, because resistance was futile, all remaining and vastly outnumbered and defenseless Christian holdings—in Beirut, Haifa, Sidon, Tortosa, Tyre—surrendered. "Thus the whole of Syria and the coastal zones were purified of the Franks," trumpeted Abu al-Fida, even though the Christians "had once been on the point of conquering Egypt and subduing Damascus and other cities. Praise be Allah!"[13] Or, in the words of the Templar of Tyre, "Thus…was all of Syria lost, taken and destroyed by the Saracens.… This time everything was lost, so that altogether the Christians held not so much as a palm's breadth of land in Syria."[14]

Islam's epic victory against and expulsion of the Crusaders in 1291 thrilled Muslims everywhere. "After Acre was lost," continues the Templar of Tyre, "it happened in the year of the Incarnation of Christ 1291 that the Saracens of Spain…saw that the sultan of Babylon [Egypt] had destroyed Christianity in Syria. So they wished to destroy their Spanish Christian neighbors—for the Saracens of Syria had long ago made a compact with the Saracens of Spain to do harm to the Christians both here and over there. What the Syrian Muslims had achieved, the others I mentioned [Moors of Spain] wanted to do so also."[15] Thus began a new chapter in the perennial jihad and counter-jihad (Reconquista) that characterized that peninsula.

Nor was the victor of 1291 forgotten: "Because of you," a Muslim panegyric was later addressed to Sultan Khalil, "no town is left in which unbelief can repair, no hope for the Christian religion! Through Ashraf the Lord Sultan, we are delivered from the Trinity, and Tawhid rejoices in the struggle! Praise be to Allah, the nation of the Cross has fallen; through the Turks the religion of the chosen Arab has triumphed!"[16]

The hubristic sultan could not contain himself and soon thereafter sent a boastful letter, also worthy of Baybars, to Hethoum the king of Cilician Armenia, who was "of the race of Christ." The sultan boasted of how

> we have conquered the city of Acre that was the seat of the true cross.… Our glittering swords consumed all the

> Hospitallers and Templars...[and] Teutonic Knights. We leveled their churches to the ground, they were slaughtered on their own altars, and the Patriarch himself was delivered into tribulation [as seen, though he was offered many chances to escape by boat, Nicolas of Hanapes remained in Acre until he drowned for trying to save other Christians on May 18]. And you can see a vast amount of treasure has come into the hands of our men...and so many women that they were sold for a drachma a piece. And you can see the towers of Acre have been razed to the ground and turned to a wasteland.... It will be to your advantage to come personally with your lords and two years' worth of tribute to our lofty doors, as a man who values his personal safety and his kingdom and does not try to evade our great power. You can be certain that nothing will escape me after the destruction of Acre.[17]

Less than two years later, this same Khalil, "the subjugator of the worshippers of the crosses,"[18] was—in keeping with the modus operandi of the Mamluk sultanate—assassinated by his own leading men, including his uncle. The final Mamluk to give him the death blow "hacked him so that he cut him in two. Thus, was Christianity avenged of the wrongs which he had committed."[19] Then the emirs, in their attempt to become the next sultan, turned against each other, eventually slaughtering one another to a man. This too offered some small comfort to the Templar of Tyre:

> Thus were killed and destroyed all the emirs, the persecutors of Jesus Christ. It may be that God permitted us to be punished by them for our evil deeds, and that it only remained for God to punish them for the evil which they had done to us...[including] the disgrace which they had brought on Christendom in knocking down the churches and dragging around the images [icons].[20]

*****

As a convenient summary—and because nothing is more authoritative than an eyewitness account—the reader is left with an excerpt of a letter that John of Villiers, the master of the Hospital, wrote days later in "sorrow and anguish"[21] from his sickbed in Cyprus, recounting to the preceptor of St. Giles the great and terrible fall of Acre:

> At last after many assaults and many defenses and many sorties, that we made against them and they against us, after great shedding of blood on one side and the other, when our people had suffered grieviously by wounds and injuries, they entered the city by the gate called King Hugh's Gate, on the 18th day of May recently passed. They had pierced and broken and thrown down the walls in several places with their engines.... They enterea the city on all sides early in the morning and in very great force. We and our Convent resisted them at St. Anthony's Gate, where there were so many Saracens that one could not count them. Nevertheless we drove them back three times as far as the Accursed Tower. And in that action and others, where the brethren of our Convent fought in defense of the city and their lives and country, we lost little by little all the Convent of our Order, which then came to an end, and belongs to the Holy Church. Among them our dear friend Brother Matthew of Clermont our Marshal lay dead. He was noble and valiant and skillfull in arms. May God be gracious unto him! On that same day the Master of the Temple also died of a mortal wound from a lance. May God have mercy on his soul! I myself on that same day was stricken nigh to death by a lance between the shoulders, a wound that has made the writing of this letter a very hard task. Meanwhile a great multitude of Saracens entered the city, on all sides, by land and by sea, moving along the walls, which were all pierced and broken, and running

> through the streets of the city until they came to our shelters. Our sergeants, lads and mercenaries, and the crusaders and others began utterly to despair, and to fly towards the ships, throwing down their arms and armor. We and our brethren, of whom the greater number were sore stricken and wounded to death, resisted them as long as we could. God knows it. And as some of us were lying thus half-dead and helpless before our enemies, our sergeants and household boys came and carried me, wounded almost to death, and our other brethren, at great danger to themselves. And thus I and some of our brethren escaped, as it pleased God, most of whom were wounded and battered without hope of cure, and we were taken to the island of Cyprus. On the day that this letter was written we were still there, in great sadness of heart, prisoners of overwhelming sorrow.[22]

In retrospect, that the master of the Hospital had survived, albeit battered and bruised, whereas the master of the Temple had been slain, was an ominous sign of things to come....

38

TIMES THAT TRY MEN'S SOULS

The fall of Acre had a traumatic impact on many a soul-searching Christian. The Templar of Tyre was "overcome by the need to put down my thoughts in rhyme, thoughts on the age and season in which have befallen so many ill things."[1] An excerpt concerning that "age and season"—which may seem uncomfortably familiar—follows:

> When Acre was despoiled and all Syria laid waste…men who were already evil now became even more vile.… No one cared anymore about anyone else. For rancor, discord and hatred have put down roots between men; Love has fled from them and Envy is sown amongst them. For they are in great contention over who should get the upper hand in this world, and prove himself superior, so that no one might be his equal.… But helping orphan girls find husbands or supporting impoverished widows…you will not see anyone setting aside coins for alms-giving. So the greater part of men are changed for the worse.… Those who are good at getting drunk, and singing dirty songs and flattering and bribing—such men can get what they want. And whoever is clever

> at deceitful things, and shows cunning, and comes up with novel ideas—that fellow is considered wise.... But a straightforward and noble soul, without malice, and of good conduct—such a one attracts no attention, but is considered a muttonhead.... Thus falls the world to ruins, when Evil is taken for Good.... [V]ile men...seek to pile up gold and silver and to lord it over better men. Such men have wrecked the world...and Christianity is sold out by everyone.[2]

For others, Acre raised disturbing questions concerning God's justice. Riccoldo of Montecroce (1243–1320) is paradigmatic of this spiritual crisis. A Dominican friar devoted to spreading the Gospel, he spent twelve years in the Middle East, primarily in Mongol-ruled Baghdad, where he learned Arabic, studied the Koran, visited mosques, and tried to proselytize Muslims (only to be beaten and nearly killed for not converting to Islam himself).[3]

Riccoldo was in Baghdad when Acre fell in 1291 and personally witnessed the tragic aftermath. Seeing countless Christians mistreated and paraded in the slave markets so tore at his heart that he unburdened his soul in five letters addressed to Heaven. "Why had such slaughter and degradation befallen the Christian people," he asked God, "and such temporal prosperity been granted to the perfidious race of the Saracens?"

> What suffering and sorrow have befallen us!... For the Saracens have killed many Christians [he later says thirty thousand in Acre alone], and many other Christians who have remained have accepted the law—nay the perfidy—of the Saracens [meaning converted to Islam].... How miserable I become when I see Christians mentally confounded, travelling on the road as if they were insane with grief and fear of the Saracens!... I have seen maidens and old women crying at the foot of the crucifix, beating their empty breasts, calling for help with worn-out voices, and waiting in vain for this crucified image to come to their aid. And they cry inconsolably for their

> children or husbands who have become the slaves of Saracens or who have been killed by them.[4]

Muslims further managed to kill two birds with one stone by exploiting their Christian slaves to empower Islam: "Children have been spared to make them into Saracens. And matrons, nuns, and virgins have been given to the Saracens as concubines and slaves, so that through them the Saracen population will increase." Apparently, "virgins and holy nuns" were especially coveted and "impregnated by the Saracens."[5]

Everywhere Riccoldo encountered the handy work of Muslims, now flush with victory: "In all of Turkey and Persia, and all the way to Baghdad, have we not found all the Christian churches destroyed, or converted into stables or mosques by the Saracens?" He tells of broken crosses mocked and dragged in the dirt and images of Jesus and the saints with their eyes gouged out.[6]

Rather than help, God had abandoned his people to that "damned tyrant Muhammad, who became a prophet through robbery and tyranny." Worse, Muslims "persecute us [precisely] because we follow you. They kill us with enmity and consider themselves saved."[7]

Like others, the friar marks the death of Templar Master William of Beaujeu as the decisive moment that presaged the fall of Acre:

> A Saracen shot a hostile arrow and it struck the Master of the Temple between the stomach and the lungs.... He died late that evening when he could have protected the city, and the next morning the city was immediately taken...and the Christians were overwhelmed by such a stupor—nay, such fear and terror.... Could it be perhaps that at that very hour, God and his angels were praying for Muhammad as it is written in the Koran? Certainly they should not pray for him any more, because if God and his angels abandon us in this way, and if the Saracens continue doing what they have been doing for the past two years in Tripoli and Acre, then I fear that soon not a single Christian will be found in the entire world.[8]

Riccoldo expresses similar regret for, and speaks directly to his fellow Dominican brother, Patriarch Nicolas of Hanapes. For refusing to quit Acre when he could and selflessly trying to take as many Christian refugees as possible into his boat, Heaven, the friar laments, rewarded the elderly man by capsizing his vessel and drowning him:

> I was miserable when I first heard that you had drowned in the sea; I was so sad that I became stupid and indolent. But now I rejoice all the more, not that you were drowned, but because by drowning you have undoubtedly delivered many people and preserved them in the faith of Christ. You were a leader who did not fear for himself, but for his people.[9]

As a father, God should "punish us as children who must be instructed, not as enemies who must be destroyed! Strike us, kill us with your own power, and do not place a sword into a furious hand, into the hand of your enemy and ours, Muhammad and the Saracens, who torture and kill us because we are unwilling to deny your faith!"[10]

So unable to comprehend why "it is to such a beast [Muhammad] that you have given so much power against the Christians for almost seven hundred years,"* Riccoldo could not but conclude that "it seems that God is his [Muhammad's] collaborator." As such, "if it pleases you that Muhammad should rule, tell us so that we may venerate him."[11]

Such was the spiritual angst that followed the fall of Acre in 1291; such were the times that tried men's souls.

Not so for the Knights of the Temple and Hospital. However they interpreted that cataclysmic event, the Holy Land was nonnegotiable for them. To their way of thinking, they had lost another battle—a rather significant one, yes—but they had yet to lose the war. It was time to regroup, recommit, and refocus. And so the Temple and Hospital relocated to and

* Riccoldo's math is accurate. From the very earliest years when Islam began conquering the ancient Christian lands of the Middle East and North Africa, beginning with Greater Syria and Egypt between 636–642, to the time of Riccoldo's writing in the 1290s, "almost seven hundred years" had indeed passed.

established headquarters in Limassol, Cyprus. Wasting no time, they developed their naval capabilities and began launching raids against the enemy.

Hope was rekindled after the Christians and Mongols formed an alliance against the Mamluks. In exchange for their swords, Ghazan Khan, the Mongol master of Persia and parts of the Middle East, would reward them with Jerusalem. By October 1299, the Templars and Hospitallers helped the Mongols take Aleppo. In the following year, the Templars garrisoned the island of Ruad. Two miles away from the Syrian mainland, it would serve as a staging post for the forthcoming Crusade.

The new Crusade never came, and in 1303, the Mamluks sent sixteen galleys to besiege the tiny island. When the vastly outnumbered knights had reached their final extremity, they accepted the Muslims' terms of surrender, which allowed the Templars to withdraw back to Cyprus. As usual, the Muslims reneged, loaded the Christian warriors with chains, and took them to Cairo, where they were all used for and killed during arrow target practice.[12]

As in all previous engagements, the knights of the military orders had the heart but not the numbers to be effective. Attacking and trying to hold any mainland Muslim domain by themselves became increasingly suicidal, causing them to become—or at least appear in the eyes of their contemporaries as—idle and purposeless. Various thinkers, including the pope, responded by suggesting a sort of "downsizing." The Temple and the Hospital—which had been known to quarrel on more than one occasion*—should, they said, merge into one order.

The masters of both orders were not amenable to the idea and for good reason (although they were both military orders, the Temple and Hospital had separate vocations, and it would not be just to require, say, a Templar knight to take vows to serve "our masters the poor," when that was never his original intention). At any rate, in early 1307, the Templar master, James (or Jacques) of Molay, traveled to France to meet with the pope to discuss this matter and other crusading plans.

---

* One of the most notorious examples occurred during 1256–1258, when conflict erupted between Venice and Genoa over property in Acre—and the Templars sided with Venice, the Hospitallers with Genoa. This led to open street fighting, naval bombardments, and even the besieging of each other's compounds.

39
FRIDAY THE 13TH

On Friday, October 13, 1307, after King Philip IV of France had heard tell of "a bitter thing, a lamentable thing, a thing horrible to contemplate, terrible to hear, a heinous crime, an execrable evil, an abominable deed, a hateful disgrace, a completely inhuman thing, indeed remote from all humanity," all Templars in his domains, including Master James of Molay, were arrested and thrown in dungeons.[1]

They were charged with heresy, including by denying Christ, spitting and urinating on the cross during their induction ceremony, engaging in homosexual activities and sorcery, worshipping demonic idols—some smeared with the fat of children they had roasted, no less—and even "worshipping a certain cat that appeared amongst them."[2]

The mass arrests and charges came as a shock to everyone. When King Philip wrote to King James II of Aragon that same month, calling on him to arrest all Templars in his domain, the latter refused. The knights of Christ, he responded, "have lived indeed in a praiseworthy manner as religious men up till now in these parts according to common opinion, nor has any accusation of error in belief yet arisen in them here; on the contrary, during our reign they have faithfully given us very great service in whatever we have required of them, in repressing the enemies of the faith."[3]

The king of England, Edward II, also found the accusations suspicious, and three weeks after launching his own investigation, on December 10, he wrote to the pope, saying that he was "unable to credit the horrible charges against the Knights Templar who everywhere bear a good name in England."[4] Edward stressed that they had been, in all their dealings with him, financial and otherwise, true and honest, and had helped his own great ancestor, Richard the Lionheart. The English king also sent letters to several other European kings, reminding them of the honor and self-sacrifice of, and urging them to defend, the Temple.[5]

It was not just that the accusations were so incongruous with the reputation of the accused; many other indicators of chicanery were apparent.

For starters, many of the charges traced back to men of ill repute—one in particular: Esquin of Floyran, a disgraced Templar and murderer who had been earlier expelled from the Order and was burning for vengeance. In 1305, Esquin had tried to sell his former Order's "secrets," which he insisted were scandalous, to the aforementioned James of Aragon. The unimpressed king had paid him no heed. When, however, Esquin took his stories to the French inquisitor, William of Nogaret, the Templar turncoat was welcomed with open arms. The vile accusations he hurled against his former brethren were precisely what the itching ears of King Philip IV were eager to hear.

Such a claim may have seemed counterintuitive to those not in the know; after all, the Templars had long been friendly and helpful to the king. In 1299, the Temple loaned Philip 500,000 livres; and in 1306, after the French king's efforts to raise taxes were met with riots, it was the strong Temple of Paris that gave him asylum. Indeed, on October 12—the very day before the Templars were arrested en masse—Templar Master James had served as a pall bearer at the funeral of Philip's sister-in-law, Catherine of Courtenay.

For those in the know, however, the French king's accusations were predictable and widely seen as a pretext for plundering the Temple of its wealth and resources—or at least to avoid paying it back his huge debts.

In short, "many contemporaries were of the opinion that the motive was greed: Philip wanted to secure the revenues of the Templars. It was a view which became so widely expressed that the French government felt the necessity to rebut it."[6]

For example, in a May 30, 1308, letter addressed to King James of Aragon, John of Burgundy, Philip's procurator at the papal court, complained of "all those slanderers" who needed to "be silent"—"those who in their desire to support the Templars in their error say that the king is motivated in his actions by his avarice and greed for the Order's goods.... The king was not motivated by greed but by the zeal of his faith."[7] Similarly, in his letter to the kings of Europe, Edward of England urged them to "turn a deaf ear to the slanders of ill-natured men, who are animated, as we believe, not with a zeal of rectitude, but with a spirit of cupidity and envy."[8]

King Philip's very own history casts suspicions on his motive. In 1291, and again in 1311, he ordered the arrest of and seized all the assets of Italian bankers. And just one year before arresting the Templars, in 1306, he subjected France's Jews to the same treatment, arresting and plundering them all in one day, before expelling them. Indeed, the whole affair was déjà vu. Not only was Philip known for targeting others for their wealth, but in 1296, after Philip's attempt to tax the church failed, the French king had a list of charges drawn up against the then-pope Boniface VIII—all of which were near identical to those leveled against the Templars—including heresy, blasphemy, sorcery, and sodomy. (When Boniface refused to back down and threatened to interdict all of France, which threatened to prompt a general uprising against Philip, the king sent an army to arrest the pope at his residence in Anagni. Although the people of the region rose up and rescued Boniface from captivity, the eighty-six-year-old died soon thereafter.)

Then there were the obvious and commonsensical arguments that naturally arose when evaluating the charges against the Knights of the Temple. For starters, how could such scandalous—nay, satanic—behavior remain hidden for so long? Consider: the Temple's recruits, drawn by sincere and pious motives, must have believed they were joining a holy brotherhood. So how is it that, upon being ordered to spit on the cross, deny Christ, commit sodomy, and worship idols, not a single one of these God-fearing men (who would have found such acts more abominable than the average medieval Christian) recoiled in horror, broke ranks, and exposed the Order? Are we to believe that thousands of Christian knights quietly submitted to a litany of diabolical rites without protest—or even so much as a whisper of dissent? That is precisely what a Templar spokesman told a papal commission on April 23, 1310:

> Many noble and powerful men from various lands and regions, some of them of considerable age and many of them well known in the secular world, honest men born of high-ranking families, had made their profession in the Temple, burning with zeal for the orthodox faith, and have remained in it till they died. If men of such standing had known, seen or heard of anything dishonorable in the order of the Temple, especially the deplorable insulting and blaspheming of the name of Jesus Christ, they would have vehemently protested, and brought everything to the notice of the whole world.[9]

Historians who specialize in the field of Templar history agree: "The order cannot have been guilty of the crimes imputed to it," Jonathan Riley-Smith flatly asserts. "It was not a secret society but a large and well-known order of the church which could not have engaged in such bizarre practices without stories leaking out."[10] Alan Forey agrees:

> Had the practices attributed to the Templars been customary throughout the order for any length of time, they would scarcely have escaped detection until the early years of the fourteenth century. It was not unusual for the brethren to leave the order, either to transfer to another—normally stricter—religious foundation or to return to the world, and these brothers would undoubtedly have made known what had been happening. As the abandoning of a religious order was a serious offense, those who had left the Temple merely to revert to secular

> life would hardly have ignored a means of justifying their flight. Nor is it credible that all who entered the order believing it to be orthodox would have stayed in it if they had been forced to submit to these practices which were said to occur at admission ceremonies.[11]

Many more particular arguments, again based purely on common sense and reason, can be and were made. How could the Knights of the Temple have denied and mocked Christ, while simultaneously fighting and dying for him? As seen, many regular Crusaders had personally witnessed various Templars willingly accept martyrdom rather than renounce Christ. Master James of Molay himself made this point during one of his later depositions: "He knew of no other Order or other people more prepared to expose their bodies to death in defense of the Christian faith against its enemies, nor who had shed so much blood and were more feared by the enemies of the Catholic faith."[12] Indeed, a full twenty thousand Templars were said to have been killed or submitted to being martyred by Muslims rather than recant since the Order's founding.[13]

Moreover, Templar records attest that various members had been punished *precisely* for what the Order was supposedly forcing initiates to do. Roger the German, who was captured at Forbie in 1244, was compelled by his Muslim captors to renounce Christ and proclaim Muhammad as God's final prophet. Although he later insisted that he did not understand the Arabic words he was made to recite—*la ilaha illa Allah, Muhammadun rasul Allah**—he was nonetheless expelled from the Order.[14]

Even the especially repugnant accusations of homosexuality were bizarre and counterintuitive. The Temple reportedly made all its new initiates "swear to be chaste as regards women and they are enjoined by their preceptors that when the desires of the flesh assail them they

* The Shahada: "There is no god but Allah; Muhammad is the messenger of Allah" (Arabic original لَا إِلٰهَ إِلَّا ٱللّٰهُ، مُحَمَّدٌ رَسُولُ ٱللّٰهِ,) Anyone who recites it before two or more Muslim witnesses, such as the hapless Roger the German, becomes a Muslim according to Islamic law.

should live one with another in carnal lust."[15] Similarly, another brother was supposedly told that "it was better to have sex between brothers of the Order than to assuage their lust with women."[16] Where is the logic in this? If the Templars were such libertines as to encourage sodomy, why would they at the same time make new recruits "swear to be chaste as regards women"? Why not copulate with all and sundry, male and female, which is much more consistent with a depraved and/or hedonistic outlook?

Incidentally, while it may be overlooked in the current climate, it should be noted that throughout history and up until a few years ago, far from being something to be "celebrated" or even acknowledged as normal, "the filthy, stinking sin of sodomy"—to quote the Templar rule—was seen as an abhorrent and vile activity. In fact, it was "so filthy and so stinking and so repugnant that it should not be named."[17] As such, this particular accusation was, no doubt, meant to demean and undermine the Templars' masculine appeal (as were accusations that Templars "kissed" one another's penises and anuses).

Still, as a reflection of its transparency, the Temple's records had openly documented that a few of its members had—as had the members of other orders who by nature had no access to women—engaged in homosexual acts. But they were severely punished for, not encouraged to engage in, such behavior. Templar documents tell of three "brothers who practiced wicked sin and caressed each other in their chambers at night; so that those who knew of the deed and others who had suffered greatly by it, told this thing to the Master and to a group of the worthy men of the house." As "the deed was so offensive," the master had them ambushed, stripped of their habits, and placed "in heavy irons." One of the convicts "escaped by night and went to the Saracens." Of the two others, one was killed while trying to escape and the other "remained in prison for a long time."[18]

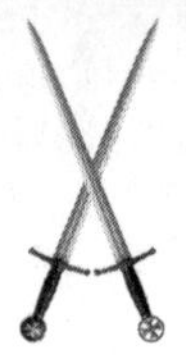

40

THE INQUISITION

Although everything pointed to the Templars' innocence, three difficulties faced them.

First, the pope who presided over their case and was most charged with providing them a fair trial was Philip's creature. The French king had learned from his difficulties with Pope Boniface VIII and made it a point to secure the pontificate for one of his own—namely, Raymond Bertrand of Got, a Frenchman and close confidant of Philip, who, as Pope Clement V, went so far as to move the papacy from Rome to Avignon, France. Although he tried to intervene on behalf of and secure a fair trial for the Templars following their October 13 arrest—which itself was illegal since all orders were subject to the jurisdiction of the Church—when push came to shove, Pope Clement all too often succumbed to Philip's expectations of conformity.

Second, the charge of heresy was, in the fourteenth century, exceedingly difficult to overcome and an almost certain way of eliminating a political rival (hence why it was used with such frequency). And although it was obvious that they were being accused of all the stock-in-trade heresies, one thing unique to the Templars, as opposed to all other European "heretics," made the charges more plausible: their familiarity with Islam, which was then seen as the king of all heresies. Denying the divinity of Christ, spitting, urinating, stomping on the cross, and even sodomy were long known to be common among Muslims. Accordingly, to many of their detractors, that the Templars had for nearly two centuries closely interacted with Muslims—worse, that some brothers could even read Arabic!—was all the proof needed that they were in league with the devil, to the point that, for some paranoids, "the Templars always favored the Saracens in the holy wars in Palestine, and oppressed the Christians."[1]

Following their arrest, this theme was amplified. Some suggested that the Temple's supposed denial of Christ was "introduced by a Templar master who had to agree to it in order to secure his release from a Muslim prison." Others believed that the Templars worshipped a bearded head, sometimes referred to as "Baphomet"—"an Old French corruption of Muhammad"—on the erroneous belief that Muslims worshipped idols. [2]

Even the good name of William of Beaujeu, the Templar master who died heroically defending Acre in 1291, was sullied. The fact that he kept close ties with Muslims and had some in his employ—all of which was done on behalf of and for the welfare of Christendom—was now presented as more "proof" that "they had gone over to the Saracens." As Felix Fabri, a Dominican from southwest Germany, concluded following Philip's propaganda campaign against the Templars: "Albeit their beginning was holy and full of virtue, yet afterward they degenerated from their forerunners after they waxed fat...forasmuch as it became known to our people that they had gone over to the Saracens, and had fallen into many vices...[and] were leading exceedingly disgraceful lives."[3] (Despite this, even he added a coda to his account stating that many still believed in the opposite view: that they were victims of Philip's avarice.)

Here, one is reminded of the Templars' response to Count Robert, when he accused them of treacherously working with the Muslims after they had advised against chasing their Egyptian enemies into Mansoura during King Louis's Seventh Crusade:

> For what purpose, O noble count, did we receive the religious habit [meaning renounce the world and lead a life of asceticism, chastity, and war]? Surely not to overturn the Church of Christ and to lose our souls through plotting treachery? Far be it from us, far be it from us, no, far be it from every Christian![4]

This could have been the same response the Templars gave to every charge now being raised against them. Why bother with the elaborate and exhausting charade of pretending to be good Christians before the world—constantly praying, fasting, and fighting Saracens—if their true desire was to live sinfully? Yet, this too was used against them; in lieu of any real evidence against the Templars, their enemies presented their virtues as vices, arguing that, "to conceal the iniquity of their lives, they made much almsgiving, constantly frequented church, comported themselves with edification, frequently partook of the holy sacrament, and manifested always much modesty and gentleness of deportment in the house, as well as in public."[5]

But it was the third obstacle facing the Temple that proved most decisive: torture. This was, after all, the great and terrible age of the inquisition—when inflicting excruciating pain on a suspect was not an uncommon way of deriving confessions.

Soon after being arrested on that fateful October 13, 1307, the knights were offered two choices: Either deny the charges and face torture, possibly death, or "confess" to them and be exonerated. The French king's procedural instructions to the inquisitors (dated September 14, a month prior to the arrests) were clear enough: "They [Templars] will be promised a pardon if they confess the truth and return to the faith of the holy Church; otherwise, they will be condemned to death."[6]

During the first week or two, when no tortures were used, the Templars denied all charges. Then the horrific torments began. The Knights of the Temple were spread-eagled and crushed with lead weights, put to the rack until their limbs were dislocated, forced to drink water with funnels till they drowned, and burned with fire; little wooden wedges were hammered between their fingers and nails, and their teeth were pulled out, exposing the nerves to further abuse. These were just some of the methods that made it in the histories.

The inquisitors—Dominican monks, also known as the "hounds of the Lord"—were experts at extracting whatever confession was desired and carried out their work with especial gusto. After rubbing lard on the feet of Brother Bernard of Vado and placing them in the fire, they were so eviscerated that the bones fell out (he later presented them at a hearing as evidence). Another Templar presented his four teeth that had been pulled out.[7]

These were the "lucky ones." The horrific nature of the inquisition is reflected in the simple fact that a full thirty-six out of 138 brethren ended up dying under torture rather than confessing.[8]

By November 24, 1307, following nearly a month and a half of interrogations and tortures, the rest of the survivors—including Master James himself—confessed to some of these charges. "That confessions were obtained from innocent men should occasion little surprise," Alan Forey correctly observes. "Persistent and skillful interrogation, deprivation and torture have often produced this result."[9] Amaury of Villiers-le-Duc, a veteran Templar in his late fifties, later said that "his tortures had been so terrible he would have confessed to anything"—indeed, to the point that he was ready to "swear to murdering God himself!"[10]

Most Templars ended up confessing to participating in this or that ritual, though only under duress and with their hearts set against it; they were simply following orders, though they did not like it. For example, when told to spit at the crucifix, some said they did so though by intentionally missing. Such a formulation was the wisest option for desperate and doomed men: It gave tormentors what they wanted to hear, while presenting the tormented as personally reluctant participants.

An important letter written three months after the Templars' arrest and subsequent confessions and addressed to the "honorable doctors and scholars of the University of Paris," summarizes their experiences well. The anonymous author begins by lambasting these

> iniquitous proceedings issued against the Templars, which contain no justice but rather savage tyranny, since

> they were arrested without warning, suddenly without right or judgement being made, shamefully and dishonorably incarcerated with destructive rage, afflicted with taunts, the gravest threats, and various sorts of torture, compelled to die or produce absurd lies which they knew nothing about, wrongly given into the hands of their enemies, who force them through those torments to read out a foul, filthy and lying list which cannot be conceived by human ears and should not enter the human heart. But when the brothers refuse to produce these lies, although they know absolutely nothing about them, the torments of the attendants who press them daily force them to speak the lies, saying that they must recite them before the Jacobins [Dominicans who interrogated them] and assert that they are true if they wish to preserve their lives and obtain the king's plentiful grace.[11]

After referencing the aforementioned thirty-six brethren in Paris (and more elsewhere in France) who, rather than confess to lies had died under torture—which only got worse the more they denied the accusations—the author continues,

> What is more, if they do not say these things, not only before but even after torture, they are always held in dark prison cells, with only the bread of sorrow and the water of affliction, in winter time with the pressing cold, lying with sighs and grief on the ground without straw or coverings. In the middle of the night, to increase their terror, now one, now another, are taken from cell to cell. Those whom they have killed in torture they secretly bury in the stable or in the garden, for fear that such horrible and savage deeds should reach the royal ears, since they had told and tell that the aforesaid brothers did not confess their crimes by violence but of their own accord.

Not only was torture used, but there were enticements and promises of rewards if the Templars would but agree to say the words:

> Anyone who is defeated by the tortures and produces the lies which the attendants and Jacobins want...is raised up to chambers where they are happily provided with everything they need, so that they will keep up the lie.... What is more, a certain monk—or more truly a demoniac—ceaselessly runs through the chambers at any hour, day and night, tempting the brothers and extending warnings of what will happen to them. And if he discovers that anyone has repented of the said lies, he sends them straight back to the aforesaid afflictions and penuries.
>
> What more is there to say? In short, I say that human tongue cannot express the punishments, afflictions, miseries, taunts, and dire kinds of tortures which have been suffered by the said innocents in the space of three months since the day of their arrest, because by day and night constant sobs and sighs have not ceased in their cells, nor have cries and gnashing of teeth ceased in their tortures. Is it amazing if they say what the torturer wants, since truth kills them and lies liberate them from death?[12]

In sum, the "Templars in France confessed because of torture and fear of torture, and knowing that the moment that they confessed—even though the confession was a lie—the agony would stop and they would be well cared for."[13]

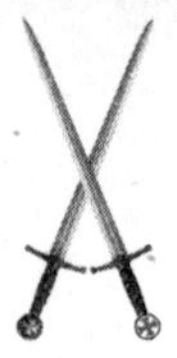

41

BURNED ALIVE

Although many tortured Templars had confessed to the charges brought against them, the matter was still not over; many within the church still had their doubts. As a result, some Templars who had confessed were independently questioned at episcopal inquiries. One of the earliest depositions, that of Ponsard of Gizy, the preceptor of Payns, was taken by a papal commission on November 27, 1309. According to Malcolm Barber, he swore that the accusations against him and his order "were all false": "Whatever he and other brothers of the Order had confessed to...were false; their previous statements... were made while being tortured by their enemies."[1] About these enemies, in a document that he had written, Ponsard said that "these are the traitors who have uttered lies and slanders." His list included Esquin of Floyran. Ponsard was returned to his cell (where he would later die under unclear circumstances).[2]

By 1310, more and more Templars—eventually six hundred—came out in the open, risking their lives on behalf of their imprisoned brothers and the good name of their order. They, too, loudly proclaimed that all the charges were false; any brother confessing to them did so to end his torments. Everything written in the aforementioned letter to the University of Paris was reconfirmed.

Brother Peter of Bologna, a canon lawyer, told the papal commissioners that all accusations were "motivated by zealous cupidity and the ardor of jealousy." Those making them had "sought out apostates or fugitive brothers" who had earlier been "thrown out" of the Order, "like sick animals because of their crimes."[3] They were all conspiring to destroy and profit from the Temple. Considering the torments the captive brothers had experienced, "it is not surprising how some tell lies, but more particularly how some maintain the truth, seeing the trials and tribulations suffered daily by those who tell the truth...and the goods, advantages, pleasures and liberties enjoyed by the liars and the generous promises made to them each day."[4]

The defense was so compelling that Pope Clement, who was always careful not to fall afoul of his benefactor, King Philip, agreed to lead a new trial, set for November 3, 1310.

Philip's response was swift and terrible. In May 1310, he had fifty-four Templars—who were expected to testify at Clement's trial—burned at the stake in Paris as relapsed heretics. On being fastened to their stakes and made to watch the fires alight, they were again offered pardon if they would but confess to the Order's guilt. They refused and were roasted over a slow fire. Of this first batch of immolated martyrs, all contemporaries "speak with admiration of the heroism and intrepidity with which they met their fate."[5]

"Those who saw them burned," reports the Templar of Tyre, "say that as they burned, they cried out with a loud voice that their bodies were in the power of the king of France, but that their souls were with God." The chronicle of William of Nangis gives a similar rendering: Even as the flames caught their flesh, all fifty-four Knights of the Temple, without exception, repeatedly refused to confess to "the crimes imputed to them, but constantly persisted in the general denial, saying always that they were being put to death without cause and unjustly: which indeed many of the people were able to observe by no means without great admiration and immense surprise."[6]

Before the year's end, a total of 120 Knights of the Temple had been burned in Paris, not counting the many that were torched throughout France. The violence-induced hatred reached such a fever pitch that

"King Philip's officers, not content with their inhuman cruelty towards the living...dragged a dead Templar...from his [Paris] grave, and burnt the moldering corpse as a heretic."[7]

The result was predictable: "Many aged and illustrious warriors, who merited a better fate, appeared before their judges pale and trembling." Although they had initially revoked their confessions as derived under torture, they now, "panic-stricken," readmitted their guilt and humbly begged forgiveness.[8] The defense collapsed; the legal representatives of the Templars, Brothers Peter of Bologna and Renaud of Provins, were either arrested or simply "disappeared." The witch hunt was such that peasants everywhere made it a point to shave any near stubble of a beard they might have—lest they be mistaken for a Templar and arrested—and "papers and certificates were granted to men with long beards, to prevent them from being molested by the officers of justice as suspected Templars."[9] On learning that they could expect little help from the outside, increasing numbers of imprisoned Templars acquiesced to confessing to anything the inquisitors wanted to hear, including that, in the provincial chapter of the Order held at Montpelier,

> the Templars set up a head and worshipped it; that the devil often appeared there in the shape of a cat, and conversed with the assembled brethren, and promised them a good harvest, with the possession of riches, and all kinds of temporal property. Some asserted that the head worshipped by the fraternity possessed a long beard; others that it was a woman's head; and one of the prisoners declared that as often as this wonderful head was adored, a great number of devils made their appearance in the shape of beautiful women.[10]

The injustice was so apparent that Clement tried to hold another, final council to determine the guilt of the Templars in Vienne in late 1311. For his troubles, he received warning that Philip "is coming in anger and with a great following."[11] The matter ended then and there: Two days after Philip's arrival, on March 22, 1312, Clement issued a bull pronouncing his final word. He began by expressing what everyone still felt—incredulity:

> It was not to be expected nor seemed credible that men so devout, who were outstanding often to the shedding of their blood for Christ and were seen repeatedly to expose their persons to the danger of death, who even more frequently gave great signs of their devotion both in divine worship and in fasting and other observances, should be so unmindful of their salvation as to commit such crimes.... Then came the intervention of our dear son in Christ, Philip, the illustrious king of France. The same crimes had been reported to him. He was not moved by greed.... He was on fire with zeal for the orthodox faith.[12]

After citing the various accusations against and confessions extracted from the Templars, Clement offered his final verdict:

> Therefore, with a sad heart, not by definitive sentence, but by apostolic provision or ordinance, we suppress, with the approval of the sacred council, the Order of Templars, and its rule, habit and name, by an inviolable and perpetual decree, and we entirely forbid that anyone from now on enter the Order, or receive or wear its habit, or presume to behave as a Templar. If anyone acts otherwise, he incurs automatic excommunication.[13]

It is telling that at no point did Clement find the Order *guilty*; rather, his reason for dissolving it was that public scandal had caused the Temple to suffer from irreparable defamation.

Following the pope's decree, most Templars who refused to confess or retracted their confessions spent the remainder of their lives in dungeons. Many of these were veteran fighters from the Holy Land who deserved so much better. Consider, for example, the fate of Brother

Himbert Blanke, the grand preceptor of Auvergne, "a knight of high honor and of stern unbending pride"[14]:

> From first to last he had boldly protested against the violent proceedings of the inquisitors, and had fearlessly maintained, amid all his trials, his own innocence and that of his order. This illustrious Templar had fought under four successive Masters in defense of the Christian faith in Palestine, and, after the fall of Acre, had led in person several daring expeditions against the infidels. For these meritorious services he was rewarded in the following manner: After having been tortured and half-starved in the English prisons for the space of five years, he was condemned, as he would make no confession of guilt, to be shut up in a loathsome dungeon, to be loaded with double chains, and to be occasionally visited by the agents of the inquisition, to see if he would confess *nothing further*! In this miserable situation he remained until death at last put an end to his sufferings.[15]

Conversely, those who stood by their confessions were released and given a small pension, though many ended their days as beggars.[16]

As for the rest of the Templars outside of France who had been arrested and tried under papal investigation, none were found guilty—no torture was used—and many of them were absorbed into other orders.

Finally, also by papal decree, all of the Temple's many properties and resources around Europe (except in Spain and Portugal) were given to the Hospital. Although protesting that decision would have utterly exposed Philip's motives, he did manage to avoid paying the huge debt he owed the Temple and confiscated much of its wealth that was due to the Hospital in "compensation" for costs he incurred against the Temple (including 200,000 livres).

*****

In 1340, nearly three decades after the dissolution of the Temple, Ludolph of Sudheim, a German priest, came across two haggard and elderly Frenchmen on the shores of the Dead Sea. He learned that they were Templars who had been captured some fifty years earlier, at the fall of Acre in 1291. They had since been living in the mountains, in complete isolation, oblivious to events in Europe.

One can only surmise the mixed emotions these septuagenarians felt as Ludolph informed them of the fate of their brethren.

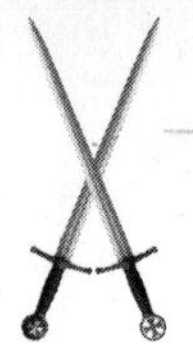

42

"GOD WILL AVENGE OUR DEATH"

Although the Temple was dissolved in 1312, the final acts of its denouement had yet to play out. On March 18, 1314, Master James of Molay and three other Templar hierarchs, who had spent the last seven years in dungeons, appeared loaded with chains on a Paris scaffold for what was expected to be a routine sentencing. In exchange for life imprisonment, they were to confess that their original confessions of guilt, which they had subsequently denied as derived under torture, were true after all.

When, however, James's turn came, he stood up, threw his bound hands to heaven, and spoke in loud defiance to the amazement of all. Now in his seventies, with nothing left to lose but a few miserable years in a dungeon, and knowing full well that if anyone was charged with defending the Temple, it was him, its master, James of Molay unburdened his soul, fully aware that the price would be a slow and agonizing death: "Before heaven and earth and with all of you here as my witnesses," cried he,

> I admit that I am guilty of the grossest iniquity. But the iniquity is that I have lied in admitting the disgusting

> charges laid against the Order. I declare, and I must declare, that the Order is innocent. Its purity and saintliness are beyond question. I have indeed confessed that the Order is guilty, but I have done so only to save myself from terrible tortures by saying what my enemies wished me to say. Other knights who have retracted their confessions have been led to the stake, yet the thought of dying is not so awful that I shall confess to foul crimes which have never been committed. Life is offered to me but at the price of infamy. At such a price, life is not worth having. I do not grieve that I must die if life can be bought only by piling one lie upon another.[1]*

Although two of Master James's other brothers, still preferring ignominy and imprisonment over death, averted their eyes in shame, Geoffroi of Charney, preceptor of Normandy, stood up alongside him in defiance. A sergeant finally silenced James by slapping him across the mouth, before dragging him and Geoffroi by their hair to a nearby chapel.[2] Once word reached King Philip of this unexpected development, he was outraged and ordered the two men burned at the stake without any further ado. The following morning, they were ferried to a small island in the Seine to be executed.

The eyewitness chronicle of Geoffrey of Paris details what happened next. Moments before he was tied to the stake, as James of Molay was being condemned and the fires were being stoked,

> the Master contradicted the cardinal [who was condemning him], and said to him that he believed in Our Lord and that there was no more loyal and better Christian than he was; and if there happened to be any

* In another translation, James says, "I do confess my guilt, which consists in having, to my shame and dishonor, suffered myself, through the pain of torture and the fear of death, to give utterance to falsehoods, imputing scandalous sins and iniquities to an illustrious order, which hath nobly served the cause of Christianity. I disdain to seek a wretched and disgraceful existence by engrafting another lie upon the original falsehood" (Addison, *History of the Knights Templars*, 279).

> evil Brother in the Order, that could well be the case, for he had often heard that there are evil people everywhere. But he did not know anything in the Order which did not originate in good faith and in the Christian law. He would not abandon his Order, but would suffer death there for God's sake, and for justice and for right. No one present was so hard-hearted that they did not cross themselves many times [for pity] when they heard him speak about his Order like this.
>
> Seeing the fire ready, the Master took off his clothes. I say what I saw: he stood there in just his shirt, happily and in good spirits. He did not tremble, no matter how they dragged and prodded at him. They took hold of him to tie him to the stake; he agreed to this, happy and rejoicing. They tied his hands with a cord, but first he said to them: "Sirs, at least, let me join my hands together for a little while and make my prayer to God, for now is the time and the season to pray. I see here my judgement, the place where I must die a short time hence; God knows that my death is wrong and a sin. So in a short time evil things will befall those who have condemned us to death; God will avenge our death.... All those who have acted against us will suffer for what they have done to us. I wish to die in this belief. See here my faith: and I beg you to turn my face towards the church of Our Lady [Notre Dame], from whom Our Lord was born." His request was met. He died like this, and met his death so sweetly that everyone was amazed.[3]

Although a partisan of King Philip, even Geoffrey of Paris could not conclude his account without a strong hint at the Templars' innocence:

> There is great debate in the world over this [the accusations against the Temple], but I don't know what to say to you about it. Some speak out of jealousy, others

> otherwise; I don't know who is telling the truth and who is lying.... You can fool the Church, but you can't fool God. I won't say any more—draw your own conclusions.[4]

The Templar of Tyre—who was not a member but an employee of the Temple during its final years in Acre—expressed the same misgivings in his account:

> The master begged them to suffer him to say his prayers, which he did say to God; and then his body [as well as Geoffroi's] was bound over to the working of their will. So they took him and cast him into the fire, and he was burnt. And if Almighty God, who knows and understands hidden things, knows that he and the others who were burned were innocent of these deeds of which they were accused, then they are martyrs before God; and if they received what they had deserved, they have been punished—but I may truly say that, to all appearances, I knew them for good Christians and devout in their masses and in their lives, and especially my lord the master, William of Beaujeu, who gave great and generous alms to many good people, both privately and openly, as anyone who cares to find out knows.[5]

As seen, before being consumed by the flames, James of Molay had called down heaven's vengeance on the Templars' persecutors. In another version, he cried, "God knows who is wrong and has sinned. Soon a calamity will befall those who have condemned us to death!"[6] Still another version had him summon Pope Clement and King Philip by name to appear before the year was out at the tribunal of God.[7] Whichever rendering is correct, Clement died one month later, in April 1314, aged fifty-one; his mortal remains were nearly consumed by flames after the church they were laid in caught fire—possibly by lightning. The French king followed him to the grave seven months later, aged forty-six; his last days were embittered with misfortune and scandal, including adultery convictions for two of his three daughters-in-law.

*****

Soon after the Temple's founding in 1119, its first master, Hugh of Payns, had warned his then-demoralized brethren of the Devil's many wiles. Having failed to tempt them through the usual lures—women, power, cupidity, pride—Satan had taken to presenting their very work—the defense of Christendom—as itself sinful. Next came nearly two centuries of warfare with Muslims, not a few of whom were almost diabolically driven to single out the knights for extirpation.

Still the Temple stood, winning the praise of all. As James of Vitry, the bishop of Acre who frequently accompanied the knights on their expeditions observed, "Lions they are in war, gentle lambs in the convent; fierce soldiers in the field, hermits and monks in religion; to the enemies of Christ ferocious and inexorable, but to Christians kind and gracious."[8]

It was, therefore, only when Christians themselves, led by Christendom's greatest leaders, the pope and king, *betrayed* the Order—through "a malign and diabolical spirit," as their defense had charged—that the Temple finally fell.[9]

Christians accomplished through treachery what Muslims could not through force.

This leads to one of the least remarked on but no doubt most decisive factors behind the Templars' initial confessions of heresy. Recall that the Order's original mandate was to protect Christians—yet here were Christians (pope, king, and monks) persecuting and torturing them to death. What were they suffering for and for whom? Was there, at this point, even a God, many a Templar must have brooded while lying wounded on the cold floors of their black cells. Why not say the words and be freed of it all—indeed, be elevated and rewarded? In short, "the Templars' worst anguish was spiritual—it must have seemed that God Himself had died—and probably many brethren went mad."[10]

From here, it becomes clear why the same men who often suffered themselves to undergo torture and martyrdom at the hands of Muslims succumbed to the torments of their coreligionists. Surely it was less the physical pain and more the spiritual anguish of knowing *who* it was that was torturing them that finally broke these men. As Desmond Seward rightly observes, "The Templars would have resisted any torment by Muslims, but now...they despaired when the torture was inflicted by fellow Christians." Despair was no doubt compounded by disillusionment. Not a few Castilian Templars were so embittered by the whole affair that these same men who had spent years fighting Muslims fled to Granada and turned Muslim.[11]

Such is how the once-mighty house of the Temple finally fell—not by sword or siege, but by treachery. And if this great injustice raised all the usual questions concerning the justice of God, it more than proved the existence of the Devil.

43

A NEW BEGINNING

Having seen the fate and destruction of the Temple, we must now go back and pick up where we left off with the Knights of the Hospital of St. John. As seen, after the expulsion of the Crusaders from the Holy Land in 1291, both the Templars and Hospitallers had withdrawn to and set up headquarters in Limassol, Cyprus. Once he had recovered from the wounds he incurred fighting at Acre, John of Villiers, the master of the Hospital, ordered the Western commanderies to send their leading men for a general assembly to discuss the Order's future. With "a countenance melancholy, indeed, but still carrying in it that air of grandeur which virtue gives, and the greatest calamities cannot deject," John shared his mind with the Knights of St. John:

> Your diligence...in observing our orders, and the courage that seems to animate you, convince me, in spite of all our losses, that there are still true Hospitallers in the world capable of repairing them. Jerusalem, my dear brethren, is fallen; fallen, as you know, under the tyranny of infidels. A barbarous but formidable power has forced us by degrees to abandon the Holy Land. For more than an age past we have been obliged to fight as many battles as we have defended places. St. John d'Acre

> [the now destroyed massive Hospital compound of Acre] is a late witness of our last efforts, and almost all our knights lie buried in its ruins. It is for you to supply their places; it is from your valor that we expect our return into the Holy Land, and you carry in your hands the lives, the fortunes, and the liberty of your brethren, not of the order only, but of the vast number of Christians that are now groaning under the chains of the infidels.

All the assembled knights, locals and newcomers, veterans and greenhorns, responded by declaring in unison that "they would sacrifice their lives to deliver the Holy Land from the tyranny of the barbarians."[1]

But first things first. Although the capital of Cyprus, Limassol, "was old and half in ruins from the continual attacks of the Saracen pirates, and there were neither fortifications, nor even accommodation sufficient for the knights," once the Hospitallers arrived, "their first care was directed to preparing some establishment for the reception of the poor and of the pilgrims," for "the order might not exist without its hospital."[2]

Next, they turned their attention to protecting Christians from Muslim attacks. Refitting their galleys, they used them "for convoying [European] pilgrims," writes the abbot René-Aubert Vertot, a chief source for the later years of the Hospitallers. These Christians, "notwithstanding the loss of Jerusalem, continued still to visit the holy places, as they were used to do before the First Crusade, paying the infidels the ordinary tribute, which they demanded at the gates of the city."[3]

English historian Augusta Drane elaborates:

> Very soon there appeared in all the chief ports of Europe little vessels of various sizes and construction, armed and manned by the soldiers of the Cross [Hospitallers], collecting pilgrims and escorting them on their way to the Syrian shores, and guarding them, a few months later, on their return. The [Muslim] corsairs, accustomed to make an easy prey of the pilgrims, were not long in attacking

> these new galleys; but they found different resistance from what they had expected.[4]

Captured Muslim ships, mostly belonging to their nemesis, the Mamluks of Egypt, were brought back to Cyprus and refitted to serve the Hospital. The Order's galleys so grew that "in a little time considerable squadrons set sail from the ports of Cyprus, and the flag of St. John at last commanded respect all over the Mediterranean," writes Vertot. "Such was the beginning of the naval armaments of the Order of St. John of Jerusalem."[5]

The Hospitallers eventually wearied of living in Cyprus, where the hitherto independent Order had to submit to the rule of Cypriot King Henry II. Gazing around the Mediterranean for a new home, their eyes finally settled on the ancient Greek isle of Rhodes, just off the southwestern tip of Asia Minor. The Order first took note of the island after many of the Muslim pirates they intercepted and fought on the high seas fled there for sanctuary. Although it was formally a part of the Eastern Roman (or "Byzantine") Empire, it "had been seized by some rebel Greeks," who "in concert with the Saracens" had turned it into a nest of pirates—many of them Muslim slavers, both Turks and Arabs. "The people of the isle of Rhodes," the Templar of Tyre adds, "allowed the passage of vessels laden with lumber and iron and Greek boys and women, which were carried to be sold to the Saracens of Babylon [Mamluk Egypt]. Even the people of Rhodes themselves often carried these goods to the Saracens."[6]

In 1305, on becoming the new master of the Hospital, Fulk of Villaret broached the idea of subduing and transforming Rhodes into a new base of holy war to the pope. Clement V gave his blessing and even provided Genoese Crusader troops to aid the Hospital in their siege of the island. The Templar of Tyre lays out the logic:

> Brother Fulk of Villaret, master of the Hospital, wanted at the beginning of his mastership to have the favor of God.... So he set about to go and take that isle of Rhodes, and determined that he would block the passage of the merchandise [including human chattel] which went to

> the Saracens. By doing this, he would also be able to subdue the neighboring areas of Turkey to Christianity.[7]

The conquest of Rhodes began in 1306 and took four long years to complete, in part because the island contained both Muslims and Christians, and the Order was careful not to harm the latter. Although the Knights of St. John could have launched an all-out assault, they resorted to blockading the island "because those within it were Christians," explains the Templar of Tyre, adding that the Hospitallers "used their strength to take it in an appropriate manner. This is why the siege lasted so long."[8]

The same mercy was not dealt out to their sworn enemies, "the infidels, who were the main strength of the place." For example, during the siege of the castle of Philermo, where "300 Turks from Turkey had come to its aid," a resentful Greek sergeant, who had been beaten and humiliated by the Muslims of Philermo, defected to and promised to lead the knights into the castle. They went with him, he secretly let them in, and they "put to the sword the 300 Turkish Saracens whom they found there. The other men and women and children went into churches to save their lives [by signifying their Christian identity]."[9] In short, as Vertot puts it, "They spared the lives of the Christian inhabitants, and gave them their liberty, but the infidels were cut in pieces."[10]

On August 15, 1310, the Hospitallers finally took possession of Rhodes. Ironically, the same four years (1306–1310) they spent subduing the isle largely overlapped with the arrest, trial, torture, and dissolution of the Templars. The contrast among the popular imagination could not have been greater. One military order was being seen—and treated as—Saracen-loving, Christ-hating homosexuals, whereas the other was still being true to its mandate: fighting on behalf of Christendom. As such, universal joy and admiration exploded throughout Europe on learning of the Hospital's conquest of Rhodes, that is, on learning that Muslim dominance of the eastern seas would no longer go unchallenged. This event also ushered in an informal change to the Hospitallers' name:

> As an eternal monument of a conquest so useful to Christendom...all nations, by common consent, gave the Hospitallers the name of the Knights of Rhodes, and it is by this name that we shall for the future speak of a body of knights that continued to make themselves as useful to Christian princes, as they were formidable to the Muslims.[11]

The conquest of Rhodes by the Knights of St. John in 1310 heralded a new phase in Crusader history. The island was well situated to resume the holy war on, and defense of Christendom from, Islam. It was close to the Holy Land and Egypt and even closer to the newest rising power of Islam: the Ottoman Turks. Indeed, the conquest of Rhodes was coterminous with the reign of that empire's eponymous founder, Osman I (or "Ottoman," r. 1299–1324). It was "as if providence had directed them thither," Vertot observed retrospectively, "to serve as a barrier against Ottoman and his successors, and stop the progress of the Turkish arms by their valor."[12]

In fact, the first assault on the knights came at the very hands of Osman himself. After conquering Rhodes in 1310, Osman led a strong force to "drive the knights out of the isle of Rhodes before they had time to establish their dominions there": "[Osman] being solicited by the Mahometans, whom the knights had chased out of Rhodes, put his troops on board a fleet, landed in the isle, and advanced towards the capital, and invested it. The master had scarce time enough to repair the walls, but the bastions and fortifications were still in a ruinous condition." Even so, this first challenge taught the knights, or rather reconfirmed, a valuable lesson: "that no place can be more securely fortified, than by the courage and valor of those that defend it. The knights stood several storms: the Turks lost abundance of men in these assaults; and Osman, that was so successful in all his enterprises, miscarried in this, and was obliged to raise the siege and embark."[13]

Following Osman's retreat, the Order fervently "worked on the fortifications of Rhodes and strengthened them," writes the Templar of Tyre, "and gathered together many good people who wanted to come to Rhodes in order to populate the place and to increase it."[14] Vertot elaborates:

> A great number of Christians, especially of the Latins, who, after the loss of the Holy Land, had dispersed themselves in different parts of Greece, flocked thither to settle themselves, and live under the standard of St. John, from which they had so often found protection. Out of this medley of knights and inhabitants, as well Greeks as Latins, a new warlike and trading state was formed, that soon became as potent by its riches as it was formidable by the courage and valor of its new sovereigns[15]

Once Rhodes was secured, the indefatigable knights expanded to and claimed many of the smaller Dodecanese islands surrounding their new home; and at least nine, the largest and most important of which was Kos, were garrisoned. This archipelago of fortresses was reminiscent of and served the same purpose as the Hospital's concentric fortifications in the Holy Land. At any time, the Order held several hundred knights—at its peak, as many as a thousand[16]—and unknown numbers of sergeants and mercenaries. The island's capital, also called Rhodes, became the Order's headquarters; and their chief fortress, which also served as the master's residence, was raised atop the ruins of an ancient castle that had itself been built atop and made from portions of the mighty Colossus of Rhodes, the tallest statue of the ancient world and one of its Seven Wonders.

Although always independent, the Order now became a sovereign state, with the master its effective king (or as the sources relay, prince) exercising temporal power over the 450 square miles of Rhodes and adjacent islands. It also began to divide its members into units by languages (or *langues*).

Being surrounded by enemies and, as it were, right smack in the middle of the growing Ottoman lion's den, many more defenses and ramparts would eventually be raised, so that by 1400 Rhodes was arguably the most heavily fortified stronghold in the world.

Despite such ongoing militarization, the Order did not forget its original vocation. If bastions and bulwarks of every size and shape surrounded the city of Rhodes, its inside resembled a monastery. As they had done when establishing themselves in Cyprus, so now in Rhodes the knights built a massive hospital containing one thousand beds. Like its predecessor in Jerusalem, this hospital also accepted anyone—from traveling merchants and pilgrims to the island's poor, Greek and Latin—and its patients slept between linen sheets and ate off silver plates. In the evenings, the brethren chanted a prayer for "Our Lords the sick."[17]

The brethren's rule was still enforced, and life remained monastic, particularly in and around the Church of St. John of the Collachium, which stood adjacent to the Order's primary fortress and the master's residence. Although it is often said that, in tandem with Europe's growing secularization, the Order's rules also began to grow lax in Rhodes—indeed, Master Fulk eventually snapped, taking to drinking and womanizing until the Order's senior leadership overthrew him—by any measure, the Hospitallers continued to follow strict discipline, including daily prayers and regular fasts, even when at sea. Records indicate draconian punishments for infractions.

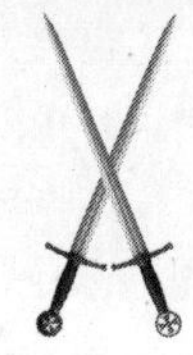

44

RISE OF THE SEA KNIGHTS

The most obvious change that took place among the Hospitallers post-Acre 1291 is that the Order went from being a land power to a sea power; from being an army to a navy. Its goals remained unchanged—protecting Christians and fighting Muslims, which were essentially synonymous—but now the waterways became its primary theater of activity. The sea knights protected all vessels containing Christians—sailors, merchants, and pilgrims—and prowled the coasts of Turkey, Syria, and Egypt, raiding the enemies of Christendom. Their maritime operations were supplemented with the Corso "which resembled licensed piracy with the element of holy war added,"[1] and most of the galley rowers were enslaved Muslims (just as most of the galley rowers of Muslim ships were enslaved Christians). One historian imagines what it was like to be on the receiving end of the knights' naval ram:

> Often the crew of an Egyptian carrack, becalmed off some exquisite Aegean island, would wake at sunrise to see beneath the violet sky a galley darting out from a silent cove. The noise in itself was terrifying: huge oars beating the water in a rhythmic stroke sounded by shrill whistle-blasts or banging on a gong. There was a jarring

> crash when the prow's iron beak buried itself in ship's timbers and then, through the smoke, along the ram or over a boarding bridge, swarmed the steel-clad brethren.[2]

These seaborne knights' early efficacy was such that the Templar of Tyre, whose chronicle ends between 1314 and 1321—meaning a mere four to twelve years following the knights' establishment in Rhodes—still found much to praise in them:

> They subdued to their obedience several parts of Turkey, all of which gave them a truce. Never did those evil [Muslim] merchants dare to pass by there again, or to pick up from Turkey either wood or skins, or any other thing to take it to Babylon [Egypt]. If anyone did make as if to go, the Hospitallers with their galleys would take them and despoil them. This was a very good thing for Christendom; thus did God arrange things for the best.[3]

As for the original goal of the Crusade—the taking and holding of the Holy Land—the knights' impact was negligible. This was less a reflection of their commitment and effort and more a reflection of growing lethargy within Christendom (certainly in comparison to 1095). Anachronistic throwbacks from the time of Duke Godfrey, the Knights of St. John almost always acted alone and, as such, were vastly outnumbered by their Muslim enemies. The best they could accomplish in the context of the Crusade was to scourge the coasts of Egypt and Syria with commando-style raids. Such hit-and-run tactics, however devastating as they were, were obviously not enough to take possession of any territory within the Holy Land.

Aside from protecting Christians and raiding Muslims, and because their tiny and remote outpost was so near to the Turks, the Knights of Rhodes quickly became a thorn in the Ottoman boot, ever thwarting the designs of what would otherwise become an Islamic behemoth that swallowed up entire kingdoms with ease.

Thus, in 1312, two years after Osman's first failed assault against Rhodes—and the same year the Templars were suppressed—the Knights of St. John learned that a Turkish fleet of twenty ships was sailing for the island of Amorgos, one hundred miles west of Rhodes. Considering that the "women of Amorgos had been famous for their beauty since classical times," the Turks, it was feared, were looking for some easy booty and plunder.[4] Master Fulk instantly dispatched a fleet to intercept the Turks, all of whom were killed or drowned in the ensuing naval melee. Several conflicts and six years later, in 1318, the Turks, concluding that the conquest of impregnable Rhodes would be no easy matter, turned to calling for tribute (jizya) from the knights. This demand was "met by a naval campaign which wreaked such havoc on the Turks that no further demands were made."[5]

In the following year, 1319, a Turkish fleet attacked Hospitaller vessels escorting the Genoese governor of Chios to his island. The knights routed the Turks; only six Muslim vessels escaped, the rest drowning to the bottom of the sea. Seeking revenge, in June 1320, eighty warships descended on and blockaded Rhodes. The pugnacious knights responded by sailing out to meet them with the Order's squadron of four galleys and twelve smaller vessels. Most of the Muslim ships were either sunk or boarded and their crews killed or captured.[6]

The governor of Chios was only one of countless Christians to owe gratitude to the Knights of Rhodes. In fact, during this period and under their guardianship, the knights

> may be said to have become the protectors of all Christendom. The numbers they rescued from captivity, or saved from falling into a bondage often worse than death, are beyond calculation; and if the crusades, though failing in their primary object, yet kept the Muslims at bay during two centuries, and thus saved Europe from that inundation of infidelity which overwhelmed the eastern nations, the maritime power of the Knights of St. John contributed in no small degree to the same end, when the old crusading enthusiasm had faded and died away.[7]

On succeeding his father, Osman, as new sultan, Orhan (r. 1323–1362) decided enough was enough and dispatched a horde of "Mahometans, Turks, Arabians, [and] Saracens" to annihilate Rhodes. On seeing their vast armada approach, the knights, rather than hole themselves up, boarded their galleys and immediately issued forth in the direction of the Muslims and "attacked them boldly."[8] Although the enemy far outnumbered them in ships and men, the sea knights, by now so "inured to that way of fighting, worked their ships with so much skill, that they sunk part of the enemy's frigates and flat bottomed vessels, and took a great number of prisoners."[9] Orhan was banking on his superior numbers, "but he had only tried them upon land, and he found enemies at sea, whose capacity and skill were superior to all his forces."[10]

With each triumph over the Muslims—whether Ottoman Turks to the north or Mamluk Egyptians to the south—the fearsome reputation of the Knights of St. John spread far and wide. In the prose of Edward Gibbon, "the noble and warlike monks were renowned by land and sea; and the bulwark of Christendom [Rhodes] provoked and repelled the arms of the Turks and Saracens."[11] Those of their victims who managed to limp back home regaled their listeners with such tales of horror that Rhodes became known in Muslim circles as the "stronghold of the hounds of Hell," or the "Abode of the Sons of Satan."[12]

Rhodes's Christian neighbors, who had long suffered from Islamic depredations, also benefited from the knights' reputation, so that a decade after their settling in Rhodes, the Muslim "corsairs durst appear no more; and the island of Cyprus, and the lesser Armenia, whose coasts were often infested by those pirates, were freed from them by the protection of the flag of St. John."[13]

Having cleared the eastern Mediterranean of Muslim pirates, the Knights of Rhodes, still seeing themselves as the sole remaining crack troops of the Crusade, took to joining any Christian league against Islam. Because of the "great reputation of the arms of the knights,"[14] in 1347, Levon, the king of Cilician (or "Lesser") Armenia, sent ambassadors to beg the master of Rhodes, Dieudonne of Gozon, to aid him against the Mamluks, who had been terrorizing and chipping away at his kingdom.

There was one problem: Armenians were Orthodox Christians not in communion with Catholic Rome; but, as Vertot explains, even though the Armenian king "was a schismatic, yet Gozon, full of zeal, and animated with the spirit of his institution, thought it his duty not to abandon any Christians to the fury of those barbarians. He prevailed upon the council of the Order to send troops into Armenia; they fitted out a strong fleet, and the bravest knights embarked on board with a considerable body of infantry." On reaching the coasts of Armenia, they joined forces with Levon's army and met the Muslims head on:

> The battle was long and obstinate, but the usual valor of the knights decided its success. The Saracens, who expected to have only to deal with the Armenians, whom they had beaten several times before, surprised to see the standards of St. John, which they distinguished still more plainly by the great blows that the knights dealt about, turned their backs and fled. The best part of them perished in the heat of the engagement; and the Christians took all their baggage, and a great number of prisoners. The king of Armenia, sustained by this powerful succor, besieged afterwards and recovered all the places which the infidels had seized on; the knights of Rhodes did not leave Armenia till they had entirely cleared the country of the Saracens, who got back into Egypt, though with great difficulty.[15]

Similarly, in 1365, Peter I of Cyprus led a new (though ultimately failed) Crusade against Alexandria, which the Knights of Rhodes eagerly joined. Though the independent warriors were not used to taking orders from others, they were happy to submit to the command of Peter—"just so long as they could fulfil their aim of chastising Islam wherever possible."[16]

Fierce in battle against the enemies of Christ, the Hospital continued to serve the servants of Christ, living up to the ideals of both St. Bernard and the founder of their order, Gerard the Blessed. Thus, Hélion of Villeneuve (r. 1319–1346), the same master who, for over a quarter of a century, led his men to many victories against the Turks and Muslim slave traders, was also reputed to have turned his kingdom into a realm of benevolence and charity:

> The inhabitants of Rhodes, and especially the poor, felt the more immediate effects of the master's care. Under so wise a government, there was not an unhappy person to be seen in all the isles of the order. The poor did not want a necessary subsistence. The sick were put in a large and magnificent hospital, where all the assistances necessary, either for the wants of the body or for those of the soul, were abundantly provided for them. The master had re-animated the zeal of his knights by his own example; and it may be said that, as long as he lived, he discharged perfectly well the functions, and justly merited the title of guardian of the poor, which had been annexed to his dignity, ever since the foundation of the order.[17]

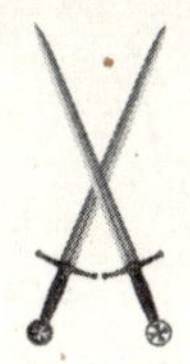

45

THE DRAGON SLAYER

We must now take a brief segue from the knights' long war with Islam to examine arguably the most famous—because most fabulous—story to emerge from Hospitaller Rhodes: the slaying of a dragon.

Sometime in the late 1330s, what sources describe as a large, scaly dragon—nearly seventy feet long from snout to tail—terrorized the locals from its haunt in the marshes near Mount St. Stephen, a few miles from the city of Rhodes. Livestock disappeared, as did shepherds who ventured too close to the beast's lair. Several knights tried to flush it out and slay it, only to be killed and devoured to a man. It reached the point that, on pain of expulsion, Master Hélion forbade them from "attempting anymore an enterprise that seemed above all human strength,"[1] and bade the populace to refrain from going anywhere near the marsh.

One knight, Dieudonne of Gozon, who had on several occasions seen the monster, refused to relent and devised a plan. He took leave to return to his father's castle in France, where he built a large replica of the monster. He then trained two large dogs (variously described as bloodhounds or bulldogs) to attack this bestial facsimile whenever they saw the young knight strike it, which he did daily as part of his own training. On returning to Rhodes sometime in 1342, he "went down the mountain with his two dogs, advanced straight to the marsh and haunt of the serpent, which, at the noise he made, ran with open mouth and eyes darting fire to devour him." Vertot continues,

> Gozon gave it a stroke with his lance, which the thickness and hardness of its scales made of no effect. He was preparing to redouble his stroke, when his horse, frightened with the hissing and stench of the serpent, refuses to advance, retires back and leaps aside, and would have been the occasion of his master's destruction, if he, with great presence of mind, had not thrown himself off. Then taking his sword in hand, and attended by his two faithful dogs, he immediately comes up to the horrible beast, and gives it several strokes in different places; but the hardness of the scales hindered them from entering, and the furious animal, with a stroke of his tail, threw him on the ground, and would infallibly have devoured him, if his two dogs, according as they had been taught, had not seized the serpent by the belly, which they tore and mangled with their teeth...though it struggled with all its strength to force them to quit their hold. The knight, by the help of this succor, gets up, and joining his two dogs, thrusts his sword up to the hilt, in a place that was not defended by scales: he there makes a large wound, whence a deluge of blood flows out.[2]

Having thus slain the great worm, all hailed Dieudonne a hero. Carrying him on their shoulders, his brother-knights rushed to Master Hélion with the joyous news. He, however, was wroth with the rebellious young man for disobeying a direct order not to engage the beast (obedience being one of the three requirements of all religious orders).

> Immediately this strict observer of discipline, without vouchsafing to hear [Dieudonne], or being moved in the least by the intercessions of the knights, sent him directly

> to prison. He next convened the council, where he represented, that the order could by no means dispense with inflicting a rigorous punishment on so notorious a disobedience that was more prejudicial to discipline than the life of several serpents would have been to the cattle and inhabitants of that quarter of the island.... But the council prevailed that [Dieudonne] should only be deprived of the habit of the order [meaning kicked out]; in short, the unfortunate knight was ignominiously degraded, and there was but a short interval between his victory and this kind of punishment, which he found more cruel and severe than death itself.[3]

This draconian response was intentionally designed to impress upon all the importance of absolute obedience in an order. As Vertot explains,

> The master, after having by this chastisement performed the obligations due to the preservation of discipline returned to his natural temper...and was pleased to be pacified, and managed things in such a manner as to make them [entreat] him to grant a pardon, which he would have solicited himself if he had not been at the head of the order. At the pressing instances made him by the principal commanders, he restored [Dieudonne] to the habit and his favor, and loaded him with kindnesses.[4]

While this medieval story of a dragon slaying may be instinctively dismissed as pure myth—Siegfriedian parallels of a fatal sword thrust to the worm's exposed underbelly are especially obvious—there are some factors to consider.

First, the fourteenth century, when this incident is said to have occurred, was not the eighth century, when "benighted" Europeans were much more consumed by and prone to spreading rumors of the fabulous. Not only were fourteenth-century people much more skeptical, but the Hospital, which recorded this incident in its annals, was an especially serious and rigorous organization that verified information.

And whereas most myths center around ahistorical figures, in the case of the dragon of Rhodes, not only are actual historical figures such as Master Hélion of Villeneuve present, but the dragon slayer himself, Dieudonne of Gozon, was so real as to be elected master of the Knights of Rhodes in 1346.

Like his predecessors, he continued leading his men against the forces of Islam. Indeed, it was Dieudonne who, in the name of Christian unity, helped the aforementioned "schismatic" Armenian king against the Mamluks. And yet—rather tellingly—on his death in 1353, he was best remembered by the words "*Extinctor Draconis*," which were inscribed on his tombstone to signify that here lies the "Dragon Slayer."

Several other factors would seem to support the veracity of this otherwise fantastic tale. For example, there are references to the skull of the dragon, which was nailed to one of Rhodes's castles and witnessed by visitors over the centuries as late as 1837. The French traveler Jean of Thévenot wrote that he saw the skull when visiting Rhodes in the seventeenth century and that "it was much bigger and larger than that of an horse, its mouth reaching from ear to ear, big teeth, large eyes, the holes of the nostrils round, and the skin of a whitish grey, occasioned perhaps by the dust which it gathered in course of time."[5]

The most compelling evidence, however, is also the least remembered or cited. From of old, since well before the ancient Greeks, Rhodes was known as a haunt of large serpentine creatures.[6] Writing in the first century BC—that is, fourteen centuries before the dragon slaying in question took place—the Greek historian Diodorus Siculus noted that "the land of Rhodes brought forth huge serpents," and that these "Serpents caused the death of many of the natives." Eventually, the hero, Phorbas, "destroyed the Serpents, and after he had freed the island of its fear he made his home in Rhodes."

The Latin *Astronomica*, written two thousand years ago during Christ's lifetime, adds that the constellation Ophiuchus, which means "master of the serpent"* and is represented by a man grappling with a large snake, is based on Phorbas's battle with the serpentine monsters of Rhodes:

> The citizens called their island, overrun by a great number of snakes, Ophiussa [Land of Serpents]. In this multitude of beasts was a snake of immense size, which had killed many of them; and when the deserted land began finally to lack men, Phorbas...killed all the beasts, as well as that huge snake. Since he was especially favored by Apollo, he was put among the constellations, shown killing the snake for the sake of praise and commemoration.

Not only does the author of the *Astronomica* assert that Rhodes was known as the "Land of Serpents," but one seventeenth-century scholar and linguist says that even before the ancient Greeks, the Phoenicians and other early Semites had referred to Rhodes as *gesirath rod*, the "Isle of Serpents."[7]

In short, it seems fairly safe to say that Dieudonne of Gozon did grapple with and slay a large serpentine or crocodile-like creature, perhaps one of the last descendants of the now extinct race of worms that anciently infested and plagued the island of Rhodes.

* Although Ophiuchus is commonly translated as "snake bearer," the word ὀφιοῦχος—made of ὄφις ("snake") and ἔχω ("to have, hold, or possess")—is better translated as "master of the snake," or more simply, "snake master."

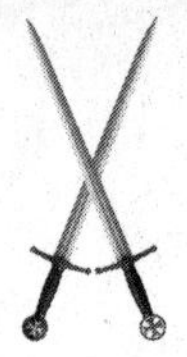

46

THE SAGA OF SMYRNA

Perhaps nothing better proves the Knights of Rhodes's uncompromising and self-sacrificial commitment to the defense of Christendom as their garrison and defense of Smyrna.

In 1344—two years after the aforementioned dragon slaying occurred—the knights, along with a coalition of Cypriots and Venetians, captured the ancient port city of Smyrna on the west coast of Asia Minor, then another nest of Muslim pirates. Once the knights stormed the port, "both Turks and Arabians were cut to pieces."[1]

The Venetians garrisoned it, but by 1374, it became next to impossible for them to withstand the growing might of the Ottomans. Rather than abandon it, Pope Gregory XI summoned the grand prior of France, Robert of Juillac, who was on his way to assume the mastership of Rhodes, and asked him to take up the defense of Smyrna. The incoming master protested that Smyrna, surrounded as it was by the Turks, was a lost cause. "The situation of the city," replied the Pontiff, "in the heart of the infidel's own country, is the very cause of my entrusting it to your order; for the Turks will not advance farther so long as they have so considerable an enemy at home; and I therefore charge you under pain of excommunication, to dispatch the necessary garrison immediately on your return to Rhodes."[2]

On reaching Rhodes, Master Robert communicated this injunction to his brethren. "All were very well aware," says René-Aubert Vertot, "that it was to send the knights to certain death; nevertheless they took the part of obedience, and many of them even generously offered themselves for service whose dangers and glory were equally certain. For it was not to be supposed that the Turks, whose power daily increased, would long leave the knights in peaceable possession of a place which was in the very center of their dominions."[3]

The knights proceeded to Smyrna, planted the standard of St. John, and successfully took up its defense for nigh thirty years. Their lonely citadel in the heart of Turkdom, surrounded by and constantly frustrating militant Islam, "is said to have delayed the fall of Constantinople, and possibly to have saved the rest of Christendom by drawing away the attack of the infidels from other quarters [and onto themselves]."[4]

And then Timur came, arguably history's most brutal and ruthless warlord. In 1402, this Muslim emir from Central Asia defeated and placed the Ottoman sultan Bayezid in a cage. (This same Bayezid had hitherto been the scourge of Christendom and had even defeated one of history's last large-scale Crusades at Nicopolis in 1396.) Timur proceeded to absorb all of the Ottomans' possessions in Asia Minor, and every eastern Christian prince took the knee and submitted to his yoke—all except for the Knights of St. John. In the words of Vertot, "There was none but the master of Rhodes and his knights, who, though eternal enemies to the Turks, would not yet crouch under the power of the Tartar."[5]

Our chief source for this episode is the contemporary Persian historian Sharaf al-Din Ali Yazdi. He begins by noting that

> Timur was informed that there was upon the sea-coast [of Asia Minor] a place exceeding strong, built of hewn stone...that there was a great number of Europeans within it; that it was called...Smyrna...[and] that there was near it...another fortress upon the ridge of a mountain...but possessed by [Muslims], who were continually

> at war with those of the other place [Smyrna], on account of their difference in religion.[6]

Sharaf continues by saying that the Knights of St. John—whom he conflates and confuses with "Greeks" and "Europeans"—waged a "cruel war" from Smyrna, and that "it had never been taken by any Muslim prince, nor ever paid tribute to anybody." Ottoman sultan Murad I "had taken the field several times at the head of a mighty army without being able to carry his point, and [his son and successor] Bayezid had kept it besieged for seven years together, without making any progress in it." In short, Smyrna "infested the Muslims exceedingly, and nothing was to be seen [there] but slaughter and streams of blood flowing continually into the sea like torrents."[7]

Now when Timur heard this, "his zeal for religion persuaded him that it was his duty to deliver the Muslims from trouble by entirely destroying their enemies." So he dispatched his generals with orders to extend Islam's three standard choices to infidels: "First," continues Sharaf, "to summon them…to embrace the Muslim religion (for such is Muhammad's order)." Should the knights comply, Timur's "pleasure was that they should be kindly treated," and told that he personally would "bestow his favors upon them." If, however, through "obstinacy," they still "desired to continue [as] Christians," they must "submit to pay tribute." But "if, unhappily for them, they should dare to stand upon their defense," Timur's generals were ordered to "put them all to the sword."[8]

Needless to say, the Knights of St. John flatly refused the first two offers—conversion or tribute—and clung to the sword. So outraged by these infidels' gall, the sixty-six-year-old warlord Timur decided to travel to and conquer Smyrna in person—so "that the merit of this [jihad] might be ascribed to him."[9]

On December 2, 1402, Timur, at the head of tens of thousands of fighters, laid siege to Smyrna. As was customary with that tyrant, a white flag appeared before his tent on the first day of his arrival, signifying to the besieged that if they surrendered now, all would be spared. On the second day, a red flag was hoisted, signifying that if they surrendered, only the captains and fighters would be killed, and noncombatants spared. On the third and final day of this silent "parley," a black flag appeared, signifying that, surrender or not, every last man, woman, child, and beast would be massacred.

Seeing how impregnable the knights' fort was and not wanting to invest too much time on this project that had little strategic value and centered around prestige, Timur tried one more time to pacify the knights by informing them that if they would merely hoist his banner atop their ramparts as a token of submission, he would peacefully withdraw. Although any other Christian prince would have submitted to the Tatar's "magnanimous" gesture, these warriors of the Lord, rather predictably, "rejected this proposition with indignation."[10]

Such defiance was less because the knights thought they stood a chance against history's notorious erecter of skull pyramids and his hordes and more because Smyrna had been entrusted to their Order—and it was not for them to abandon, surrender, or even sully it with a barbarian's banner.

On their rejection, war instantly broke out over Smyrna. Above their heads, a deluge of missiles rained down, and beneath their feet, sappers and tunnels undermined the fortifications. Smyrna's tiny garrison of two hundred brothers and the few remaining mercenaries who did not flee before the Tatar advance, all under the command of the aptly named Brother Iñigo—meaning the "fiery or ardent" one—fought "like a band of enraged devils," to quote the Persian historian.[11] Indeed, not content to remain behind their walls, "the knights made frequent sallies to hinder their works from advancing; there was every day some skirmish or other in which those soldiers of Jesus Christ strove with emulation to signalize their valor against the infidels."[12]

Two weeks of incessant warfare later, a Hospitaller relief fleet was espied along the distant horizon, prompting Timur to redouble efforts and give "orders for the general assault."[13] What followed was apocalyptic; the Mongols' all-out effort continued for over twenty-four hours under black clouds and windswept rains. Even the contemporary Muslim chronicler, though unaware of the Christian defenders' knightly identity, could not help but give them their due:

> The brave men on both sides performed actions of wonderful vigor. If the attack was obstinate and resolute, the defense was equal to it, and nobody had time to rest a moment; the engines and battering rams beat down the walls and towers, and the besieged, still undaunted, were continually throwing pots of naphta, wildfire, and showers of stones and arrows from engines as well as bows, without the least intermission. All this while the rain was so excessive, that it looked as if the universe was going to be overwhelmed with a second deluge; yet notwithstanding this prodigious storm, the indefatigable Timur was every moment giving orders to his generals, and encouraging his soldiers in person.[14]

The Christian stronghold was at last overwhelmed, and Timur's hordes rushed "into Smyrna, crying out victory, and praising Allah, to whom they offered the heads of all their enemies by way of thanksgiving for their success"—that is, they built yet another pyramid, this time of Hospitaller heads.[15]

On reaching the shoreline, the Order's relief vessels were shocked to discover that there was absolutely nothing left of Smyrna but fire and smoke: Timur ordered every last standing edifice razed to the ground and hurled into the sea. As a parting gift, the Tatar had some of the knights' heads catapulted toward the fleet, and some of these ghastly visages landed at the feet of, and were recognized by, some of the relief knights, who withdrew in sorrow.[16]

Of this saga at Smyrna, Drane offers the following reflection:

> The defense of Smyrna, first undertaken under religious obedience, had been persisted in from the same honorable motive. They had been avowedly stationed in that remotest outpost of Christendom to offer themselves, if need were, as victims for the safety of Europe; and the destiny, far from appalling them, had only seemed glorious in the eyes of men whose vow and vocation it was to die for the Cross they bore upon their breasts. So when

> the black flag of Timur was hung but on the last day of the siege—his accustomed signal of "universal destruction"—they knew very well that the hour of sacrifice was come, and welcomed it, as the martyrs did their torments. The dawn saw them at the altar; Mass, and last communion, and an offering of their life to God, made solemnly, yet withal with certain joy and exultation, preceded the last struggle at the ruined ramparts.[17]

No doubt the knights had also remembered and were comforted by Christ's exhortation to their ancient predecessors, the Christians of first century Smyrna, to "not fear any of those things which you are about to suffer," but rather, "be faithful until death, and I will give you the crown of life " (Revelation—or more literally and appropriately, Apocalypse—2:8–11 NKJV).

If the fall of Smyrna underscored the knights' commitment, its aftermath demonstrated their tenacity to the cause. Convinced that it was still the Order's responsibility to provide succor to whichever Christian remained in the vicinity of Smyrna, Master Philibert of Naillac quickly reconnoitered the coastline in the hopes of establishing a new garrison. He eventually found a castle on the ruins of ancient Halicarnassus full of Timur's men. Leading his small fleet, he cut them to pieces, took possession of and refortified the fort (including with material from another of history's Seven Wonders, the then-dilapidated Mausoleum of Halicarnassus). He dedicated it to St. Peter and inscribed in Latin over one of its gates, "Unless the Lord keep the city, he who keeps it watches in vain." It "became the asylum of refuge on the coast of Asia, for such Christian slaves as found means to affect their escape from Turkish or Tartarian bondage."[18]

> It also became in one sense another hospital of the order. A strong garrison was put into it, and a number of vessels were constantly at anchor in the harbor, ready at the first note of alarm to issue forth and...sweep the seas of the

> hordes of pirates and corsairs that infested the coasts.* Many too were the Christian slaves who, escaping from the chains of the infidels, found refuge within its walls; and the inmates were never weary of inventing and practicing new devices for the relief of the refugees.[19]

All this was done because "the master's care was not confined to the bare preservation of the isles of the order," says Vertot; "he equally concerned himself in the defense of all the Christian states in the East: he was a sort of general in ordinary to them."[20]

*****

As a final reflection of the quality of the Knights of Rhodes, the reader is left with a brief notice of John (or Juan) Francis of Heredia (1310–1396) as a paradigmatic representation of the Order. At the age of eighteen, he became a Knight of the Hospital in Aragon; half a century later, at the age of sixty-seven, he became master of the Knights of St. John in 1377.

* Among the other ways they sought to help fugitive Christians, "the knights kept a race of large and sagacious dogs, whom they trained to go out and seek for those who might have sunk exhausted on the mountains unable to reach the castle walls. The instinct of these dogs was extraordinary: we read of one Christian who, escaping from the hands of his masters, threw himself into a well when closely pursued, rather than fall again into their hands. Here he was tracked by one of these watchdogs, who, unable to get him out, at least succeeded in saving his life. The well was dry, and the man had received no injury from his fall, but would infallibly have died of hunger but for the fidelity of the Hospitallers' dog. For many days did the noble animal bring him in its mouth all the share of food given him for his own daily support, dropping it down into the well below. At length it was observed that the dog was growing thinner every lay; and his continual excursions after breakfast in the same direction exciting curiosity, some of the servants of the garrison set out to watch what he was about; the truth being thus discovered, the man was saved, and the dog given his place in the history of the Order, of which he had proved himself so worthy a member" (Drane, *Knights of St. John*, 49). According to another source, "The Hospitallers waged a constant war against the Turks which was 'as violent as it was just.' They had some fifteen huge dogs which roamed free within two or three miles of the fortress on Rhodes. If these happened upon Turks they would career back to the fortress, raising the alarm; but if they chanced upon Christians they would welcome them and escort them on their way" (Heers, *Barbary Corsairs*, 54).

Although he is mostly known as a scholar and patron of literary projects—he sponsored the earliest translations into any Western language of Plutarch's *Parallel Lives* and Thucydides's *History of the Peloponnesian War*—he was also a great man of war.

One example suffices: After setting sail from Naples to assume his new position as master of the Knights of Rhodes, he and his men encountered a Venetian fleet off the coast of Morea battling the Turks, who had just seized the town of Patras from Venice. Coming aboard the master's vessel, the Venetian general begged him "for the common good of Christendom" to join forces with him to recover Patras "out of the hands of the infidels." Although the newly minted master's presence was urgently needed in Rhodes, "his courage prevailed over his interest, and he embraced with joy an occasion of signalizing his warlike talents against the eternal enemies of his order." So the two fleets joined, landed their troops, and marched straight to Patras. The siege was long and hard, and

> the order lost several knights of distinction; but at last the machines made use of in those times, having made a breach, the master impatient of so long a resistance, takes a ladder, claps it to the breach, mounts up first sword in hand, and without minding whether he was followed or no, throws himself into the place. The [Turkish] governor, on his side, opposes his progress with great courage; a sort of duel ensues between them, till the Christian, more expert, or else stronger than the infidel, runs him through, kills him, cuts off his head, whilst his knights, uncertain of his fate, mount up the breach in crowds to his succor, bear down all before them, and breaking into the place, put the garrison to the sword.[21]

Not content, and apparently now taken by a war frenzy, the sixty-seven-year-old master and veteran of many battles against the Moors of Spain continued alongside the Venetians deep into Morea until he was captured by the Turks. On learning of his identity, they sent him to a castle in Corinth and kept him under strict guard.

His men compelled the Venetians to offer to return Patras to the Turks in exchange for their master's release, but the Muslims haughtily refused, saying that, "being masters of the Morea, they knew how to recover that place in less time than the Christians had employed in reducing it." His inconsolable knights would not relent, and "offered, besides Patras, a very considerable sum, and three grand priors in hostage, to be kept till the whole was paid." The Turks agreed—but when they informed the master of the good news of his upcoming release, he refused to consent that three grand priors should become hostages on his account.

Preferring riches and Patras to some old "infidel," the Turks allowed his knights to visit and implore Heredia to reason, but "in vain did his knights…labor by their prayers and tears to gain his consent for this exchange; nothing could shake his resolution."[22] He would not even allow the Order to pay his ransom: "If it must be paid," said he, "my family hath received estate enough from me to give this proof of their gratitude."[23] Otherwise, "Let me alone, my dear brethren; suffer a useless old man, that cannot live much longer, to die in prison, and do you that are younger, reserve yourselves to be serviceable to the order."[24]

Not knowing what to do, the confused Turks sent him away into captivity; he was "shut up in a close prison, and instead of enjoying his new dignity [as master] at Rhodes, he was kept above three years in a rigorous slavery."[25] His family eventually managed to ransom him; rather than retiring with every possible honor, Heredia, now seventy, picked up right where he left off: He sailed to Rhodes, resumed his mastership, and led his knights into many more victorious battles against the Muslims until 1396, when the eighty-six-year-old battle-scarred master did at last succumb to mortality.[26]

47

WRATH OF EGYPT'S SLAVE-KINGS

Because their island base was (intentionally) right smack in the middle of enemy territory, it was not long before the Knights of Rhodes's problems were compounded: "Whilst the knights and the Turks," Vertot begins his entry for the 1440s, "equally animated against one another, were roving up and down the seas, ravaging the coasts, where they could make any descent, and laboring to surprise one another, there started up a new enemy to the order."[1] This was the new Mamluk sultan of Egypt, Barsbay. Among the many Circassian boys to be enslaved or "sold…by their unnatural parents," he was converted to Islam and trained to become, and became, a great warrior. By the age of fifty-three, he had ascended the Mamluk ranks to become sultan in 1422.[2]

In 1426, Barsbay began his jihad against the more proximate Christian kingdom of Cyprus. He sent an enormous fleet of 180 galleys demanding that Cypriot King Janus submit to vassalage. Janus instantly called on the Knights of St. John for aid. This was not an easy decision for the Order. Being an already tiny force surrounded by a sea of Islam—sandwiched as they were between the Turks to the north and the

Saracens to the south—their strategy had long been "to maintain peace with one of those infidel princes, whilst it was engaged in war with the other,"[3] and, as it happened, they were then at peace with Mamluk Egypt, the more distant of their existential enemies.

So the Order tried to mediate peace between Cyprus and Egypt. It failed; war broke out and "the order, as an ally of the crown of Cyprus, sent over considerable succors at different times. The war proved long and bloody." In the end, a great many Christians were slain—including "several knights of St. John"—the king was captured, and "the Saracens had a complete victory."[4] They torched and ravaged much of the Christian island. During their triumphant return to Cairo, Janus, who was also titular king of Jerusalem, was paraded through the streets on a donkey, his arms tied behind his back, and his bare feet shackled beneath its belly; nine times he was released to dismount and kiss the ground before the sultan.

Despite this major setback, the master of Rhodes, Anton Flavian, intent on helping Cyprus recover, "sent over new succors of men and money" and urged the remaining lords of that imperiled kingdom that "the order would never abandon them, provided they would not abandon themselves; and that they should take up a noble resolution to die sword in hand rather than submit to the Muslims."

"But those lords," continues Vertot, "divided among themselves, and effeminated by pleasures, not discovering any great courage and resolution," opted to parley with Barsbay. He, banking that "his troops would soon reduce the whole island," obfuscated and dissembled. But the wily sultan soon "found a stop put to the progress of his arms by the valor of the knights. By way of revenge, he ravaged the great commandry…which the order possessed in [Cyprus], demolishing the houses, cutting down the trees, and rooting up the vines."[5]

Peace was at last established in 1427. A huge ransom of 200,000 ducats, which the Order contributed to, was paid to release Janus, though he was ever after known as the king "who never smiled again"—not least due to the obscene humiliations he was exposed to during ten months' captivity.[6]

Henceforth, Cyprus would become a vassal state of Egypt, leaving Rhodes as the last and final heir of the Crusader legacy. This was not lost on the brethren who appeared to have developed a renewed sense of dedication, including by referring to their Order as "our holy religion." Similarly, Vertot notes that, during this time, "in the middle of the fifteenth age [or century], near 400 years after the first institution of the Order," when so many other Europeans had long since lost any semblance of Crusader zeal, "all the commandries of it were like so many seminaries and academies, where the knights were alike educated in piety and the exercise of arms, two qualities, which, though they happen not to meet together in secular persons, may nevertheless form great men in each particular kind, but which ought to be ever united in a knight of the order of St. John."[7]

Once the Mamluks had reduced Cyprus, they eyed and planned on taking that last Christian stronghold, Rhodes, as its master learned from his spies in Egypt. Various vicissitudes stalled this, including a severe famine that struck Egypt. With the rise of Sultan Sayf al-Din (or "Saphadin," yet another "Sword of Islam") Jaqmaq—also a Circassian who was sold to Egypt by his brother, and who as an adult was "known for his devout religiosity"—jihadist fervor was rekindled. Even though he was "moderate in his rule when compared to Barsbay, his predecessor," during his reign, and for the offense of being Christian, "many Copts were burned and killed, while others were nailed to wooden planks and paraded on the backs of camels on the streets of Cairo."[8]

In 1440, two years after becoming sultan, Jaqmaq sent a large fleet consisting of eighteen fully armed and equipped galleys against Rhodes. Master Anton acted fast and had eight galleys, as well as four cargo ships with high decks, fitted out and filled with his warriors. Once the Muslim fleet was sighted on September 25, 1440, the Order's marshal, Louis of St. Sebastien "advanced boldly" to the sound of gunfire and martial music "and offered them battle." Meanwhile, the hardened inhabitants of Rhodes, emulating the knights, took up arms and lined the coasts "resolute to oppose the infidels, if they should offer to make a descent."

Hoping to avoid such an intrepid reception—the sea knights' reputation still instilled terror among the denizens of Islam—the unnerved

Muslims ran their vessels close to shore, lying alongside each other with their sterns turned seaward. They held the brethren off with a barrage of cannon fire—only to be "answered in the same manner."

Once darkness descended, the Egyptian fleet absconded, seemingly toward Turkey. In reality, they were headed for and planning on devastating Lango, a small island garrisoned by the Order. The marshal, however, "whose experience supplied the place of spies, guessing at their design," put out to sea at the same time, "so that the Saracens, when they came up [to Lango], were strangely surprised to find him in their front, drawn up in the order of battle, and offering to fight them a second time."

Not wishing to reengage the sea knights, the admiral ordered a retreat to a nearby Turkish island. Although the Ottomans and Mamluks were longtime rivals, the Turkish inhabitants of the island, due to "the religion which they professed in common with the Saracens, ran to their succor against the Christians," and the two Muslim peoples fortified the island. On the admiral ship, Marshal Louis summoned a war council to decide what to do next. Many of the officers offered strong arguments to return to Rhodes: the Muslims far outnumbered them; the island had sandy shallows, which were dangerous for the large cargo vessels; and besides, the knights could already claim the victory, having driven the Egyptians from the Order's domains.

The marshal, however, was of the old cast; he "did not know what danger was," and informed them that "the knights of St. John were never used to count the number of their enemies, and that he would sooner choose to meet with a grave in the sea, than lie under the reproach of seeing the barbarians so near him, without daring to attack them."

Without any further ado, he transferred his men-at-arms from the carracks to his fleets and sailed straight for the island's coast. Both sides opened cannon fire on one another; a wild battle ensued, "and the Saracens, supported by the Turks, exerted themselves to the utmost, in order to hinder the Christians from approaching their gallies." When night finally parted the combatants, seven hundred Muslims and fifty Christians were dead. Having made his point, and as a sea storm was brewing, the marshal, "covered over with the blood of his enemies, and wounded in five several places," finally set sail for Rhodes. The sullen Mamluks set sail back to Egypt though, and by "way of revenge," they first made a stop in Cyprus and torched another of the Order's great commanderies, and this, concluded Vertot, "was all the advantage the sultan had from an armament and expedition which had put him to a considerable expense."[9]

Sultan "Sword of Islam" Jaqmaq never forgot nor forgave these humiliations and began building a vast fleet in 1442, specifically to annihilate Rhodes. On August 10, 1444, the largest armada ever to attack Rhodes—eighty-five ships and eighteen thousand men—appeared, blockaded, and laid siege to its capital. Over the course of six weeks, the Muslims wreaked havoc on the island and devastated its capital and convent with cannon fire and heavy artillery. We do not, unfortunately, possess extant records of the siege—of the sallies made by the knights, the storming they opposed, or even the number killed and wounded on both sides. Apparently "these knights knew much better how to handle their swords than their pens," observes Vertot, before lamenting that this lacuna "has deprived us of so curious and so important a relation":

> All that is to be found in the registers of the chancery, is, that the siege lasted forty days; that the infidels battered down the place with a great train of artillery; that there were several assaults given, in which they were always repulsed; and that their general, having lost the best part of his troops, re-embarked with the remainder, and was the first that carried to his master [in Egypt] the news of the ill success of his arms.[10]

Other sources suggest that the final battle came when the walls of the city of Rhodes were on the verge of being breached. Sometime before—and precipitating the Mamluk retreat on September 18—the master, John of Lastic, made an unexpected and furious cavalry charge under the cover of darkness into the Muslim camp to the blast of horns and cries of "St. John! St. John!"[11]

What was meant to be a supreme victory for the Mamluks and a decisive defeat for the knights was reversed. On learning that "the knights had drove the infidels out of their isle," a large number of inspired young knights left Europe and eagerly sought to join the Order. This was fortuitous and "helped to fill up the forces of the order, which had been much diminished by losses which are inseparable from war." Mamluk Egypt, on the other hand, would never again dare attack Rhodes. It instead signed a peace treaty in 1446, and the Hospitallers' joy was complete when the envoy returned from Egypt bringing "back with him into the island a great number of Christian slaves and prisoners."[12]

48

"FIRST CONSTANTINOPLE, THEN RHODES"

No sooner did the Egyptian threat withdraw than the Turkish one resumed in earnest. During the 1430s and 1440s, Ottoman Sultan Murad II revived the Ottoman Empire from its stupefaction at the hands of Timur and began making inroads into the Balkans. There, he was met with strong resistance, particularly under the leadership of two Christian warlords: John Hunyadi of Hungary and Skanderbeg of Albania. Confronting these two defenders of the faith taxed the Ottomans of so much of their manpower* that they had nothing left for Rhodes, even making a peace treaty with the sea knights lest their dreaded ships appeared in Murad's rear. Indeed, the same year that witnessed Rhodes's greatest siege, 1444, also witnessed John Hunyadi's "Long Campaign," which devastated the Ottoman realm. All of this was fortuitous for the knights, as it allowed them to meet and repulse the Mamluk armadas in 1440 and 1444.

In 1451, the most ferocious of all Ottoman sultans, Muhammad II, ascended the throne at the age of twenty-one. Although "he had very

* See chapters 6 and 7 of *Defenders of the West: The Christian Heroes Who Stood Against Islam*, which are respectively dedicated to Hunyadi and Skanderbeg.

superior talents, immense views, and an admirable genius...his thirst after glory and pleasures was insatiable, and he abandoned himself to those abominable sensualities which nature cannot think of without horror; he had no honor, no humanity." For three decades, Muhammad the Conqueror would be the scourge of Christendom and author of countless atrocities. Although "nothing escaped his cruelty but the handsomest young persons of both sexes, whom he reserved for the abominations of his seraglio," he still knew how to command his men's respect.

For example, when a seventeen-year-old Christian slave woman, Irene, probably a Greek, was gifted to him, he was so "struck with her exquisite beauty," and spent countless hours with her that it seemed to his leading men that "war was no longer his reigning passion." On learning of such grumbling, he ordered his captains and generals to assemble on the following day, before retiring to Irene's chambers. While there, Muhammad renewed his "tender marks of love," and ordered "her women to exert all their art and skill in dressing her." On the following day,

> When she was thus set out and adjusted to appear in public, he took her by the hand, and led her into the middle of the assembly, when throwing aside the veil which covered her face, he demanded haughtily of the pashas that stood round him, if they had ever seen a more finished beauty? All the officers, like good courtiers, were lavish of their praises, and congratulated him on his happiness. Upon which, Muhammad taking the fair Greek by the hair with one hand, and drawing his scimitar with the other, he cut off her head at one stroke, and turning himself about to the grandees of the court, "This sword," says he to them, with a wild and furious air, "can, when I please, cut asunder the bonds of love." The whole assembly was seized with horror, and shuddered at the sight: the dread they were all seized with, of being treated in the like manner, made the most mutinous of them tremble: everyone thought he saw the fatal scimitar lifted over his own head.[1]

Such was the ruthless nature of the man whose mantra was first "Constantinople—and then Rhodes!"[2] Constantinople, or New Rome, was chosen for being the symbolic head of Christianity since the time of Islam's prophet Muhammad (who promised any Muslim who conquered it great rewards in the here and hereafter), and Rhodes, for being the last heir and representative of the old Crusader spirit.

On May 29, 1453, Muhammad accomplished his first goal. Writing one week later, on July 6, to one of his commanderies, Master John of Lastic described how "the Great Turk, the greatest enemy of the Christians" had captured the city through "force of arms with a great massacre of the Christians. In this campaign, he carried out every kind of cruelty, impiety, and abomination to such an extent that it is impossible to speak of or think of acts of such great cruelty."[3]

The well-recorded atrocities committed at Constantinople—including the outright slaughter of as many as forty thousand Christians[4]—are indeed abominable. According to eyewitness accounts,

> When they had massacred and there was no longer any resistance, they were intent on pillage and roamed through the town stealing, disrobing, pillaging, killing, raping, taking captive men, women, children, old men, young men, monks, priests, people of all sorts and conditions.... There were virgins who awoke from troubled sleep to find those brigands standing over them with bloody hands and faces full of abject fury.... [The Turks] dragged them, tore them, forced them, dishonored them, raped them at the cross-roads and made them submit to the most terrible outrages.... Tender children were brutally snatched from their mothers' breasts and girls were pitilessly given up to strange and horrible unions, and a thousand other terrible things happened besides.... One Turk would look for the captive who seemed the wealthiest, a second would prefer a pretty face among the nuns.... Each rapacious Turk was eager to lead his captive to a safe place, and then return to secure a second

> and a third prize.... Then long chains of captives could be seen leaving the church and its shrines, being herded along like cattle or flocks of sheep.[5]

On breaking into the great cathedral of Hagia Sophia, the Muslim conquerors "engaged in every kind of vileness within it, making of it a public brothel." On "its holy altars" they enacted "perversions with our women, virgins, and children." The daughter of a leading nobleman was tied to an altar and, with a crucifix mockingly placed behind her head, repeatedly gang-raped.[6]

The usual jihadist hate for all things Christian naturally accompanied the sack of Constantinople. Churches were everywhere desecrated, and crucifixes broken, spat upon, and dragged into the dirt to mocking cries of "Behold the god of the Christians!" Bibles and icons were torn to pieces, broken up, and cast into the flames.

Once Hagia Sophia had been "cleansed" of its crosses, statues, and icons—the sultan himself had knocked over and trampled its altar—Muhammad ordered a muezzin to ascend the pulpit and sound "their detestable prayers. Then this son of iniquity [the sultan], this forerunner of Antichrist, mounted upon the Holy Table to utter forth his own prayers," thereby "turning the Great Church into a heathen shrine for his god and his Mahomet."

Like others before and after him, Muhammad found no conflict in moving from piety to perversion. Drunk that night at his victory banquet, he sent word to Grand Duke Loukas Notaras—the nobleman whose aforementioned daughter was gang-raped on the altar of Hagia Sophia—commanding him to surrender his youngest son to the sultan's sexual gratification. "When the boy's father heard this, his face turned ashen as though he had been struck dead." He replied that "it would be far better for me" to die than to "hand over my own child to be despoiled by him." On hearing this, Muhammad, "in a rage," ordered Loukas executed. Before being killed, the grand duke—citing "Him Who was crucified for us, died and arose"—exhorted his terrified sons to reject Muhammad's advances and not fear the outcome. Encouraged, they too "were ready to die," and were executed.[7]

In short, "everywhere there was misfortune, everyone was touched by pain," following the sack of New Rome, which Constantine founded over a millennium earlier in 330. "There were lamentations and weeping in every house, screaming in the crossroads, and sorrow in all churches; the groaning of grown men and the shrieking of women accompanied looting, enslavement, separation, and rape." Muhammad capped off his victory by dragging out the "wretched citizens of Constantinople" before his men and having them "hacked to pieces, for the sake of entertainment." The rest of the city's population—between forty-five thousand and sixty thousand people—were hauled off in chains to be sold as slaves.[8]

Sounding like Riccoldo of Montecroce following the sack of Acre in 1291—though without any accusations against Heaven—by February 1454, the master of Rhodes, John, wrote of the fate of those hapless captives: "Like sheep, streams of Christian captives bound with chains and ropes were brought through Europe and Asia, sold into slavery, and treated so shamefully that nothing more miserable can be said." Unless the kings and lords of Europe stopped squabbling among each other and turned their attention to the east, "this fire," continued the master, "will spread far and wide and will devour other provinces and the name of Our Lord, Jesus Christ, will be brought under the reproach of all."[9]

Having achieved his first goal, the master fully expected Muhammad to turn to his second goal, the conquest of Rhodes: "The Great Turk has our island of Rhodes in his heart and is constantly moving his jaws to swallow it up."[10] Throughout the rest of the 1450s and 1460s, however, Muhammad had his hands full—and by the same men who had plagued Murad II, his father: Hunyadi and Skanderbeg.*

---

* "[Sultan Muhammad II] ravaged those great provinces [of the Balkans], making most of the sovereigns tributaries to him, and would have extended his conquests still farther, had not a stop been put to them by Skanderbeg, the son of John Castriot king of Albania, on one side, and by John Hunyadi Voivode of Transylvania, and general of the troops of Hungary, on the other, both of them the greatest captains of their age, who with an inconsiderable number of forces, but supported by an intrepid courage, and the most exquisite experience in war, checked the rapid progress of his arms" (Vertot, *History of the Knights*, vol. 2, 269).

So the sultan consented to demanding jizya from Rhodes; ever recalcitrant, the knights refused. "Muhammad, the haughtiest and proudest man breathing, enraged at the resolute answer the knights made his ambassador, swore their ruin, and the destruction of Rhodes."[11] He periodically sent whatever available men he had to raid and harry Rhodes and its neighboring islands. They were never enough. "On four separate occasions," notes William Caoursin, a contemporary, Muhammad "readied his fleet for battle and invaded, besieged, and attacked the castle and fields of the Rhodians; from these actions he gained dishonor, damage, and disaster. Many of the Turks were slaughtered: impaled on stakes, hung from gallows, struck by arrows, crushed by stones, brought down by flaming missiles, slain by swords, and torn apart limb from limb. By land and sea the enemy perished."[12]

The wily sultan next "decided to try cunning and trickery" in an effort to seduce the knights into becoming his allies—"but they rejected an alliance with one who persecuted the Christian faith," prompting Muhammad to develop an even greater, more "inexorable hatred" for the Order.[13] And when he tried to turn Orthodox Greek against Catholic Latin in Rhodes, telling the former that he would offer them "unlimited exercise of their religion free from all Latin domination," his efforts were ignominiously met with the indignant cry of "We are all of one belief! here there is neither Greek nor Latin; for we are Christians."[14]

The mighty conqueror of Constantinople gnashed his teeth in rage but could do little as most of his resources were tied up to his wars against Hungary, Albania, and Wallachia. Worse, as feared, in 1458, Master James of Milly took advantage of the Ottomans' quagmire in the Balkans and launched a series of highly successful raids: The knights "ravaged the coasts of his [Muhammad's] dominions, blocked up his ports, did infinite damage to the commerce of his subjects, and secured that of the Christians."[15]

In 1459, the pope called for a Crusade, which the knights were eager to join. The only prince to respond—Hunyadi was dead and Skanderbeg, still defiant, was holed up in the fastness of Albania—was Vlad III Dracul, the dread lord impaler of Wallachia (Romania). In 1462, his vastly outnumbered men terrorized and defeated Muhammad's vast army—almost assassinating the sultan in the process. Greatly moved by this victory, the Knights of Rhodes "tolled the bells and have sung Te Deum to worship the glory of the Romanian prince," wrote Chalkokondyles, a contemporary.[16] Otherwise, few Christian leaders resisted, and Pope Pius II lamented that "if all the other Christian princes...had shown themselves as tireless in their hostility to the Turks as the single island of Rhodes had done, that impious people would not have grown so strong."[17]

During this time, the image of the knights was also becoming cemented in the European consciousness. Based on writings from the mid-to-late fifteenth century, the knights now represented a

> sense of European ethnic identity (the knights are not fighting to regain Jerusalem but to prevent the extermination of Christianity both as a faith and as a people). Frequently-used phrases presented the Knights as warriors for the faith, full of love for Christ; they defended the weak, and they protected and respected the Eastern Christians who, since the fall of Constantinople, came under their care. The Ottomans were characterized as the polluters of Christianity and the destroyers of the Christian people. The Hospitaller chancery listed Ottoman atrocities [which occurred after the 1453 sack of Constantinople]: the killing of men, pregnant women, women, and babies; raping virgins; and abducting young boys. The chancery re-iterated to its European audience that the celibate Knights defended the Church, all Christians (including, since the fall of Constantinople, Eastern Christians) and protected the weak in their care to preserve the purity of the Christian race.[18]

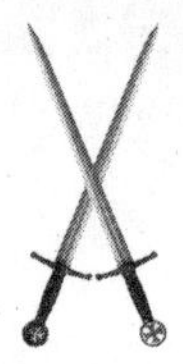

49

"WHAT IS HAPPIER THAN TO FIGHT FOR CHRIST?"

Whatever resistance the Knights of St. John and a few Christian leaders offered following the fall of Constantinople in 1453, the noose continued to tighten around Rhodes. Sultan Muhammad II conquered numerous smaller islands in the vicinity—Lerro, Calamo, Nassaro, Lango, and Simia—taking a "barbarous pleasure" in slaughtering and enslaving their Christian inhabitants. Such atrocities "gratified his rage against the knights: he left them [conquered Christian islanders] only the choice of dying or abjuring their religion."[1]

In 1462, Muhammad attacked the island of Lesbos. Master Peter Raymond Zacosta sent his knights to aid the Greeks, and they caused "torrents of blood" to "stream down in all their sallies," until the island was betrayed to the Muslims, at which point the knights "died all with their weapons in hand." Following the conquest of Lesbos, "the harshest destruction was carried out...so many crimes, such carnage, such cruelty could be seen."[2] A great many of Lesbos's Christian inhabitants were hauled off in slavery and/or forcibly converted to Islam.

In 1470, Muhammad took the Venetian fortress of Negroponte in the Greek island of Euboea, west of Rhodes. More atrocities followed, beginning with its governor Erizzo. He had surrendered on the sultan's oath that he would "not be touched," but once Muhammad had "him in his power, he ordered him sawed in two; and mixing raillery with cruelty...he said that he had indeed given Erizzo assurance for his head, but that he had never meant to spare his sides."[3]

Erizzo's daughter, Anna, "a young lady of surprising beauty," underwent a different trial. Before being sawn asunder, "her father, fearing she would be afterwards exposed to the brutish lust of the soldiers, begged of the executioner to put her to death before they dispatched him; but they replied, that she was reserved for the sultan's pleasures." Anna was taken to Muhammad; enamored by her beauty, he tried to cajole her, but she responded that

> she was a Christian and a virgin, and that she did not so much fear death as she abhorred the debauchery of his seraglio and the poisonous flattery of his promises. Muhammad tried all ways to seduce her, but in vain. They presented her with fine cloths and jewels in his name, but she refused them with a noble disdain. Muhammad, naturally more proud than sensual, enraged at her refusal, changed his love into hatred, and in one of his furious fits cut off her head with his scimitar at one blow; thus fulfilling the wishes of that heroine, who by the sacrifice of a short transitory life, and a frail beauty, acquired immortal glory and felicity.[4]

As for the rest of the hapless Christians of the island of Negroponte, Master John Baptiste Orsini detailed the all-too-typical aftermath in a letter to the prior of France:

> Once the city surrendered to the Turks...the citizens were overcome and miserably butchered. Children were slaughtered; virgins, widows to their disgrace were raped. Youths denied the faith and promiscuous unions were celebrated with the Turks from which children instructed in Muslim rites were conceived and born. Nearly all the

> poor on the island were reduced to the yoke of slavery. The islanders who did not subject themselves voluntarily to this yoke were annihilated. Slaughter, plunder, rape, and the defilement of the holy places was everywhere. No place, entrance, or view was devoid of cruelty and savagery. Who can keep himself from tears in talking of such great things?[5]

In response, the knights continued to do what they had always done—prepare for the inevitable and call for aid from their commanderies:

> Therefore day and night, we ready this city of Rhodes for defense.... Witness therefore, dear brothers, that we are placed in such dangers, precarious situations, anxieties, disasters, and penury!... We wish you could hear the cries, laments, and shouts of our [Rhodian] people who implore your protection, aid, and help and who are unnerved by such great terror concerning an attack on the city. Indeed, these Christian people are committed to our faith and we are about to render an accounting concerning this before the judge and eternal creator.... Understand why you are marked by the Cross! Understand what you have professed! Understand, most dear brothers, what you have vowed to God! Speed up your pace and come to our rescue and relieve us with every firm protection!... [J]ust as true athletes of Christ you must be committed with us to the protection of the city of Rhodes.

John Baptiste made especial request for "a band of warriors" and those of "our brothers who we know are qualified in the use of weapons."[6]

At long last, "in the year of our Lord Jesus Christ one thousand four hundred eighty, the great Turk, infidel enemy of the Christian faith, full of pride, envy, and presumption, made four large armed expeditions to destroy the Catholic faith and Christianity, to subjugate the Christians, and to conquer countries and kingdoms."[7] So begins the account of

Ademar Dupuis, a member of the Order of the Hospital. Two of these expeditions were directed against Hungary and Portugal, but the most famous, or notorious of these jihads, was directed against Otranto, Italy.

After Muhammad's forces captured it on August 11, 1480, more than half of its twenty-two thousand inhabitants were massacred, and five thousand were hauled off in chains. Another eight hundred were offered Islam or death. In keeping with the words of one of their numbers—"My brothers, we have fought to save our city; now it is time to battle for our souls!"—they all spurned the Muslim offer and were all ritually beheaded, their archbishop sawn in half.[8] (The skeletal remains of some of these defiant Christians can still be seen in the Cathedral of Otranto.)

The fourth of Muhammad's jihads in 1480 was directed against Rhodes. Its time had finally come; the sultan vomited forth as much of his resources as he could spare.

Unlike the conquests of other Christian territories, which were strategically important or offered up much by way of booty and plunder, tiny Rhodes offered little of either. It was, however, home to not cowed and tribute-paying Christians but rather uncompromising and militant ones—the very last of the hated Crusaders—and therefore an affront to the imperial dignity of the sultan. Accordingly, in the spring of 1480, Muhammad sent the largest Muslim force ever to besiege tiny Rhodes—160 galleys and 70,000 Turks.

Even John Kay, the author of an important account that appeared in distant England in 1482, two years after the siege, understood Muhammad's ultimate motive in taking tiny Rhodes: "The intent and purpose of the great and cruel Turk was to persecute and utterly undo the Christian faith. Therefore, after the space of 24 years, when he had conquered many empires, kingdoms, and lordships, he was wroth to see the little city of Rhodes standing so nigh his kingdoms and lordships: not subject nor tributary to him."[9]

It was left to Master Peter of Aubusson to defend Rhodes against the largest siege it had ever been subjected to. A charismatic and handsome Frenchman who entered the Order in his early twenties, Peter was fifty-seven when the conflict began in 1480. He, too, was under no illusions as to the source of the upcoming siege: Because "we have stood against him for the faith of Christ," he wrote, that "raging dragon" Muhammad had "conceived an inexorable hatred against us and our Order.... His insane fury has been increasing since the city of Constantinople was assaulted twenty-four years ago," and "now the tyrant of the Turks has plotted to complete his efforts against Rhodes."[10]

In the months and years preceding the arrival of Muhammad's forces in 1480, the master, like his predecessor, summoned the commanderies in Europe to send aid to Rhodes, "the refuge, asylum, and home of Christians in the east."[11] He reminded them of all the "destruction, violent outrages, and injuries that have been caused to the Christian name"; of "how with such great cruelty and fury of spirit he [Muhammad] savaged some of the holy sanctuaries, churches, and monasteries"; of "how many extremely modest maidens, virgins, and matrons he drove into the most shameful disgrace and how many adolescents and youths marked with the sign of baptism he ordered compelled to deny the Catholic Faith."[12]

Although numbers were as ever against the knights of Christ, because theirs was the righteous cause, they were not to hesitate—for "we demand no more experience in war than a willing sword." Below are a few more excerpts from the extant letters Master Peter sent to the commanderies.

> The infidel does not understand the clemency and power of Our Lord, Jesus Christ, who perceiving that one never fails who bases victory not on arrogance or the number of troops, but on a true and just cause.... There is no greater and truer cause to think of than the protection of the Catholic Faith, for which we fight; for which we spill our blood; and for which without hesitation we tread underfoot our corporeal and transitory goods.... We exercise such a firm hope in Jesus Christ that we wear his triumphal sign [the crucifix] on our chests and are not put off by difficulties. To strongly defend this hope, we implore the forces and aid of our fellow knights, the

> protection of our most holy Lord, and of the Catholic kings and princes, and the protection that in matters of the faith at no time should be denied...: May we be crowned with the diadem of a martyr.[13]

He closed by asking each of them to search their own souls: "How much blood will you spend to protect the orthodox faith?... What is happier than to fight for Christ?"[14]

Although many knights responded to the call, how many is unknown. Among those to respond to the master's call was his own elder brother, Anthony of Aubusson, lord of Montelyon, France—"whose great manhood was well known to all the Knights of Rhodes." He was preparing to go to and likely die in Jerusalem during a final pilgrimage, "but when he understood that the great Turk should come and lay siege to Rhodes, he purposed to help and defend the city of Rhodes with jeopardy of his life and all his company," writes John Kay, "for he thought, in no manner place, nor in no manner wise, he might spend his blood better and more for the welfare of his soul than there, where he should fight for the precious name of our Lord Jesus Christ, and for the rightful quarrel of all Christian faith."[15]

As the master's letters indicate, when the vast Ottoman armada arrived in May 1480, the knights were hardly taken unawares. Since his election in 1476, Peter had worked feverishly to further impregnate the island, including by deepening ditches, creating moats, installing artillery, fortifying the wall and towers, and stockpiling food and supplies. To prevent the enemy from finding any shelter, he turned everything outside the walls of the city of Rhodes into a desert: buildings and entire suburbs were destroyed; trees and gardens hewn down; and even churches razed. Considering the onetime beauty of the island, this was a harsh but necessary measure for the people to bear. Peter finally evacuated the Rhodians, and placed their women, children, elderly, and sick in bunkers and underground shelters, and trained and formed the farmers into garrisons. "Day and night," he wrote, "we are preparing for defense so that with the protection of God, in whose power we are waging war, we may achieve victory over our abominable enemies."[16]

50

THEY "MADE A RAMPART WITH THEIR BODIES"

In May 1480, the Muslims came to put an end to the Knights of Rhodes once and for all. A massive Ottoman armada consisting of 160 ships and 70,000 fighters appeared along the horizon. Facing this behemoth, all the master could muster to defend Rhodes were six hundred men of the Order—knights and sergeants—and between two thousand and at most four thousand local militia and mercenaries.[1] In other words, for every one Christian defender, there were between fifteen and twenty-eight Muslim aggressors.

Jacobo Curte, an Augustinian friar living in Rhodes, recorded the common people's consternation on first espying the Turkish fleet:

> On a certain day, when the sun had nearly set, several of the Rhodians, who had slipped away to the mountains to view the sunset, seemed to catch sight of a huge fleet. Although we all already suspected it, there was one who gave voice to our suspicions, saying, "I seem to see the fleet of the most terrible Turks...." Indeed, there in the distance was a huge fleet of galleys stretching over fifty miles. Then, like women, the ignorant mob began to

> shout to high heaven and to raise their hands up to the sky. We went without sleep that night.

A measure of comfort soon returned to them on learning that, "in preparation for this event, the most reverend Peter brought into the city such a great supply of grain, wine, oil, cheese, salted meat, and other supplies that we could have endured a Turkish siege for two years."[2] The sight of around four thousand soldiers "who carried helmets, arms, shields, and hauberks as armor, as well as 500 knights of St. John, covered with iron plate," further encouraged them.[3]

The supreme commander of the Muslim armada whom Sultan Muhammad entrusted with the conquest of Rhodes was Mesih Pasha. As indicated by his first name (*masih* is Arabic for "Christian") this twenty-first grand vizier of the Ottomans was not just originally a Christian but also the nephew of Constantine XI—the last Eastern Roman emperor, who had died heroically defending Constantinople from Muhammad in 1453. As a youth, his captive nephew "had turned Muslim to prevent his being put to death, a punishment which Muhammad inflicted on all the heirs of the empire," writes Vertot; and "the cause of the Cross had no deadlier enemy than this miserable renegade, who sought to secure the favor of his new master by an excess of fury against the Christian name…and especially against the master and the knights of Rhodes."[4]

The siege of Rhodes began on May 22; a week later, Master Peter summarized what had taken place in a letter: Mesih Pasha, "having gathered for the attack of our city a great number of guns, war machines, bombards, and wooden towers as well as engineers and suitable soldiers, he assaulted, besieged and surrounded it. The enemy stationed nearly 70,000 men in a camp opposite us, who sought out, invaded, and attacked us with constant assaults. We have resisted them with an efficient, energetic, and strong spirit." Sounding like an ancient Spartan scoffing at Persians, he condemned the Turks for "waging war with Asiatic effeminacy using engines, machines of war and bombards against a few men."[5]

In another letter dealing with these early days of the siege, the master emphasized the religious hostility fueling the Turks:

> The extremely powerful enemy, maddened by a frenzy against the Catholic Faith, occupied passes, ports, and very suitable sites; readied fleets from far and near; drew up armies and prepared war machines. Nor did we lack an extremely aggressive spirit and we made very many preparations for earthly victories. For the tyrant of the Turks, follower of the faithless prophet Muhammad who wished to overturn the Biblical law, had conquered two imperial capitals, very many realms, extremely rich cities, and fertile islands.[6]

Skirmishes occurred in the early days. "Some of the Turks on horseback and on foot, the most hardiest of them, ran to the walls," writes John Kay, but the knights, "with great manhood went against them, and put them to flight, and slew many of them." The Turks were soon avenged; several knights were captured and publicly beheaded or impaled. On seeing their men split on stakes, the Christians "marveled at the impaling, which is a manner of martyrdom," Hospitaller Ademar Dupuis explained to Western readers, "that the Turks perform on Christians to make their death more agonizing and a greater martyrdom."

Rather than marvel, the master acted. He ordered five of his Muslim captives impaled: "They were staked high on the wall in sight of all the Turks to show them that for each Christian they killed he would kill two Turks."[7]

The primary focal point of the assault was St. Nicholas tower, which strategically guarded the city's two harbors. It was ceaselessly bombarded, but every time a portion of the wall crumbled, the Christians feverishly worked to erect another from the rubble behind it, making the tower impregnable in its ruin.

Meanwhile, the man who called on his brethren to come and sacrifice their all did not just talk the talk but walked the walk. Wherever the bombardment and assaults were thickest, there too was Master

Peter seen, "always armed and in the front lines, constantly checking on each guard-post and bearing himself as valiantly as could be imagined," writes Ademar, who was present during the siege. The master inspired his men to no end: "His armor," another eyewitness notes, "was gilt or golden, and always kept highly polished and shining; and at the head of his chosen and valiant squadron he sat on his horse the whole night long without moving, or taking a moment's repose; and the splendor of the moon reflected from that gilt cuirass rendered his figure a clear and striking object."[8]

Discussing the contemporary accounts' fixation on Peter, Augusta Drane observes,

> This long night-watch, and the spectacle of the master in his golden armor, has been noticed by almost every historian of the order; and doubtless there must have been something unusually solemn and beautiful in his appearance, which distinguished him from the numbers around him, whose conduct was nevertheless scarcely less devoted than his own. He had all the true courtesy and modesty of chivalry; listening to the counsel of all, before declaring his own sentiments, which never failed of being received as law; he had a smile and patient word for all; and yet withal his prompt resolution never suffered itself, when once formed.[9]

Due to the sustained bombardment, by early June, the once impregnable St. Nicholas tower had been much compromised and primed for a frontal assault, which came on June 9. According to the contemporary accounts, "In the middle of the night…with loud shouts thundering all the way to the stars,"[10] the Turks, "wailing the profane name of Muhammad"[11] had "advanced with thirty galleys to attack the tower [of St. Nicholas], which was extremely well fortified with guns and men."[12] But the Christians "stood up to the enemy well, valiantly, and with great courage, and served them very well, very violently, and very strongly with bombards, serpentines, showers of stones and blows by hand. They fought well and tirelessly; they withstood, turned, and forced them back strongly and valiantly. The evil and infidel Turks advanced and retreated, each time all discomforted and all disconcerted."[13] Then "as dawn broke they reluctantly retreated."[14]

Based on the Hospital's archives, Vertot offers more details, including of Peter's exploits:

> [On reaching the much-pulverized wall, the Muslims clapped on ladders] with an air of intrepidity to that heap of stones which the cannon had beat down, and which served as a forewall to the place, and mounted to the storm, sword in hand, with a resolution great enough to astonish any other men but the knights. The master was upon the breach, and performed the office of a captain and a soldier at one and the same time. His armor was pierced through in several places in this engagement, and a shard of stone having carried off his helmet without wounding him, he, without any concern at all, took off the hat of the first soldier that stood next him [and put it on]. The fear of other accidents still more fatal made the knights, who knew not what it was to tremble for themselves, to be under the greatest apprehensions for the safety of the master.

When the commander, Caretto, begged him to take cover and leave the care of defending the breach to his knights, "The post of honor is here," responded Peter, and "belongs to your master." Besides, he added with a friendly smile to Caretto, "if I am killed there, you have more to hope than I have to fear." The master said this to have Caretto "understand that his great valor made him think he merited to be his successor"—which, in fact, he eventually became.

Continues Vertot,

> The knights following the example, and fighting in the presence, of the master, lined the breach; and for want of a wall, made a rampart with their bodies. Some

> overturn the scaling ladders; others throw down masses of vast weight that crush the besiegers to pieces in their fall; nor are there wanting some who throw fire-works and boiling oil on the assailants: everyone has a share in the attack, and all exert themselves in a resistance that seems to be superior to human strength. The Turks don't appear any way daunted; not one of them draws back from danger. If the knights strike any of them down from the ladders, their places are immediately supplied by others who press on to mount. Such as could not get to the posts of danger at the foot of the wall, fired up on the breach with their muskets, annoyed the knights with their arrows, or else tried to lay hold of them with cramp-irons fastened to cords, and so pull them down to the ground in order to cut them to pieces.... At length fire, whose strength is greater and more terrible than that of men, determined the fate of this furious attack. The fireships of the order, fastening themselves to several of the Turkish gallies, set them on fire; the cannon of the city played upon the rest; and the knights, whose force and courage seemed to redouble with the heat of the attack, made such a dreadful fire with their small shot, that the infidels, after the loss of their principal leaders, took to their heels, and in their precipitate retreat, were drowned or killed in great numbers on the seashore, as they were crowding to get aboard their vessels.[15]

In this first major engagement, the Turks lost between five hundred to seven hundred men.

Eager to avenge this setback, Mesih Pasha increased the bombardment in preparation for a final, all-out assault, which came around midnight of June 16, when the exhausted knights could barely keep their eyes open. Making a bridge or floating pontoon of his light ships, he personally led thousands of the Ottomans' elite crack troops, the Janissaries, to the breaches of St. Nicholas with extreme stealth.

Once in position, "those in the vessels began to make a great noise, crying out and invoking Muhammad," recalled Ademar, "and causing a great racket with horrible and terrifying sounds of large taborins, gitterns, hurdy-gurdies, and other instruments, all barking and swirling together in such a way that it seemed that the sky was falling with the firing of cannons and bombards. They approached the tower and mole in such fashion that the noise of their approach was horrible, marvelous, and awful to hear."[16]

Interestingly, all of the sources marvel at this jihadist din. Unable to recognize or describe the (today universally recognized) battle cry of "Allahu Akbar," John Kay merely described it as the "stout and horrible cry," with which the Turks "begin to fight."[17] For Jacobo, the Muslims were "letting out the most shameful wailing, invoking the name of the Prophet Muhammad and blaspheming Jesus Christ. The heavens were filled with their voices."[18]

The cries were unnecessary; even before the assault, the knights, who were not taken unawares, had stealthily positioned all their artillery to bear upon the weakest part of the wall, which they expected the enemy to target. Holding matches to their cannons, and with their muskets well aimed, they but waited for the word from Peter to open fire. And that word came once the ululating Muslims were close enough. Then the knights unleashed all hell on the encroaching enemy. The explosion—from cannons and muskets, Greek fire, bursting grenades, and flares of all sorts—reportedly turned night into day.

In the midst of this latest Armageddon between Christian and Muslim, "a long and obstinate engagement ensued," writes Vertot. "The bridge and galiots supplied the Turks continually with fresh troops. Never did those Infidels show so much valor and so resolute a courage."[19] The battle raged for nearly twelve hours, into late morning and, according to Drane,

> Horrible was the confusion—the roaring of the flames; the incessant cannonading; the fire-balls blazing and

> flaming; the yells of the combatants; the shrieks and groans of the maimed and the dying.... In spite of the tremendous fire poured on them from all sides, the infidels plant their ladders at the foot, and, brandishing their scimitars, scale the bastions. The assault is all along the front: the master stands at the breach, and around him his gallant knights, making a rampart with their bodies. The ladders are thrown down, only to be raised again by the determined foe; massive stones and boiling oil and streams of flaming fire are launched upon them—still they press on.[20]

In short, a repeat of the June 9 assault occurred, though on a much larger scale; and before long, "those barbarians, not able any longer to bear up against the Christians gave over the attack, notwithstanding the prayers and threats of their officers, and fled for their lives to the vessels in which they first came."[21]

Not content, and now in a battle frenzy, the victorious Christians issued forth from their keep and plunged into the harbor, chasing and mowing down the retreating Muslims. Conspicuous among them was Anthony Fradin, a Franciscan friar who, having plunged shoulder deep into the water, was seen pulling fleeing Turks out of their boats and back into the water with him, where he lopped off their heads with his sword "or hacked them into pieces, and then flung them into the sea. As brief as his wonderful feats of arms were, those who saw them assert that he struck hard blows. When it was over he was badly wounded and hurt. The Master thought well of the deed, and gave him the reward of having a brand new habit made."[22]

The grisly aftermath of the Muslim rout was visible for days. Countless sodden corpses and turbans—heads still inside—were seen either beached or floating in "the sea [which] was made red from the enemy gore."[23] As the Christians later learned from deserters, a full 2,500 Muslims were slain or drowned in the assault, including three principal commanders, one of which was Ibrahim Bey, the sultan's son-in-law and lord of Anatolia.*

As for Mesih Pasha, "when he saw that his people once again had been violently beaten back, and that he had lost so many men and officers, he had such great pain and melancholy that he went into his tent, where he stayed for three days without speaking to any of his people[24]... [being so] absorbed by monstrous grief."[25] It did not help that the Christians—whose tiny casualties included only twelve knights—"hung many of the Turkish heads on our towers."[26]

---

* Because primary sources are so valuable, and at the risk of redundancy, Master Peter's own modest and succinct account of this battle follows: "In the middle of the night...the Turks, inflamed with a desire to fight, approached the citadel in complete silence and then with a great charge attacked from all sides. Our men had not slept but strained their ears to hear. When it was discovered that the enemy was approaching, soldiers fired stones from guns, drew their swords, and loaded their crossbows with bolts. Stones were fired from the tower, and they drove the enemy from the mole. The battle was fought with tremendous force from midnight until ten the following morning. A great number of the Turks who had disembarked from the skiffs and galleys on the mole were cut down. A floating bridge loaded down with Turks was demolished by artillery fire and those on top of it were plunged into the sea. Four of the galleys and the ships that had been loaded with bombards and stones were shattered by the barrage of stones and sank beneath the waves. Also, the fire that had been hurled into the fleet compelled the defeated Turks to withdraw. During this glorious battle, some of the great men who commanded the Turks died and their death caused all of the [Muslim] army to mourn. Deserters brought within our lines after the battle claimed that the Turks had suffered a great massacre in the battle and that approximately 2,500 of their troops had been killed" (Vann and Kagay, *Hospitaller Piety*, 161).

51

THREATS OF IMPALEMENT, RAPE, AND SLAVERY

Following his failed and costly storming of St. Nicholas on June 16, Mesih Pasha redirected his fury from that tower to the city walls themselves, particularly the southeast wall adjacent to the Jewish quarter of the city of Rhodes, which had already been much compromised from the initial bombardment. "Eight tremendous cannons," wrote the master, "of the largest size ever seen, ceased not night and day." Others confirmed that they "shook the walls with vehement fury" so that, "as in an earthquake, the buildings of the city swayed." Islands within a hundred-mile radius around Rhodes reported hearing the Turks' raging.[1]

The master, as usual, tried "to pay the pasha in his own coin," and "set the carpenters of the town at work to make a wooden engine that would also throw quarries of stone of a prodigious bulk." These vast stones wrought havoc among and "crushed…to pieces" all Turkish fighters within reach. "The knights out of raillery called this machine 'the Tribute,' alluding to that which Muhammad demanded of the Order, and giving him withal to understand, that he was to expect no other kind of payment."[2]

Finally, after "a steady Turkish barrage of 3,500 round stone," much of the wall was "tore to pieces, destroyed, and demolished...and a huge pile of dead bodies lay on the ground."[3] Still, wherever the wall crumbled, the people—young and old, men and women—built a new ditch and wall from the rubble: "Nobody shirked work," writes William ("Guillaume") Caoursin, vice-chancellor of the Order who was also present at the siege, "not the master, bailiffs, priors, knights, citizens, merchants, matrons, brides, nor virgins. They carried stones, soil, and lime on their shoulders. Neither gold, nor silver, nor household goods were spared to care for the public safety."[4]

Vertot adds that "the Jewish women as well as the Christian, being threatened with an odious slavery, and dreading still more the indignities they should be exposed to if the city should be taken by storm, drudged at the work, as well as the men. The very nuns came out of their convents and assisted the workmen with an incredible zeal. Everybody was then a soldier."[5]

This widely reported alacrity and "good will of the people"—which was "a great pleasure and a beautiful thing to see," to quote Ademar—was a byproduct of the master's inspiring example.[6] Peter never "spared himself," writes William. "Not refusing any hard labor, he stayed in the empty space left by the fallen walls, where he snatched what little sleep he could, ate, and remained at the ready. The most courageous of the Rhodians followed the master's example; neither the upper, nor middle, nor poorest refused duty."[7]

Constantly being frustrated by the master and convinced that if he could only cut off the head of this Rhodian snake, the island would quickly fall, Mesih Pasha sent double agents and assassins to dispatch the master by dagger or poison. Many of them were former Christians who appeared before the walls, claiming to want to defect from the Ottomans and rejoin the Christian name. The sources especially focus on one "Meister George," a German artillery expert. Claiming that he regretted helping the Muslims against his coreligionists of Rhodes and was eager to repent by offering his formidable skills to the Christians, he was admitted but also closely watched. His true purpose was to ascertain and inform his Muslim masters where the walls were weakest.

The meister was eventually exposed—"It was he who caused many cities of Christians to perish and many souls to be driven into the seraglio," charged Jacobo—and hanged by order of the master.[8] Another deserter was found with "a vial of poison to find a way to poison my Lord, the Master," writes Ademar. On being discovered, "the Master had a large stone bound to his neck and then flung into the sea."[9]

While the cannons continued to pummel the city, the Muslims began to build a causeway of stones and dirt across a portion of the ditch surrounding the crumbling walls. The plan was to raise a mound on level with the ramparts and use it for an all-out assault to take the city by storm. The knights did what they could to frustrate these designs, for example,

> My Lord, the Master, ordered sixty men to sally forth one morning to the ditches and defenses. With great courage they pursued all the Turks who were there, and made them retreat all the way to their camp. They slaughtered ten within the refuges and carried their heads into the city, and put them on the point of their lances on the wall. They directed and conducted the fire into the Turkish ditches and refuges, and they slaughtered them; therefore, the people of the town were glad for their bravery.[10]

Ever inspired by their knightly lords, the Rhodians themselves crept out every night, clandestinely removed stones from the watery foundation of this causeway, and used them to refortify their own city walls, so that the Turks were surprised to find their causeway constantly shrinking in height.

Despite the Christians' stalwart resistance, six weeks after the bombarding began and much of the wall had been reduced to rubble, a causeway—one which "a squadron of horse might easily march over"—was completed alongside the Jewish sector. Now nothing stood between the Christians and the hordes clamoring for their blood outside—"neither ditches nor walls nor towers." But because Mesih Pasha by now "dreaded the heroic valor of the knights more than he did the fortifications of art," he magnanimously offered to parley with the knights and sent his ambassadors to negotiate a peaceful surrender.[11]

Standing atop their causeway before the breach, the Muslims began by congratulating the Christians for their stalwart courage and impressive resolution. However, now that it was evident that the Turks were poised to take the city in a day, Mesih Pasha was pleased to offer the knights one last chance. If they would but take the knee, "make peace and forge a union with our lord [Sultan Muhammad]," not only could the knights "retain possession of the city and its territory," but "there will be great benefit and profit for the city and of those inside it."[12]

Besides, now that there was a breach in the wall and a causeway above it large enough for a squadron of horses to gallop atop—not to mention over fifty thousand Turks eager to storm the city—continued resistance was madness, not courage, added the Muslim emissaries. If the knights did not care for themselves, at least "take pity" on the people of Rhodes, they urged, for, if the city is taken by storm, Mesih Pasha will "allow it to be plundered with all manner of cruelty," with "the men enslaved, and the women led off to rape and dishonor."[13]

> O most splendid men of fame in war, highly distinguished for prudence that everyone admires, what reason exists, what power, what weapons, in short, what force that you are willing to [continue to] do battle on the same scale as he who rules over almost the entire world [Sultan Muhammad II]? Are you not surrounded by a fleet? Are you not ringed by an entrenched army? Are you not by now entirely battered by artillery and death?[14]

Undaunted, Anthony Gautier, the castellan of the city of Rhodes, began by inquiring "if your Lord Turk is as powerful as it is said, why do you exhort us to make peace and union with him, and then threaten us?" The fort commander then spoke like many knights of Christ had from of old:

> We do not know if our deeds prove our courage and will; but know you that all that you have said to us, and

> all that you have done here, does not drive us to do a thing that is harmful to our faith and to our religion; nor do your threats make us fear at all. We are all one in courage, and we believe fervently in our Lord Jesus Christ, who is the true God, and for whom we are all prepared and ready to fight and to die; and rather than join with your Muhammad, whose law that you hold is false and evil, we will keep with all our power our law, which is good and right. Since you have come in great power, complete what you have begun: and in the grace of Jesus Christ, we will respond to you so well and with such good courage, that you will know that you do not deal with Asians, or with people lacking in courage.[15]

Anthony closed by telling the ambassadors to return and inform Mesih Pasha—that Christian apostate "who is so bold and who so loves the profit of the Turk his Lord"—that "we are hardly afraid of your power."

> We have no dread of your weapons. Besides, we in no way desire to conclude an alliance or make peace with your king. Christians have not been subject to the people of this king by law, tribute, or treaty. He wants a treaty between Christ and the Devil! If you wish peace, you should not besiege the island and city with a fleet. We are not wiser than any of those men who pay annual tribute to your king and yet are no less well resolved in our courage. Indeed, we proclaim that our soldiers defending the faith of Jesus Christ, and girded with weapons, desire to be slaughtered rather than subordinated to you. Leave! Don't desire to approach our walls any longer if you want to keep living your precious life![16]

As the shamefaced ambassadors withdrew, one of their numbers, unable to restrain his passions, blurted out,

> Not many days will pass, oh Rhodians, and you will see your virgins raped and the soil will be thoroughly sodden with your blood spilled by the sword! It will disgust you. The most select of your children will become the most deceitful Janissaries and we will become intoxicated with your spoils! The kneeling, excuses, and tears of your powerful men will then accomplish nothing!

At that, four knights instantly pounced off the ramparts in the direction of the insolent Muslim; they fought and killed his defenders and seized and spirited him back into the city.[17]

On learning of the knights' continued insolence in the face of certain death, the Turks "were whipped into a frenzy," writes William. "It shamed them that so great an army as theirs did not prevail, and the terrible power of their tyrant was slighted by the Rhodians."[18] As for Mesih Pasha, he "became very irate with the Rhodians, and swore by Muhammad that if he should capture the city that he would spare no one, and that all would be put to the stake. He ordered four hundred stakes for the purpose."[19] Next, he had what was in store for Rhodes publicly announced before the city walls:

> The herald of the Turks cried out from the camp that the goods of the city would be taken as plunder and that the beardless boys would be sent into slavery so that they might come to deny their faith. The throats of the older boys reaching manhood would be cut, and the Turks had prepared 8,000 stakes for those captured alive to be impaled.[20]

The Knights of St. John responded by bringing forth the insolent Muslim they had earlier seized and impaling him before the entire Ottoman army, "in accordance with Turkish custom."[21]

"After these threats were made public," writes William Caoursin concerning the aforementioned Ottoman proclamations of forthcoming impalement, rape, slavery, and forced conversion, "the Turks hastened to attack the city. Before the assault, they cried out in their customary way to Muhammad, and washed and cleansed their bodies. They prepared sacks to carry off plunder, and they attached cords to their belts to tie up captives." (Ademar adds that there was not a single Muslim "who did not carry one or two girded cords in order to bind the Rhodians.")[22]

Meanwhile, inside the city of Rhodes, everyone prepared to meet their Maker:

> The people of the city, the great as well as the small, Knights, men, women, and children, made good confessions and repented of their sins and were all well-ordered like good Christians, since they were expecting to die day by day and hour by hour. They were often in churches for prayer and worship, devoutly entreating God to save them and the city, and defend them from the hand of the Turks, the false dogs who persecuted them daily and hourly without any respite.[23]

Not everyone was so resolved to meet death. Seeing, as the Muslim ambassadors had pointed out, that Rhodes would be taken at the first assault, followed by a bloodbath and worse, a few knights concluded that, "since there was no saving of Rhodes, it was not just to sacrifice what knights were still left to the desperate humor of the master, a man who did not care to survive the loss of his principality; but that they, whatever he had resolved to the contrary, ought to save the knights and inhabitants by an honorable composition."[24]

On learning of these "murmurs and scandalous projects," the master summoned those indecisive knights and, formally addressing them as "gentlemen," said, "if any of you do not feel secure here, the port is not yet so entirely blockaded but shall be able to find means for you to retire. If, however," he continued with rising indignation, "you choose to remain, let me hear no more talk of surrender, otherwise I shall certainly put you to death."[25]

Such an address—including the fact that he referred to them as "gentlemen," a cold term never used between brother-knights—"stung them to the quick."[26] They hurled themselves at his feet, swearing they were his obedient subjects. As Vertot writes, "These terrible words filled those knights with shame and confusion," prompting them to "detest their own weakness and all promised to make atonement for it by the sacrifice of their own blood or of that of the Infidels, and they were afterwards always the first to expose themselves to the greatest dangers."[27]

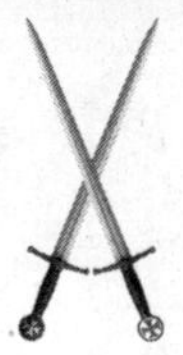

52

THE "INDOMITABLE SPIRIT OF MARTYRS"

Once jihadist ceremonies and preparations were complete, on July 26, 1480, the Turks unleashed one final barrage of hellfire on the city of Rhodes; all their cannons incessantly blasted and continued reducing the walls to rubble. Neither time nor cover was granted the Christians to make any repairs. After nearly twenty-four hours of this ceaseless pulverization, Mesih Pasha ordered two hundred ladders thrown up along the most compromised sections of the wall.[1]

Finally, as the morning sun rose on July 27, a tremendous war cry was heard throughout the Muslim camp, as an advance troop of two thousand Turks charged, overran, and easily took possession of and planted their banners on the wall. On their heels came four thousand other Muslims, charging to and ascending the ladders. The few remaining Christian defenders on the wall were quickly mowed down in the onslaught (except for eight nameless warriors espied by Jacobo, who "victoriously clashed in combat," and apparently continued to do so "until the sounding of the final trumpet"[2]).

As panic was on the verge of spreading among the Rhodians, the voice of the master was heard to boom: "Come, my brothers," cried he, "let us fight for the faith and for Rhodes, or be buried under the ruins!" And with that, he ordered "the trumpet sounded immediately, and the Knights and the townspeople sallied forth under arms," writes Ademar.[3]

Leading the charge with a half-pike in hand, he threw a ladder against the wall, ascended it, and "skillfully and courageously attacked the first row of enemy soldiers." Thrice was the fifty-seven-year-old hurled back to the ground—a distance of between ten and twenty feet—and thrice rose again, grunting his way back up the ladder. Once on top, "striking with his own hand, he killed several of them," until "this Samson, this true Joshua, recalled to the battle our people who had almost turned and run away from it. He unleashed a violent attack along with the defenders." Despite such ferocity in the midst of battle, Master Peter, as was his wont, maintained a "calm expression and friendly banter," continues Jacobo.[4]

There is no exaggerating the pivotal role played by the master; all contemporary and eyewitness chronicles emphasize it. "Peter of Aubusson," writes William Caoursin, "with a large retinue of men and a strong will, climbed the ladders; he himself slew enemy soldiers. He attacked the enemy manfully; he repulsed them; he slaughtered them. He and the knights in his retinue fought on behalf of the Catholic faith and of the Christian commonwealth.... Not fearing any danger, he suffered five wounds in his body, any one of which could have been fatal."

From Ademar's vantage point, "My Lord Master...came at once to the heights, and began immediately to climb. With great courage he climbed up carrying out marvelous feats of arms. But in climbing he received great and bad blows, and also gave some good ones. Two or three times he was thrown down from the wallwalk, but was valiantly helped by the Knights who were with him, all of whom supported him so well and so valiantly that in spite of the Turks they climbed the wall."[5]

Following the example of their master, "a huge mass of people rushed to the attack" to "the pealing of bells and clatter of weapons," recalled those present, and "a tremendous cry arose from all sides." Now did a strange thing unfold: The Christians and Muslims seemed to have switched positions "because the defenders of the town were like the attackers," writes Ademar. "With great courage, they climbed up by degrees to retake their wall, fighting with blows of lances, of vouges, and of arrows. The Turks on the wall defended themselves strongly and spiritedly by firing bolts, hurling stones and throwing all they could down upon the people of Rhodes."[6]

On reaching the top of the wall, the outnumbered Christians "locked in hand-to-hand combat" with "2,500 magnificently-armed Turks," who were, nonetheless, "tightly packed on top of the wall… with our men, striving to drive them back by force of arms. But our front ranks, persisting with unconquerable courage, supported by divine protection, did not yield an inch."[7]

Everyone was there for "this glorious struggle," writes William Caoursin: "The bailiffs and knights of Jerusalem, the merchants, and many natives and strong men of each nation. Some of them were killed, fighting bitterly among the tightly packed enemy; others survived after receiving many wounds." Knowing that their fate was in the balance, even the meanest folk, "both men and women," observed Ademar, joined the fray and "comported themselves so well and valiantly that it was marvelous. They did what was necessary, and there were not many who did not bear some wound." As the battle reached a fever pitch, "all of Rhodes cried on Jesus Christ," for "they fought against the enemies of Christian faith," even as "the Turks cried on Muhammad," writes John Kay.[8]

Still, what could such faith and courage do against tens of thousands? According to William,

> Besides the Turks who had occupied the walls, another huge group of them had so filled the field bordering the wall, the ruins, the rampart, and the ditch that the ground could barely be seen. Deserters confirmed that forty thousand of the Turks were involved in the attack. The fighting went on for two hours with no clear result;

> sometimes victory tipped to our men, sometimes to the Turks.[9]

At one point, Mesih Pasha, who was advancing "saber in hand," espied the master, "not so much by his gilt arms as by the deadly blows he gave." "As he had not been able to destroy him by poison," he promised the Janissaries accompanying him "a great reward" to kill the master. Twelve of these elite warriors "devoted themselves, as it were to death, in order to dispatch him. They rush headlong into the midst of the engagement, charge the Christians with vigor, pierce their ranks, open a way to the master, and in spite of the knights that surrounded his person, attack him, and give him five great wounds at once."[10]

Such might have been the heroic end of a lesser man, but the master was not quite ready to give up the ghost: The adrenaline and "ardor with which he was enflamed in the heat of the combat," propelled him to fight "on some time longer with his usual valor," before falling back on and waving a banner of Christ crucified. When his knights entreated their bloodied master to withdraw, "Let us die in this place, my dear brethren!" cried he, for "can we ever die more gloriously than in the defense of our faith and religion?"[11]

Such words, such a sight—their beloved master and father, stained by his own blood and that of his enemy, collapsed on one knee, yet still holding aloft Christ's banner in defiance—"animated the knights and Christian soldiers in such a manner that, mad with vexation…they throw themselves like furies into the thickest of the enemies, and make an horrible slaughter of them."[12]

The pivotal moment had come. The knights' fury, haloed, as it were, by Christ's banner—which, once unfurled, caused the Turks "to hang their heads," writes Ademar, "like someone who had seen a ghost"*—worked to unnerve the Muslims.[13] Due to the superhuman blows they began to receive, "which rage inspired with an uncommon force," the bewildered Turks now took the knights "for other men—or for something more than man. Terror seizes their spirits; they lose all sense and judgment...and all take to their heels."[14]

Here, it is perhaps meet to consider the words of Augusta Drane on the source of such superhuman feats:

> Doubtless the Knights of St. John, as sworn companions in arms, vowed to fight and to die in the same great cause, felt themselves bound to each other by no ordinary tie, and were ever ready to sacrifice their lives for the sake of their brethren; but it was not in this that their strength lay. It lay in the simple power of divine faith, in a religious devotion as humble as it was ardent, and a burning enthusiasm for the cause of God in the world. This it was that elevated their valor to a supernatural

* According to most eyewitness sources, a miracle occurred in connection with this banner. According to William Caoursin, the same deserters who "divulged that nine thousand Turks perished from the siege, [and] fifteen thousand were wounded," also "confirmed a persistent rumor spread among the Turks of a miraculous vision that frightened them out of their wits. So great was their trepidation they broke ranks and retreated on foot. They affirmed that when the banner of our lord Jesus Christ and the Virgin Mary, as well as that of St. John the Baptist and the Order of Jerusalem were raised in battle by order of the prince, the enemy saw the most splendid golden cross raised aloft in the air. In addition, a glistening white maiden bearing a shield and spear appeared, with a man in peasant garb, surrounded by a most splendid company of retainers who came there in defense. This vision instilled such a terror in the enemy that none dared to advance despite every agreement made among them." Ademar shares a similar account: "when my Lord Master had unfurled the banner of the crucifixion, the Turks saw in the air above the banner a great cross of gold, and to one side above the wall was revealed to them a beautiful virgin clothed in white who held a lance in one hand and a white shield in the other. She was attended by a man very poorly dressed, who was accompanied by many beautiful people. These things made them so fearful and afraid that they did not know what to do, and they lacked the power to defend themselves.... The Turks, false dogs, and enemies of the Catholic faith...God by His grace had destroyed and confused. Amen" (Vann and Kagay, *Hospitaller Piety*, 137–143, 279).

> virtue, and gave them the calm intrepid bearing and the indomitable spirit of martyrs.[15]

Still aflame with rage, the knights gave chase and made quick work of the retreating enemy. Panicky Muslims everywhere were hewn down or hurled off the walls. Now the Muslims' vast numbers worked against them; fleeing before Christian steel in such tightly packed and confused throngs, "the Turks killed one another...snapping at each other like dogs." Now even the "townsmen stabbed and slaughtered them like pigs." Before long, "the Turks were scattered, repulsed, and killed," to quote William; "they were slaughtered to a man," and "it was a wonder for us to witness the feats that our men performed in this battle."[16]

Despite entreaties and threats for his men to fight on, Mesih Pasha—this apostate to Islam who was preparing to celebrate his jihadist victory by impaling eight thousand Christians—was himself carried off in ignominious flight back to the safety of his fleet; for the advancing knights, now on horseback, had already overrun the pasha's camp around the city, putting its dismayed defenders to the sword.

And that was that. A few days later, a much-traumatized Mesih Pasha quit Rhodes and set sail for safer waters, and "there was nothing left of their vast armament but the corpses that strewed the battlefield as thick as the forest-leaves in autumn." Indeed, 3,500 Turks were slain in that final battle. During the entire three-month siege, a total of 9,000 were killed and 15,000 wounded. After describing how "our men entered the city [after routing the Turks] amidst great applause through the ruined walls," William writes that "the cadavers of the enemy were discovered laying within the city, on the top of the city walls, in the ditch, on the ramparts, and in the sea. Afterward, to avoid plague, our men burned the deformed and mangled corpses." Ademar adds, "there were so many that it took days to burn them, and the women who saw them burn gave thanks, cursed them, and hurled at them rotten figs and other fruits from their gardens."[17]

On the Christian side, only fifteen knights and forty Rhodians were killed in this final clash, and about five hundred seriously wounded. Among those who vacillated between life and death was the master.

After the battle, Peter, covered with his own blood and that of his enemies—but even more so with honor and glory—was borne by his men as if on a funerary bier to the infirmary. There he spent the next three days fighting for his life. He eventually emerged alive but even more scarred than before 1480. Once he was able to walk, he went to the Church of St. John and fell to his knees in thankful prayer. He built several churches and established foundations within them "to pray to God forever for the souls of the knights that were killed in this bloody siege."[18]

He then sent several letters to the Western commanderies describing the battle. As a reflection of the man's modesty, while repeatedly praising the valorous efforts of his fellow knights and Rhodians, he never mentioned his pivotal role in the fight, which is otherwise confirmed in every other contemporary and eyewitness account. Even the distant Englishman John Kay, after extolling the master for "his great manhood and noble heart to God and his order," added that, following 1480, "throughout all Rhodes [he] was called the very father and defender of the city and of the faith of Jesus Christ."[19]

Indeed, Peter only mentions himself once—and that as a suppliant of Christ: "In the sight of the enemy, we raised the standard of the image of our lord Jesus Christ and of our religion. The two sides had fought with all their might for two hours. At last, the Turks, hard pressed, harassed, terrified, and badly wounded, turned tail and fled in such a rush that they got in their own way and constituted a danger to themselves and their troops."[20] The conclusion of Peter's account is even more pious in nature:

> Those of us who were wounded gave thanks to God and tended our wounds. After a strong garrison was posted on the walls and our troops returned, it seemed that these events had occurred with divine aid that shielded us from such great destruction.... With hopes of capturing the city, the Turks had prepared many ropes to tie up captives and had ordered that sharpened stakes be made to impale them alive. Indeed, had we not saved the

> city from Turkish control, they would have killed all the men, slaughtered all the women over ten (impaling them all on stakes), sent into slavery everyone of a tender age, compelled them to abjure their faith, and plundered all the booty of the ruined city. But they were frustrated in their nefarious desire and were killed like swine.... Thus, they returned beaten and in shame.[21]

As for the author of this entire passion play, on learning of his army's defeat, Sultan Muhammad II flew into a rage and nearly had Mesih Pasha strangled—the standard Ottoman punishment for failed generals—but eventually consented to banishing him to Gallipoli. After his initial paroxysm had blown over, Muhammad consoled himself by concluding that his men were never successful without his personal leadership. Less than one year later, he had two hundred thousand men mustered, and the general rendezvous was in Bithynia, a province adjoining to Lycia. Whether this massive campaign was to be directed against the knights, as it was widely believed, or another target was never known.

While in Bithynia, on May 3, 1481, the sultan died, aged forty-nine, possibly poisoned by his own son and successor, Bayezid II, who was impatient to prove his worth. Muhammad's corpse was carried back to and interned in Constantinople. And although that sultan and scourge of Christendom had conquered two empires, twelve kingdoms, and hundreds of cities and towns, the epitaph that he reportedly had made for himself made no mention of these but rather consisted of a few Turkish words to the following effect: "I Designed to Conquer Rhodes and Subdue Proud Italy."[22]

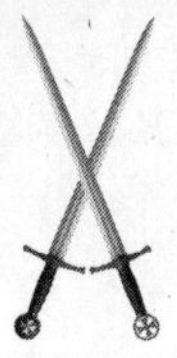

53

THE "STANDING PROTECTORS OF CHRISTIAN NATIONS"

The Knights of St. John's triumph over the Turks in 1480 resulted in a dramatic return of the prestige they had once enjoyed before the loss of Acre nearly two centuries earlier. William Caoursin's account of the siege was, thanks to the printing press, spread all over Europe where it became an instant "bestseller." Although they had little interest in the knights' naval battles with Muslim vessels in the distant and eastern Mediterranean, Western Christians were increasingly terrified of the Turk's growing might and conquest of European regions. The same year that Rhodes was besieged, 1480, witnessed the Turks invade and create a pyramid of skulls in Otranto, Italy.

As such, that a band of Christian knights on a tiny island that was practically attached to Turkdom had accomplished what entire Christian kingdoms could not—defeating everything the Turks could hurl at them—inspired Western Europeans to no end. A renewed burst of enthusiasm ensued, and the Order was recipient to many more recruits and donations.

Always, it was those who most appreciated what the knights stood for and against—that is, other piously militant Christians who were themselves at war with Islam—who most supported them. Thus, when the infamous Borgia pope, Alexander VI, tried to seize upon and bestow the priory of Catalonia to one of his (bastard) sons, there was outrage from King Ferdinand II of Aragon and Castile, who was also at war against Islam, for "in his wars against the Moors of Granada, he had found no succor so surely to be depended on as those of the Spanish knights [of the Hospitaller and other military orders]." So Ferdinand wrote to the pope, reminding him that

> those illustrious knights were the standing protectors of all the Christian nations that sailed in the Mediterranean; that ever since the foundation of the order, they had always served as a convoy to pilgrims that went out of devotion to visit the holy land and the Sepulchre of the Savior of mankind; that since the increase of their power by the conquest of the isle of Rhodes, they made no use of their forces, as his holiness well knew, but only to succor Christian princes against the infidels; that they spent their revenues, their blood, and their lives in that service; that the order was daily losing some of its bravest knights in those holy wars; and that very few of them came off without wounds.[1]

While the knights were, moreover, sacrificing their blood and treasure in the war against Islam, other Christians chose a more pragmatic course. Thus, when Venice and Hungary made peace with the tyrannical Turks, "none stood out but the knights of Rhodes, who, without having the least succor from the pope and the other princes of Europe, continued the war against the Turks with the single forces of the order." Alone and vastly outnumbered, they still managed to score several naval victories against the Muslims of both Egypt and Turkey throughout the first decade of the sixteenth century.[2]

Numbers, which the Muslims almost always dwarfed the Christians with, may have been decisive for land battles. On the sea, however, the knights' naval skills and seafaring technology neutralized and made Muslim numbers count for nothing—except, perhaps, as more food for the fish. As such, by 1504, the Ottomans and Mamluks, both "being exasperated against the knights, who were masters of the sea...secretly made a league together to destroy a power which ruined the commerce of their subjects." Muslim pirates from everywhere were ordered to "make descents on the isles belonging to the knights, and destroy all with fire and sword." Despite the initial massacres and havoc these corsairs caused, most of them "were cut to pieces" by the "sword of the knights."[3]

In one instance, in 1506, five hundred Turks landed on tiny Lerro—more a rock than an island—which was garrisoned by a tiny band of knights. The Muslims battered the castle all night long. In the morning, as they prepared to storm its ruins, they were shocked to see the breach filled with many more knights than they had anticipated, causing them to tuck tail and run. In fact, what they saw were peasant men and women whom the small knight garrison of Lerro had dressed in their habit, with the large pectoral white cross, in order to intimidate the Turks.[4]

In 1512, the Order received something of a slight reprieve. On becoming Ottoman sultan, the second thing "Selim the Grim" did—after assassinating his father, his brothers, their wives, and all their children—was marshal the full might of his empire against the Turks' longtime rival, the Mamluks, centered in Egypt and Syria. Although they were both Sunni Muslims, Selim's war was, he said, a jihad, as the Mamluks had long interfered with his ability to wage jihad against Christians and heretics (the latter being Shias, including the Mamluks' Persian allies). By 1517, he had "entirely destroyed the empire of the Mamluks," at which point he "immediately set to work fitting out two hundred gallies, which he designed for the conquest of the isle of Rhodes."[5]

"Now that the terrible Turk has Egypt and Alexandria and the whole of the Roman eastern empire in his power," lamented Pope Leo X, "he will swallow not just Sicily and Italy but the whole world!"[6] If large western states had much to fear, what about tiny Rhodes in the east? Aside from a small window to the west, it was surrounded by the same implacable enemy: Anatolia to the north, Syria to the east, and Egypt and most of North Africa to the south were now all Ottoman domains.

Even so, like Muhammad II, Selim died while preparing for this grand jihad against the knights in 1520. His son and successor, Suleiman the Magnificent—who also came to power by slaughtering all his brothers—was no less ambitious than his ancestors. In 1521, Belgrade finally fell to the Turks under his leadership. Underscoring that his was a pious jihad, Suleiman, "according to established custom…took formal possession of the place in the name of the false prophet by 'saying prayers' in the cathedral, which thus became a mosque, and was then…'purged from idolatry' by the destruction of the altars and the removal of every Christian ornament and symbol."[7]

After Belgrade, Suleiman, who was always "zealous for his religion," turned his gaze to Rhodes, not least because the grand mufti was "continually [complaining] to him that those Christian capers [of the knights] disturbed the pilgrimages to Mecca and that he was obliged in conscience to put a stop to their cruisings."[8] Suleiman responded by renewing the treaty with Venice to ensure its neutrality, and, in early 1522, began vast preparations to destroy the Knights of Rhodes once and for all. Engulfed by a semicircle—or crescent-shaped *hilal*—of hostile Islam from north, east, and south, the knights called for aid from the west, but the "unified response of Christendom was exactly zero," not least as "Martin Luther's reformation was beginning to split the Christian world into factitious shards."[9]

By the spring of 1522, Suleiman was finally ready to launch his grand jihad against tiny Rhodes. Although the knights implored Europe for aid—and although "the eyes of all the universe were then fixed upon Rhodes"—none would come.[10]

On June 25, 1522, it was déjà vu all over again. A vast Ottoman fleet of four hundred ships appeared over the Rhodian horizon, bringing a total of two hundred thousand men. Against this monstrous horde, the knights had no more than seven thousand fighting men, led by six hundred knights. For every one Christian defender there were twenty-eight jihadist warriors with which to contend.[11] The knights were fortunate, however, to be led by yet another especially capable master, Philip Villiers of L'Isle-Adam, then fifty-eight.

He and his men were living reminders that, even now, in the early, and rather secularized, sixteenth century, and in the face of certain annihilation, the knights of Christ continued to be living fusions of those two ancient virtues—piety and militancy. Thus, an "excellent engineer," Gabriel Martinengo, who went to Rhodes to help its fortifications, "saw these knights and warriors preparing themselves, like Christians and true religious, for the defense of religion. Under a soldier's habit, and with a military equipage, he admired their contempt of the world, their lively faith, and sincere disengagement from the things of this life."

On witnessing such noble behavior, this onetime secular "businessman" from Venice was so touched to the core, that "he ran to the master's palace, threw himself at his feet, and, inflamed with zeal to sacrifice his life for the defense of the faith, entreated that prince to honor him with his cross. The master took him up and embraced him tenderly." After a brief council concerning Gabriel's "pious intentions," it was unanimously agreed that he be accepted into the Order: "the master gave him the habit, and administered the vows to him, in a full assembly," where they also acknowledged "the generosity wherewith he had abandoned his patrimony, and the great pensions he had from the republic of Venice."[12]

54

"LET US DIE FOR THE DEFENSE OF OUR HOLY LAW"

Once the latest Ottoman siege began in July 1522—when Suleiman himself arrived—and throughout August, the Turks ceaselessly battered, bombarded, and undermined the walls of Rhodes. Several skirmishes took place between the opposing forces, and the outnumbered knights always put the Muslims to flight. Disgusted by this early display, Suleiman, who supervised the siege from high atop a special throne built for him, whence he cast "dreadful looks on every side," chastised a large group of soldiers for behaving not like soldiers, but "wretched slaves, weaker and more fainthearted than women…base and effeminate!" Did they think the knights were "greater cowards than yourselves," he asked, who would "come in a servile manner, to offer their hands and feet to the irons with which you should be pleased to load them?"

> In order to undeceive and cure you of such a ridiculous mistake, know that, in the person of these knights, we are to fight with the flower of the Christian world, with brave men, trained up from their infancy in the profession of arms; we are to fight with cruel and fierce lions,

> greedy of the blood of Muslims, and who will not quit their haunt but to a superior force.

By way of good measure, Suleiman closed by assuring his men that an "exemplary" punishment awaited any Ottoman fighter who did not give his all—his very life—fighting the knights. Upon concluding his diatribe, Suleiman's personal guard, which surrounded the hapless group of Muslims being chastised, "drew their swords as if they were going to massacre their comrades. Those wretches, at the sight of the drawn swords, fell upon their knees, and cried aloud to the sultan for mercy." Given one final chance, they instantly rushed the knights' bastions with drawn swords and to hollering cries of Allah's name.[1]

On September 4, two gunpowder mines violently blew up much of the English bastion; its ruins helped fill the ditch. To the bang of drums and the braying of horns, throngs of sword-waving Turks instantly rushed in for the kill. "The master was, at the very time that the mine sprung, in a church not far off, where he was before the altar, imploring from heaven the succor which the princes of the earth refused him." Knowing what that terrible din meant, Philip Villiers of L'Isle-Adam instantly rose from his knees—right at the part of the liturgy when the priest was saying, "O God, make haste to deliver me."

"I accept the omen," said the master, and, turning to some elderly knights who were praying alongside him, "Let us go, my brethren," cried he, "to change the sacrifice of our praises into that of our lives, and die, if it must be so, for the defense of our holy law." The history continues: "He advances immediately with his half-pike in his hand, mounts upon the bastion, comes up to the Turks, breaks, overturns, and kills all that dare oppose him: he pulls down the enemies' ensigns, and recovers the bastion with an irresistible impetuosity."[2]

Before long, the knights, fighting once again with a fell fury, had so terrified the invaders that the Turks began to retreat. The overall general in charge of the siege, Mustapha, who was bringing the rear, cut down the first of these fleeing fugitives with his scimitar and showed "the rest that they would find less safety near their general than they would upon the breach." He drove them back, and "the engagement begins afresh;

the dispute grows bloody; fire and sword are equally employed on both sides; they kill one another both at a distance and near with musket shot and the sword."

Hours later, three thousand Turks lay dead before the ruined English bastion. Although far fewer Christians died, several still did, and "the loss of one knight was of greater consequence" to Master Philip "than fifty soldiers to [Suleiman]."[3]

Despite this Ottoman setback—or perhaps because of it—from now on, "scarce a day passed but was signalized by some new attack." General Mustapha personally led several more assaults throughout September, including one where "columns of the Children of the Prophet, a thousand deep, came roaring over the barricades." They were all cut down and beat back, with heaps of more dead Turks in the wake.[4]

On September 24, the entire southern section of the wall, including the bastions of England, Aragon, Provence, and Italy, were mercilessly bombarded and undermined. Then, from the smoke and ruins, thousands of rushing Janissaries appeared: Mustapha had ordered the largest general assault yet. Watching the hordes of Islam approach, the master, who would not deign to offend his men's courage through an affected harangue, simply told them to "consider only, my dear brethren, that we are going to fight for our order, and for the defense of our religion, and that a glorious victory must be the reward of our valor, or else Rhodes, the strongest rampart of Christendom, must serve us for a grave." He also exhorted the Rhodians that "besides the defense of the faith, you have taken up arms for your country, for your wives, your maidens, and your children: fight gallantly, my friends, in order to rescue them from the infamy that the barbarians threaten them with."[5]

The battle of September 24 was the fiercest yet, and despite the Janissaries' own ferocity, "never had they met men like these [knights], fanatics fiercer than the wildest dervish. Over 2,000 Turkish corpses remained." Burning with shame, Suleiman had General Mustapha—his own brother-in-law—paraded before the army in preparation for his execution (death by arrows), relenting only after an old vizier pled for the general's life.[6]

Despite all these setbacks, Suleiman, like all Ottoman sultans, had numbers on his side; his men were legion, and the siege continued unabated. By October, "the breaches were so large, that the Turks could mount in formed battalions to the assault of the bastion of England. The knights, that had undertaken the defense of it, lined the ramparts, sword in hand, and with their bodies made a new parapet for its defense."[7]

As might be imagined, all sorts of storied feats of heroism took place during this siege. Knowing that his readers may well doubt his history (which itself is based on eyewitness testimony), Vertot attributed the knights' valor to seasoned leadership and commitment to their vows to spill every last drop of blood in defense of Christendom:

> It would appear very surprising that, so small a number of Christians, who had nothing to cover them but some barricadoes and weak entrenchments, should be able to hold out so long against such a prodigious number of assailants, if this handful of men had not been composed of old knights, whose valor had been experienced on a thousand other occasions, and who on this, were unanimously resolved, to sacrifice their lives for the defense of their religion. Men are very strong, and very formidable, when they are not afraid of death. Historians, speaking of their zeal and courage, use but one sort of eulogium for all these noble soldiers of Jesus Christ.[8]

The same jihadist threat that elicited valor from the knights elicited desperate acts of madness among the beleaguered general populace. As one example, when a Greek woman, who had mothered two children with an English knight, came across his slain body, she, "resolving not to survive him," kissed her two children and made the sign of the cross on their foreheads. "'Tis better for you, my dear children," she then said, with tears in her eyes, "to die by my hands, than by those of our merciless enemies, or to be reserved for infamous pleasures more odious than death itself."

> Then, inspired with fury, she takes up a knife, cuts their throats, throws their bodies into the fire, puts on the officer's clothes, that were still dyed with his blood, snatches up his sabre, runs to the breach, kills the first Turk she meets, wounds several others, and dies fighting.[9]

By mid-November, the Turks had managed to cross the moat and breach the inner curtain wall of Italy and Aragon. Still, for every inch they gained, the knights made them pay bitterly with their lives. In early December, after yet another general assault failed,

> [Suleiman] could not see his troops coming back in disorder, and in a downright flight, without falling in to a passion: he had been almost six months with 200,000 men before the place, without being able to take it: the vexation he felt, and his apprehensions that the [Western] Christian princes might at last unite their forces in order to oblige him to raise the siege, made him shut himself up some days in his tent, without suffering any of his captains to come near him.[10]

55

THE END OF AN ERA

The turning point in the siege came after one of Suleiman's more "subtle ministers" conceded that "they had indeed to deal with a set of desperate men, who would suffer themselves to be all killed to a man, rather than surrender." Even so, the vizier went on to remind the sultan that the knights had been so reduced in number, whereas the majority of the people behind the wall were mostly Greek peasants, who "had not the same courage, nor indeed the same interest to be obstinate in the defense of the place."[1]

From that point on and throughout December, the sultan sent messages, through false deserters and spies, spreading word among the people that there was no stalling the inevitable; that if they surrendered now, the sultan promised to treat them well. If not, nothing but slow torture and impalement awaited them.

Suleiman also dispatched emissaries to try to parley with the knights, including by offering them a safe and honorable withdrawal from Rhodes. The warden only scorned such overtures, adding that "the knights of St. John never treated with the infidels but sword in hand." Knowing that they were offering poisoned honey to weaken his men's resolve, the master ordered his men to open fire should such envoys approach the wall again.

Still, Suleiman's vizier was right: What would not work with the knights was working with the desperate Greek locals. After debating the situation, they concluded that surrender was their best option and begged their head prelate to beseech the master to capitulate in their name. He did as asked and told Master Philip that, if he did not treat with the sultan, not only would all the people be "the first victims of the fury of the victorious soldiers," but that "he, himself, would see the churches profaned…and the women and virgins exposed to the brutality of the Infidels." The master refused to relent, saying that he and his brethren were resolved to be buried in the ruins of Rhodes and that he had "hoped the inhabitants would follow their example and show the same courage."[2]

Nor were all the Rhodians committed to surrender. On learning that the majority had petitioned the master to surrender, another smaller group of wild young men "ran in a tumultuous manner," saying that "they were treating with the enemy without their consent, and that would be delivering them up to a perfidious nation, that gloried in breaking their faith with Christians, and that they all chose to die with their weapons in their hands, rather than be cut to pieces after the capitulation as the inhabitants of Belgrade had been."[3]

Adding to all this internal turmoil was something else—something especially pernicious: Right from the start, a number of spies, double agents, and traitors had been fervently working from within to betray Rhodes. The sources focus especially on a false Jewish convert to Christianity who, to appear more convincing and natural, had been planted in Rhodes many years earlier, during Selim's reign. On being caught shooting arrow messages to the Turks, he was drawn and quartered.

But perhaps nothing was worse for morale than the discovery that one of their own knights—a senior brother no less—had also betrayed the Order. Andrew d'Amaral, the chancellor of the Order, had long coveted the post of and expected to be elected master. When Philip Villiers of L'Isle-Adam was elected in his place in 1521, Andrew developed a maniacal hatred for the knights and, through the agency of a Turkish slave, opened secret talks with Suleiman's court, exposing all of the Order's secrets and weaknesses. (In fact, it was in large measure due to this betrayal that Suleiman's fleet came when it did, less than a year later.) After one of his servants was also caught shooting arrows to the Turkish camp, Brother Andrew was questioned, exposed, and executed, along with his servant: "Their bodies were afterwards quartered, and exposed to the view of the Turks."[4]

With so much inner discord and distrust in the air, and fearing lest a revolt ensue, Master Philip held a council to discuss whether it was better to "die to the last man, or save the people?"[5] All the council concluded that, without outside aid, defeat was inevitable—hence, surrender in the interest of the people was acceptable. Only the master clung to the old way of thinking; Philip reminded them that "in the whole course of so many ages, as the Order had been making war upon the Infidels, the knights had, in the most perilous occasions, always preferred an holy, and glorious death, before a frail and precarious life; that he was ready to set them an example, and begged of them, before they took so grievous a step, to reflect once more upon it in the most serious manner." The entire council agreed with his sentiments, saying that if the question only concerned their lives,

> They would all follow his example, and freely die by his side; that they were ready to sacrifice their lives, that they had devoted them to God when they took the habit, but that the safety of the inhabitants was the business in question: that if the Infidels should carry the place by storm, and enter it sword in hand, they would force the women and children and all weak persons to renounce the faith; that they would make the most of the inhabitants either slaves or renegadoes [converts to Islam], and that the churches...would be profaned by the Infidels, and be made the subject of their contempt and raillery. The master yielded at length to these pious considerations.[6]

This decision could not have come at a better time for Suleiman. He had never planned on spending so much time (six months) or so many lives (forty-four thousand killed by the knights and nearly as many more from sickness and disease) for a tiny and otherwise insignificant island.[7] Such, however, was the price for any who challenged the knights—and on their own turf.

On December 20, the sultan offered them excellent terms. In exchange for surrender, not only would he permit the Order to leave with their goods, but he would provide transport. No church would be "profaned" or turned into a mosque; no Rhodians would be compelled to "deny Christ," but would rather be "allowed the free exercise of the Christian religion," exempt from having to pay jizya for five years, and not "obliged to deliver up their children to be made [Janissaries]." On December 22, the master signed the agreement.[8]

Two days later, on Christmas Eve 1522, a vizier informed Master Philip that Suleiman wished to see him and that quitting the island without paying the sultan a visit would be interpreted as a great insult. Although the master was not overly eager to place himself in the sultan's hands—this man that he had so frustrated for half a year—he also did not want to give Suleiman a pretext to renege once the knights let their guard down. Accordingly, the head of the Order "who had, during the siege, exposed himself to the greatest dangers," ignored the threat to his person and "resolved to sacrifice himself once more for the safety of his brethren."

And so it was that, in the early hours of Christmas Day—a day of immense cold, snow, and "hail [that] fell in abundance"—Master Philip set out for the sultan's tent. The Turks, "out of pride and a barbarous kind of grandeur," suffered him to wait outside in the harsh weather for the entire day, without so much as offering him food, water, or cover. It was only toward evening that they permitted him inside.

Despite all that he had gone through—or perhaps precisely because of it—Suleiman was so "struck with the majesty" of this grim old knight that he spoke to him (through an interpreter) as an equal, consoling him over the vicissitudes of war and fortune. Nor could the sultan help but add that, seeing how all the other "Christian princes…had so scandalously abandoned him," if the master would but submit to Islam, "there was no post or dignity in the whole extent of his empire" that Suleiman would not happily bestow on him.

The master, "who was as zealous a Christian as he was a great captain," thanked him but politely declined. He adroitly explained that it would be a dishonor for so great a sultan as Suleiman to take into his service a "traitor" who was willing to betray his faith for profit and gain. All that he asked of the sultan was that he prevent his men from "giv[ing] him any disturbance" as he prepared to quit Rhodes—which they had already done (five days after signing the agreement, a band of zealous Turks had desecrated several churches, even overturning the tombs of several masters, though they were quickly restrained). Suleiman agreed and, "as a token of friendship, though perhaps out of ostentation of his grandeur, he gave him his hand to kiss." As the master took his leave, the sultan, turning to his vizier, quietly remarked, "It saddens me to be compelled to force this brave old man to leave his home."[9]

On January 1, 1523, the Turks were shocked to see the knights, to the blast of a single, solitary horn, issue out of the city of Rhodes in parade order—armor burnished, drums beating, standards flying—as they marched to their ships in preparation of forever quitting the isle. With them came those Rhodians who preferred exile under the Order rather than life under the Turks. From the master's galley flew a half mast of the sorrowing Virgin, holding her dead Son, with the words, "In all which afflicts us, thou art our only hope."[10]

And so, on New Year's Day 1523, the Knights of the Hospital of St. John of Jerusalem, who had lived on—and utterly frustrated the Muslims from—Rhodes for almost 220 years, once again became, as had happened in 1291 after Acre, the homeless Hospitallers.

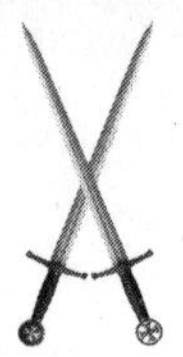

56

HOMELESS HOSPITALLERS AND MUSLIM MASTERS

The same year the knights forever quit Rhodes in 1522, their new flagship, the *Santa Anna*—which would come to be known as the "Great Carrack"—was launched. Like a floating and self-sufficient town, this massive vessel could hold nearly a thousand sailors, had fifty large cannons and, of course, had a hospital. Not only did it quickly become the most powerful ship of its time but, alongside the rest of the Order's fleet, it served as a home for the sea knights and those five thousand Rhodian men, women, and children who voluntarily joined them into exile.

For eight years, the homeless Hospitallers either lived on the high seas, where they not infrequently continued to combat their Muslim enemies, or had temporary settlements, mostly in Italy. During this trying time, it is widely attested that, had it not been for the strong character of Master Philip Villiers of L'Isle-Adam—whom the Rhodians looked to and called "Father," a name which "gave this great man more pleasure than the title of lord and prince that was due to his dignity"—the Order would most likely have followed the Templars into extinction.

Indeed, for Philip, it was not enough that the Order stay intact; it must also live up to its mandate. Thus, on their first landing in Messina in 1523, the knights, true to their ancient calling, set up a tent hospital on the beach, where the master and his brethren ministered to all "the knights that were sick and wounded" from their defense of Rhodes. For the Italian onlookers, "'twas indeed a very moving sight to see these men, who used to appear so terrible with their weapons in their hands, now, animated only by a spirit of charity, devote themselves to the meanest services, carry broth to the sick, make their beds, and show a disregard to everything, but what might contribute to their relief and recovery."

Once all those who could recover recovered, and the rest were laid in peace, all the knights' thoughts were set on revivifying their other vow of charity: finding a new headquarters from "where the order, agreeable to its institution, might continue the succors, it had given for so many ages to the Christians that sailed in those seas."[1]

In 1530, after years of negotiations, Charles V (1500–1558), Holy Roman emperor and king of Spain, ceded to the Knights of St. John the small and rather barren island of Malta. Just north of the Muslim statelets of North Africa—the barbarous, or Barbary states, whence countless devastating slave raids had over the years issued against Spain, Sicily, and Italy—Charles had prudently placed these crack-warriors on the front lines of the Crusade and jihad: "Geographically, they were now far removed from Jerusalem, but their vocation was the same as ever: to defend Christendom against the aggression of Islam."[2]

On settling in Malta, the master established the Order's convent and had the island refortified, though for long he refused to accept this barren rock as his permanent home and continued harboring high hopes of eventually reclaiming Rhodes. The knights also continued to hone and develop their navy, which, though at first consisting of seven or so oared galleys and irregular ships, was still the most efficient in the Mediterranean.

Nor did they forget their original calling. As at Rhodes, so too in Malta did the knights establish a hospital, which soon became "the envy of Europe. In its day it was without any doubt the greatest hospital in the world. The Order despite its militant role, had never at any time forgotten its principal function in the world—care for the sick. This was at a time when, throughout most of Europe, the sick were no more than sad casualties abandoned on the battlefield of life."[3]

Although initially wary of them, the denizens of Malta began to warm up to their new masters on seeing them arrive with Muslim slaves. Rough Catholic peasants who spoke a form of Arabic (from when Malta was conquered and governed by Arabs in the ninth century), the Maltese were habitually on the receiving end of Muslim slave raids: seeing that their new masters practiced a form of tit for tat was a promising sign.[4]

The knights' relocation to Malta could not have come at a better time for Christendom. Although North Africa had for centuries been a nest of Muslim pirates and jihadists (such as the Almoravids and Almohads), following the expulsion of the Moors of Granada in 1492, it became infused with a new and vengeful population that lived for nothing more than to terrorize and prey on the hated Christians.

Due to the horror these piratical statelets visited upon the Christians, they were soon known among contemporaries as "the flail of the Christian world…the terror of Europe…the pinnacle of cruelty in all its forms and the asylum of impiety." These Muslims subsisted entirely on raiding and devastating the Mediterranean coasts of Spain, France, and Italy, whence they enslaved hundreds of thousands of Christians. Indeed, from the very year the knights received Malta in 1530 to just 1640, "it would not be stretching the truth to say that they have put a million [Christians] in chains."[5]

For many years (c. 1510–1546), these Muslim pirates were led by the so-called Barbarossa brothers (due to their reddish beards). Born of an unholy union between a Muslim Turk and a Christian slave woman on the conquered Greek isle of Lesbos, they exhibited an extreme hatred for Christians and engaged in vile and wanton behavior—shocking even for those times. The eldest brother, Aruj, was notorious for such obscenities as biting into and tearing open the throats of his Christian captives—before devouring their tongues. He also once tied and twirled a rope around a Knight of St. John until his eyes popped out of their sockets.[6]

The even more successful and sadistic slave raids launched by Aruj's younger and much longer-lived brother, Hayrettin (1478–1546), were such that he was known among Christians as the "king of evil" and, by corollary, among Muslims as the "goodness of Islam" (or *khayr al-din*, hence Hayrettin). He had vowed never to cease his raids on Christendom "until I have killed the last one of you and enslaved your women, your daughters, and your children." Considering his long career, this vow naturally resulted in the capture of countless Christians over the years. For example, from just the two hundred–mile coastline between Valencia and Barcelona alone, he seized and enslaved ten thousand Christians. In another, especially devastating raid, he carried off three hundred children and nuns. Suleiman, so impressed by Hayrettin's raids—it was the sultan who first dubbed him the "goodness of Islam"—elevated this former pirate to the rank of grand admiral of the Ottoman navy in 1533. Now, with the full might of the Turks' navy, the terror he visited upon Christendom skyrocketed.[7]

It may be hard to imagine how devastating these slave raids were (especially in the current climate, when slavery is often seen as an exclusively European enterprise). Suffice to say, during these times, in the sixteenth century, the average number of Africans sold by other Africans to Europeans in one year (3,200) was about how many Europeans were enslaved by Muslims during just a few successful raids.[8]

The surviving record of the Frenchman Du Chastelet reflects the terror and trauma Christians experienced when being enslaved by the denizens of Barbary: "As to me," he wrote of the moment when he was captured,

> I noticed a great Moor approaching me, his sleeves rolled up to his shoulders, holding a sabre in his large hand of four fingers; I was left without words. And the ugliness of this carbon face, animated by two ivory eyeballs, moving about hideously, terrified me a good deal more

> than were frightened the first humans at the sight of the flaming sword at the door of Eden.[9]

There was good reason for such terror; whereas the European transatlantic slave trade of Africans was fueled by cold business, the Muslim slave trade of Europeans was fueled by hate for infidels. This point comes out repeatedly in the sources. Thus, captives seized during these raids that were, upon inspection, deemed useless or unprofitable (too old or infirm, for example) were cruelly tortured before their mutilated bodies were dumped back on Europe's coasts—often with notes mocking Christianity pinned to their corpses.[10]

Similarly, when French priest Jerome Maurand, who, as part of the then (utterly scandalous) French-Ottoman alliance against Charles V, witnessed the corsairs' conquest of the Italian island of Lipari in 1544, he failed to comprehend why the Muslims so wantonly tortured the now enslaved population—including by slowly gutting alive and dismembering their old and weak captives with knives, "out of spite." Unable to hold his tongue, he "asked these Turks why they treated the poor Christians with such cruelty, [and] they replied that such behavior had very great virtue; that was the only answer we ever got."[11]

Likewise, in his sixteenth-century book, *Book of Martyrs*, John Foxe wrote, "In no part of the globe are Christians so hated, or treated with such severity, as at Algiers," where the slaves were regularly treated "with perfidy and cruelty." Centuries later, nothing had changed: "In almost every case," wrote Robert Playfair in the late nineteenth century, "they [European slaves in Algiers] were hated on account of their religion."

Not only were most women sexually enslaved, but—and perhaps as part of the sadism felt for Christians—so too were almost all of the boys and the handsomer men. They were purchased by "persons who are so abominable that they only buy slaves with this idea…of making them give in to their horrid desires." In fact, "All the Barbary capitals—but especially Algiers—had open and flourishing homosexual cultures: male prostitutes [almost all of whom were white, Christian slaves] were… widely available."[12]

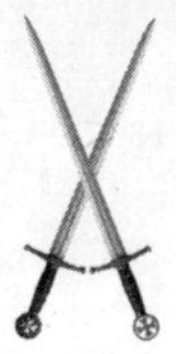

57

THE KNIGHTLY "TERROR OF THE INFIDELS" RETURN

In response to the horrific rise of Islamic piracy and slave raids on the European coastline, Charles V launched several Crusades against the Barbary states of North Africa, particularly those under the command of that dread pirate–turned Ottoman grand admiral, Hayrettin Barbarossa. Thus, when the Knights of Rhodes became the Knights of Malta, the central Mediterranean, where their new island headquarters was located, had already become the latest front line in that old war between Islam and Christendom.

As such, Charles V's bequeathal of Malta to the knights was not altruism; it was smart policy. For "he was of the opinion that the knights, who were the terror of the infidels, would keep them in awe by their valor; and that the squadrons of the Order would serve for an invincible rampart against the enterprises of the [Ottoman sultan]." Nor did the Order disappoint, "for the knights, agreeable to the spirit of their institution, and out of gratitude for the favors they had received from Charles V, were always ready to furnish him with the most powerful succors, whenever war was to be made against the infidels."[1] In the words of one historian,

> The Muslims were soon to find out…that the sea along the barbary coast—for so long exclusively their preserve—was to become a dangerous one in which to venture.… [and] the Knights of St. John were soon to find that their new island home, although it could never replace Rhodes in their hearts, was to be the ideal base for their eternal warfare against the enemies of the Cross.[2]

True to their original mission of providing aid to their coreligionists, once stationed in Malta, the Knights of St. John also eagerly sought to find and free Christian slaves, many of whom were galley slaves either to the Ottoman or Barbary Muslims. During one sea battle, the knights liberated two hundred Christian galley slaves, "the Turks were chained down, and the renegadoes [Christian apostates to Islam] hanged." In another, in 1536, the knights returned to Malta with four hundred liberated Christian slaves and an unknown number of their former slavers enslaved. And when a large Muslim galley tried to escape the knights by sailing back to Barbary, "the knights, with sabre in hand, attempted to board her," causing the panicked Muslims to accidentally sink their galley "in the fight, and to the regret of the knights, who were more afflicted for the death of the Christian slaves that were drowned on that occasion, than the loss of a prize, which could not possibly have escaped them."[3]

In short, once they settled in Malta, "there were few engagements" to beat Muslims or free Christians, "either in Asia or Africa, wherein the standards of St. John were not seen waving in the emperor's army."[4]

In 1535, Charles called on the knights to join his expedition to conquer Tunis, Hayrettin's personal den, whence issued numerous slave raids. The order enthusiastically seized the occasion and "put to sea four of the largest and best equipped gallies, with 18 brigantines, all well-armed; not to mention the Great Carrack, which alone was more formidable, and did more service in this expedition than a whole squadron."

On reaching the fortress of Goletta, which guarded the road to Tunis, the emperor ordered his squadrons to unleash a hail of fire, which continued for twelve hours. Although the knights' Great Carrack stood behind Charles's war vessels, "it was so high built, that it easily fired over them all, and it made so dreadful and uninterrupted a fire, that it dismounted all the cannon of the tower."

Before the Muslims could repair the breaches, the emperor ordered a general assault on the fortress. As usual, the Knights of St. John led the charge: "Plunging in [the sea] above the waist," they "advanced boldly, sword in hand, got to the shore, and, in spite of a shower of musket-shot, advanced to the storm." After an hour of savage fighting, they managed to climb atop and make themselves masters of the tower, though "this victory cost the order many of its bravest knights, and scarce one of them returned back without wounds."[5]

Meanwhile in Tunis, Hayrettin was preparing to lead his motley crew of piratical Arabs, Bedouins, and Turks against the encroaching knights. Before leaving Tunis, he contemplated slitting the throats of every last one of his twenty-two thousand Christian slaves, lest, as a fifth column, they aid their coreligionists. He held off, however, to see how the forthcoming battle went, reasoning that, if he won, it would have been a great shame and waste to needlessly dispatch so many slaves who could have otherwise fetched him a pretty penny.

His hopes were frustrated. The battle was an utter rout, and three hundred Muslims were butchered—good at surprise, piratical raids, they could not withstand melee combat—with only eighteen Christians slain.[6]

As he fled back to Tunis, Hayrettin sent advance word for his men to blow up the dungeons holding his twenty-two thousand Christian captives. But before they could act, one of their prisoners, Paul Simeoni, a young Knight of St. John who was captured years earlier while defending Ero, broke free of his chains and helped free the others. They broke into the armory, "armed themselves with everything that first came to hand, cut to pieces all such of the Turkish soldiers as had remained in the castle, and made themselves masters of it"—and not a moment too soon.

Hayrettin and his retreating army were just then arriving and trying to gain entry into the castle, when Paul and the other liberated slaves barricaded themselves against and opened fire on the pirates—all while signaling to the advancing Christians with a white flag. "All is lost," Hayrettin was heard to cry in a fit of rage, "since those dogs are masters of my castle, and of my treasures." He hopped on a light skiff and sailed to Ottoman territory.

On gaining entry into the castle of Tunis and learning what had happened, Charles embraced Paul, exclaiming, "Brother knight, blessed be forever your courageous resolution, which has made you break your chains, has facilitated my conquest, and heightened the glory of your order!"[7] The release of twenty-two thousand Christian slaves following the conquest of Tunis was widely celebrated throughout Europe, including through art.

As in olden times, if the knights of Christ were always at the fore of advances against Christendom's enemies, so too were they always at the rear of withdrawals. In both cases, they were on the front lines of attacks on and defenses against their foes.

This was notably demonstrated in Charles V's 1541 campaign against Ottoman-held Algiers, another stronghold of piratical activities since 1529, when Hayrettin captured it from the Christians. Once the knights learned that this would be a "holy war, which he [Charles] assured them was designed only for the destruction of the corsairs and the enemies of the order," virtually every Knight of St. John tried to enlist, meaning "that Malta and the convent would have been left deserted, had not the Master prudently limited the succor to four hundred knights."

Going against the advice of his leading generals, Charles launched his armada in late autumn, when weather and sea conditions were notoriously mercurial. In fact, severe storms rose against and destroyed several Christian ships before they could even reach and anchor near Algiers in late October 1541. Even then, a surviving eyewitness account of the Knights of St. John describes them as advancing before the rest of the army, with their usual "intrepidity," their surcoats over their armor being "all of damask or crimson velvet,"* and their large white crosses glittering in the sunlight, the combined effect of which "gave terror to all such Barbarians as durst approach."[8]

Before long, however, yet another storm broke out, with torrential rains flooding the Christian camp. Although most of their horses were dead, and they themselves were drenched and "benumbed with cold," the knights advanced against the Muslim army from the fortress of Algiers: "though on foot, [they] fell in furiously among the Turkish and Moorish cavalry, so that they killed a great number of them, and dismounted several." Being slaughtered by cross-wearing, sword-waving knights, who by now were so "inflamed with the highest ardor," and all under black clouds and pouring rains was too much; and before long, the Muslims fled back to Algiers with the knights in hot pursuit.

On seeing this mad rush, the Muslim pasha and lieutenant of Hayrettin, "who was resolved to sacrifice all his soldiers, who were out of the city, to the fury of the Christians, ordered the gates to be shut"—though not before the standard-bearer of the Order, Ponce of Savignac, who was furiously leading the charge, stabbed and fixed his dagger into the gate just as it slammed in his face, "as a proof that he had advanced as far as it was possible for him to go."

Algiers's fate seemed sealed, until worsening weather came again to its rescue. Storms caused fifty more Christian galleys and carracks to sink and dispersed more, leaving the emperor's forces without much needed reinforcements and supplies—even as more Muslim reinforcements reached Algiers and began sallying against the Christians. By late November, after a total of 150 Christian ships had been lost to fate, Charles sounded the retreat, at which point "the Knights of Malta, though most of them were wounded, had yet the post of honor, and were put in the rear," to protect the main army as it withdrew. It is only

---

* In the fourteenth century, the knights began adopting red surcoats with a white cross for combat purposes. As with the Templars before them, red continued to be associated with martyrdom and military valor, while the white cross remained a symbol of religious devotion and purity. Their original black mantle with a white cross remained for formal and religious occasions, with the red surcoat reserved specifically for combat.

because they continued fighting off the now unbridled and massive Muslim assaults that Charles barely managed to escape.[9]

Algiers would be one of the emperor's worst defeats to the Ottoman-Barbary alliance, as thousands of Christians were slain. As usual, the Order lost a disproportionate number of men relative to their much smaller numbers: seventy-five knights and four hundred sergeants and soldiers killed. Many more thousands of soldiers were chained alongside those other Christian slaves they had come to liberate. Indeed, it was after this campaign that Algiers's slave markets became so glutted that a Christian cost the "price of an onion."[10]

The remnants of the Knights of St. John returned home to more bad news: Muslim pirates had taken advantage of their absence by launching several raids against Malta and Gozo (also a possession of the knights) "and carried off all such inhabitants as had the ill fortune to fall in their hands."

Over at Constantinople, Hayrettin, "incensed that the knights should appear at the head of all the enterprises that the Christians engaged in against the African Turks," was begging Suleiman to retaliate and avenge the honor of Islam. This would be just one of the first of many complaints concerning the knights to reach the sultan's ears, each bringing more and more unwanted attention against them.[11]

Despite the setback of Algiers, and throughout the 1540s, Charles continued to launch various, often successful, raids on the corsair strongholds of North Africa, with the knights always, "pursuant to custom," in the front lines, whence they "advanced first to the storm."[12]

58

KILL THEM LEST THEY "REVIVE THE ANCIENT SPIRIT OF THE CRUSADES!"

During the summer of 1550, Charles V's forces and the Knights of St. John besieged the Ottoman fortress of Mahdia, about 130 miles southeast of Tunis. It was defended by the notorious pirate, Dragut—"the drawn sword of Islam"—a disciple of Hayrettin (who, after a lifetime of piracy, finally died peacefully in his bed, surrounded by his harem, aged almost seventy, in 1546).

After a sustained bombardment of the fortress, the signal for a general assault was given, and the knights were once again first to throw themselves into the sea, wading out with swords drawn, as the Muslims opened a hail of fire on them—with cannons, guns, arrows, firepots, and boiling oil—killing many: "However, the knights, not daunted at the number of their dead, surmounted all these obstacles, and forced their way to the top of the breach." Their commander managed to plant the Order's standard atop the tower before being shot dead. For over two months, the siege raged on with various vicissitudes until September 8, when the Christians finally took Mahdia.[1]

Like his master Hayrettin before him, so now "Dragut, enraged at the loss of the town of Africa...ascribed it chiefly to the knights of Malta; and, accordingly, made his complaints" known to Suleiman's court. He further put it into the sultan's mind that, based on the knights' wider "pretense of delivering Jerusalem and Palestine from the dominion of the Ottomans," and now that they had captured and controlled a chain of fortresses across North Africa, they "might penetrate into those countries, revive the ancient spirit of the Crusades, and bring into their party the forces of the Christian princes, who were formidable when united together." This last point pricked Suleiman's ears, and Dragut was assured that the sultan would soon "drive the knights, those declared and eternal enemies of the Koran, out of all Africa, as he had done already out of Asia [meaning Rhodes, 1522]."[2]

Less than a year later, a large Ottoman fleet, carrying some ten thousand soldiers, was launched. Although its primary mission was to attack the knights in their African holdings, upon the incessant urgings of Dragut to "fall with fire and sword upon" Malta, "for the extirpating of those knights, who, notwithstanding their being few in number," were always at the fore "whenever a war was carrying on against the Muslims," the Ottoman fleet first paid Malta a visit, arriving in mid-July 1551.[3]

Although "a general terror seized the inhabitants," who fled and hid wherever possible, the knights prepared for a fight to the death. On surveying how well fortified Malta was, and knowing that victory would not come except by "kill[ing] all those warriors to the last man," the Ottoman admiral Pasha Sinan al-Din (the "teeth of Islam") concluded that punishing the knights should suffice for now before turning to and rooting them out of North Africa, which was of greater concern to Suleiman. So the Turks invaded Malta and "spread themselves up and down in all its villages and hamlets, and destroyed all before them with fire and sword. They set the houses on fire, so that nothing was to be seen, wherever one turned one's eyes, for the country was entirely buried in a smoke."[4]

Next, because "a thirst for plunder is the prevailing passion of those Barbarians," they quickly set sail for Gozo, the second-largest island after Malta in the Maltese Archipelago, and one of the Order's possessions. It was governed by a knight of the Order, Galatian of Sesse, who "proved a horrible coward." Rather than prepare for a staunch resistance, he immediately sent a monk messenger to Sinan al-Din asking for honorable terms of surrender, "which," Vertot is quick to add, "are never granted but to those only who make a brave defense."[5]

The monk told Sinan that they were prepared to surrender on condition that none of the inhabitants be molested. The Muslim general "rejected the proposal with disdain, and told the envoy that if the governor did not quit the place that very moment, he would hang him up at the gate." On receiving this unexpectedly harsh response to his otherwise friendly gesture of surrender, Galatian, rather than finally bracing for battle, sent the monk back to the "teeth of Islam," saying that, on reconsideration, the governor was now willing to surrender the island in exchange for just his own life and liberty and that of two hundred other "principal" inhabitants that he would name. The pasha reduced the number to forty and told the monk that was the best they could expect—and that if he dared return to him again with another counteroffer, he would have him hung. On learning of Sinan al-Din's offer—his own life and that of forty others—Governor Galatian, this Knight of the Order of St. John, "seized with panic [and] fear, commanded the gates to be opened to the enemy, which was the only order he had given ever since the Turks had entered the island" two days earlier.

Once in Gozo, the Muslims ran amok, plundering the small island of everything animate and inanimate. Not only was the governor's lodging the first to be stripped of all its possessions, but to show their contempt for the commander, they made Galatian carry atop his head and shoulders some of the booty—his very own belongings—back to their ships. Once there, "they stripped his clothes off, and chained him down like a galley-slave."

When he protested that Sinan al-Din had broken their agreement, the pasha proceeded to release forty of the very oldest, infirm, and useless captives—mockingly claiming that he had indeed kept his word of releasing forty of the "principal" inhabitants, since "the oldest ought to be looked upon as the principal."* Along with the cowardly governor, all the rest of Gozo's inhabitants—6,300 men, women, and children—were loaded with chains and hauled off into slavery. As always, some, including one Sicilian man, preferred death to slavery: He slaughtered his wife and two daughters and killed two Turks with a crossbow before charging them with his sword, wounding several until he was cut down.

It would take a century of resettling before Gozo's population, which disappeared on that day, could recover.[6]

This Gozon interlude is important for something else: It demonstrates the objectivity of Abbe Vertot, the Order's historian. Although his praises for the Knights of St. John and their exploits may strike some as exaggerated, he is, in fact, throughout his history, often critical and unsparing of the actions of several individual knights, as he is here with the knight Galatian. If his intention was to present the Order as without blemishes, he might have quickly passed over the knights' less-than-impressive deeds, rather than censoriously dwelling on them as he often does. A few pages after the Gozon debacle, for example, he summarizes the life of Master John of Homedes (r. 1536–1553) as follows: "He had distinguished himself by his valor at the siege of Rhodes [1522], was religious, and affected a great air of regularity and devotion, but was withal of an imperious and vengeful nature. He was covetous, and so bent on enriching his family, that he almost ruined the Order by the

* Sinan al-Din was employing the little-known Islamic doctrine of tawriya, which permits the deception of others through the use of double entendres. Tawriya is when a speaker uses a word that means one thing to the listener, though the speaker means something else—and his words technically support this alternative meaning. For example, X asks Y if he can borrow a dollar, and Y says he doesn't have a penny in his pocket. Although X understands this to mean that Y has no money on him, Y, in fact, has many dollar bills—just no pennies. Thus, Y, according to this Islamic doctrine, did not lie. In certain Eastern languages, the word for "old" and "great" (or, as translated in the above text, "principal") are the same and differentiated through context. For example, the Arabic word *kibir* can mean "great" or "old." In short, Sinan let Galatian think that he would release the "great/principal" persons, though in his mind he only meant the elderly. For more on tawriya, see https://www.raymondibrahim.com/2012/02/28/tawriya-lying/

grants he made in his lifetime to his relations, in contempt of the laws and statutes of the society."[7]

After the despoliation of Gozo, the Ottoman fleet sailed for the knights' stronghold in Tripoli. In 1510, Charles V had wrested it from the Muslim pirates and given it to the knights to defend as part of the same deal of taking Malta for a new home in 1530. Being right smack in the midst of hostile Muslim territory, Tripoli was, from the very start, a hopeless and expensive drain on the brethren. As one knight, Commander Botigella, once told a council of the Order, "experience ought to have made them sensible, how impractical it was for the Christians ever to make any fixed and durable conquests on the coast of Africa, and among the Moors," who, "either from the aversion which a difference of religion is apt to inspire, or from the natural inconstancy of those people, were altogether as unfaithful to sovereigns of their own nation, as they were to foreigners."[8]

By 1551, when the Ottomans came, Tripoli was defended by a skeleton crew of knights and a few hundred common soldiers from the emperor's domains. Although the knights made their customary stand, they too were betrayed by a conspiracy between the local Muslims and a soldier from Provence. A Christian who had been at Tripoli for a long time, this soldier had earned the knights' trust, "but, having been seduced by a criminal commerce with some Moorish women, he had secretly renounced the faith, embraced Islam, and, being as false to the order as he had been to God, he stayed at Tripoli for no other reason than to serve as a spy" for the Turks. Once their fleet arrived, he absconded to them and exposed the weakest points of the fortress, which the Turks mercilessly cannonaded. Terrified by the inevitable, the rest of the common soldiers threatened to revolt unless the knights surrendered Tripoli to the Turks in exchange for the soldiers' lives and freedom.[9]

Marshal Gaspard of Vallier—"an old knight...universally esteemed for his valor"—eventually conceded to their pleas and went out to parley with Sinan al-Din. But on seeing the marshal approach, the Ottoman admiral "assumed that air of haughtiness and pride, an air which such Barbarians generally put on when fortune has declared herself on their side." Vexed because the knight would not give in to his threats and demands, Sinan cried, "It is not with such dogs as you...that a man is to keep his word!" and ordered the marshal who had come out under a flag of truce stripped, placed in irons, and sent to his ship. As he was being so unceremoniously handled, Gaspard, "still resolute and undaunted," turned to a knight by his side and asserted, "If you, brother, are allowed to go back into the city, tell my lieutenant, and the Commander Copier from me, that they consider me no longer but as a dead man; and as for the rest, that they behave themselves as their duty and honor may require of them on this occasion." The fortress capitulated soon thereafter, on the demands of the common soldiery.[10]

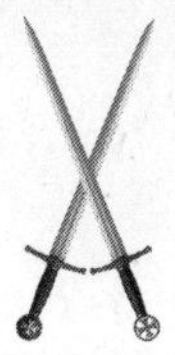

59

THE "ENEMIES OF JESUS CHRIST" DESCEND ON MALTA

In 1553, two years after the fall of Tripoli, Emperor Charles V sought to give the Knights of St. John Mahdia in Tunis, which they helped take, as a base for them to expand into Africa. After deliberating in council, the knights concluded that their Holy Land "predecessors, though much more powerful than they were, had never attempted to enlarge their territories by conquests, which generally clash with justice," but rather were dedicated to helping defend and liberate Christians. The knights politely declined the offer.[1]

The years passed, and they continued to attack and frustrate their enemies throughout the Mediterranean. By 1564, "the continual war which the order made upon the infidels, the frequent ravages upon their coasts, the taking of such numbers of corsairs and merchant ships, and the security which their succors gave to the commerce of the Christians, drew upon them the resentment of Sultan Suleiman."[2] As seen, many Muslims—from Hayrettin to Dragut—had long complained to and urged the sultan to snuff out that "den of vipers" once and for all, and that day of reckoning was fast approaching.

Then came September of 1564, when the knights played yet another pivotal role in helping Spain take Peñón de Vélez de la Gomera, a small island connected by an isthmus to Morocco (it remains a Spanish possession to this day): "The noise of this conquest gave a terrible alarm to all the corsairs of Barbary, who carried the news to Constantinople, where they complained about it to Suleiman," insisting that, with this latest conquest added to Goletta and Tunis, the knights "kept all the coast of Barbary, as it were, in chains."

But the real straw that broke the sultan's back—which "railed [his] resentment to the highest pitch, and made him more eager in fitting out his armada"—came after the knights commandeered a large Ottoman ship that was defended by over two hundred Janissaries. This vessel "belonged to Kislir Aga, chief of the black eunuchs of the seraglio... minister of his master's pleasures, and the guardian of those young ladies and beauties who were reserved for his use." As might be imagined, "this capture made a greater noise at Constantinople" than anything before it, and the black eunuch and others of Suleiman's entourage "threw themselves at the sultan's feet, and entreated him to revenge them on the knights," to which he "swore by his head that he would extirpate the Order."[3]

As an attack on the sultan's harem was an attack on the sultan's dignity—if not manhood—everyone now, especially the "Mahometan priests," or leading *ulema*, exploited this latest outrage to incite Suleiman against the knights. The grand mufti reminded him that all Muslims must pilgrimage to Mecca, but that these "Christian pirates" were interrupting their safe passage from Europe, and that "Malta was crowded with Turkish slaves." And the grand imam, on a Friday when he knew the sultan would be attending mosque prayers, expounded on the horrors of being a Muslim enslaved to Christians and how that could lead to apostasy. He climaxed his sermon by praising all of Suleiman's magnificent achievements—with just this one thing lacking: saving Islam from the fury of the knights. Even old Dragut, now eighty, was still there, whispering in the sultan's ear and reminding him that "this island, which was no more than a rock, was the only barrier that braved his power," preventing Islam's conquest of the West.[4]

"Those sons of dogs"—barked the usually tranquil and now seventy-year-old sultan as he finally snapped—"whom I have already conquered and who were spared only by my clemency at Rhodes forty-three years ago!"[5] Like the Assassins before him, Suleiman was learning of the undying reach of the Order. Once he cooled down, he laid out the empire's objective to his leading men: "I intend to conquer the island of Malta," because "Malta is a headquarters of infidels."[6]

Once again, a massive Turkish force, consisting of Suleiman's finest vessels—nearly two hundred of them—and nearly thirty thousand of his finest fighters were mobilized and assembled in the east. Among their numbers, a Christian eyewitness would later describe "four thousand Adventurers, all religious fanatics...who were accustomed to spending their leisure hours in the mosques." Dressed in white robes and green turbans to signify that they were hajjis, they had "begged the sultan to allow them to go and fight for their faith, for they believed that their souls would be saved if they died in battle."[7]

On March 22, 1565, after morning prayers, this vast armada—with "multicolored banners bearing verses from the Koran, crescent moons, and pictures of scimitars fluttering in the breeze"—left Constantinople for that tiny rock known as Malta.[8] Another fifteen to twenty thousand Muslims from Barbary would rendezvous with them, for a combined total of nearly fifty thousand men.[9]

As in 1480 and 1522, no one came to the knights' aid. Pope Pius IV repeatedly implored the kings of Europe to Malta's defense, to no avail. The king of Spain "has withdrawn into the woods," complained the pope of Philip II, "and France, England and Scotland [are] ruled by women and boys."[10] Only the Spanish viceroy of neighboring Sicily, Garcia Alvarez, responded, but he needed time to raise recruits.

Happily for the knights, however, they did have another capable master, John (or Jean) Parisot of Valette—a "totally dedicated man, a Christian of the old crusader breed," who "was as ardent in his religious practices as he was upon the field of battle."[11] Everything about this man made him the ideal commander for the upcoming siege—down to his very lineage (his knightly ancestors had crusaded alongside St. Louis). He took his vows in 1515, at age twenty, and never once looked back or even visited his native France. Over the following half century, John had seen and experienced every aspect of war. He was there as a twenty-seven-year-old fighting knight when the Order was ejected from Rhodes and remembered the bitter years of exile and wandering. He had been severely wounded in several battles and knew what it meant to be a galley slave. After a sea battle with the Muslims in 1541, he was captured, chained to an oar, whipped, and made to toil for a year until an exchange between prisoners was made.

In 1557, John was elected master of the Order. According to Peter of Bourdeille, who met him, he was "a very handsome man, tall, calm, and unemotional, speaking several languages fluently—Italian, Spanish, Greek, Arabic and Turkish." (The latter two were learned during his captivity among Muslims.)[12]

In 1565, however, when the vast Ottoman armada was coming to annihilate Malta, Master John Parisot of Valette was seventy-one years old; and while confirming that he was "tall and very well built," and "for his age…very robust," another eyewitness source noted that John was, perhaps unsurprisingly and based on all that he had seen and experienced, "rather melancholy" in spirit, though still "a very devout man."[13]

No doubt, as the master watched yet another vast Muslim fleet approach, he was reminded of events forty-three years earlier, when he was among those who fought for but lost Rhodes. It was a grim reminder that the knights could be defeated and ejected—and this time there would be no coming back; they would likely perish as an order: "Malta was literally the last ditch, and it was here that the ultimate battle between Cross and Crescent—the Armageddon of the Crusades—must take place."[14]

This final showdown was to be the climax of what started decades ago; and its two supreme leaders—Master John and Suleiman the Magnificent—were throwbacks of the exact same age, seventy-one. But while the Muslim potentate was enjoying his gardens and harems, the Christian master was preparing for war.

Against the sultan's nearly fifty thousand men—six thousand of whom were wild Janissaries—all that the master had at his disposal were a total of some seven thousand men: five hundred knights and some sergeants; about four thousand arquebusiers and mercenaries, mostly Spanish and Italian; and three thousand irregular Maltese men, crudely dressed and poorly armed.

Once all the defenses of Malta had been made, John assembled his brethren and gave a speech that captured his mood—one of piety and resolution, one becoming of the ancient Temple and Hospital:

> A formidable army, composed of audacious barbarians, is descending on this island; these persons, my brothers, are the enemies of Jesus Christ. Today it is a question of the defense of our faith, as to whether the book of the Evangelist is to be superseded by that of the Koran? God on this occasion demands of us our lives, already vowed to His service. Happy will those be who first consummate this sacrifice. But that we may indeed be worthy to render it, come, my dear brothers, to the foot of the altar, where we may renew our vows.[15]

The Turks arrived on May 18, 1565, and began reconnoitering the island on May 20. They were immediately met with ambushes. In one instance, a Maltese man killed a Turk and stuffed a pig's snout in his mouth, outraging Muslim sensibilities. During a Christian sortie on May 21, one hundred Turks were butchered against only ten Christians. A veteran French knight from La Riviere was, however, captured and taken to Mustapha Pasha, the commander of the Ottoman infantry, a man who "was harsh and severe in command, cruel and bloody to all such enemies as fell into his hands; and, particularly, was not ashamed to glory in breaking his word and oath with the Christians."[16]

To get whatever information he could from the captive knight, Mustapha ordered him tortured at the rack and questioned, though all the Christian would say is that the knights would die to the last man before the Turks took Malta. When the tortures became excruciating, he finally broke and confessed that the weakest and least fortified point on the island—which the pasha wanted to know to start the siege there—was the port of Castile. Content that he had broken the knight, Mustapha wasted much valuable time getting to and reconnoitering the port; but when he was in the vicinity and asked the captive knight which one was Castile, and the latter pointed it out, the pasha was shocked to see that it was, in fact, among the best fortified of the island's bastions, which "put him in such a rage that he gave him a blow with his cane, after which the soldiers of his guard knocked him on the head."[17]

Deciding where to start the siege remained a difficult task—not least as Suleiman had appointed two commanders: the aforementioned Mustapha, in charge of the land forces, and Piali Pasha, the sultan's grandson-in-law, in charge of the navy. Not only were they co-commanders—and not only were they both jealous of and eager to outdo each other—but Suleiman further hampered them by insisting that they also heed the advice of that old pirate, Dragut, who was also coming with his own men.

Without taking Malta's Grand Harbor, the Turks could accomplish little, so they began there. On one promontory, defending the town of Birgu, was the knights' headquarters, Fort St. Angelo, by far the best fortified. Next to it, on another promontory, was the town of Senglea, defended by Fort St. Michael. Across from them both, on Mount Sciberras, the island's highest point, stood Fort St. Elmo, a small star-shaped fort which, after St. Angelo, was Malta's second-best fortified.

There the war would begin.

60

BETTER THAT ONE SHOULD DIE THAT MANY SHOULD LIVE

On May 24, 1565, the Turks concentrated their forces against and began bombarding Fort St. Elmo. It was commanded by an eighty-year-old knight, Luigi Broglia. Before the siege, another elderly knight, known only as the bailiff of Negroponte, was also "thrown into it with sixty knights," as well as a large company of Spanish soldiers under John of la Cerda, for a total of about one hundred men. That number would constantly be replenished and augmented. As St. Elmo was just across from the master's headquarters in St. Angelo, passage was open across the small strait separating them, and communications were regularly exchanged by expert Maltese divers.

On June 3, after a massive and sustained bombardment, the Turks attempted a general storming. The much-outnumbered defenders responded with everything they had—hurling rocks and liquid fire atop the heads of their assailants. After five hours of brutal fighting, five hundred Muslims and sixty Christians, including twenty knights, lay dead.[1]

When the Christians tried to carry one young knight, Abel of Bridiers, who had been shot through the body with a musket ball, "Don't trouble yourselves about me," said he, for "I am a dead man; your care will be better employed in the defense of our surviving brethren." And with that, "he crawled to the chapel of the fort, and, commending his soul to God, expired before the altar, where he was found dead."[2]

Not all were so noble. Among those who placed themselves with the wounded ferried to St. Angelo was John of la Cerda. On inspecting that commander, however, the master noted that his wound was "scarcely visible." Master John was so incensed that, "though he pitied his weakness, he nevertheless had him arrested and sent to prison."[3]

Because the senior commanders of St. Elmo, Luigi Broglia and the bailiff of Negroponte, were both elderly, sick, and had been injured in the fighting—the bailiff took an arrow during the aforementioned assault—the master sent word that they had leave to return to the convent, "but they, though wounded, and very ancient, refused it with great resolution." The bailiff's only request was that "if the Master wanted to send someone to take his place, he would willingly serve under him, but he was determined to stay in St. Elmo as a simple knight, and to die for the Order."[4]

> [Thereafter] these venerable knights, whose faces were burnt and disfigured by the heat of the sun [the siege took place during one of Malta's most blistering summers], were always under arms, and never stirred from those places where there was most danger; and though they were almost worn out with old age, they nevertheless labored in carrying earth to those places that stood in need of being fortified, and were continually lending a helping hand to the other knights; some of whom, by reason of the narrowness of the place, were continually wounded. Nothing was there seen but cripples, arms hanging in slings, and mangled limbs that had been shot off, and which lay scattered up and down for want of their having had time to bury them; and nevertheless, these men...did service about the artillery, crawled to the breaches, and appeared with intrepidity in all places.

All this time, the master sent whatever reinforcements he deemed appropriate. A few brave souls, including another elderly knight, known only as la Miranda, much "reverenced for his piety as his courage," was so "prompted by his zeal," that he "obtained leave of the Master to throw himself into the Fort of St. Elmo." Although this boosted the garrison's morale, the nonstop bombardment and destruction of Elmo continued apace.[5]

On Friday, June 8, the Turks launched another assault to storm the fort, which, after much incessant bombardment, was now much dilapidated. Fierce fighting lasted for seven hours; more than five hundred Turks were slain, "among them many Janissaries and fanatics," noted Francis (or Francisco) Balbi of Correggio, an Italian soldier stationed in Fort St. Michael whose eyewitness account of the siege is indispensable and largely informs this history.[6]

By now, St. Elmo's tiny garrison had been so reduced from deaths and injuries that the holed-up knights concluded that its defense was untenable—that it was only a matter of time before the Turks took (whatever remained of) the fort and chopped them down to a man. Lest they be accused of cowardice, however, they sent another venerable knight, Medran, to make their case before the master. Being an honorable and trustworthy man, Medran confirmed that the situation was indeed hopeless; nothing was in store for those few Christians barricaded in St. Elmo but death. The master held a council, and all therein also agreed that the fort was no longer tenable and that its knights should abandon it and come to and refortify St. Angelo or St. Michael.

Only the master disagreed. While acknowledging that St. Elmo was a lost cause, John, employing Caiaphasian logic,* argued that it is sometimes necessary and better to sacrifice "some of the limbs to save the whole body," particularly since the whole fate of Malta "depended entirely on the length of the siege." (He had heard it said that if any forts were taken or abandoned, the Sicilian viceroy, who was already

---

* This just-coined word is a reference to the trial of Jesus Christ, when Jewish high priest Caiaphas argued before the Sanhedrin "that it is expedient for us, that one man should die for the people, and that the whole nation perish not" (John 11:50 KJV).

evincing some equivocation, would not bother coming or risking his men, as Malta would already be doomed.)

So Master John told Medran that everything, the very existence of the Order, "depended on the time" that the knights defending St. Elmo "should hold out the place; that they should call to mind the vows they had made at their profession; and that they were obliged to sacrifice their lives for the defense of the order."

On hearing the master's response, "several knights, especially the most ancient among them, professed they would bury themselves under the ruins of the fort, rather than abandon it." However, the overwhelming majority of St. Elmo's garrison thought the master's answer was "harsh and cruel."[7]

Even so, they continued to do their duty and hold the fort. On the evening of June 10, the Turks attacked again, "shouting war cries and making a fearsome noise," recalled Francis. "Although it was night, the immense number of flares and incendiaries used by both sides meant that there was no darkness. We, who were in the garrison of St. Michael, could see Fort St. Elmo quite clearly." The attack continued till dawn. The Turks lost over one thousand men, the Christians about sixty with many wounded.[8]

On June 15, Mustapha ordered all the artillery, both on land and sea, to bombard St. Elmo without intermission, until "the wall was entirely demolished, to the very rock on which it had been built." Once night fell, silence descended on the Turkish camp—only for a new, more ominous sound to rise and wax all night long, reaching a crescendo by dawn: thousands of assembled Muslims, preparing for jihad and martyrdom, beseeching their deity, ululating, and "shouting at the top of their voices, as is their custom when praying," recalled Francis, who did not manage to sleep a wink that night, though he added that "the men of St. Elmo were ready to meet them."[9]

Once the call for the general assault was given, thousands of Turks to wild cries of "Allahu Akbar" flung themselves into the water and ditch, much of which was nearly filled, and savagely climbed up the pulverized fort. Although its wall was rubble, they were met with "a kind of new wall"—one made of every last Christian soldier, with a knight placed among every three of them, "in order to sustain and encourage them. This was the only strength and defense of the castle."[10]

Now the most savage battle of the war ensued. "So great was the noise, the shouting, the beating of drums, and the clamor," recalled Francis who witnessed everything from across the harbor at St. Michael, "that it seemed like the end of the world." The Christians gave every last ounce of themselves: First they spent all their artillery and fire and burned a great many Muslims alive; then, they engaged those who reached them in melee combat, breaking their swords and pikes in and on them; at last, Christians and Muslims were seen rolling on the ground in a death grip, "when the dagger determined the fate of the combatants."

So it went from morning till dawn: "The cries…the groans of the wounded and expiring, the noise and thunder of the cannon and muskets; all this spread a kind of terror on both sides, which nevertheless could not make the Turks retire, nor would the knights abandon an inch of ground."

Everyone across the harbor in the forts of St. Angelo and St. Michael watched helplessly. "From St. Michael we could see one of our soldiers fighting like one inspired, with a trump in his hands," recalled Francis, of a fighter who was incinerating his enemies with a hollow metal tube filled with a flammable liquid mixture—the ancestor of fire throwers. As for the master, being "always determined to inflict the greatest possible damage on the enemy of the Christian Faith," he instantly used this occasion to blast his cannons on strategic and now unguarded Turkish locations.

Seven hours later—and after between one and two thousand Muslims had been killed—a disgusted Mustapha called off the attack. St. Elmo had proved its mettle yet again. As the Turks retreated, a great cry of defiance emanated from the Christian fort; it was answered by another, even greater cry of joy from across the harbor—all of which was too much for the pasha to bear. Any sense of triumphalism was tempered by the sobering fact that three hundred Christians had been killed or lay dying in the fort. Indeed, as Francis later learned, had the Muslim assault lasted a moment longer, it would have prevailed, as not a single one of those still-breathing Christians could even stand, much less swing their sword arm, from fatigue.

As the final rays of the sun set on this sanguine day, two elderly knights, the bailiff of Negroponte and la Miranda, were espied from the two forts across the harbor taking care of the sick and wounded, "like true knights hospitallers."[11]

Considering the utterly ruined state of St. Elmo, its defenders tried once again and sent a letter to the master bearing the signature of fifty knights. It said that unless boats were sent "to carry them off from a place, where they were all going to be destroyed, they were absolutely bent to take a desperate resolution, to sally out and be killed sword in hand," and thus at least die with honor, "rather than continue in the fort, to no other purpose than to be smothered under its ruins; or, in case of its being taken by storm, to have their throats cut like so many beasts, and be exposed to all the torments, which the ingenious cruelty of the Barbarians is ever sure of inventing."[12]

The master received their arguments with mixed emotions. First came rising "indignation" that knights sworn to obedience unto death would so question direct orders; but that their situation was indeed hopeless—and that he was consigning them to death—also "weighed heavily" on him. So he wrote them back saying "it was not enough for them to lose their lives, sword in hand, in order to die with honor, which they seemed so fond of"—like those vain secular knights St. Bernard had so long ago warned against—"but that they must likewise lose them in the practice of the obedience which they owed him, and in the occasions which he should prescribe them." He also emphasized that time was of the essence and that the longer they held the fort, the better Malta's chances of deliverance.[13]

Master John also resorted to a bit of reverse psychology: He informed the knights of St. Elmo that he had found others—including regular Maltese peasants—who had volunteered to relieve them, adding, "Return, my brethren, to the convent; you will be more in safety there; and as for me, I shall then be less in pain about the preservation of Fort St. Elmo, though it be of such importance, that the preservation of the island, and all our Order, depends entirely on it."[14]

At this, and the shame they expected to face if they were to take the master's offer, the knights of St. Elmo finally resolved to end their days in the fort. They went to its chapel, made their confessions, received communion, said their prayers, and prepared to die. As for Master John, no one, Francis repeatedly observes, really knew how he felt inside, consigning his brethren to what he knew was certain death. St. Elmo was and had to be a sacrifice—for time.

The Christians did receive one bit of good news around this time. On June 18, Dragut—the "drawn sword of Islam," that ancient scourge and slaver of Christians, and nemesis of the Order—was killed by friendly fire, "his brains spattered from his mouth, nostrils, and ears." With one less enemy, the news "comforted the Master."[15]

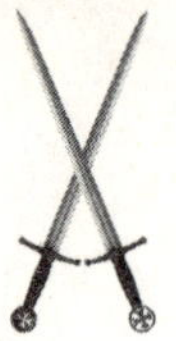

61

CRUCIFIED AGAIN

After the bloodbath of June 16, Mustapha gave his men time to rest and collect themselves, while his artillery continued to rain down on and pulverize St. Elmo. Meanwhile, Master John sent another 150 fresh men to reinforce the fort—all volunteers inspired by and happy to fight and die alongside the knights.

On Friday, June 22, Mustapha called for another storming of the fort. Once again, "so great was the noise, and so violent their attack, that it was truly terrifying—it was by far the most bloody and effective one they had made." The living Christians within St. Elmo "resisted with cold steel, with fire, and with rocks."[1] They fought with such desperation and ferocity—some were seen combing through their slain comrades' pockets for ammunition—and had apparently become "something more than men, who, by a noble contempt of death, still made their enemies tremble."[2]

The assault lasted for six hours, at the end of which two thousand more Turks lay dead and double that number severely wounded—but so too were five hundred Christian defenders killed. All that remained within the rubble pile that was once Fort St. Elmo were barely one hundred men, all wounded and hardly able to stand.

That night, a swimmer was sent to inform the master of their desperate situation "and to beg him for assistance. The messenger said that there was not a man left in St. Elmo who was not covered with his own blood as well as that of his own enemy, and that they had no ammunition left at all." Unwilling to send any more men to their death, and also aware that he, of all men, could not now show weakness or despair, Master John responded with bravado. He praised the Christians and scoffed at the Turks, adding, "I trust in God that they will never take the fort!" "Such were his words," observed Francis, "but no man can tell what his feelings really were."[3]

Left forsaken, the remaining one hundred Christians of St. Elmo spent the final hours of the night making "themselves ready to die in the service of Jesus Christ." Huddled inside the dilapidated remains of their chapel, they called on God "in their great anguish" while consoling and listening to one another's confessions, "like men who know the next day will be their last on earth"—even as the Turks, "to add to their trials," continued "their bombardment all night, sounded alarms and made sporadic attacks" to ensure that "when morning came, the defenders would be worn out."[4]

Once the undaunted knights of Christ had made their peace and "nothing remained but the giving up their souls to God, they embraced one another with tenderness" and went to their posts "in order to die with their weapons in their hands." As for those ancient and worthy knights, including Broglia, la Miranda, the bailiff of Negroponte, and others who could not stand or walk due to age or wounds, they "had themselves carried in chairs to the side of the breach, where, armed with swords, which they held with both their hands, they awaited" an honorable death.

Once the hot summer sun of June 23 rose, the final assault was sounded, as throngs of Janissaries chanting "kill, kill" rushed into St. Elmo, which, considering its utterly dilapidated condition, was an easy affair. The Christians tried to make a final valiant effort, but they were overwhelmed by sheer numbers. Shot down in their chairs, the elderly and incapacitated knights were not given a chance to swing their swords. A lone knight, making a final stand atop the summit of Mount

Sciberras, was espied from St. Angelo hacking and hewing with his two-handed sword, before being blotted out under a hail of scimitars.

Thus did St. Elmo at last fall to the Turks; and before the dust of war had settled came the much-anticipated and all-too-typical retribution—of a sadistic quality that far outdid what Saladin did to the knights of Christ following Hattin, 378 years earlier.

Mustapha had any Knights of St. John that "were found lying among the dead" with "any marks of life left, to be ripped open, and their hearts to be plucked out." In clear view of the other forts across the harbor, he ordered those still-breathing knights hoisted upside down from iron rings before allowing the Janissaries—the "sons of the sultan" as they prided themselves—to vent all their rage on their fallen Christian enemies. Those fierce Muslim warriors mutilated the knights' faces, gouged their eyes, and crushed their skulls; they gutted them open and pulled out and hurled their hearts and entrails to the dirt.

Next, "the pasha, in order to insult the instrument of our salvation, which the knights wore as the badge of the order, had gashes made over their body in the form of a cross." Finally, and in another parody of the crucifixion, he had these former knights turned into mutilated mockeries nailed to wooden crosses and set adrift in the Grand Harbor. Such, the message was clear, was to be the fate of all who dared to resist the sultan.

As for any other living Christians found within St. Elmo, they too were methodically killed, many by being tied to stakes and riddled with arrows by jeering Turks working on their aim. "As if this cruel deed was not enough to satisfy Mustapha," writes Francis, "he bought from the Corsairs some Christians who had surrendered, and had them beheaded in front of the army."[5]

In the end, all the defenders of St. Elmo, about 1,500 Christians, were killed. Most of them met their end during—the unlucky ones, after—the siege. (A rumor persisted that nine knights were spirited away as prisoners and never heard from again.)

News of the fall of St. Elmo was quickly spread far and wide, creating fear and consternation among nearby Christians so that "even Protestant England said prayers for Catholic Malta."[6]

Considering the cost in time and Muslim lives (between six and eight thousand), this Turkic victory seemed more a pyrrhic victory. As Francis writes, "They captured the fort, but at so high a price that they had little reason to rejoice." Indeed, on entering St. Elmo, Mustapha is said to have blurted, "Allah! If so small a son has cost us so dear, what price will we have to pay for so large a father?" in reference to the much better fortified St. Angelo.[7]

On the following morning, June 24—ironically, the feast of John the Baptist, the patron saint of the Order—the Christians of St. Angelo awoke to yet another grisly sight: the heads of many of those ancient knights and commanders who had voluntarily thrown themselves to die in St. Elmo staring at them from atop the points of spears planted in front of the fort. "Their intention was to terrify us with so revolting a sight and to cow us into submission," wrote Francis of this and the previous mutilation of the knights. "But if such was their idea they failed, for the sight of our dead friends roused in us a desire for vengeance."[8]

This was especially the case with John. Although he had privately wept, in public, the seventy-one-year-old master was determined not to let the Christians of St. Elmo's sacrifice be in vain. He delivered a thundering speech of defiance, praised the martyrdom of those Christians who had bought them so much time, forbade the people from any shows of public grief, and ordered that the feast of St. John commence as usual. He even made the rounds among and encouraged the common Maltese people: "We are, my brave comrades, the Soldiers of the Lord Jesus Christ—as are you!"[9]

Next came the necessary retribution from these knights who always gave as well as they took: All Turkish prisoners were brought onto the ramparts and beheaded before the Muslim army. Then, "ramming their heads into his cannon," the master ordered them fired "all covered with blood as they were, into the camp of the infidels." This last move was not just meant to avenge his fallen brethren; it was to make the rest of the Christians know that they were in a do-or-die situation—for the Muslims would never show any mercy after this act of defiance.[10]

62

CONFRONTING "THE FATHER"

Having seen how much it had cost to take "the son" (Fort St. Elmo), Mustapha was not overly eager to contend with "the father" (Fort St. Angelo, the island's headquarters and master's residence). So, on June 29, a small delegation of Turks under a white flag approached St. Angelo in an effort to parley. But when the ostentatiously clad leader, with equal ostentation, shot his gun in the air to haughtily indicate that he wanted to talk, the fort immediately responded in like manner—shooting cannon fire at him and causing him to jump off his horse for cover, thereby ruining his fine plumes in the mud.

Next came a human apparition running wildly to the fort in an effort not to be blown up. It was a seventy-year-old Christian slave of Spanish origin, who had rowed in the sultan's galley for over thirty years. He was let into the fort. After much prompting from the master, the slave, who was reluctant to deliver his message under the steel-cold eyes of John, finally and with much trepidation relented.

The Ottoman envoy was here, the old slave began, "to demand the surrender" of the island, with the warning that "you do not display the same obstinacy as at St. Elmo, or he will be forced to mete out the same treatment to you." The slave then breathlessly added, "While there is still time, accept his clemency. All they want is this barren island. They will grant you, and all your people, your property and your artillery, a free passage to Sicily." It was, in short, the same offer that Suleiman had made to the knights forty-three years earlier in Rhodes: They could surrender and have free and safe passage to Sicily.

Once the slave was finished speaking, the master, looking at a nearby knight, barked, "Take him out and hang him!" As usual, this too was for public morale—a show of no compromise. John was recalling the lessons of 1522, when the knights lost Rhodes. Then, because they had opened the door, even a little, to the idea of surrender, the people had begun to clamor for a "deal," with the eventual result being capitulation. He, John, would have none of it. The message to every last person in Malta was that they would either prevail by the force of arms or else all die trying.

Privately, however, he had mercy on and allowed the Spanish slave to return to his masters, with a message for them: "Let this be known among the Turkish army: if any other man comes here with such proposals, I will hang him without mercy!" A separate and special message was sent to Mustapha: "Do your worst. My trust is reposed in Our Lord Jesus Christ. He will deliver us from your hands. More than that, He will give us victory over you!"[1]

An interesting episode, highlighting the role of religion and heritage, occurred during these early days when the Turks, having gained the Sciberras Peninsula, began to transport their shipping into the harbor and place their guns to assault the rest of the forts from all sides. As usual, among the Turkish army were many former slaves-turned-Muslim-converts. One of these, a Greek whose name had been Philip Lascaris, was enslaved as a child and converted to Islam; due to his abilities, he eventually rose through the ranks to become an important officer. On seeing all the sufferings that the Christians had gone through and "being touched with a sudden remorse of conscience," he decided to abandon his former kidnappers to aid his former coreligionists—including by exposing Mustapha's plans.

> The sight of Malta, ready to sink under the power of the infidels, revived in his memory, the indelible character of a Christian, which he had received at his baptism. The heroic valor, of which the knights gave such distinguished proofs, raised his compassion, and he could not forbear reproaching himself for fighting on the side of the barbarians, who had put most of the princes of his family to death.[2]

On June 30, he managed to escape the Turks and make his way to the Christians. When they took him to the master, "I wish to be a Christian," he cried, "as were my ancestors!" to which John responded, "You are welcome indeed." He took the Greek in, thanked him, considered his counsel, and gave him a pension. Having retaken his birth name, Philip continued in the war but now on the side of the Christians.[3]

By July 5, all the Turks' guns and batteries were in place and the ceaseless bombardment of Malta began from all sides. By July 13, the Muslims especially focused on and pounded the town of Senglea, which was defended by Fort St. Michael. By way of terrorizing the Maltese in an effort to get them to demand that the knights capitulate, the Muslims "concentrated on the houses, and killed many women and children who were in the streets," wrote Francis, who was stationed in St. Michael.[4]

Once darkness put an end to the incessant shelling, and because they were now camped so close, "every night the Turks used to make their prayers and devotions with such a shouting and screaming that it was really laughable," remembered Francis. He describes how one imam would start chanting, before the rest would reply "with a monstrous caterwauling."[5]

As had happened at Rhodes in 1522, double agents and renegades were sent to subvert the people's morale. At one point, a "corrupt Maltese" man approached "two very fine old Maltese" defenders, both named Paul (Micho and Daula).* He began by cataloging how badly

---

* Because he was shipwrecked at, and evangelized the people of, Malta (Acts 28), St. Paul is especially revered in, and is the patron saint of that island—with not a few Maltese men, past and present, named after him.

the knights had supposedly treated the people of Malta since taking possession of the isle and assured his listeners that, if the people rebelled now against the knights, who were, anyway, so outnumbered, the Ottomans, as the Maltese people's new rulers, would treat them better than they could ever imagine.

"You are lower than a dog!" responded Paul Daula. "We want no advice from a man so damned as you. We would rather be slaves of St. John than companions of the sultan!" The apostate Maltese ignored him and, turning his attention to the other Paul, oily suggested that he tell him where he would be hiding, so he, the corrupt Maltese, having "some influence with Mustapha," would tell that pasha not to harm Paul or his family. "Look where the battle is fiercest," was Paul Micho's reply. "There you will find me, old as I am with my sword and my shield, defending my God, my country, my wife, and my children!"[6]

After the Turks had spent several days ceaselessly bombarding Senglea, all throughout the night of July 14, "their priests kept up an endless chanting—just as they had done before their general assault of St. Elmo." And sure enough, all such "caterwauling" did indeed presage yet another major assault—this time on the fort of St. Michael, where Francis was stationed.

On the morning of July 15, three thousand hardened Muslim fighters—"they all wore splendid turbans," recalled the Italian soldier—made for the much-damaged fort aboard countless boats. The lead vessels contained long-haired dervishes and other "Mahometan priests" loudly crying their deity's name, reading jihad verses from the Koran and casting "imprecations against the Christians."[7] Francis and his fellow soldiers braced themselves for the shattering impact of the Islamic war boats against the palisade.

Meanwhile, an even larger assault was being directed against the landside of the fort, led by Hassan, the viceroy of Algiers, who had recently arrived with two thousand Algerians. As Hayrettin Barbarossa's son and Dragut's son-in-law, he had some rather large jihadist boots to fill and was eager to prove his quality. On arriving in Malta a few days earlier, he had boasted to Mustapha that, had he been there, St. Elmo would have fallen much sooner. As such, he asked the pasha to allow him to take charge of this attack on St. Michael to bring the war to a swift close. To such cheek, "Mustapha, who was an old general, and who would not have been sorry that this bold youth should learn, at his own expense, how dangerous it was to come within reach of the sword of the knights, answered him in a very obliging manner." He even contributed six thousand of his own men and assured Hassan that he would be coming up just behind him.[8]

These eight thousand Turks "met a resistance they had never expected, and not one of them managed to reach the top of the wall alive." The knights' incessant gunfire "was responsible for decimating the Turks attacking at this point." But the battle raged for hours, and the determined Algerians eventually gained the top entrenchment of St. Michael, where a bitter fight between the vastly outnumbered knights—aided by stone-slinging Maltese boys—and the Muslims raged.[9]

Over at the palisade, the knights, who had been warned of this coming attack by Philip Lascaris, the aforementioned Ottoman deserter, had silently waited until the sailing Turks were in point-blank range, at which point they unleashed all hell on them, including with a special, sea-level battery of five cannons at the base of St. Angelo, designed for just such an amphibious attack.

Of the first ten large ships, nine were instantly destroyed under the hail of fire—killing eight hundred Janissaries. The guns of the knights' batteries were not just filled with shot, "but fired bags full of stones, pieces of chain, and iron caltrops. It was these that caused the carnage. Those of the men who were not killed or wounded, were drowned." (The Christians later learned that all the Muslim fighters sent in were intentionally chosen for not knowing how to swim—ensuring that they would fight to the death.)[10]

No matter how many Muslims were killed, more, especially on the landside, appeared, and the assault would not let up. "I don't know if the image of hell can describe the appalling battle," wrote the Order's contemporary historian, Giacomo Bosio: "the fire, the heat, the continuous flames from the flamethrowers and fire hoops; the thick smoke, the stench, the disemboweled and mutilated corpses, the clash of arms, the groans, shouts, and cries, the roar of the guns…men wounding, killing, scrabbling, throwing one another back, falling and firing."[11]

In this infernal backdrop, Francis saw "our preacher," Brother Robert, at "all the various posts, crucifix in one hand and sword in the other, encouraging us to fight for the Faith of Jesus Christ, and to die well."

In the end, the Muslims finally retreated, and in the rout, many more were killed or drowned, as Christian fighters chasing them down showed no mercy, crying that "they should have St Elmo's pay!" Before long, the water was "covered with dead bodies, with heads, arms and mangled limbs." Slaughtered on that day were some four thousand Turks and two hundred Christians, half of whom were knights.[12]

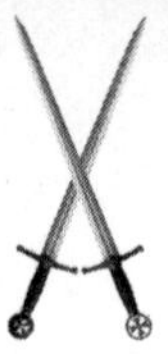

63

"WE FIGHT FOR OUR LORD JESUS CHRIST, OUR LIVES, AND OUR LIBERTY!"

Once again, where direct assaults failed, Mustapha turned to nonstop bombardments. Between July 22 and 27, all of the Turks' heavy artillery—sixty-four guns and cannons and fourteen batteries—ceaselessly pummeled both Senglea and Birgu. The pasha also engaged in psychological warfare, launching un-strategic but terrifying night raids, sometimes shooting randomly, all to make the Christians snap. "During this period there were a thousand alarms and excursions," wrote Francis, "as well as a number of attacks which caused us great anxieties." At one point, the "Christians, parched with heat and thirst, and quite spent with fatigue, were forced to take up arms" against thousands of howling Janissaries. Maltese women and children joined the fray—hurling stones, fireworks, and boiling oil at their would-be murderers and masters. Although the Turks fled again, they took the lives of two hundred Christians and forty knights—one whose head was blown off by a cannon.[1]

On July 18, Master John, being no respecter of persons, ordered his own nephew Henry of La Valette to lead a desperate sally, reminding him that "it was the duty of a knight of Malta to dare more than any other warrior." The youth, who was already eager to prove himself, happily complied and was promptly killed. When someone tried to console the master, "All the knights are alike dear to me," he responded with a stern look. "I consider them all as my children."[2]

To keep the people's spirit alive, John had assured them that the Sicilian viceroy would most assuredly arrive on July 25, as that was not only the feast day of Spain's patron saint—St. James Matamoros, the "Moor Slayer"—but viceroy Garcia Alvarez himself was a member of Spain's Order of St. James. When July 25 came and still no relief force appeared along the horizon, mass demoralization set in among the people—even as the Turkish bombardment continued unabated.

In a fury, the master appeared on a high place and, as missiles whizzed above his head, delivered another thundering speech on how "it was in God alone that we should put our trust!" According to Francis,

> [Master John] hoped for no help save that of God. It was God who was our true relief, and He who had preserved us up to now, would certainly deliver us from the hands of the enemies of His Holy Faith.... He did not know what to say about the promises of Don Garcia, since the time of their fulfillment was now past, but he asked every one of us to bear in mind that we were Christians. We were fighting above all for the faith of Our Lord Jesus Christ, and for our lives and liberty. Each one of us must remember that there was no hope of any more mercy from the Turks than had been shown to the defenders of St. Elmo, and that in all our dangers we would find him in the vanguard.

The speech had the desired effect, and "there was not a man who did not resolve to die rather than fall into the hands of the Turks. We were all determined to sell our lives dearly and to waste no more time in hoping for outside help."[3]

Between July 28 and 30, the incessant bombardment of St. Michael and Senglea was so devastating as to kill a great many women and children; their splattered remains weighed heavily on the master. All he could do was follow his own order. So the elderly man "exposed himself in places of the greatest dangers" and "was frequently the first man to engage the enemy." Otherwise, he often "went alone to the Church of St. Lawrence and said his prayers, something that he never neglected to do whenever he had a moment to spare." Interestingly, as a reminder of his philosophical disposition, the master also kept a jester about his person. According to Francis, this fellow "informed him of what was happening at the various posts, as well as trying to amuse him with his quips—although there was little enough to laugh about."[4]

On August 4, a group of knights went out on a sally. When they returned with eight less fighters, the master was vexed as these were "men from whom the Turks might extract information about the weakness of the defenses." The following morning, he saw all eight of their heads adorning Muslim spears, and "the Master knew then that they had kept their word, and had died rather than surrender."[5]

On August 7, after Castile, one of the major bastions protecting the city of Birgu, had been nearly razed to the ground, Mustapha ordered another double assault. Following the usual pre-morning cries of Islam, chants, and beating of drums, eight thousand Muslims fell upon Senglea and four thousand upon Birgu, but "they were received like men who were well-expected." The defenders had prepared and hurled all sorts of incendiary fire and boiling oil atop their heads. "The attacks made on this day were violent," recalled Francis—which was certainly saying something—"and fought out on both sides with much bloodshed and cruelty."

When a knight informed the master that the Turks were on the verge of taking Castile, the master, "without showing a trace of emotion," raised his voice: "Come, my knights, let us all go and die there! This is the day!"

Then, with "a pike in his hand, as if he were no more than a common soldier," the seventy-one-year-old master, "with exemplary courage led the way to Castile, followed by all the reserves." On seeing him grimly stalk toward them, the startled knights already stationed there "tried to prevent him from going to the post of danger. But, to their dismay, he insisted on going forward, and even tried to climb up the spur of the cavalier of Castile, where the enemy were already established." On being prevented, John went to another area "thick with Turks" and "he seized an arquebus from a solider and aiming at the enemy opened fire, calling out at the same time, 'This way, boys, this way!'"[6]

By now, the assaults had spilled into the streets of Birgu and Senglea, where the women and children fought with equal desperation, the former especially, as "the fear of losing their honor and their liberty, if they should fall into the hands of the infidels, inspired these brave women with a contempt of all the horrors of impending death."[7]

Nine hours after the assaults began, the Turks, having so inundated the two cities by their sheer numbers, were poised for victory when what they had most dreaded happened—the Sicilian viceroy Garcia had finally arrived with his many thousands and was closing in behind and making quick work of the Muslims' ranks. When word reached those in the Ottoman front lines, panic ensued, followed by a stampede of fleeing Turks: "We were completely astounded by this sudden retreat," recalled Francis, "for we had no idea what had happened."

In fact, Garcia had not come at all. A group of one hundred knights and Maltese militia had, on seeing the Turkish camp emptied, made a sally from Mdina. Turkish scouts mistook them for the front line of the many thousands of Christians that they assumed had landed. Although Mustapha quickly learned the truth of the matter, it was too late. With sword in hand, he tried to halt the panicked retreat—and even chopped down two fleeing Janissaries—but the stampede would not be stayed: "It is impossible to describe how humiliated the pashas, and indeed all their army, felt when they saw how small a force had caused them such grievous harm and instilled such fear into their hearts. Mustapha was the angriest of all, and, in his fury, he turned on [and upbraided] Piali."

Not only had the Turks forfeited an assured victory—Castile was reclaimed by the Christians—but they also lost yet another two thousand fighters, against sixty dead Christians.[8]

64

JUDGMENT DAY

It was now mid-August, and to say that Malta looked like a war zone or graveyard would be a grand understatement. Over one hundred thousand cannonballs had pulverized it, and thousands of bloated corpses surrounded its harbor. Even so, the front lines of this apocalyptic wasteland—marked by tattered flags and the rotting trophy heads of each side mounted atop spears—were as defiant as ever, with the master ready to strike down any who dared even hint at surrender. "Our men are in large part dead," wrote one knight, Vincent Anastagi, "the walls have fallen; it is easy to see inside, and we live in danger of being overwhelmed by force. But it is not seemly to talk of this. First the master, and then all the Order, have determined not to listen to anything [defeatist] that is whispered outside."[1]

John was, as ever, the first to follow his own words and set an example. Despite his age and suffering, "There was no type of work from which he spared himself, whether physical or mental, in keeping us on our toes and ready for every emergency," writes Francis. "He would sleep in the most exposed positions, and made night rounds constantly, even though the knights in charge begged him not to risk his life but to take care of himself." When the master was advised to abandon Castile and that he and the people take refuge deep inside St. Angelo, still the best fortified fort on the island, he refused, saying that just as the knights of St. Elmo had died to the last man defending it, so too must they all now fight and die to the last man for Castile.

Inspired by such perseverance, even now, "Christian renegades in the Turkish ranks, moved by our plight, called across to our men from their trenches, taking pity on us as they had many times before." They avoided the scrutiny of the rest of the Ottoman army by yelling out code words and phrases designed to sound as typical Muslim insults. For example, they would mockingly yell, "You dogs, hold out! You haven't got many oxen to kill. There are only sheep left, and they are weak ones, weak ones!" To any Muslim ear, such words were taken as taunts that the Christians—whom Muslims always referred to as "dogs"—had little suitable food left. In fact, it meant that the stronger Turks (the oxen) were dead or injured, and that all the Christians had to contend with were weak ones (sheep).[2]

Following the near successful assaults of August 7, Mustapha resumed the ceaseless bombardment. On August 18, a mine blew up much of the bastion of Castile. Before the dust and debris had settled, hordes of white-robed fighters screaming Allah's name poured through the breach into Birgu. The Muslims' victory was all but complete; the Christians were on the verge of panicking and fleeing, until a lone figure—Master John, looking like so many masters and knights of yesteryear—was seen leading a countercharge, sword in hand, right into the breach. Such a sight emboldened everyone, and all those Christians—including women and children—who were on the verge of fleeing the Muslim advance, followed old John into the fray.

Once again, battle reached a fever pitch, and even convalescent Christians arose from their beds to fight, "for they preferred to die in battle rather than be cruelly slaughtered in the hospital." The master was wounded by a grenade and urged to withdraw. "Never will I withdraw," cried he, pointing with his sword at a Turkish standard planted at the breach, "so long as those banners wave in the wind!" (That the elderly master could fight in full armor in 100-degree weather is a reflection of the hardihood a lifetime of war had inured into such men as these fathers of knights.)

The Muslims, unable to make any headway, again retired. On being thanked for leading the defense at a time when everyone was ready to break, John responded, "Will it be possible for me, at the age of seventy-one, to end my life more gloriously than in fighting with my brethren and my friends for the service of God, and the defense of our holy religion?"[3]

By August 29, when yet another Turkish assault came, it took swords, whips, and sticks to prod the by-now dispirited Turks—who were indeed more like sheep than oxen—to attack. And although Castile and St. Michael had been so utterly devastated—"We were now so close to the enemy at every point, that we could have shaken hands with them"—the Christians continued to fend off their assailants.[4]

At long last, on September 7, Sicilian Viceroy Garcia landed in Malta with about ten thousand Christians (mostly Spaniards and Italians). Although Master John was unaware of this development, on the following morning, September 8, which was the Feast of the Nativity of the Virgin, he ordered the bells of the conventual church of St. Lawrence to ring out over the ruins of Birgu; the unexpected chimes were caught up and answered by more bells from the ruins of Senglea. "Never, I believe, did music sound so sweet to human ears as did the peals of our bells on this day," remembered Francis. A solemn Te Deum was offered up to the "God of Victories" and the gates were, for the first time, opened, with a few knightly squadrons now even making sallies against the Turks.[5]

Although fear and dread took the Turks on learning that the viceroy had arrived, a two-faced Morisco—an insincere Muslim convert to Christianity who had arrived with the relief force—defected to the Turks and assured them that Garcia's force was smaller, weaker, and more poorly supplied and organized than they had thought.

On September 11, Mustapha tried one last-ditch effort. Demoralized as they were, his Muslim forces still outnumbered the Christians, and he would try to meet the relief force head on. Yet, so eager were the recently arrived Christians to chastise the Muslims that "not even at the point of their sword could [the commanders] restrain their men, so great was the desire of all to come to blows with the Turks."[6] As might be imagined, these eager-to-fight and fresh Christians utterly routed their weary adversary. In an effort to show his own men that flight was not an option, Mustapha killed his own horse and shouting "Allah" ran, scimitar in hand, to the front lines—to no avail: The rout was complete. The Turks were fleeing en masse back to their gallies, chased down by the Christians.

The final scene of this Armageddon played out across St. Paul's Bay, where the apostle was shipwrecked fifteen centuries earlier. When all was said and done, the beach was littered with floating turbans, scimitars, shields, and countless bodies. Only a few of those tens of thousands of Turks that left Constantinople six months earlier on March 22 amid much jihadist fanfare escaped. In total, over thirty-five thousand Muslim soldiers were killed during the course of the siege.[7]

Meanwhile, in the midst of the devastation that was once Malta, all that stood were a total of six hundred defenders still capable of bearing arms. Of the original five hundred knights, three hundred had died fighting and most of the other two hundred were maimed or crippled for life. Nearly three thousand of the Spanish and Italian soldiers were also dead. "Seven thousand Maltese men, women, girls, and boys"—about a third of the island's entire population—"were also killed," noted Francis.[8]

Yet, the few standing survivors had much to celebrate. Their tiny island had withstood what was till then history's most sustained bombardment, as the largest empire in the world hurled everything it had at them—including 130,000 cannonballs. Moreover, though no one knew it at the time, this would be the last real Ottoman effort to break into the western Mediterranean and complete the encirclement of Europe from the south. Had Malta fallen, in ten years' time, the face of western Europe could have been dramatically altered, possibly permanently. Even England's Queen Elizabeth—certainly no friend to the Catholic order and a frequent ally and supporter of their Muslim enemies—observed, "If the Turks should prevail against the isle of Malta, it is uncertain what further peril might follow to the rest of Christendom."[9]

Just as the knights' stellar defense of Rhodes against Muhammad II's forces nearly a century earlier in 1480 had catapulted their reputation and prestige throughout Christendom, so too now did their victory in Malta against the same foe in 1565.

Meanwhile, over in Constantinople, the mood was glum. Suleiman's ministers tried to deceive the people, saying that the Ottoman mission—which they now pretended was never meant to capture but to level Malta to the ground—had been accomplished. The city's many Christian *dhimmi* subjects "could not walk in the streets for fear of the stones which were hurled at them by the Turks."[10] Like his great-grandfather, Muhammad II, the aged Suleiman concluded the matter with self-flattery: "I see now that it is only in my own hand that my sword is invincible." He gave orders for a new expedition against Malta in a year's time, "which I will lead myself against this accursed island. And I swear by the bones of my fathers—may Allah brighten their tombs—that I will not spare one single inhabitant!"

But also like his forefather, Muhammad II, who made the same boast following his defeat against Rhodes in 1480, only to die prematurely, so too did Suleiman die before he could realize his vow against the Knights of St. John.[11]

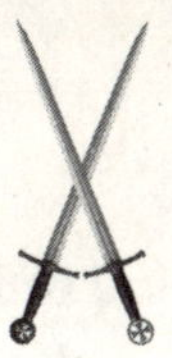

65

HOLY WAR MORIBUND

The histories of the Knights of the Hospital of St. John almost always end with the 1565 siege of Malta and for good reason. As Vertot writes in his magisterial tome,

> Among the several authors who have writ the general history of the Order of St. John of Jerusalem, whether in Italian, Latin, French, or Spanish, not one of them has carried his account of it past the last siege of Malta: all these writers leave off, as it were by concert, at that famous epoch, fancying, probably, that they could not better end their works, than with the conclusion of that bloody war.... Whatever might have been their different motives, I have followed the same method in the plan and distribution of my work.[1]

Indeed, nor will I try to supersede or outdo the chroniclers of old (not least seeing how long this book has already become), save by offering a brief summation to cap off the knights' history.

As had happened following the victorious defense of Rhodes in 1480, after the siege of 1565, the Order's prestige once again catapulted, resulting in an increase in recruits and donations. With more men and resources, the Order continued as before, frustrating the Turks on the high seas and helping and freeing their captive coreligionists whenever they could.

The decades passed; religion continued to fall by the wayside; and more and more European powers engaged in realpolitik, making alliances with the Muslims. Not so for the Order: "the most infamous enemies of the Christian rite, the Turks, initiates of the sect of Muhammad," to quote Master Peter of Aubusson, hero of Rhodes, 1480, remained the same.[2] Their war was so total and so existential to the point that whoever aided the Turks became their de facto enemy.

Not long after 1565, for example, the Knights of St. John attacked and plundered Venetian vessels for being allied with the Ottomans. Although the Republic of Venice accused the knights of being nothing more than "corsairs parading crosses"—hypocrites using religion as a pretext for plunder—"the brothers' own writings indicate that they truly believed that their activities formed part of a holy war against the Turks. In contrast, the brothers believed that the Venetians were too ready to sacrifice the interests of Christendom in their own commercial interests." The Order's ancient commitment to Christendom remained total. On the one hand, "the Hospitallers refused to join the duke of Osuna's expedition to the Adriatic in 1617 because the duke was unable to guarantee that it would not be used to attack Christians."[3] On the other hand, they were always ready to lend a helping sword to any Christian fighting the Muslims—including the very same Venetians they often fought against for being allied with the Turks.

Thus, during the Cretan War (1645–1669), when a Muslim alliance of Turks and Barbary pirates invaded and conquered most of Venetian Crete, the fortress of Candia continued to hold out for many years, falling only after a brutal twenty-seven-month-long siege in 1669. As usual, the knights were there from the start, spearheading the defense, and were among the last of the Venetians' allies to leave. In a letter to the Republic, Francesco Morosini, the Venetian commander of Candia, wrote, "I lose more by the departure of these few, but most brave, warriors than by that of all the other forces."[4]

Perhaps most remarkable of all is that the fusion of piety and prowess that marked the ancient Knights of the Temple and Hospital remained on display even in the latter's latter years. One anecdote from well over a century after the 1565 siege of Malta suffices.

In 1672, "five great vessels of Tripoli" intercepted and attacked a small boat commanded by a twenty-two-year-old brother knight who is now remembered only as the "knight of Thémércourt" (in France). He responded "with much courage and intrepidity," including by "shooting the masts of two" Muslim ships and "killing [an] abundance of their men" so that "the infidels, despairing to take him…left him at liberty to keep on his way; but he was soon after caught in a dreadful storm, which drove him upon the coast of Barbary, where his vessel was cast away, and he himself was taken by the Moors."

Loaded with chains, he was eventually sent to Adrianople. On hearing of his presence, Ottoman Sultan Muhammad IV paid him a visit. He asked the knight if he was indeed the man who had fought off five vessels from Barbary. "It was I," replied the young Christian. When Muhammad asked him his nationality, and he responded French, "You are a deserter then," said the sultan, "for I am in strict peace with the king of France." After confirming that he was indeed a Frenchman, the captive added, "but I am likewise a knight of Malta, a profession which obliges me to expose my life against all the enemies of the Christian faith."

Impressed by this knight's exploits and overall bearing, the sultan, "desiring to get him into his service," sent him to a much finer prison, "where he was treated with great humanity." Muhammad further

> made him all those advantageous offers that might possibly tempt a young warrior who was but 22 years old; and, to encourage him to change his religion [to Islam], he promised to marry him to a princess of his blood, and to make him a pasha, or his great admiral. But these pompous offers had no effect upon the young knight; he resisted them with as much courage and resolution as he had done their arms. The sultan, incensed at his

> steadiness, resolved to try if harsh usage could not shake his constancy, and accordingly ordered him to be thrown into a dungeon for a fortnight. They there gave him the bastinado, put him to the torture, and mangled his limbs, during which this noble confessor of Christ Jesus did nothing but call upon his holy name, and implore his grace that he might die for the confession of it. In fine, the sultan ordered his head to be cut off.[5]

Such martyrdoms are seldom remembered these days; rather, Malta is remembered and criticized by modern historians for being little more than a mass slaving machine of innocent Muslims throughout the seventeenth and eighteenth centuries:

> In their early days [in Malta] the Knights had been content if they could but fill the oar-benches of their galleys and have a work-force of slaves available for building and maintaining the fortifications. Gradually, however, as they acquired a surplus, they began to follow the practice of the Turks, the Tunisians, and the Algerians. Slaves were regularly sold to traders from Genoa, Venice, and other Italian cities. Even as late as the eighteenth century there were still about two thousand slaves employed in Malta. They were either Turks captured from Ottoman trading or fighting vessels, Arabs or Berbers from the North African coast, or Negroes who had themselves been enslaved to oar-benches of Arab galleys.[6]

What to make of this rather unflattering description?

First, as seen in an earlier chapter dealing with the sixteenth century, it was the Muslims who were mass slavers of Christians, not the other way around. Muslim enslavement of Christians continued to wax over the following centuries so that virtually no part of Europe was untouched.

From 1627 to 1633, Lundy, an island off the west coast of Britain, was actually occupied by Barbary pirates, who pillaged England at will. In 1627, the Muslim corsairs raided Denmark and even far-off Iceland, hauling a total of some eight hundred slaves. Such raids were accompanied by the trademark hate. Writing around 1614, one English captive noted that the Muslim pirates "abhor the ringing of the church bells being contrary to their Prophet's command" and so destroyed them whenever they could. In 1631, nearly the entire fishing village of Baltimore and elsewhere in Ireland were raided and "237 persons, men, women, and children, even those in the cradle" seized.[7]

Despite attempts by some modern historians to paint the Knights of Malta as mass slavers extraordinaire, slaving around the Mediterranean remained "a prevalently Muslim phenomenon."[8] Thus if, according to one tally, "over the course of the seventeenth and eighteenth centuries, at least thirty-five thousand to forty thousand [Muslim] slaves passed through Malta,"[9] according to another tally for roughly the same timeframe, "between 1530 and 1780 there were almost certainly a million and quite possibly as many as a million and a quarter white European Christians enslaved by the Muslims of the Barbary Coast."[10] In other words, for every one Muslim enslaved by the Christians, thirty-one Christians were enslaved by the Muslims.

Moreover, being a Muslim slave of Christians was often much more enviable than being a Christian slave of Muslims. As seen, the latter were exposed to horrific abuses, including forced homosexuality and sodomy; they were pressured into becoming Muslim and were certainly denied freedom of worship, let alone churches. Punishments for those who resisted or in any way spoke negatively of Islam, Muslims, and especially Muhammad, beggared description and included being "impaled alive" and "roasted alive." Other European slaves were "thrown from the city walls, and caught upon large sharp hooks, on which they hang till they expire." After a Muslim man tried to engage in homosexual relations with his young male Christian slave, and the latter, outraged, killed him,

> He was dragged to the place of execution over the rough and pointed stones, subjected to the insults of an excited and brutal crowd. On his arrival there each of

> the spectators seemed to take a pleasure in assisting at the work. He was crucified against the wall with four large nails; a red-hot iron was thrust through his cheeks to prevent him from speaking, and, in this condition, he was slowly burnt to death with firebrands. Such acts of cruelty were by no means uncommon.[11]

Compare and contrast this with the following anecdote that revolves around one Hali, a Muslim slave of the Knights of Malta. After they allowed him to be ransomed by the Ottomans in the 1720s, he implored the Turks to besiege Malta. Although it may be assumed that, having been horribly mistreated by the knights, he was justly burning for revenge, in reality, "this slave, who was beloved of the knights, and in favor with the master, had served in the navy, and had been for ten years imam or chief of the Turkish slaves that were at Malta." (Muslim slaves were permitted freedom of worship in Malta.) Even so, on arriving at Constantinople, Hali gave the leading ministers "an account of the forces of the Order, and persuaded them it would be an easy matter to surprise the island."[12]

The final consideration as to why slaving among Muslims and the knights was different came out during an exchange between the Turks and Anthony Manuel of Vilhena (the same master who had once "favored," elevated, and allowed the ransoming of Hali the aforementioned slave). Master Anthony wrote that the knights' business was not "to scour the seas in view only of making slaves, but to cruise with their ships for securing the liberty of the seas to all Christian vessels; that they attacked such as only disturbed commerce, and who deserved to be made slaves for endeavoring to make Christians so; that they had nothing so much at heart as the delivery of such of theirs as were in slavery."[13]

In sum, Muslims were mass enslavers of Christians, not the other way around. However, the same knights who always sought to give Muslims a taste of their own medicine—including by beheading them—again responded in kind and only made slaves of those who "*deserved to be made slaves for endeavoring to make Christians so.*" Despite this, and as seen, the number of Muslims the knights enslaved was roughly 3 percent the number of Christians enslaved to Muslims. Finally, while all slavery is deplorable, according to the descriptions in sources, it seems to have been preferable to be a Muslim slave of Christians than a Christian slave of Muslims.

At any rate, inasmuch as the Order tried to persevere, time and secularization stood against it—against what many had come to see as an embarrassing anachronism. During the "Enlightenment" in the seventeenth and especially eighteenth centuries—when "drinking, whoring, gambling, and dueling were the leisure activities of young nobles"—a certain moral laxity began to infiltrate the Order, even if at a markedly less rate than the average noble:

> Certainly they would go out whenever required upon the caravans, and certainly they would do battle against the infidel whenever the opportunity offered, but they were not going to wear hair shirts and behave like monks when they were back home in Malta. Rhodes had been cut off, isolated geographically and spiritually from the western world, and it had been possible there to maintain an anachronistic society. Malta was quite different. Before long, even the statutes of the Order, although frowning upon open immorality, more or less admitted that sins of the flesh existed—and that it was only the open display of them that must at all costs be avoided.[14]

To a certain extent, it was a moot point. By 1732, the holy war was over: French and Venetian pressure caused the Order to stop harassing Ottoman shipping. (That said, whenever any European power happened to fight a Muslim power, the knights were quick to be there, including when France fought Tunis in 1752 and 1770 and when Spain fought Algiers in 1772, 1775, 1783, and 1784.)

In June 1798, Napoleon Bonaparte's fleet stopped in Maltese waters in order to take the island for commercial and strategic reasons. So moribund had it become that "of the 332 knights on the island, fifty were too old or ill to fight," and the "ancient guns had not been fired in anger for a century. Powder was found to be rotten and shot defective. The Maltese urban militia was inexperienced and undisciplined.... In two days and with hardly any bloodshed the garrison...had been overcome. The master and his knights were ignominiously expelled." As Napoleon himself later wrote, Malta "certainly possessed immense physical means of resistance, but no moral strength whatsoever."[15]

Worst of all was the cruel irony. In the words of Ernle Bradford,

> This time it was not the Turks, not the eternal Muslim enemy, but the French—once the foremost of all crusaders—who achieved...what all the cannons, fleets, sappers and miners, Janissaries, Generals, and Admirals of the Sublime Porte, together with the innumerable private raiders of the Barbary coast, had failed to do.

Indeed, further adding insult to injury, Napoleon, who was on his way to Egypt, had brought with him a copy of the Koran: "It was a strange quirk of fate that it should be a Frenchman who now read the words of Muhammad as he prepared to capture the island that had resisted the onslaughts of the followers of the Prophet for so many centuries."[16]

Still, the homeless Hospitallers persevered and continue to exist till this day. Although long since demilitarized, the Sovereign Military Hospitaller Order of St. John of Jerusalem, now based in Rome, continues to focus on its original mandate of charity, including healthcare, disaster relief, and social services, while maintaining its sovereignty and diplomatic relations with various countries.

As something of a closing tribute to the original fighting knights of the Order, we close with an encomium from Augusta Drane's history:

> The determined courage and heroic devotion of the Knights of St. John have commanded the admiration, of every noble and generous mind, whatever may have been its religious convictions or prejudices. At Acre, at Smyrna, at Rhodes, and lastly at Malta, these brave champions of the faith occupied what for the time being

was the outpost of Christendom. At times almost annihilated, they rose again before the eyes of their enemies with more than recovered strength; abandoned, or but tardily and grudgingly succored by the powers of Europe, who were too much engaged with their own political quarrels, and too deeply absorbed by their own selfish and immediate interests, to look to the future or unite against the common foe, they confronted single-handed the enormous hosts of the infidels in their descents upon Europe, arrested their triumphant march towards the West, retreated from one position only to rally in another, and renew a contest which in appearance was hopeless; and at length, when all seemed lost, by sheer fortitude and perseverance they baffled and beat back the barbarian invader in the very pride of his strength, so that he never dared to approach their stronghold again.[17]

66

WHITHER THE TWO SWORDS OF CHRIST?

From the very start, one of the biblical verses that actuated the knights of the military orders told of how one man could "chase a thousand, and two put ten thousand to flight" (Deuteronomy 32:30 KJV). For biblical commentators of the time, as well as the knights themselves, this rather inspiring scripture meant that, no matter the odds or how badly outnumbered, even a few men could defeat hordes—not because of their personal prowess, but because God, not numbers, ultimately decided the outcome.*

But was it true? Figuratively, yes: The Knights of the Temple and Hospital repeatedly defeated and set to flight Muslim numbers that vastly outnumbered them.

* The full verse in context: "How should one chase a thousand, and two put ten thousand to flight, except their Rock had sold them, and the LORD had shut them up?" (KJV). As the latter half of this verse makes clear, this verse is not celebrating how an outnumbered Israel defeated a larger enemy force, but rather the opposite: that a small number of non-Israeli soldiers were able to rout great multitudes of Israel's people—something only possible because God, the Israeli people's "Rock," had abandoned and handed them over. For the Crusaders, however, the salient point was that God—not numbers—decided battles.

This is because they were throwbacks to and resembled the First Crusaders of 1097–1099, pious warriors such as Duke Godfrey, who were willing to sacrifice their all, including their lives, on behalf of Christendom, with the addition that the knights of the orders further embraced a vigorous monastic rule. They became the embodiment of the Crusader spirit—if not always "gentler than lambs," certainly "fiercer than lions" in war[1]—and, as such, were pivotal to the Crusader states. Even that cynical Enlightenment historian Edward Gibbon could not but remark that "in their most dissolute period the knights of the Hospital and Temple maintained their fearless and fanatic character: they neglected to live, but they were prepared to die, in the service of Christ."[2]

We have already seen numerous examples of their prowess against the Muslim hordes that regularly dwarfed them. Here is yet another that captures both the essence and ultimate weakness of the military orders. After complaining about how the king and nobles of Hungary were slow to fight off a Mongol invasion in 1241, the eyewitness chronicler, Thomas of Spalato, praised the Templars for their opposite behavior:

> As befitted active men, they did not give themselves over to quiet slumber like the rest but kept watch the whole night under arms. As soon as they heard the shout, they at once burst out of the camp. Then, girded in military arms and grouped in one wedge they rushed boldly into the enemy army and fought with them for some while with much fortitude. But, *since they were very few in number* in comparison with the infinite multitude of Mongols, who bubbled from the ground everywhere like locusts, they returned to their camp, after killing more than they had lost themselves [emphasis added].[3]

"Since they were very few in number"—such, in a nutshell, was the ultimate downfall of the military orders, which time only exacerbated. With every passing century (if not decade), the Crusader zeal that had led to the miraculous triumph of the First Crusade lessened, and fewer and fewer Western Christians went to or lent support to the Holy Land, causing the military orders' already small numbers to become that much more pronounced. It is precisely for this reason that, if ten years after their founding in 1119, the Templars were still so insignificant as not to warrant a mention in Fulcher of Chartres's chronicle, by 1291, when the Crusader states were finally expelled from the Holy Land, it was the military orders and their castles that dominated the landscape.

Nor was it long before the West's growing indifference turned into outright hostility, especially among those Christians who, not realizing that it was *their* beliefs that were changing, balked at the knights' conservatism and "old ways." Thus, in the years preceding the Temple's destruction in the early fourteenth century, "when religious belief was increasingly emphasizing the mercy of God, the humanity of Christ and the benign intervention of His Mother, the Templars' harsh and apparently merciless discipline seemed to outsiders to be not only inhuman but even ungodly."[4]

In short, from once epitomizing all that was good, noble, pious, and manly, the Knights of the Temple and Hospital became strange and eventually unwelcome aberrations. Alan Forey explains this evolution well:

> Despite calls for crusades and the proliferation of crusading plans and proposals, the defense—and later the recovery—of the Holy Land was left increasingly to the military orders.... [T]he orders' ability to defend the Holy Land was at the same time being diminished by the actions of Westerners. Just as crusading activity declined, so the initial enthusiasm for military orders waned. Their privileges and exemptions were reduced, and increasing financial demands were made on them by popes and Western secular rulers.... At times even their dispatching of men and supplies to the East was impeded by Western kings. Although the Temple, the Hospital and the Teutonic order provided garrisons for numerous castles in the crusader states...and could usually put a disciplined and experienced force into the

> field, they could not by themselves undertake the defense of the Holy Land, and their ability to render assistance was being reduced.

As for those growing numbers of Europeans who habitually harped against the knights for "constantly failing to achieve what they were capable of doing," they were, in fact,

> seeking in part to relieve themselves of responsibility for the Holy Land and therefore to exonerate themselves from blame for the lack of success against Islam in the eastern Mediterranean. The failure was, in fact, that of Western Christendom as a whole, without whose continuous support it was impossible to maintain a distant Christian outpost amidst surrounding Muslim territories. Although most Westerners continued to pay lip-service to crusading ideals…the Holy Land was a cause which had lasted too long.[5]

In short and to reiterate, yes, even as they increasingly stood alone, the Knights of the Temple and Hospital could *figuratively* defeat and drive off "ten thousand," which is to say that they could and did defeat those who far outnumbered them (though obviously not by a 2-to-10,000 ratio). However, when the West abandoned them to the point that the knights *literally* began to face the odds of "two" against "ten thousand," defeat was inevitable.

*****

That medieval and premodern Christians cooled to and turned against the knights leads to a timely question: How are the Knights of the Temple and Hospital viewed today? Interestingly, the answer is not unlike that concerning those other *Defenders of the West*: As I explained in the conclusion of that book, the modern West's response to those great Christian heroes who stood against Islam has been twofold: (1) demonizing and knocking down from their pedestal those who are well known in the West (such as Richard the Lionheart and El Cid) and (2) letting sleeping dogs lie by ignoring those whom the West has already forgotten about (such as Skanderbeg and Hunyadi).

Something of a similar approach has been meted out to the Knights of the Temple and Hospital—with the former being demonized and the latter ignored.

The false accusations that brought an end to the Temple in the early fourteenth century—that they were a secret order of cat-worshipping, Muslim-loving sodomites—continued to snowball down the ages so that, till this day, "the Templars" remain popular, though in a way that would be totally alien to the Templars themselves. Today, they are widely believed to have been great occultists, wielders of esoteric knowledge, and invisible movers and shakers of world events.

As with the former charges that led to the Temple's downfall, so too are these newer ones wholly unfounded.* Even that most popular and widespread of all beliefs, that they continued thriving underground becoming today's Freemasons, was in fact fabricated in Germany around 1760—that is, some 450 years *after* their extinction. As Riley-Smith (somewhat exasperatedly) notes, "it is amazing how often it has to be pointed out that the Templar myth is an eighteenth-century German invention."[6]

---

* Although several modern organizations claim descent from the Knights Templars—most notably the Freemasons, the Ordo Templi Orientis, and the Rosicrucians—there are no historical links whatsoever between the knightly order that was suppressed in 1312 and these later esoteric/occultist upstarts that were born in the eighteenth century and after. All serious historians of the Templars make clear that these groups merely appropriated the honorable name of *Templar* in an effort to legitimize themselves and their activities—many of which any historic Templar would have viewed with shock and disgust. As Jace Stuckey says in his essay, "Templars and Masons: An Origin Myth," "perhaps no other aspect of the history of the medieval crusades has become more attractive to modern enthusiasts than the rise and fall of the…Templars. However, at the same time there has been no topic more misunderstood or more misused than the Templars." He also argues that no matter how staunchly actual historians of the Temple argue otherwise, the myths surrounding the Order are "ingrained…in our culture" and continue to receive "a kind of currency or 'street credit' among the general population…" (*Seven Myths of the Crusades*, 106, 124–125).

As for the Knights of the Hospital of St. John, because no fabulous stories or sensational gossip was attached to their name, time has done the secular, if not increasingly anti-Christian, West's work for it: completely blotting them out of memory. This is evident in the simple fact that virtually no one today associates the ubiquitous and important word "hospital" with its actual founders, the Knights of the Hospital of St. John of Jerusalem.

*****

Now that we have seen all the many characterizations of the Knights of the Temple and Hospital—from those written by themselves to those written by their accusers—perhaps it is best to close with arguably the most objective testimony of all, that of their contemporary enemies: Muslims. Not only did Muhammad's followers experience—and feel the swords of—the knights firsthand but, while hating and fearing them, Muslims also seemed to respect and speak honestly about them, especially among fellow Muslims.

For starters, there are numerous references attesting to the fact that Muslims saw the knights as the most dangerous and "evil enemies of Islam" or "fanatical warriors of Christ."[7] As we saw following the Battle of Hattin in 1187, more than one Muslim contemporary commented that Saladin singled out the Knights of the Temple and Hospital for slaughter "because they were the fiercest of all the Frankish warriors, and in this way he rid the Muslim people of them," to quote Ibn al-Athir.[8] After describing their ritual execution in graphic detail, to the point that some of the formerly willing executioners no longer had the stomach to continue in the grisly work, one Muslim eyewitness concluded with seeming—and telling—relief: "How many ills did [Saladin] cure by the ills he brought upon a Templar."[9]

Similarly, one year after Hattin, in 1188, two "chiefs of the Hospitallers" were captured and brought to Saladin. They reportedly showered the sultan with compliments to avoid execution because "it was his custom to massacre the Templars and Hospitallers on account of the violent hatred that they had for the Muslims, and their bravery."[10] For many other Muslims, such as Imad al-Din, the much-feared knights were naught but "demons...with their castles built on inaccessible crags which were the lairs of wild beasts."[11]

All that said, perhaps the soberest example of Islam's understanding of the Knights of the Temple and Hospital comes from a Muslim manual of war prepared by military theorist and strategist Abu al-Hasan Ali bin Abi Bakr al-Harawi (1145–1215). In it, he presents the Holy Land's Latin clergy as corrupt and pliable, easily manipulated:

> [The sultan] should not neglect to write to the clergy [concerning surrender].... For they have little religious sentiment and are capable of treachery and disloyalty; they desire the things of this world and are indifferent to the things of the next; [they are] irresponsible, thoughtless, petty, and covetous...being concerned with rank and status among kings and nobles; [they] have a permissive religious judgment regarding their own [actions].

Such unflattering characterizations of the Crusader state's clergymen can easily be dismissed as biased Muslim caricatures of the Christian enemy. The problem, however, is that al-Harawi completely changes tack when talking about the sincerity and dedication of the military orders:

> [The] sultan should beware of [the Templar and Hospitaller] monks...for he cannot achieve his goals through them; for they have great fervor in religion, paying no attention to the [things of this] world; he cannot prevent them from interfering in [political] affairs. I have investigated them extensively, and have found nothing which contradicts this.[12]

Clearly, then, and based on none other than the enemy's testimony, not only were the Knights of the Temple and Hospital Christendom's greatest warriors, they were also among its most sincere and pious. In the end, and as a collective, they had indeed lived up to Bernard of Clairvaux's exhortations and expectations:

> This is a new kind of knighthood and one unknown in ages past. It indefatigably wages a twofold combat, against flesh and blood and against spiritual hosts of evil in the heavens [Ephesians 6:12].... For a man to powerfully gird himself with both swords [spiritual and secular] and nobly mark his belt [with the Cross]—who would not consider this worthy of great admiration...? Truly, a fearless knight and secure on every side is he whose soul is protected by the armor of faith just as his body is protected by armor of steel. Doubly armed, surely, he need fear neither demons nor men.[13]

Such were the Knights of the Temple and Hospital—the Two Swords of Christ—back in those ancient days when Christians were expected to fight both fell spirits *and* fallen humans.

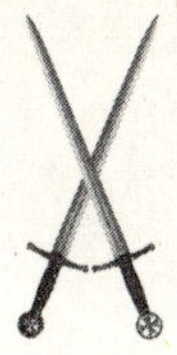

WORKS CITED

1. Addison, Charles G. *The History of the Knights Templars.* Oxford: Oxford University Press, 1842.
2. Andrea, Alfred J. *Encyclopedia of the Crusades.* Westport: Greenwood Press, 2003.
3. Allen, S. J. and Emilie Amt, eds. *The Crusades: A Reader.* Toronto: University of Toronto Press, 2010.
4. Andrea, Alfred, and Andrew Holt, eds. *Seven Myths of the Crusades.* Indianapolis: Hackett Publishing Company, 2015.
5. Barbaro, Nicolò. *Diary of the Siege of Constantinople.* Translated by J. R. Jones. New York: Exposition Press, 1969.
6. Barber, Malcolm. "Supplying the Crusader States: The Role of the Templars." In *The Horns of Hattin*, edited by B. Z. Kedar. Jerusalem: Yad Izhak Ben-Zvi and Israel Exploration Society, 1992.
7. Barber, Malcolm. *The New Knighthood: A History of the Order of the Temple.* Cambridge: Cambridge University Press, 1994.
8. Barber, Malcolm. *The Templars.* Translated by Keith Bate. Manchester: Manchester University Press, 2002.
9. Bernard of Clairvaux. *In Praise of the New Knighthood.* Trappist: Cistercian Publications, 2000.
10. Bertrand, Louis. *The History of Spain.* 2nd ed. London: Eyre & Spottiswoode, 1956.
11. Bostom, Andrew, ed. *The Legacy of Jihad: Islamic Holy War and the Fate of Non-Muslims.* New York: Prometheus Books, 2005.

12. Bradford, Ernle. *The Knights of the Order.* New York: Dorset Press, 1972.
13. Brundage, James A. *The Crusades: A Documentary Survey.* Milwaukee: Marquette University Press, 1962.
14. Burgess, Glyn S., trans. *The Song of Roland.* London: Penguin Books, 1990.
15. Campbell, G. A. *The Knights Templars: Their Rise and Fall.* London: Duckworth, 1937.
16. *Christianity Today.* "Turkish Police Foil Assassination of Christian Pastor." January 18, 2013. https://www.christianitytoday.com/2013/01/turkish-police-foil-assassination-of-christian-pastor/.
17. Correggio, Francisco Balbi di. *The Siege of Malta, 1565.* Translated by Ernle Bradford. London: Penguin Books, 2003.
18. Crawford, Paul. *The Templar of Tyre.* Aldershot: Ashgate, 2003.
19. Crowley, Roger. *Empires of the Sea.* New York: Random House, 2009.
20. Crowley, Roger. *The Accursed Tower: The Fall of Acre and the End of the Crusades.* New York: Basic Books, 2019.
21. Currey, E. Hamilton. *Sea Wolves of the Mediterranean.* Ithaca: Cornell University Library, 2009.
22. Daniel, Norman. *Islam and the West: The Making of an Image.* Edinburgh: Edinburgh University Press, 1962.
23. Davis, Robert C. *Christian Slaves, Muslim Masters: White Slavery in the Mediterranean, the Barbary Coast, and Italy, 1500–1800.* New York: Palgrave Macmillan, 2003.
24. Din ibn Shaddad, Baha' al-. *The Rare and Excellent History of Saladin.* Translated by D. S. Richards. Burlington: Ashgate, 2001.
25. Doukas. *Decline and Fall of Byzantium to the Ottoman Turks.* Translated by Harry J. Magoulias. Detroit: Wayne State University Press, 1975.
26. Drane, Augusta. *The Knights of St. John: with the Battle of Lepanto and Siege of Vienna.* London: Burns and Oates, 1858.
27. "Drakones Rhodioi." *Theoi Greek Mythology.* Accessed December 10, 2024. https://www.theoi.com/Ther/DrakonesRhodioi.html.
28. Einhard and Notker the Stammerer. *Two Lives of Charlemagne.* Translated by David Ganz. London: Penguin Books, 2008.

29. Fernandez-Morera, Dario. *The Myth of the Andalusian Paradise: Muslims, Christians, and Jews under Islamic Rule in Medieval Spain.* Wilmington: ISI Books, 2016.
30. Forey, Alan. *The Military Orders: From the Twelfth to the Early Fourteenth Centuries.* London: Macmillan, 1992.
31. Foxe, John. *An Universal History of Christian Martyrdom.* London: J. G. Barnard, 1807.
32. Frankopan, Peter. *The First Crusade: The Call from the East.* London: Vintage Books, 2013.
33. Fuller, J. F. C. *Military History of the Western World. Vol. 1, From the Earliest Times to the Battle of Lepanto.* New York: Da Capo Press, 1987.
34. Gabrieli, Francesco, trans. *Arab Historians of the Crusades.* New York: Barnes & Noble, 1993.
35. George-Tvrtković, Rita. *A Christian Pilgrim in Medieval Iraq: Riccoldo da Montecroce's Encounter with Islam.* Turnhout: Brepols Publishers, 2012.
36. Gibbon, Edward. *The Decline and Fall of the Roman Empire.* Vol. 2. Chicago: University of Chicago, 1952.
37. Guibert of Nogent. *The Deeds of God through the Franks.* Middlesex: Echo Library, 2008.
38. Guindy, Adel. *A Sword over the Nile: A Brief History of the Copts under Islamic Rule.* London: Austin Macauley Publishers, 2020.
39. "Hadith 4:271." Hadith of Bukhari. *Internet Sacred Text Archive.* Accessed May 5, 2024. http://www.sacred-texts.com/isl/bukhari/bh4/bh4_274.htm.
40. Hamblin, William J. "Muslim Perspectives on the Military Orders during the Crusades." *BYU Studies.* Accessed September 10, 2024. https://byustudies.byu.edu/article/muslim-perspectives-on-the-military-orders-during-the-crusades.
41. Heers, Jacques. *The Barbary Corsairs: Warfare in the Mediterranean, 1480–1580.* New York: Skyhorse Publishing, 2018.
42. Hillenbrand, Carole. *The Crusades: Islamic Perspectives.* New York: Routledge, 2000.
43. Hugh. "Hugh 'The Sinner': Letter to the Knights of Christ in the Temple at Jerusalem." Translated by Helen J. Nicholson. *De Re*

Militari (blog). Accessed September 4, 2024. https://www.deremilitari.org/RESOURCES/SOURCES/templars2.htm.

44. Humphreys, R. Stephen, "Ayyubids, Mamluks, and the Latin East in the Thirteenth Century." Paper presented at the second annual *Mamluk Studies Review*, January 17, 1997. https://doi.org/10.6082/M12N50D8.
45. Ibn Ishaq. *The Life of Muhammad: A Translation of Ibn Ishaq's Sirat Rasul Allah*. Translated by A. Guillaume. Oxford: Oxford University Press, 1997.
46. Ibrahim, Raymond, ed. and trans. *The Al Qaeda Reader*. New York: Doubleday, 2007.
47. Jackson, Peter, trans. *The Seventh Crusade, 1244–1254: Sources and Documents*. London: Routledge, 2016.
48. Jacob, Uri. "*Chevalier Mult Estes Guariz* and the 'Pre-Chansonnier' Vernacular Lyric." *Plainsong and Medieval Music* 30, no. 2 (2022): 119–140. https://doi.org/10.1017/S0961137121000115.
49. Jacques de Vitry. "Jacques de Vitry: Sermons to a Military Order." Translated by Helen J. Nicholson. *De Re Militari* (blog). Accessed October 15, 2024. https://www.deremilitari.org/RESOURCES/SOURCES/vitry.htm.
50. Joinville, Jean, and Geoffroi of Villehardouin. *Chronicles of the Crusades*. Translated by Sir Frank Marzials. Mineola: Dover Publications, 2007.
51. Jordan, William Chester. *The Apple of His Eye: Converts from Islam in the Reign of Louis IX*. Princeton: Princeton University Press, 2019.
52. King, E. J. *The Knights Hospitallers in the Holy Land*. London: Methuen & Co., 1931.
53. Kizilov, Mikhail. "Slave Trade in the Early Modern Crimea from the Perspective of Christian, Muslim, and Jewish Sources." *Journal of Early Modern History* 11, nos. 1–2 (2007): 1–31. https://doi.org/10.1163/157006507780385125.
54. Knowles, David. *Christian Monasticism*. London: Weidenfeld & Nicolson, 1969.

55. Lane-Poole, Stanley. *The Story of the Barbary Corsairs*. London: T. Fischer Unwin, 1890.
56. Lewis, Bernard, ed. and trans. *Islam: From the Prophet Muhammad to the Capture of Constantinople*. Vol. 1, *Politics and War*. New York: Oxford University Press, 1987.
57. Lewis, Bernard. *The Assassins: A Radical Sect in Islam*. London: Weidenfeld & Nicolson, 1967.
58. Madden, Thomas F. *The New Concise History of the Crusades*. Lanham: Rowman & Littlefield Publishers, 2007.
59. Malan, S. C., trans. *A Short History of the Copts and Their Church*. London: D. Nutt, 1873.
60. Manning, Scott. "The Siege of Ascalon (1153) According to Contemporary or Near-contemporary Western European Sources." *De Re Militari* (blog). March 4, 2013. https://deremilitari.org/2013/03/the-siege-of-ascalon-1153-according-to-contemporary-or-near-contemporary-western-european-sources/.
61. Maqqari, Ahmad ibn Muhammad. *The History of the Mohammedan Dynasties in Spain*. Vol. 1. Translated by Pascual de Gayangos. New York: Johnson Reprint Corp, 1964.
62. Maqqari, Ahmad ibn Muhammad. *The History of the Mohammedan Dynasties in Spain*. Vol. 2. Translated by Pascual de Gayangos. New York: Johnson Reprint Corp, 1964.
63. Maqrizi, Taqi al-Din. "Medieval Sourcebook: Al-Makrisi: Account of the Crusade of St. Louis," Fordham University. Last modified April 14, 2025. https://sourcebooks.fordham.edu/source/makrisi.asp.
64. Matthew of Edessa. *Armenia and the Crusades, Tenth to Twelfth Centuries: The Chronicle of Matthew of Edessa*. Translated by Ara Edmond Dostourian. Lanham: National Association for Armenian Studies and Research; University Press of America, 1993.
65. Maxwell, Herbert. *The Chronicle of Lanercost*. Glasgow: James Maclehose and Sons, 1913.
66. Melville-Jones, John R. *The Siege of Constantinople 1453: Seven Contemporary Accounts*. Amsterdam: Hakkert, 1973.

67. Michaud, Joseph François. *History of the Crusades*. Vol. 1. Translated by W. Robson. Philadelphia: George Barrie, [n.d., ca. 1880].
68. Makarem, Sami. *Al Taqiyya f'il Islam*. London: Mu'assisat at-Turath ad-Druzi, 2004.
69. Mourad, Suleiman A. and James E. Lindsay. *The Intensification and Reorientation of Sunni Jihad Ideology in the Crusader Period*. Leiden: Brill, 2015.
70. Nicholson, Helen J. *The Knights Hospitaller*. Woodbridge: Boydell Press, 2001.
71. Nicholson, Helen J. *The Knights Templar: A New History*. Stroud: Sutton Publishing, 2001.
72. Nicholson, Helen J., trans. *Chronicle of the Third Crusade: A Translation of the Itinerarium Peregrinorum et Gesta Regis Ricardi*. Burlington: Ashgate, 1997.
73. Nicholson, Helen J., trans. "Military Orders: Anonymous, Lament for the Templars." *The ORB*. Accessed April 10, 2024. https://the-orb.arlima.net/encyclop/religion/monastic/anonlamt.html.
74. Nicolle, David. *Knights Hospitaller*. Oxford: Osprey Publishing, 2001.
75. North, William L., trans. "Account of the Taking of Constantinople, Thomas the Eparch and Joshua Diplovatatzes (?)." *Carleton College*. https://apps.carleton.edu/curricular/mars/assets/Thomas_the_Eparch_and_Joshua_Diplovatatzes_for_MARS_website.pdf.
76. O'Callaghan, Joseph F. *Reconquest and Crusade in Medieval Spain*. Philadelphia: University of Pennsylvania Press, 2004.
77. Perry, Frederick. *Saint Louis (Louis IX of France): The Most Christian King*. London: G. P. Putnam's Son, 1902.
78. Peter, D. R. M. "The Founding of the Templars." *De Re Militari* (blog). January 11, 2014. https://deremilitari.org/2014/01/the-founding-of-the-templars/.
79. Peters, Edward. *Christian Society and the Crusades, 1198–1229: Sources in Translation including the Capture of Damietta by Oliver of Paderborn*. Philadelphia: University of Pennsylvania, 1971.
80. Playfair, R. Lambert. *The Scourge of Christendom: Annals of British Relations with Algiers Prior to French Conquest*. New York: Books for Libraries Press, 1972.

81. Polo, Marco. *The Travels of Marco Polo*. Edited by Manuel Komroff. New York: Modern Library, 2001.
82. Read, Piers Paul. *The Templars*. New York: St. Martin's Griffin, 1999.
83. Rega, Frank M. *St. Francis of Assisi and the Conversion of the Muslims*. Rockford: Tan Books, 2007.
84. Richards, D. S., trans. *The Chronicle of Ibn al-Athir for the Crusading Period from al-Kamil fi'l-ta'rikh*. Part 1. Burlington: Ashgate, 2006.
85. Richards, D. S., trans. *The Chronicle of Ibn al-Athir for the Crusading Period from al-Kamil fi'l-ta'rikh*. Part 2. Burlington: Ashgate, 2007.
86. Riley-Smith, Jonathan. *A History of the Order of the Hospital of St. John of Jerusalem*. London: St. Martin's Press, 1967.
87. Riley-Smith, Jonathan. *Hospitallers: The History of the Order of St. John*. London: Hambledon, 1999.
88. Rubenstein, Jay, ed. *The First Crusade: A Brief History with Documents*. Boston: Bedford/St. Martin's, 2015.
89. Seward, Desmond. *The Monks of War: The Military Religious Orders*. London: Penguin Books, 1995.
90. Shirley, Janet, trans. *Crusader Syria in the Thirteenth Century: The Rothelin Continuation of the History of William of Tyre with Part of the Eracles or Acre Text*. Aldershot: Ashgate, 1999.
91. Philippides, Marios, trans. *The Fall of the Byzantine Empire: A Chronicle by George Sphrantzes, 1401–1477*. Amherst: University of Massachusetts Press, 1980.
92. Rowton, Erik. "The Last Templar: The Prophetic Final Words of Grand Master Jacques de Molay." *Paranormal Scholar*, April 5, 2019. https://www.paranormalscholar.com/the-last-templar-the-prophetic-final-words-of-grand-master-jacques-de-molay/
93. Stark, Rodney. *God's Battalions: The Case for the Crusades*. New York: Harper One, 2009.
94. Stewart, Devin. "Dissimulation in Sunni Islam and Morisco Taqiyya." *Al-Qantara* 34, no.2 (2013): 439–490. https://doi.org/10.3989/alqantara.2013.016.
95. Sweetenham, Carol, trans. *Robert the Monk's History of the First Crusade (Historia Iherosolimitana)*. Burlington: Ashgate, 2005.

96. The Battle of Jacob's Ford. Northumberland, n.d., https://northumberlandkt.com/?page_id=2210.
97. Treptow, Kurt W., ed. *Dracula: Essays on the Life and Times of Vlad the Impaler*. Oxford: Center for Romanian Studies, 2019.
98. Upton-Ward, J. M., trans. *The Rule of the Templars: The French Text of the Rule of the Order of the Knights Templar*. Woodbridge: Boydell Press, 1992.
99. Vann, Theresa M. and Donald J. Kagay. *Hospitaller Piety and Crusader Propaganda: Guillaume Caoursin's Description of the Ottoman Siege of Rhodes, 1480*. London: Routledge, 2015.
100. Vertot, L'Abbé de. *The History of the Knights Hospitallers of St. John of Jerusalem, Styled afterwards, the Knights of Rhodes, and at present, the Knights of Malta*. 5 vols. London: John Donaldson, 1775.
101. Walsh, Michael J. *Warriors of the Lord: The Military Orders of Christendom*. Grand Rapids: William B. Eerdmans Publishing, 2003.
102. Welsh, William E. "A Day of Terrible Slaughter: The Battle of Montgisard, 1177." *Medieval Warfare*, March/April 2016, 28–35.
103. Wheatcroft, Andrew. *Infidels: A History of the Conflict between Christendom and Islam*. New York: Random House Trade Paperbacks, 2005.
104. White, Joshua M. *Piracy and Law in the Ottoman Mediterranean*. Stanford: Stanford University Press, 2017.
105. Wilken, Robert L. *The Land Called Holy: Palestine in Christian History and Thought*. New Haven: Yale University Press, 1992.
106. William of Tyre. *A History of Deeds Done Beyond the Sea*. Vol. 1. Translated by Emily Atwater Babcock and A. C. Krey. New York: Columbia University Press, 1943.
107. William of Tyre. *A History of Deeds Done Beyond the Sea*. Vol. 2. Translated by Emily Atwater Babcock and A. C. Krey. New York: Columbia University Press, 1943.
108. Ye'or, Bat. *The Decline of Eastern Christianity under Islam: From Jihad to Dhimmitude*. Cranbury, NJ: Associated University Presses, 2010.
109. Zenkovsky, Serge A., ed. and trans. *Medieval Russia's Epics, Chronicles, and Tales*. New York: Penguin/Meridian, 1974.

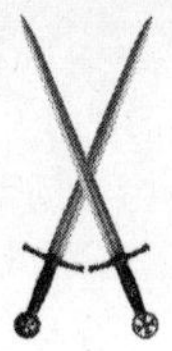

ENDNOTES

Author's Note

1 Vertot, *History of the Knights*, vol. 5, 44.

Chapter 1

1 Wilken, *Land Called Holy*, 88.
2 Ibid, 104.
3 Ibid, 91, 102.
4 Riley-Smith, *Hospitallers*, 3.
5 Wilken, *Land Called Holy*, 92.
6 Bostom, *Legacy of Jihad*, 392; Riley-Smith, *Hospitallers*, 5.
7 Malan, *Short History of the Copts*, 86.
8 Stark, *God's Battalions*, 84.
9 Frankopan, *First Crusade*, 59–60.
10 Ibid, 61; cf. Guibert of Nogent 2008, 33.
11 Ye'or, *Decline of Eastern Christianity*, 292.
12 Rubenstein, *First Crusade*, 56.
13 Addison, *History of the Knights Templars*, 2–3.
14 Nicholson, *Knights Templar*, 18.
15 Addison, *History of the Knights Templars*, 3–4.
16 Forey, *Military Orders*, 6.
17 Barber, *New Knighthood*, 3.
18 Ibid, 6.

Chapter 2

1 Barber, *The Templars*, 29.
2 Campbell, *Knights Templars*, 21.
3 Some other sources push the date of the Templars' founding to January 1120, at the Council of Nablus.

4 Read, *The Templars*, 92.
5 Seward, *Monks of War*, 36.
6 Barber, *The Templars*, 29–30.
7 Nicholson, *Knights Templar*, 24.
8 Barber, *The Templars*, 25–26; cf. William of Tyre, *A History of Deeds*, vol. 1, 524–527.
9 Read, *The Templars*, 92.
10 Alfred, *Encyclopedia of the Crusades*, 41.
11 Knowles, *Christian Monasticism*, 77–78.
12 Barber, *New Knighthood*, 13; cf. Read, *The Templars*, 101.
13 Campbell, *Knights Templars*, 29–30.
14 Bernard of Clairvaux, *In Praise*, 11.

Chapter 3

1 Addison, *History of the Knights Templars*, 5.
2 Campbell, *Knights Templars*, 29.
3 Ibid, 29.
4 Bernard of Clairvaux, *In Praise*, 19.
5 William of Tyre, *A History of Deeds*, vol. 1, 522; vol. 2, 29.
6 King, *Knights Hospitallers*, 2.
7 Ibid, 2.
8 Ibid, 2–3.
9 Forey, *Military Orders*, 143.
10 Barber, *New Knighthood*, 260.
11 Barber, *New Knighthood*, 261.
12 O'Callaghan, *Reconquest and Crusade*, 48.
13 Maqqari, *History of the Mohammedan Dynasties*, vol. 2, 309.
14 Barber, *The Templars*, 161.
15 Ibid, 162.
16 Seward, *Monks of War*, 143.
17 Barber, *New Knighthood*, 32.
18 Forey, *Military Orders*, 23; cf. Barber, *The Templars*, 94.
19 Barber, *The Templars*, 95; cf. Barber, *New Knighthood*, 24.
20 Nicholson, *Knights Templar*, 94.
21 William of Tyre, *A History of Deeds*, vol. 1, 526.
22 Addison, *History of the Knights Templars*, 98.
23 Forey, *Military Orders*, 142.
24 Addison, *History of the Knights Templars*, 27.
25 Forey, *Military Orders*, 6.
26 Addison, *History of the Knights Templars*, 11.
27 Campbell, *Knights Templars*, 22.
28 Peter, "The Founding of the Templars."

Chapter 4

1 Barber, *New Knighthood*, 41.
2 Nicholson, *Knights Templar*, 36; cf. Barber, *New Knighthood*, 61.
3 Ibid, 37.
4 Hugh, "Letter to the Knights of Christ."
5 Ibid.
6 Ibid.
7 Ibid.
8 Ibid; cf. Barber, *The Templars*, 54–59.
9 Burgess, *Song of Roland*, 89.
10 Peter, "The Founding of the Templars."
11 Hugh, "Letter to the Knights of Christ"; cf. Barber, *The Templars*, 54–59.

Chapter 5

1 Bernard of Clairvaux, *In Praise*, 33.
2 Ibid, 33–34.
3 Jacques de Vitry, "Sermons to a Military Order."
4 Ibid.
5 Bernard of Clairvaux, *In Praise*, 35.
6 Ibid, 39.
7 Ibid, 37.
8 Ibid, 46–47; Forey, *Military Orders*, 195.
9 Ibid, 38.
10 Bernard of Clairvaux, *In Praise*, 39.
11 William of Tyre, *A History of Deeds*, vol. 1, 444.
12 Bernard of Clairvaux, *In Praise*, 40.
13 Ibid, 40.
14 Ibid, 40–41.
15 Ibid, 49–50.
16 Ibid, 45.
17 Ibid, 45–46.
18 Ibid, 47–48.
19 Ibid, 48.

Chapter 6

1 Read, *The Templars*, 97.
2 Barber, *New Knighthood*, 182.
3 Upton-Ward, *Rule of the Templars*, 19.
4 Campbell, *Knights Templars*, 56–57.
5 Walsh, *Warriors of the Lord*, 164.
6 Upton-Ward, *Rule of the Templars*, 27.
7 Ibid, 26.
8 Ibid, 172.

9 Ibid, 31.
10 Ibid, 31.
11 Ibid, 83; Campbell, *Knights Templars*, 64.
12 Ibid, 36.
13 Read, *The Templars*, 97.
14 Upton-Ward, *Rule of the Templars*, 36.
15 Ibid, 74, 120.
16 Nicholson, *Knights Templar*, 140.
17 Campbell, *Knights Templars*, 64.
18 Walsh, *Warriors of the Lord*, 157.
19 Barber, "Supplying the Crusader States," 317–318.
20 Barber, *New Knighthood*, 191.
21 Ibid, 18.
22 Ibid, 185–186.
23 Upton-Ward, *Rule of the Templars*, 59.
24 Addison, *History of the Knights Templars*, 50.
25 Barber, *New Knighthood*, 193.
26 Upton-Ward, *Rule of the Templars*, 60.
27 Barber, *New Knighthood*, 193.
28 Upton-Ward, *Rule of the Templars*, 24–25.
29 Read, *The Templars*, 103; Nicholson, *Knights Templar*, 124.
30 Forey, *Military Orders*, 203.
31 Upton-Ward, *Rule of the Templars*, 23, 90, 113; Forey, *Military Orders*, 136.
32 Forey, *Military Orders*, 137; Read, *The Templars*, 135.
33 Barber, *New Knighthood*, 192; Read, *The Templars*, 104.
34 Upton-Ward, *Rule of the Templars*, 170.
35 Read, *The Templars*, 134.
36 Barber, *New Knighthood*, 212.
37 Barber, *The Templars*, 28.

Chapter 7

1 Hillenbrand, *The Crusades*, 111; William of Tyre, *A History of Deeds*, vol. 2, 85, 158.
2 Gabrieli, *Arab Historians*, 49–50.
3 William of Tyre, *A History of Deeds*, vol. 2, 143.
4 Michaud, *History of the Crusades*, 243.
5 Ibid, 243.
6 Bostom, *Legacy of Jihad*, 607.
7 Matthew of Edessa, *Armenia and the Crusades*, 44
8 Michaud, *History of the Crusades*, 243; Hillenbrand, *The Crusades*, 112.
9 William of Tyre, *A History of Deeds*, vol. 2, 163–64.
10 Ibid, vol. 2, 164.
11 Michaud, *History of the Crusades*, 252–253.
12 Jacob, "Chevalier Mult Estes Guariz," 125.

13 Michaud, *History of the Crusades*, 255.
14 Ibid, 259.
15 Addison, *History of the Knights Templars*, 38.
16 William of Tyre, *A History of Deeds*, vol. 2, 171.
17 Michaud, *History of the Crusades*, 262.
18 William of Tyre, *A History of Deeds*, vol. 2, 175.
19 Michaud, *History of the Crusades*, 263.
20 William of Tyre, *A History of Deeds*, vol. 2, 176.
21 Michaud, *History of the Crusades*, 266.
22 Ibid, 266.

Chapter 8

1 William of Tyre, *A History of Deeds*, vol. 2, 176–177.
2 Barber, *New Knighthood*, 67.
3 Addison, *History of the Knights Templars*, 39.
4 Ibid, 73.
5 Campbell, *Knights Templars*, 47.
6 Michaud, *History of the Crusades*, 266.
7 Barber, *New Knighthood*, 67.
8 Campbell, *Knights Templars*, 47.
9 Michaud, *History of the Crusades*, 266–267.
10 Barber, *New Knighthood*, 69.
11 Campbell, *Knights Templars*, 50.
12 Addison, *History of the Knights Templars*, 40–41.
13 Barber, *New Knighthood*, 69; Campbell, *Knights Templars*, 50.
14 William of Tyre, *A History of Deeds*, vol. 2, 193.
15 Barber, *New Knighthood*, 70.
16 Addison, *History of the Knights Templars*, 43–44.
17 Ibid, 44.
18 Upton-Ward, *Rule of the Templars*, 187.

Chapter 9

1 Gabrieli, *Arab Historians*, 18.
2 Rubenstein, *First Crusade*, 157–158.
3 Hillenbrand, *The Crusades*, 123.
4 Gabrieli, *Arab Historians*, 70–71.
5 Mourad and Lindsay, *Intensification and Reorientation*, 151.
6 Ibid, 163.
7 Ibid, 155.
8 William of Tyre, *A History of Deeds*, vol. 2, 146.
9 Ibid, vol. 2, 199.
10 Addison, *History of the Knights Templars*, 52.
11 William of Tyre, *A History of Deeds*, vol. 2, 210.

12 Addison, *History of the Knights Templars*, 46.
13 Ibid, 47.
14 Campbell, *Knights Templars*, 71; Addison, *History of the Knights Templars*, 53.
15 Addison, *History of the Knights Templars*, 47.
16 Ibid, 53.
17 Barber, *New Knighthood*, 88.
18 Ibid, 89.
19 Sweetenham, *Robert the Monk's*, 204, 209.
20 William of Tyre, *A History of Deeds*, vol. 2, 202–203.
21 Barber, *New Knighthood*, 73.
22 William of Tyre, *A History of Deeds*, vol. 2, 203.

Chapter 10

1 William of Tyre, *A History of Deeds*, vol. 2, 220.
2 Ibid, vol. 2, 220.
3 Michaud, *History of the Crusades*, 285.
4 William of Tyre, *A History of Deeds*, vol. 2, 223.
5 Ibid, vol. 2, 221, 223.
6 Ibid, vol. 2, 220.
7 Campbell, *Knights Templars*, 53.
8 Manning, "Siege of Ascalon"; cf. William of Tyre, *A History of Deeds*, vol. 2, 227–228.
9 William of Tyre, *A History of Deeds*, vol. 2, 227.
10 Ibid, vol. 2, 227.
11 Nicholson, *Knights Templar*, 75.
12 William of Tyre, *A History of Deeds*, vol. 2, 227.
13 Ibid, vol. 2, 232.
14 Ibid, vol. 2, 227–228.
15 Manning, "Siege of Ascalon."
16 William of Tyre, *A History of Deeds*, vol. 2, 229–230.
17 Ibid, vol. 2, 236.

Chapter 11

1 Seward, *Monks of War*, 47–48; cf. William of Tyre, *A History of Deeds*, vol. 2, 251. There appears to be some confusion on whether Nasr murdered the caliph, or whether Nasr's father, who had used his son to get close to the caliph, murdered him. That is William's rendering.
2 William of Tyre, *A History of Deeds*, vol. 2, 253.
3 Barber, *New Knighthood*, 76.
4 Addison, *History of the Knights Templars*, 74.
5 William of Tyre, *A History of Deeds*, vol. 2, 391, 77.
6 Komroff, *Travels of Marco Polo*, 53.
7 Ibid, 54.

8 William of Tyre, *A History of Deeds*, vol. 2, 392.
9 Addison, *History of the Knights Templars*, 74.
10 Peters, *Christian Society*, 91–92.
11 Barber, *The Templars*, 75–76; William of Tyre, *A History of Deeds*, vol. 2, 393.
12 Barber, *The Templars*, 77.
13 William of Tyre, *A History of Deeds*, vol. 2, 391–392.

Chapter 12

1 Abu Ja'far Muhammad at-Tabari, *Jami' al-Bayan 'an ta'wil ayi'l-Qur'an al-Ma'ruf: Tafsir at-Tabari* (Beirut: Dar Ihya' at-Turath al-'Arabi, 2001), vol. 3, 267, author's translation.
2 Ibrahim, *Al Qaeda Reader*, 73; cf. 'Imad ad-Din Isma'il Ibn Kathir, *Tafsir al-Qur'an al-Karim* (Beirut: Dar al-Kutub al-'Ilmiya, 2001), vol. 1, 350, author's translation.
3 "Hadith 4:271."
4 Guillaume, *Life of Muhammad*, 367–8; Makarem, *Al Taqiyya fil Islam*, 32–33.
5 Fernandez-Morera, *Myth of the Andalusian Paradise*, 55.
6 Stewart, "Dissimulation," 482.
7 Stewart, "Dissimulation," 445; Bertrand, *History of Spain*, 154.
8 Allen, *The Crusades*, 339.
9 Stewart, "Dissimulation," 445.
10 William of Tyre, *A History of Deeds*, vol. 1, 494–495.
11 Lewis, 1967, *The Assassins*, 25.
12 The Templar of Tyre offers several examples; see Crawford, *Templar of Tyre*, 63–68 and Hillenbrand, *The Crusades*, 515.
13 Barber, *The Templars*, 76; William of Tyre, *A History of Deeds*, vol. 2, 393.
14 William of Tyre, *A History of Deeds*, vol. 2, 393.
15 Ibid, vol. 2,394.
16 Riley-Smith, *A History of the Order*, 127–128.
17 Walsh, *Warriors of the Lord*, 152.

Chapter 13

1 Wheatcroft, *Infidels*, 157.
2 Einhard, *Two Lives*, 19.
3 Shirley, *Crusader Syria*, 37.
4 Ye'or, *Decline of Eastern Christianity*, 292.
5 Rubenstein, *First Crusade*, 69.
6 William of Tyre, *A History of Deeds*, vol. 2, 243.
7 Ibid, vol. 2, 243.
8 Ibid, vol. 2, 243–245.
9 Rubenstein, *First Crusade*, 56.
10 William of Tyre, *A History of Deeds*, vol. 2, 245.
11 Ibid, vol. 2, 245.
12 Ibid, vol. 2, 245.

13 Riley-Smith, *Hospitallers*, 21.
14 William of Tyre, *A History of Deeds*, vol. 2, 335.
15 King, *Knights Hospitallers*, 20.
16 Riley-Smith, *Hospitallers*, 21.

Chapter 14

1 Riley-Smith, *Hospitallers*,19, 21.
2 Ibid, 25.
3 King, *Knights Hospitallers*, 157.
4 Ibid, 24.
5 Ibid, 33–34.
6 Nicholson, *Knights Hospitaller*, 13.
7 Riley-Smith, *Hospitallers*, 37.
8 King, *Knights Hospitallers*, 34; Nicholson, *Knights Hospitaller*, 10.
9 Nicholson, *Knights Hospitallers*, 21.
10 Ibid, 20.
11 King, *Knights Hospitallers*, 51; cf. William of Tyre, *A History of Deeds*, vol. 2, 229.
12 King, *Knights Hospitallers*, 60.
13 Ibid, 67.
14 Ibid, 67.
15 Ibid, 60.
16 Ibid, 69.
17 Drane, *Knights of St. John, 2–3.*
18 King, *Knights Hospitallers*, 154.
19 Riley-Smith, *Hospitallers*, 29.
20 Seward, *Monks of War*, 37.

Chapter 15

1 William of Tyre, *A History of Deeds*, vol. 2, 306.
2 Ibid, vol. 2, 306–307.
3 Barber, *The Templars*, 99.
4 William of Tyre, *A History of Deeds*, vol. 2, 312.
5 Nicholson, *Knights Hospitaller*, 21.
6 Nicholson, *Knights Templar*, 65.
7 William of Tyre, *A History of Deeds*, vol. 2, 357.
8 Ibid, vol. 2, 303.
9 Gabrieli, *Arab Historians*, 1993, 90, 99–100.
10 Hillenbrand, *The Crusades*, 182.
11 Guindy, *A Sword Over the Nile*, 127, 131, 141, and 142.
12 Gabrieli, *Arab Historians*, 101.
13 Nicholson, *Chronicle of the Third Crusade*, 27.
14 Addison, *History of the Knights Templars*, 62.
15 Campbell, *Knights Templars*, 78.

[16] Addison, *History of the Knights Templars*, 63.
[17] William of Tyre, *A History of Deeds*, vol. 2, 377.
[18] Campbell, *Knights Templars*, 78.
[19] William of Tyre, *A History of Deeds*, vol. 2, 443.

Chapter 16

[1] William of Tyre, *A History of Deeds*, vol. 2, 398.
[2] Hillenbrand, *The Crusades*, 295.
[3] William of Tyre, *A History of Deeds*, vol. 2, 426.
[4] Welsh, "A Day of Terrible Slaughter," 30.
[5] Ibid, 30.
[6] William of Tyre, *A History of Deeds*, vol. 2, 427.
[7] Ibid, vol. 2, 428–429.
[8] Ibid, vol. 2, 429.
[9] Ibid, vol. 2, 430.
[10] Welsh, "A Day of Terrible Slaughter," 28.
[11] William of Tyre, *A History of Deeds*, vol. 2, 429.
[12] Ibid, vol. 2, 430.
[13] Ibid, vol. 2, 429–430.
[14] Ibid, vol. 2, 430.
[15] Ibid, vol. 2, 430.
[16] Welsh, "A Day of Terrible Slaughter," 35.
[17] William of Tyre, *A History of Deeds*, vol. 2, 430.
[18] Hillenbrand, *The Crusades*, 446.
[19] William of Tyre, *A History of Deeds*, vol. 2, 431.
[20] Welsh, "A Day of Terrible Slaughter," 35.
[21] Addison, *History of the Knights Templars*, 76.
[22] William of Tyre, *A History of Deeds*, vol. 2, 431.
[23] Ibid, vol. 2, 434.
[24] King, *Knights Hospitallers*, 107.
[25] Campbell, *Knights Templars*, 81–82.

Chapter 17

[1] Barber, *The Templars*, 79.
[2] Ibid, 79–80.
[3] Michaud, *History of the Crusades*, 306.
[4] Addison, *History of the Knights Templars*, 77.
[5] Gabrieli, *Arab Historians*, 119.
[6] Addison, *History of the Knights Templars*, 119.
[7] Seward, *Monks of War*, 51.
[8] Hillenbrand, *The Crusades*, 342.
[9] King, *Knights Hospitallers*, 120.
[10] Read, *The Templars*, 157–158.

11 Seward, *Monks of War*, 53.
12 Michaud, *History of the Crusades*, 306.
13 King, *Knights Hospitallers*, 121.
14 Walsh, *Warriors of the Lord*, 95.
15 Gabrieli, *Arab Historians*, 118.
16 Ibid, 117.

Chapter 18

1 Barber, *New Knighthood*, 181.
2 Nicholson, *Chronicle of the Third Crusade*, 25–26.
3 Ibid, 26.
4 *The Battle of Jacob's Ford*, Northumberland.
5 Addison, *History of the Knights Templars*, 77; Barber, *New Knighthood*, 86.
6 Nicholson, *Knights Templar*, 152.
7 Addison, *History of the Knights Templars*, 78.
8 Barber, *The Templars*, 81.

Chapter 19

1 Nicholson, *Chronicle of the Third Crusade*, 26.
2 Barber, *New Knighthood*, 112.
3 Gabrieli, *Arab Historians*, 120.
4 Nicolle, *Knights Hospitaller*, 44; Seward, *Monks of War*, 53.
5 Chapter 5 of my *Sword and Scimitar*, which is devoted to this battle and its significance, quotes liberally from primary sources and offers a close reconstruction of this decisive military encounter.
6 Campbell, *Knights Templars*, 104.
7 Addison, *History of the Knights Templars*, 122–123.
8 Fuller, *Military History*, 426.
9 Gabrieli, *Arab Historians*, 132.
10 Gabrieli, *Arab Historians*, 22.
11 Addison, *History of the Knights Templars*, 123–124.
12 King, *Knights Hospitallers*, 128.
13 Gabrieli, *Arab Historians*, 137.
14 Addison, *History of the Knights Templars*, 129; cf. Barber, *New Knighthood*, 115.
15 Gabrieli, *Arab Historians*, 135–136.
16 Ibid, 134.
17 Ibid, 123.
18 Barber, *New Knighthood*, 113.
19 Ibid, 113.
20 Ibid, 113.

Chapter 20

1 Read, *The Templars*, 160; Nicholson, *Knights Templar*, 153.

2 Addison, *History of the Knights Templars*, 127.
3 Nicholson, *Chronicle of the Third Crusade*, 34.
4 Hamblin, "Muslim Perspectives"; cf. Gabrieli, *Arab Historians*, 124.
5 Hillenbrand, *The Crusades*, 335.
6 Gabrieli, *Arab Historians*, 138–139; cf. Mourad and Lindsay, *Intensification and Reorientation*, 95–96.
7 Nicholson, *Knights Templar*, 153.
8 Din ibn Shaddad, *Rare and Excellent*, 75.
9 Addison, *History of the Knights Templars*, 129–130.
10 Addison, *History of the Knights Templars*, 129.
11 Gabrieli, *Arab Historians*, 144.
12 Addison, *History of the Knights Templars*, 131.
13 Hillenbrand, *The Crusades*, 191.
14 Hamblin, "Muslim Perspectives"; cf. Hillenbrand, *The Crusades*, 305.
15 Nicholson, *Chronicle of the Third Crusade*, 39.
16 Guindy, *A Sword Over the Nile*, 127, 131, 141, and 142.
17 Campbell, *Knights Templars*, 106.
18 Gabrieli, *Arab Historians*, 163–164.

Chapter 21

1 Seward, *Monks of War*, 55.
2 Riley-Smith, *A History of the Order*, 110.
3 Addison, *History of the Knights Templars*, 136–137; cf. Barber, *New Knighthood*, 116.
4 Nicholson, *Knights Hospitaller*, 24.
5 Nicholson, *Knights Hospitaller*, 24–25.
6 Riley Smith, *A History of the Order*, 110; Seward, *Monks of War*, 55.
7 Riley-Smith, *A History of the Order*, 111.
8 Ibid, 112, 122.
9 Alfred, *Encyclopedia of the Crusades*, 73.
10 Addison, *History of the Knights Templars*, 137.
11 Hillenbrand, *The Crusades*, 380.
12 Addison, *History of the Knights Templars*, 111.
13 Addison, *History of the Knights Templars*, 138–139.
14 King, *Knights Hospitallers*, 139.
15 Nicholson, *Chronicle of the Third Crusade*, 79.
16 Ibid, 78–79.

Chapter 22

1 Nicholson, *Chronicle of the Third Crusade*, 68.
2 Addison, *History of the Knights Templars*, 142.
3 Nicholson, *Chronicle of the Third Crusade*, 83.
4 Richards, *Chronicle of Ibn al-Athir*, part 2, 387.
5 Nicholson, *Knights Templar*, 211.

6 Nicholson, *Chronicle of the Third Crusade*, 209.
7 Richards, *Chronicle of Ibn al-Athir*, part 2, 390.
8 Nicholson, *Chronicle of the Third Crusade*, 240.
9 Barber, *New Knighthood*, 119; Addison, *History of the Knights Templars*, 149.
10 Nicholson, *Chronicle of the Third Crusade*, 244; Richards, *Chronicle of Ibn al-Athir*, part 2, 390.
11 Nicholson, *Chronicle of the Third Crusade*, 244.
12 Din ibn Shaddad, *Rare and Excellent*, 170–171.
13 Nicholson, *Chronicle of the Third Crusade*, 250.
14 Ibid, 248.
15 Ibid, 256.
16 Ibid, 249.
17 Ibid, 251.
18 Ibid, 251–252.
19 Ibid, 252.
20 Ibid, 252–253.
21 Ibid, 253.
22 Ibid, 254.
23 Ibid, 254.
24 Ibid, 255.
25 Richards, *Chronicle of Ibn al-Athir*, part 2, 391.
26 King, *Knights Hospitallers*, 152.
27 Nicholson, *Chronicle of the Third Crusade*, 258.
28 Ibid, 258.
29 Ibid, 258.
30 Richards, *Chronicle of Ibn al-Athir*, part 2, 391.

Chapter 23

1 Nicholson, *Chronicle of the Third Crusade*, 268.
2 Ibid, 268.
3 Ibid, 269.
4 Ibid, 269.
5 Ibid, 270.
6 Ibid, 271.
7 Ibid, 271.
8 Din ibn Shaddad, *Rare and Excellent*, 34; Richards, *Chronicle of Ibn al-Athir*, part 2, 387.
9 Nicholson, *Chronicle of the Third Crusade*, 279.
10 Ibid, 280.
11 Ibid, 336.
12 Riley-Smith, *A History of the Order*, 115.
13 Nicholson, *Chronicle of the Third Crusade*, 371.
14 Gabrieli, *Arab Historians*, xvi.

15 Addison, *History of the Knights Templars*, 146.
16 Riley-Smith, *A History of the Order*, 113–119.
17 Nicholson, *Knights Hospitaller*, 23, 25.
18 Ibid, 25.
19 Bradford, *Knights of the Order*, 42.
20 Addison, *History of the Knights Templars*, 151.

Chapter 24

1 Barber, *The Templars*, 100.
2 Peters, *Christian Society*, 57.
3 Barber, *The Templars*, 83; cf. Peters, *Christian Society*, 58.
4 Peters, *Christian Society*, 64.
5 Campbell, *Knights Templars*, 136.
6 Peters, *Christian Society*, 80.
7 Ibid, 79–80.
8 Ibid, 80.
9 Ibid, 66–67.
10 Ibid, 70.
11 Ibid, 70–71.
12 Ibid, 72.
13 Ibid, 73.
14 Campbell, *Knights Templars*, 136.
15 Peters, *Christian Society*, 75.

Chapter 25

1 Campbell, *Knights Templars*, 134–135; cf. Peters, *Christian Society*, 86.
2 Campbell, *Knights Templars*, 134.
3 Ibid, 135.
4 Peters, *Christian Society*, 81.
5 Ibid, 82.
6 Ibid, 82.
7 Ibid, 83.
8 Rega, *St. Francis of Assisi*, 53–54.
9 Ibid, 63.
10 Ibid, 34, 60.
11 Ibid, 65–69.
12 Ibid, 70.
13 Read, *The Templars*, 211.
14 Rega, *St. Francis of Assisi*, 70.

Chapter 26

1 Peters, *Christian Society*, 94.
2 Ibid, 88.

3 Barber, *New Knighthood*, 129.
4 Nicholson, *Knights Hospitaller*, 28.
5 Peters, *Christian Society*, 106.
6 Barber, *New Knighthood*, 129; cf. Peters, *Christian Society*, 106.
7 Peters, *Christian Society*, 141.
8 Ibid, 115.
9 Ibid, 127.
10 Ibid, 128.
11 Ibid, 128–129.
12 Addison, *History of the Knights Templars*, 157–58; cf. Peters, *Christian Society*, 144.
13 Peters, *Christian Society*, 131.
14 Addison, *History of the Knights Templars*, 158.
15 Madden, *New Concise History*, 155.

Chapter 27

1 Madden, *New Concise History*, 162.
2 Gabrieli, *Arab Historians*, 271.
3 Gabrieli, *Arab Historians*, 270.
4 Shirley, *Crusader Syria*, 37.
5 Ibid, 13.
6 Campbell, *Knights Templars*, 161.
7 Addison, *History of the Knights Templars*, 160–161.
8 Ibid, 161.
9 Riley-Smith, *A History of the Order*, 146.
10 Barber, *The Templars*, 86.
11 Ibid, 84.
12 Ibid, 86.
13 Ibid, 86.
14 Ibid, 87.
15 Ibid, 88.
16 Addison, *History of the Knights Templars*, 166.
17 Barber, *The Templars*, 91–92.
18 Barber, *New Knighthood*, 167.

Chapter 28

1 Shirley, *Crusader Syria*, 64.
2 Ibid, 64.
3 Ibid, 64.
4 Maqrizi, "Medieval Sourcebook."
5 Campbell, *Knights Templars*, 166.
6 Perry, *Saint Louis*, 134.
7 Shirley, *Crusader Syria*, 65.
8 Barber, *New Knighthood*, 230.

9 Shirley, *Crusader Syria*, 132; cf. Campbell, *Knights Templars*, 166.
10 Maqrizi, "Medieval Sourcebook."
11 Hillenbrand, *The Crusades*, 222.
12 Hillenbrand, *The Crusades*, 306.
13 Addison, *History of the Knights Templars*, 167.
14 Ibid, 167–168.
15 Ibid, 168.
16 Ibid, 168–169.
17 Maqrizi, "Medieval Sourcebook."
18 Addison, *History of the Knights Templars*, 169; cf. Shirley, *Crusader Syria*, 65.
19 Addison, *History of the Knights Templars*, 169–170.
20 Barber, *New Knighthood, 149.*
21 Addison, *History of the Knights Templars*, 172.
22 Ibid, 174.
23 Maqrizi, "Medieval Sourcebook."

Chapter 29

1 Shirley, *Crusader Syria*, 85.
2 Ibid, 86.
3 Maqrizi, "Medieval Sourcebook."
4 Perry, *Saint Louis*, 168; cf. Jackson, *Seventh Crusade*, 89.
5 Jackson, *Seventh Crusade, 88.*
6 Shirley, *Crusader Syria*, 87.
7 Jackson, *Seventh Crusade*, 91.
8 Ibid, 131.
9 Ibid, 136.
10 Jordan, *Apple of His Eye*, 29.
11 Guindy, *A Sword Over the Nile,* 154–155.
12 Joinville and Villehardouin, *Chronicles*, 157.
13 Shirley, *Crusader Syria*, 137.
14 Ibid, 91.
15 Ibid, 93–94.
16 Ibid, 94.
17 Nicholson, *Knights Hospitaller*, 28; cf. Barber, *New Knighthood*, 150.
18 Nicholson, *Knights Hospitaller*, 29.
19 Shirley, *Crusader Syria*, 96.
20 Barber, *New Knighthood*, 150.
21 Perry, *Saint Louis*, 178.
22 Shirley, *Crusader Syria*, 95.
23 Ibid, 96.
24 Ibid, 96.
25 Ibid, 97.
26 Ibid, 97.

[27] Barber, *New Knighthood*, 150; Addison, *History of the Knights Templars*, 177.

Chapter 30

[1] Shirley, *Crusader Syria*, 98.
[2] Ibid, 99–100.
[3] Jackson, *Seventh Crusade*, 101.
[4] Shirley, *Crusader Syria*, 102.
[5] Ibid, 102.
[6] Jackson, *Seventh Crusade*, 101.
[7] Barber, *New Knighthood*, 151; cf. Joinville and Villehardouin, *Chronicles*, 175.
[8] Jackson, *Seventh Crusade*, 160.
[9] Campbell, *Knights Templars*, 188.
[10] Jackson, *Seventh Crusade*, 102.
[11] Joinville and Villehardouin, *Chronicles*, 188.
[12] Jackson, *Seventh Crusade*, 101–102.
[13] Ibid, 112.
[14] Shirley, *Crusader Syria*, 107.
[15] Ibid, 108.
[16] Ibid, 107.
[17] Joinville and Villehardouin, *Chronicles*, 214.
[18] Ibid, 216.
[19] Ibid, 215–217.

Chapter 31

[1] Zenkovsky, *Medieval Russia's Epics*, 6, 201, 247.
[2] Gibbon, *Decline and Fall*, vol. 2, 484.
[3] Crowley, *Accursed Tower*, 42.
[4] Shirley, *Crusader Syria*, 118.
[5] Barber, *New Knighthood*, 157.
[6] Barber, *The Templars*, 101.
[7] Ibid, 103.
[8] Ibid, 105.
[9] Ibid, 104–105.
[10] Shirley, *Crusader Syria*, 118–119.
[11] Ibid, 119.
[12] Barber, *New Knighthood*, 158.
[13] Hillenbrand, *The Crusades*, 227.
[14] Ibid, 231.
[15] Ibid, 230.
[16] Sahih Bukhari 52:269; Sahih Bukhari 8:78:618–619.
[17] See Adel Guindy's highly detailed *A Sword Over the Nile*, 179–200.
[18] Hillenbrand, *The Crusades*, 516.

Chapter 32

1 Allen, *The Crusades*, 358–359
2 Nicolle, *Knights Hospitaller*, 22
3 Nicholson, trans., "Lament for the Templars."
4 Ibid
5 Seward, *Monks of War*, 80.
6 Crawford, *Templar of Tyre*, 51.
7 Hillenbrand, *The Crusades*, 231.
8 Addison, *History of the Knights Templars*, 182.
9 Crawford, *Templar of Tyre*, 52–53; cf. Riley-Smith, *A History of the Order*, 126.
10 Crawford, *Templar of Tyre*, 55.
11 Ibid, 59.
12 Gabrieli, *Arab Historians,* 310.
13 Madden, *New Concise History*, 181.
14 Crawford, *Templar of Tyre*, 59; Seward, *Monks of War*, 80–81.
15 Gabrieli, *Arab Historians,* 311; cf. Hillenbrand, *The Crusades*, 320.
16 Nicholson, *Knights Hospitaller*, 36.
17 Bradford, *Knights of the Order*, 47.
18 Riley-Smith, *A History of the Order*, 192; Seward, *Monks of War*, 81.
19 Seward, *Monks of War*, 81.
20 Crawford, *Templar of Tyre*, 68.
21 Stark, *God's Battalions*, 234.
22 Gabrieli, *Arab Historians,* 101; Hillenbrand, *The Crusades*, 237.

Chapter 33

1 Crawford, *Templar of Tyre*, 77.
2 Riley-Smith, *A History of the Order*, 141; cf. Gabrieli, *Arab Historians,* 334; Bradford, *Knights of the Order*, 47.
3 Nicholson, *Knights Hospitaller*, 36; Gabrieli, *Arab Historians,* 337.
4 Gabrieli, *Arab Historians,* 342.
5 Daniel, *Islam and the West*, 111–112.
6 Read, *The Templars*, 239.
7 Addison, *History of the Knights Templars*, 185.
8 Gabrieli, *Arab Historians,* 331.
9 Crowley, *Accursed Tower*, 99.
10 Crowley, *Accursed Tower*, 97; Crawford, *Templar of Tyre*, 102.
11 Guindy, *A Sword Over the Nile,* 185–186.
12 Crawford, *Templar of Tyre*, 105.
13 Hillenbrand, *The Crusades*, 238.
14 Crowley, *Accursed Tower*, 109–110.
15 Ibid, 112.
16 Ibid, 109.
17 King, *Knights Hospitallers*, 292; Crawford, *Templar of Tyre*, 103.

18 Addison, *History of the Knights Templars*, 187; Crawford, *Templar of Tyre*, 69.
19 King, *Knights Hospitallers*, 301.
20 Crowley, *Accursed Tower*, 129.
21 Addison, *History of the Knights Templars*, 186.
22 Ibid, 186–187.

Chapter 34

1 Gabrieli, *Arab Historians*, 345; cf. Riley-Smith, *A History of the Order*, 196.
2 Crowley, *Accursed Tower*, 139.
3 Addison, *History of the Knights Templars*, 187; Crowley, *Accursed Tower*, 138.
4 Addison, *History of the Knights Templars*, 188.
5 Crawford, *Templar of Tyre*, 107.
6 Ibid, 107.
7 Ibid, 108.
8 Crowley, *Accursed Tower*, 149.
9 Crawford, *Templar of Tyre*, 108.
10 Crowley, *Accursed Tower*, 150.
11 Addison, *History of the Knights Templars*, 188.
12 Maxwell, *Chronicle of Lanercost*, 79–80. Although the dates appear to be skewed, this chronicle says that Palm Sunday was on April 15.
13 Addison, *History of the Knights Templars*, 188.
14 Crowley, *Accursed Tower*, 160.
15 King, *Knights Hospitallers*, 296.

Chapter 35

1 King, *Knights Hospitallers*, 294.
2 Addison, *History of the Knights Templars*, 188–189.
3 Nicolle, *Knights Hospitaller*, 23; cf. King, *Knights Hospitallers*, 295; Crowley, *Accursed Tower*, 166–68.
4 King, *Knights Hospitallers*, 294; Addison, *History of the Knights Templars*, 189.
5 King, *Knights Hospitallers*, 295.
6 Crowley, *Accursed Tower*, 169.
7 Crawford, *Templar of Tyre*, 110.
8 Crowley, *Accursed Tower*, 172.
9 Ibid, 172.
10 Crawford, *Templar of Tyre*, 110.
11 Ibid, 111.
12 Crowley, *Accursed Tower*, 177.

Chapter 36

1 Crawford, *Templar of Tyre*, 111.
2 Seward, *Monks of War*, 89.
3 Crawford, *Templar of Tyre*, 111.

4 Ibid, 112.
5 King, *Templar of Tyre*, 297.
6 Crawford, *Templar of Tyre*, 112–113.
7 Ibid, 113.
8 Ibid, 116.
9 Crowley, *Accursed Tower*, 182.
10 Ibid, 179.

Chapter 37

1 Crowley, *Accursed Tower*, 184; King, *Knights Hospitallers*, 297.
2 King, *Knights Hospitallers*, 297.
3 Crawford, *Templar of Tyre*, 113–114.
4 Ibid, 116.
5 Crowley, *Accursed Tower*, 187.
6 Crowley, *Accursed Tower*, 187; King, *Knights Hospitallers*, 297–298.
7 Addison, *History of the Knights Templars*, 190; Crawford, *Templar of Tyre*, 114.
8 Crowley, *Accursed Tower*, 190–191.
9 Crawford, *Templar of Tyre*, 117.
10 Ibid, 117.
11 Ibid, 117.
12 Crowley, *Accursed Tower*, 198.
13 Gabrieli, *Arab Historians*, 346.
14 Crawford, *Templar of Tyre*, 119.
15 Ibid, 129.
16 Hillenbrand, *The Crusades*, 240.
17 Crowley, *Accursed Tower*, 196.
18 Hillenbrand, *The Crusades*, 241.
19 Crawford, *Templar of Tyre*, 122.
20 Ibid, 123.
21 King, *Knights Hospitallers*, 301.
22 King, *Knights Hospitallers*, 301–2; Nicholson, *Knights Hospitaller*, 37–38.

Chapter 38

1 Crawford, *Templar of Tyre*, 123.
2 Ibid, 124–127.
3 George-Tvrtković, *A Christian Pilgrim*, 142.
4 Ibid, 138, 156–162.
5 Ibid, 155–168.
6 Ibid, 148–149.
7 Ibid, 140.
8 Ibid, 169.
9 Ibid, 166–167.
10 Ibid, 164.

[11] Ibid, 145.
[12] Barber, *New Knighthood*, 294; Seward, *Monks of War*, 205.

Chapter 39

[1] Barber, *The Templars*, 244.
[2] Addison, *History of the Knights Templars*, 203; Barber, *The Templars*, 273.
[3] Read, *The Templars*, 286.
[4] Barber, *The Templars*, 218.
[5] Addison, *History of the Knights Templars*, 206; cf. Forey, Military Orders, 73.
[6] Forey, *Military Orders*, 335.
[7] Barber, *The Templars*, 264–265.
[8] Addison, *History of the Knights Templars*, 206.
[9] Forey, *Military Orders*, 233–234.
[10] Riley-Smith, *A History of the Order*, 52.
[11] Forey, *Military Orders*, 233.
[12] Barber, *The Templars*, 294.
[13] Read, *The Templars*, 311.
[14] Barber, *New Knighthood*, 227.
[15] Barber, *The Templars*, 257.
[16] Ibid, 251.
[17] Upton-Ward, *Rule of the Templars*, 112.
[18] Ibid, 148.

Chapter 40

[1] Addison, *History of the Knights Templars*, 265.
[2] Forey, *Military Orders*, 232; Barber, *New Knighthood*, 321.
[3] Forey, *Military Orders*, 232; Barber, *New Knighthood*, 315.
[4] Nicholson, *Knights Hospitaller*, 28.
[5] Addison, *History of the Knights Templars*, 204.
[6] Barber, *The Templars*, 248.
[7] Addison, *History of the Knights Templars*, 205.
[8] Seward, *Monks of War*, 212.
[9] Forey, *Military Orders*, 234.
[10] Seward, *Monks of War*, 218.
[11] Nicholson, "Military Orders."
[12] Ibid
[13] Nicholson, *Knights Templar*, 219; cf. Addison, *History of the Knights Templars*, 235.

Chapter 41

[1] Barber, *The Templars*, 289–290.
[2] Ibid, 290.
[3] Ibid, 300.
[4] Ibid, 299.

5 Addison, *History of the Knights Templars*, 240.
6 Crawford, *Templar of Tyre*, 180; Read, *The Templars*, 281.
7 Addison, *History of the Knights Templars*, 241.
8 Ibid, 241.
9 Ibid, 287.
10 Ibid, 242.
11 Forey, *Military Orders*, 228.
12 Barber, *The Templars*, 311.
13 Ibid, 318.
14 Addison, *History of the Knights Templars*, 277–278.
15 Ibid, 278.
16 Seward, *Monks of War*, 219.

Chapter 42

1 Seward, *Monks of War*, 221.
2 Crawford, *Templar of Tyre*, 180.
3 Nicholson, *Knights Templar*, 223.
4 Ibid, 223.
5 Crawford, *Templar of Tyre*, 180–81.
6 Rowton, Erik. "The Last Templar: The Prophetic Final Words of Grand Master Jacques de Molay."
7 Seward, *Monks of War*, 221; Read, *The Templars*, 300.
8 Addison, *History of the Knights Templars*, 50.
9 Read, *The Templars*, 287.
10 Seward, *Monks of War*, 218.
11 Ibid, 212.

Chapter 43

1 Vertot, *History of the Knights*, vol. 2, 6-7.
2 Drane, *Knights of St. John*, 22; cf. Vertot, *History of the Knights*, vol. 2, 8.
3 Vertot, *History of the Knights*, vol. 2, 8
4 Drane, *Knights of St. John*, 22–23.
5 Vertot, *History of the Knights*, vol. 2, 8.
6 Vertot, *History of the Knights*, vol. 2, 52, 41; Crawford, *Templar of Tyre*, 170.
7 Crawford, *Templar of Tyre*, 170.
8 Ibid, 171.
9 Ibid, 170-171.
10 Vertot, *History of the Knights*, vol. 2, 56–58.
11 Ibid, vol. 2, 58.
12 Ibid, vol. 2, 62.
13 Ibid, vol. 2, 62–65.
14 Crawford, *Templar of Tyre*, 172.
15 Vertot, *History of the Knights*, vol. 2, 67.

16 Ibid, vol. 2, 242.
17 Seward, *Monks of War*, 225.

Chapter 44

1 Riley-Smith, *Hospitallers,* 98.
2 Seward, *Monks of War*, 237–238.
3 Crawford, *Templar of Tyre*, 172.
4 Bradford, *Knights of the Order*, 69.
5 Nicholson, *Knights Hospitaller*, 53.
6 Seward, *Monks of War*, 230–231.
7 Drane, *Knights of St. John*, 23–24.
8 Vertot, *History of the Knights*, vol. 2, 108.
9 Ibid, vol. 2, 108–109.
10 Ibid, vol. 2, 117–118.
11 Gibbon, *Decline and Fall*, vol. 2, 488.
12 Seward, *Monks of War*, 223; Bradford, *Knights of the Order*, 90.
13 Vertot, *History of the Knights*, vol. 2, 123.
14 Ibid, vol. 2, 132.
15 Ibid, vol. 2, 145.
16 Bradford, *Knights of the Order*, 71.
17 Vertot, *History of the Knights*, vol. 2, 123.

Chapter 45

1 Vertot, *History of the Knights*, vol. 2, 114.
2 Ibid, vol. 2, 116.
3 Ibid, vol. 2, 117.
4 Ibid, vol. 2, 117–118.
5 Ibid, vol. 2, 118.
6 "Drakones Rhodioi."
7 Vertot, *History of the Knights*, vol. 2, 118.

Chapter 46

1 Vertot, *History of the Knights*, vol. 2, 136.
2 Drane, *Knights of St. John*, 38.
3 Ibid, 38.
4 Ibid, 38.
5 Vertot, *History of the Knights*, vol. 2, 224.
6 Ibid, vol. 2, 197.
7 Ibid, vol. 2, 197.
8 Ibid, vol. 2, 228–229.
9 Ibid, vol. 2, 198.
10 Ibid, vol. 2, 225.
11 Seward, *Monks of War*, 240.

12 Vertot, *History of the Knights*, vol. 2, 226.
13 Ibid, vol. 2, 199.
14 Ibid, vol. 2, 199–200.
15 Ibid, vol. 2, 231.
16 Ibid, vol. 2, 231.
17 Drane, *Knights of St. John*, 47.
18 Ibid, 48.
19 Drane, *Knights of St. John*, 48–49; cf. Vertot, *History of the Knights*, vol. 2, 235.
20 Vertot, *History of the Knights*, vol. 2, 235.
21 Ibid, vol. 2, 171.
22 Ibid, vol. 2, 172.
23 Ibid, vol. 2, 173.
24 Ibid, vol. 2, 172.
25 Ibid, vol. 2, 173.
26 Ibid, vol. 2, 187–188.

Chapter 47

1 Vertot, *History of the Knights*, vol. 2, 236.
2 Ibid, vol. 2, 270.
3 Ibid, vol. 2, 237.
4 Ibid, vol. 2, 238.
5 Ibid, vol. 2, 271–274.
6 Seward, *Monks of War*, 241; the amount of ransom differs according to source.
7 Seward, *Monks of War*, 243; Vertot, *History of the Knights*, vol. 2, 277.
8 Guindy, *A Sword Over the Nile*, 197.
9 Vertot, *History of the Knights*, vol. 2, 281–284.
10 Ibid, 286-287.
11 Seward, 244.
12 Vertot vol. 2, 287-288.

Chapter 48

1 Vertot, *History of the Knights*, vol. 2, 296–301.
2 Drane, *Knights of St. John*, 58.
3 Vann and Kagay, *Hospitaller Piety*, 57–58.
4 Vertot, *History of the Knights*, vol. 2, 299.
5 Barbaro, *Diary of the Siege*, 65–67; Philippides, *Fall of the Byzantine Empire*, 130–131; Melville-Jones, *Siege of Constantinople*, 98–123.
6 Melville-Jones, *Siege of Constantinople*, 123; Philippides, *Fall of the Byzantine Empire*, 131; North, "Account," 235; Lewis, *Islam*, 146.
7 Doukas, *Decline and Fall*, 234–235; Melville-Jones, *Siege of Constantinople*, 103–112; Gibbon, *Decline and Fall*, vol. 2, 552.
8 Melville-Jones, *Siege of Constantinople*, 124; Vertot, *History of the Knights*, vol. 2, 299.

[9] Vann and Kagay, *Hospitaller Piety*, 57–59.
[10] Ibid, 59.
[11] Vertot, *History of the Knights*, vol. 3, 1.
[12] Vann and Kagay, *Hospitaller Piety*, 87–88.
[13] Ibid, 89.
[14] Drane, *Knights of St. John*, 66.
[15] Vertot, *History of the Knights*, vol. 3, 5.
[16] Treptow, *Dracula*, 348.
[17] Crowley, *Empires of the Sea*, 7.
[18] Vann and Kagay, *Hospitaller Piety*, 56.

Chapter 49

[1] Vertot, *History of the Knights*, vol. 3, 7.
[2] Ibid, vol. 3, 21–22; Vann and Kagay, *Hospitaller Piety*, 315.
[3] Vertot, *History of the Knights*, vol. 3, 30.
[4] Ibid, vol. 3, 30–31.
[5] Vann and Kagay, *Hospitaller Piety*, 317.
[6] Ibid, 315–321.
[7] Ibid, 217.
[8] https://italiantribune.com/the-battle-of-otranto-2/
[9] Vann and Kagay, *Hospitaller Piety*, 182.
[10] Ibid, 341–343.
[11] Ibid, 343.
[12] Ibid, 333.
[13] Ibid, 325, 335.
[14] Ibid, 345; Bradford, *Knights of the Order*, 92.
[15] Vann and Kagay, *Hospitaller Piety*, 196.
[16] Ibid, 325.

Chapter 50

[1] Bradford, *Knights of the Order*, 90.
[2] Vann and Kagay, *Hospitaller Piety*, 289.
[3] Ibid, 291.
[4] Drane, *Knights of St. John*, 71; Vertot, *History of the Knights*, vol. 3, 56.
[5] Vann and Kagay, *Hospitaller Piety*, 341.
[6] Ibid, 353.
[7] Ibid, 259.
[8] Ibid, 223; Drane, *Knights of St. John*, 72.
[9] Drane, *Knights of St. John*, 72.
[10] Vann and Kagay, *Hospitaller Piety*, 297.
[11] Ibid, 299.
[12] Ibid, 297.
[13] Ibid, 233.

[14] Ibid, 297.
[15] Vertot, *History of the Knights*, vol. 3, 66–67.
[16] Vann and Kagay, *Hospitaller Piety*, 233.
[17] Ibid, 194.
[18] Ibid, 299.
[19] Vertot, *History of the Knights*, vol. 3, 73.
[20] Drane, *Knights of St. John*, 74.
[21] Vertot, *History of the Knights*, vol. 3, 73.
[22] Vann and Kagay, *Hospitaller Piety*, 249.
[23] Ibid, 301.
[24] Ibid, 251.
[25] Ibid, 123.
[26] Ibid, 301.

Chapter 51

[1] Vann and Kagay, *Hospitaller Piety*, 111.
[2] Vertot, *History of the Knights*, vol. 3, 69–70.
[3] Vann and Kagay, *Hospitaller Piety*, 133.
[4] Ibid, 111.
[5] Vertot, *History of the Knights*, vol. 3, 68.
[6] Vann and Kagay, *Hospitaller Piety*, 238.
[7] Ibid, 135.
[8] Ibid, 293.
[9] Ibid, 243.
[10] Ibid, 245.
[11] Vertot, *History of the Knights*, vol. 3, 77–78.
[12] Vann and Kagay, *Hospitaller Piety*, 261.
[13] Ibid, 261.
[14] Ibid, 301.
[15] Ibid, 263.
[16] Ibid, 301–303.
[17] Ibid, 303.
[18] Ibid, 133.
[19] Ibid, 265.
[20] Ibid, 135–136.
[21] Ibid, 303.
[22] Ibid, 137, 277.
[23] Ibid, 241.
[24] Vertot, *History of the Knights*, vol. 3, 70.
[25] Drane, *Knights of St. John*, 78.
[26] Ibid, 78.
[27] Vertot, *History of the Knights*, vol. 3, 76–77.

Chapter 52

1 Vann and Kagay, *Hospitaller Piety*, 265.
2 Ibid, 309.
3 Drane, *Knights of St. John,* 79; Vann and Kagay, *Hospitaller Piety*, 269.
4 Vann and Kagay, *Hospitaller Piety*, 309.
5 Ibid, 139, 271.
6 Ibid, 309, 269.
7 Ibid, 139.
8 Ibid, 137, 273, 201.
9 Ibid, 139.
10 Vertot, *History of the Knights*, vol. 3, 74–75.
11 Ibid, vol. 3, 75.
12 Ibid, vol. 3, 81–84.
13 Vann and Kagay, *Hospitaller Piety*, 271.
14 Vertot, *History of the Knights*, vol. 3, 81–84.
15 Drane, *Knights of St. John*, iv.
16 Vann and Kagay, *Hospitaller Piety*, 271, 140–141.
17 Drane, *Knights of St. John,* 81; Vann and Kagay, *Hospitaller Piety*, 141, 275.
18 Vertot, *History of the Knights*, vol. 3, 81–84.
19 Vann and Kagay, *Hospitaller Piety, 201.*
20 Ibid, 171.
21 Drane, *Knights of St. John,* 80–81.
22 Vertot, *History of the Knights*, vol. 3, 81–84.

Chapter 53

1 Vertot, *History of the Knights*, vol. 3, 126.
2 Ibid, vol. 3, 130.
3 Ibid, vol. 3, 137, 139.
4 Ibid, vol. 3, 140.
5 Ibid, vol. 3, 153–154.
6 Crowley, *Empires of the Sea*, 9.
7 Drane, *Knights of St. John*, 96.
8 Vertot, *History of the Knights*, vol. 3, 165.
9 Crowley, *Empires of the Sea*, 10.
10 Vertot, *History of the Knights*, vol. 3, 230.
11 Ibid, vol. 3, 181.
12 Ibid, vol. 3, 177–178.

Chapter 54

1 Vertot, *History of the Knights*, vol. 3, 198.
2 Ibid, vol. 3, 208.
3 Ibid, vol. 3, 200, 208.
4 Ibid, vol. 3, 209; Seward, *Monks of War*, 261.

5 Vertot, *History of the Knights*, vol. 3, 213–215.
6 Seward, *Monks of War*, 261.
7 Vertot, *History of the Knights*, vol. 3, 225.
8 Ibid, vol. 3, 224.
9 Ibid, vol. 3, 217.
10 Ibid, vol. 3, 236.

Chapter 55

1 Vertot, *History of the Knights*, vol. 3, 236.
2 Ibid. vol. 3, 238.
3 Ibid. vol. 3, 242.
4 Ibid. vol. 3, 229.
5 Ibid. vol. 3, 240.
6 Ibid. vol. 3, 240.
7 Ibid. vol. 3, 242.
8 Ibid. vol. 3, 262, 246.
9 Bradford, *Knights of the Order*, 119.
10 Seward, *Monks of War*, 265.

Chapter 56

1 Vertot, *History of the Knights*, vol. 3, 253–254, 261, 266.
2 Nicholson, *Knights Hospitaller*, 67.
3 Bradford, *Knights of the Order*, 197.
4 Ibid, 124.
5 Davis, *Christian Slaves*, 8.
6 Crowley, *Empires of the Sea*, 29.
7 Ibid, 29; Heers, *Barbary Corsairs*, 83.
8 Davis, *Christian Slaves*, 24.
9 Crowley, *Empires of the Sea*, 73.
10 Crowley, *Accursed Tower*, 31.
11 Crowley, *Empires of the Sea*, 70.
12 Foxe, *Universal History*, 250–251; Playfair, *Scourge of Christendom*, 12; Davis, *Christian Slaves*, 125.

Chapter 57

1 Vertot, *History of the Knights*, vol. 3, 279; Vertot, *History of the Knights*, vol. 4, 19.
2 Bradford, *Knights of the Order*, 130.
3 Vertot, *History of the Knights*, vol. 4, 62–72.
4 Ibid, vol. 4, 19.
5 Ibid, vol. 4, 46–50.
6 Ibid, vol. 4, 54.
7 Ibid, vol. 4, 55–56.
8 Ibid, vol. 4, 87–89.

[9] Ibid, vol. 4, 91–96.
[10] Lane-Poole, *Story of the Barbary Corsairs*, 122.
[11] Vertot, *History of the Knights*, vol. 4, 97.
[12] Ibid, vol. 4, 126.

Chapter 58

[1] Vertot, *History of the Knights*, vol. 4, 127.
[2] Ibid, vol. 4, 130–132.
[3] Ibid, vol. 4, 130–131.
[4] Ibid, vol. 4, 143–148.
[5] Ibid, vol. 4, 155.
[6] Ibid, vol. 4, 155–157.
[7] Ibid, vol. 4, 232.
[8] Ibid, vol. 4, 80–81.
[9] Ibid, vol. 4, 164.
[10] Ibid, vol. 4, 160–175.

Chapter 59

[1] Vertot, *History of the Knights*, vol. 4, 241.
[2] Ibid, vol. 4, 246.
[3] Ibid, vol. 4, 288–291.
[4] Ibid, vol. 4, 291–293.
[5] Bradford, *Knights of the Order*, 141.
[6] Crowley, *Empires of the Sea*, 91.
[7] Correggio, *Siege of Malta*, 36.
[8] Crowley, *Empires of the Sea*, 96.
[9] Correggio, *Siege of Malta*, 36.
[10] Crowley, *Empires of the Sea, 102.*
[11] Bradford, *Knights of the Order*, 140.
[12] Correggio, *Siege of Malta*, 13.
[13] Ibid, 27.
[14] Bradford, *Knights of the Order*, 143.
[15] Currey, *Sea Wolves*, 265–66; cf. Vertot, *History of the Knights*, vol. 4, 301–302.
[16] Crowley, *Empires of the Sea,* 112; Correggio, *Siege of Malta*, 50; Vertot, *History of the Knights*, vol. 4, 297.
[17] Vertot, *History of the Knights*, vol. 4, 311.

Chapter 60

[1] Correggio, *Siege of Malta*, 66.
[2] Vertot, *History of the Knights*, vol. 4, 322.
[3] Ibid, vol. 4, 323.
[4] Ibid, vol. 4, 323; Correggio, *Siege of Malta*, 70.
[5] Vertot, *History of the Knights*, vol. 4, 323–326.

6 Correggio, *Siege of Malta*, 73.
7 Vertot, *History of the Knights*, vol. 4, 328–330; cf. Correggio, *Siege of Malta*, 72.
8 Correggio, *Siege of Malta*, 78.
9 Vertot, *History of the Knights*, vol. 4, 338; Correggio, *Siege of Malta*, 81.
10 Vertot, *History of the Knights*, vol. 4, 338.
11 Correggio, *Siege of Malta*, 28, 81–82; Vertot, *History of the Knights*, vol. 4, 338–344.
12 Vertot, *History of the Knights*, vol. 4, 328–330; cf. Correggio, *Siege of Malta*, 72.
13 Vertot, *History of the Knights*, vol. 4, 331–334; cf. Correggio, *Siege of Malta*, 72.
14 Vertot, *History of the Knights*, vol. 4, 334.
15 Correggio, *Siege of Malta*, 84.

Chapter 61

1 Correggio, *Siege of Malta*, 87.
2 Vertot, *History of the Knights*, vol. 4, 346.
3 Correggio, *Siege of Malta*, 88–89.
4 Ibid, 89.
5 Vertot, *History of the Knights*, vol. 4, 346–348; Correggio, *Siege of Malta*, 93.
6 Crowley, *Empires of the Sea*, 157.
7 Correggio, *Siege of Malta*, 91; Vertot, *History of the Knights*, vol. 4, 347.
8 Correggio, *Siege of Malta*, 93.
9 Vertot, *History of the Knights*, vol. 5, 3.
10 Ibid, vol. 4, 347–348.

Chapter 61

1 Correggio, *Siege of Malta*, 97–98.
2 Vertot, *History of the Knights*, vol. 5, 9.
3 Correggio, *Siege of Malta*, 101.
4 Ibid, 105.
5 Ibid, 109.
6 Ibid, 109–110.
7 Ibid, 109–112; Vertot, *History of the Knights*, vol. 5, 19.
8 Vertot, *History of the Knights*, vol. 5, 18.
9 Correggio, *Siege of Malta*, 116.
10 Ibid, 115–116.
11 Crowley, *Empires of the Sea*, 152.
12 Correggio, *Siege of Malta*, 117; Vertot, *History of the Knights*, vol. 5, 23.

Chapter 62

1 Correggio, *Siege of Malta*, 129; Vertot, *History of the Knights*, vol. 5, 26.
2 Vertot, *History of the Knights*, vol. 4, 336; Vertot, *History of the Knights*, vol. 5, 28–29; cf. Correggio, *Siege of Malta*, 120.
3 Correggio, *Siege of Malta*, 129.
4 Ibid, 134, 130; Vertot, *History of the Knights*, vol. 5, 40.

5 Correggio, *Siege of Malta*, 138.
6 Ibid, 143–144.
7 Vertot, *History of the Knights*, vol. 5, 33.
8 Correggio, *Siege of Malta*, 147.

Chapter 63

1 Crowley, *Empires of the Sea*, 173.
2 Correggio, *Siege of Malta*, 156–157.
3 Bradford, *Knights of the Order*, 158–163; Vertot, *History of the Knights*, vol. 5, 42–43.
4 Correggio, *Siege of Malta*, 161–165.
5 Ibid, 168; Bradford, *Knights of the Order*, 165.
6 Crowley, *Empires of the Sea*, 183.
7 Correggio, *Siege of Malta*, 187.
8 Vertot, *History of the Knights*, vol. 5, 69–70; Riley-Smith, *Hospitallers*, 111; Correggio, *Siege of Malta*, 189.
9 Bradford, *Knights of the Order*, 168.
10 Crowley, *Empires of the Sea*, 185.
11 Bradford, *Knights of the Order*, 166.

Chapter 65

1 Vertot, *History of the Knights*, vol. 5, 89.
2 Vann and Kagay, *Hospitaller Piety*, 347.
3 Nicholson, *Knights Hospitaller*, 126–129.
4 Bradford, *Knights of the Order*, 194.
5 Vertot, *History of the Knights*, vol. 5, 171–172.
6 Bradford, *Knights of the Order*, 189.
7 Davis, *Christian Slaves*, 40; Playfair, *Scourge of Christendom*, 52.
8 Davis, *Christian Slaves*, 9.
9 White, Joshua, *Piracy and Law*, 27.
10 Davis, Christian Slaves, 23.
11 Foxe, *Universal History*, 251; Kizilov, "Slave Trade," 15; Playfair, *Scourge of Christendom*, 12.
12 Vertot, *History of the Knights*, vol. 5, 203.
13 Ibid, vol. 5, 203–204.
14 Bradford, *Knights of the Order*, 183.
15 Riley-Smith, *Hospitallers*, 122–23.
16 Bradford, *Knights of the Order*, 211–213.
17 Drane, *Knights of St. John*, iii-iv.

Chapter 66

1 Bernard of Clairvaux, *In Praise*, 48.
2 Gibbon, *Decline and Fall*, vol. 2, 403.
3 Nicholson, *Knights Templar*, 106–107.

4 Ibid, 195.
5 Forey, *Military Orders*, 241.
6 Riley-Smith, *Hospitallers*, 54.
7 Nicholson, *Knights Templar*, 80.
8 Walsh, *Warriors of the Lord*, 96.
9 Hamblin, "Muslim Perspectives"; cf. Gabrieli, *Arab Historians*, 138–139; Mourad and Lindsay, *Intensification and Reorientation*, 95–96.
10 Riley-Smith, *Hospitallers*, 76.
11 Nicholson, *Knights Templar*, 54.
12 Hamblin, "Muslim Perspectives."
13 Bernard of Clairvaux, *In Praise*, 33–34.

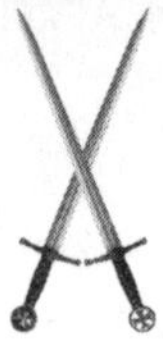

PHOTO CREDITS

Roland sounds his olifant for aid at Roncesvalles (1873).
Wolfgang von Bibra /Wikimedia Commons / CC BY-SA 4.0

Raymond of Puy (1842).
Alaspada / Wikimedia Commons / CC BY-SA 4.0

A Templar knight (12th-century fresco from the Templars' chapel at Cressac, France).
JLPC / Wikimedia Commons / CC BY-SA 3.0

Ruins of Baghras, a Templar fortress in the Amanus Mountains.
Godfried Warreyn / Wikimedia Commons / CC BY-SA 3.0

Krak des Chevaliers, the Hospitallers' "mountain" fortress, cursed by Muslims as "a bone stuck in the throat."
Ergo / Wikimedia Commons / CC BY 2.0

The Oriflamme ("golden flame") symbolized holy, no-quarter warfare for the Frankish kings since Charlemagne.
Tomasz Steifer, Gdansk / Wikimedia Commons / CC BY-SA 3.0

Hospitaller castle of Rhodes (Master's palace and knights' headquarters).
Antiquarian / Wikimedia Commons / CC BY-SA 3.0 / Enhanced

Reconstruction of Muslim (or Barbary) corsair flag.
RootOfAllLight / Wikimedia Commons / CC BY-SA 4.0

Fort St. Elmo today.
Dion Hinchcliffe / Wikimedia Commons / CC BY-SA 2.0

Master John of Valette praises God for the lifting of the 1565 siege of Malta (c. 1850).
PHGCOM / Wikimedia Commons / CC BY-SA 3.0